The
AMA
Handbook for
Employee Recruitment
and Retention

The
AMA
Handbook for
Employee Recruitment
and Retention

Mary F. Cook, Editor

American Management Association

New York · Atlanta · Boston · Chicago · Kansas City · San Francisco · Washington, D.C.
Brussels · Toronto · Mexico City

Library of Congress Cataloging-in-Publication Data

*The AMA handbook for employee recruitment and retention / Mary F.
    Cook, editor.*
        p.   cm.
        Includes bibliographical references and index.
        ISBN 0-8144-0109-0
        *1. Employees—Recruiting.   2. Employee selection.   3. Personnel
management.   I. Cook, Mary F., 1937–   .   II. American Management
Association.   III. Title: American Management Association handbook
for employee recruitment and retention.*
HF5549.5.R44A45   1992
658.3'11—dc20   *92-17352*
                                                                          CIP

Printing number

10 9 8 7 6 5 4 3 2 1

Contents

Acknowledgments

Many people made valuable contributions to this book and deserve recognition and thanks. Entire chapters were written and contributed by the top consultants in their fields today. Many thanks to executives of Hay Management Consultants, Dr. Andrew Geller, Robert Ochsner, Steven Gross, and Robert James, who contributed chapters in the important areas of compensation, executive compensation, and performance management. Dr. Lyle Spencer, CEO of McBer and Company, and Dr. David C. McClelland, founder and chairman of the board of McBer and Company and professor emeritus from Harvard, contributed to the chapter on selection with their work on competency assessment. Dr. Dale Masi, an expert and consultant on employee assistance programs, contributed the EAP chapter, and Diane Arthur provided her special expertise in the area of testing of applicants and employees. Carol Benjamin, a consultant with the Dallas office of The Wyatt Company, was a tremendous asset both in writing the chapters on benefits and in acting as a sounding board on other HR issues surrounding recruitment and retention.

Barney Olmsted, a nationally recognized consultant in the area of alternative work programs, contributed that chapter to the book and was most responsive to requests for information. Charles Newcom, a partner with the Denver law firm of Sherman & Howard, was especially helpful on many issues that came up in the writing of this book and personally contributed the chapter on the legal and regulatory considerations of recruitment and retention. I am grateful to Dr. William Tracey, who interrupted work on his current book to write the chapter on training and development, and to Dr. Ray Collins, for contributing a great deal of timely information in the chapter on work and family issues, which are foremost in the minds of many employees and organizations today.

Thanks also to Adrienne Hickey, my editor at AMACOM Books, for the idea for this handbook and for her guidance and support, and to Jacqueline Laks Gorman, whose editorial instincts made this an excellent product. Thanks also to Margaret Montoya, who provided the word-processing support. Without it, the book would still be an idea.

Finally, thanks to my husband, Fred Cook, who has been so supportive through the years in all my writing endeavors and who picks up the slack when family matters need attention—always with a smile.

Introduction

Mary F. Cook
President
Mary Cook & Associates

The recruitment and retention elements of the human resources (HR) function are the fastest changing, most visible, and most highly regulated functions in business today. New issues in these areas arise every year, and many form trends that HR managers need to watch. *The AMA Handbook for Employee Recruitment and Retention* focuses on these key HR issues and trends. The book also provides practical, easy-to-use policies and procedures for finding and keeping the best, most productive work force available in these times.

A major problem for organizations now and in the coming years is the mismatch between the types and numbers of people who are available to work and the types of available jobs. The United States has changed drastically from an industrial society to an information and service society. This change has had a significant impact on the creation of jobs—and on the people who must be recruited and retained to fill those jobs.

Moreover, a powerful tide is sweeping across all organizations today—a tide that is bringing tremendous changes in organizational structure, in types of employees, in the way we work, in productivity, in human rights, and in employee motivations and values. This same tide is gradually eating away at the old traditional ways organizations do things—how we handle people and our policies and procedures.

In addition, new types of organizations are emerging. They are the downsized corporations, the merged megacorporations, the fast-growing midsize companies, and the small businesses started by entrepreneurs. These companies use a variety of organizational and working styles, flexible work hours and benefits, multiple compensation strategies including two-tier wage plans and salaried plans, futuristic training and telecommunications programs, and more flexible personnel policies. They have different organizational cultures than most traditional companies are used to, and all of us—in both traditional and nontraditional companies—have already begun to experience these organizational changes at work as well as in the way we are raising our families, planning our careers, and structuring our lives.

A New Generation of Workers

Today, 75 million people in the baby boom generation are working, and they represent one out of every three Americans. Just below this huge baby boom generation is an emerging class of individuals, sometimes called "baby busters," who are challenging the meaning of the American dream. About 22 million strong, they are the young to middle-age adults who program America's computers, manage its fast-food stores, type its letters, teach its children, and nurse its sick. They hold jobs in the gray area between the professional and laboring ranks. They continue the workhorse role of their mothers and fathers, but culturally—and, to a significant degree, politically—they are a different breed. Economically they are between the poor and the affluent. They work hard but are not obsessed with their careers. Many of them are disappointed to find that a college degree and a white-collar job don't guarantee financial security; in fact, many find their college education has little application to their current job. That current job is not the one they aspired to when they went to college, but because of the tremendous mismatch between jobs and talent, they have had to take jobs they don't particularly want, in order to work at all. It is these people that companies must attract and retain, and it's at this huge group of workers where most HR programs and policies must be directed.

In the meantime, there is a squeeze for technically skilled labor that is forcing many employers to take special steps—from raising starting salaries to expanding re-training programs—to get the people they need. The big winners in coming years will be the educated and experienced baby busters. Some, forced to take jobs for which they were overqualified, will get second chances to shift directions and move up. Companies paying top dollar are figuring out they can find thirty-year-olds with experience who will gladly work nearly as cheaply as the top new graduates.

The scramble for skilled workers could herald a decade of rising salaries and greater job opportunities for anyone trained to handle advanced technologies and complex in-formation. More women will get the chance to move up to managerial and technical positions. There will be opportunities for many baby busters sidetracked in the 1980s. Skilled immigrants will be sought, and older employees will be encouraged to keep working.

But for people without a college education or technical expertise, this decade could be difficult. There is a widening gap between what the economy requires and what the new labor force can provide. Through the end of the 1990s, three-fourths of all new jobs will require some college education and technical skill, while only about half of all new workers are likely to have gone beyond high school. Moreover, computerization of the workplace will move millions of today's lower-level jobs out of the reach of the less skilled. As a result, the labor force may well include a growing army of unskilled workers facing limited employment opportunities.

Recruiting and Retaining a Productive Work Force

What does this mean for employers? The message for all employers who want their organizations to run smoothly and stay competitive is to become more adept at recruiting and retaining the best, most qualified, and most productive workers they can find. Con-stant turnover will be too expensive and too disruptive for organizations striving to compete in today's business world.

This Handbook provides current information from top authorities in areas critical to the recruitment and retention of a productive work force. That information can be put to work immediately to help your company become more effective and competitive. Some of the key recruitment and retention issues discussed in the pages that follow are:

- Advanced HR planning: identifying needs as far in advance as possible and assessing the demographics and skills of your applicant base
- Innovative, quality recruitment and selection programs
- Effective performance management
- Constant training and retraining
- A participative management style
- Honesty and candidness with employees
- Flexibility in work arrangements, compensation, benefits, and personnel policies addressing work and family issues

Not only will organizations need to be more flexible in their recruitment and retention policies, but they will have to look beyond the traditional recruitment methods. One solution, discussed in this Handbook, is low-cost technology. Companies will use telephone job lines, electronic database recruiting, and telerecruiting much more in the future.

Another important issue in the recruitment and retention of a top-level productive work force will be the greening of America. The best and brightest people will want to work for organizations that have a positive social consciousness. Companies that pollute or expose their workers to unsafe working conditions will not be able to attract and retain the best people.

In putting together this Handbook, we've gathered some of the top consultants working today on the newest elements of human resources management, including alternative work arrangements, work and family issues, and employee assistance programs. We've looked at what's new in testing, competency-based assessment, recruitment techniques, and competitive but affordable compensation and benefits programs. We've tried to put a bottom line to the issue of recruitment and retention for the future.

PART I

PREPARING FOR WORKFORCE 2000

1

Workplace 2000: Prospects and Challenges

Mary F. Cook
President
Mary Cook & Associates

Even though the last few years have seen a tremendous corporate downsizing, America is hanging out a "help wanted" sign, and organizations are doing everything they can to keep their top performers. Not only is the skilled labor pool shrinking, but there is a significant mismatch between the types of jobs that are available and the skills of the workers who are in the job market. This mismatch makes it difficult to recruit and retain the best, most productive workers and creates a huge challenge for U.S. corporations.

Snapshot of the Changing Work Force

According to the Bureau of Labor Statistics (BLS) there were tremendous changes in the work force in the 1990s. Most of these changes were triggered by the baby boom generation. Born between 1946 and 1964, they number 75 million people, one out of every three Americans. They are the largest generation in U.S. history.

• *Aging population.* One result of the influx of baby boomers is the aging of the U.S. population. In 1983 the median age of the population reached 30.9, the oldest ever, and is expected to exceed 36 by the year 2000. One out of four Americans is now over the age of 50. By the turn of the century, more than 100,000 Americans will be 100 years or older, about three times the number today. In the year 2025, 64 million people will be over the age of 65, and the United States will have fewer than four working-age individuals for every retirement-age person. The superelderly, as they are sometimes called, represent the fastest-growing segment of the U.S. population.

• *Changing family structure.* There are 50 million single people in the United States today, and single people now account for 23 percent of all U.S. households. As many as 8 percent of today's adults will never marry. In addition, the number of families with single heads of household grew by 69 percent from 1970 to 1983. Today one out of every five children and more than half of all black children live in a one-parent household. Another interesting statistic is that more than 20 million young adults have had to move back home or cannot leave home because they can't afford to rent or purchase a home of their own.

As a result of these developments, "typical" is no longer an adjective that can describe the American family. In the mid-1970s, 40 percent of all households consisted of husband, wife, and children; today the stereotypical nuclear family of mom, dad, and two kids accounts for only 11 percent of all households. The number of female-headed households with one or more children under age 18 doubled in the last decade, from 2.9 million to 5.9 million.

• *Increasing diversity.* According to government projections, 75 percent of new workers in the 1990s will be women, minority group members, or immigrants from widely diverse cultural backgrounds. This will pose tremendous challenges for managers who are not accustomed to dealing with nontraditional employees, certainly not in such large numbers.

• *Decline in income.* Average household income in constant dollars is dropping steadily, from $21,400 in 1980 to $20,600 in 1990. In 1991 fewer than a third of all households headed by a person under age 35 had any discretionary income. These baby busters are having a hard time matching the living standards to which they were accustomed as children. Demographers call it the promotion squeeze: There is not enough room at the top. Today the combined income of a young married couple, both of whom are working, is likely to be less than either of their fathers earned at the same age. Baby busters are not able to afford the houses they grew up in, they make between $20,000 and $30,000 a year, and they will be the work force of the late 1990s and early 2000s.

• *Illiterate workers at the bottom.* Today as much as a quarter of the total U.S. labor force—anywhere from 20 million to 27 million adults—lacks the basic reading, writing, and math skills necessary to perform in the increasingly complex workplace. A Society for Human Resource Management/CCH survey on workplace literacy indicates that 63.5 percent of the companies questioned knowingly and unknowingly hire workers lacking basic skills, and 92 percent of those companies report still having employees without basic skills working for them today. These statistics reflect the reason so many companies have to provide basic skills training for their workers.

The total problem, however, is not just that large numbers of entry-level workers can't read or write. Never before in U.S. history have so many jobs required such high levels of technological and mathematical expertise. What was considered basic knowledge and skill levels even five years ago is below basic acceptable standards today. Now even low-level service employees must be computer-literate and must have eleventh- to twelfth-grade math skills. In addition, over this decade, Hispanics, Asians, and immigrants, who will be the fastest growing entrants in the labor force and who make up more than half of all entry-level job applicants, may speak English poorly. The long-term solution to the literacy problem lies with the nation's overall educational system, but in the meantime, organizations must train workers. U.S. industry spends $25 billion annually teaching newly hired employees to read, write, and count, and will have to continue such training for the foreseeable future.

• *The effects of immigration.* It's expected that the Immigration Reform and Control Act, which was not fully implemented until 1988, will gradually reduce the level of undocumented immigration to the United States. The number of illegal aliens is projected to drop from 200,000 in 1988 to 100,000 in 1998. Legislation passed in 1991 will increase the number of documented (legal) immigrants allowed from 560,000 annually to 700,000 annually.

Other immigration reforms will nearly triple, from 54,000 to 140,000, the number of skilled workers who can enter the United States legally each year because U.S. employers sponsor them. As a result, businesses and universities will have a greatly expanded opportunity to import professionals they cannot find in the United States.

Growth of the U.S. labor force is expected to slow during the 1990s, making room for more skilled foreign workers, especially in fields such as chemistry, biology, physics, engineering, and mathematics.

Labor Force Projections to the Year 2000

The growth of the U.S. labor force is expected to slow perceptibly between 1988 and 2000, according to projections by the BLS.[1] Under the most moderate of three alternative projections, the total labor force is estimated to grow 1.2 percent annually, compared with the 1976–1988 growth rate of 2 percent. The labor force is projected to total 141 million persons in the year 2000, a net addition of almost 19.5 million. In contrast, the work force grew by over 25.6 million people between 1976 and 1988. (Under the more extreme alternative BLS projections, the work force in 2000 varies from a low of 137.5 million to a high of 144 million.)

Women composed only 40.5 percent of the labor force in 1976; by 2000, they are projected to be 47.3 percent. The labor force will also be older. The proportion of youths (those sixteen to twenty-four years old) dropped from 24.3 percent of the labor force in 1976 to 18.5 percent in 1988, and it is projected to fall further, to 16 percent in 2000. The proportion of workers in the broad age span 25 to 54 is projected to increase from 69 percent in 1988 to almost 72 percent by the year 2000.

The proportion of blacks in the labor force is projected to rise from almost 11 percent in 1988 to almost 12 percent by 2000. Hispanics are projected to increase their share of the labor force from 7.4 percent in 1988 to just over 10 percent by 2000. The proportion of the Asians, American Indians, Alaskan natives, and Pacific Islanders is expected to rise from 3 percent in 1988 to 4 percent in 2000.

Where the Jobs Will Be

As the industrial profile changes, jobs will be appearing in different sectors.[2] Certain industry divisions will see sustained growth, while others will experience declines.

Services

The services division is the largest and fastest growing industry division. The division provided 34.5 million jobs in 1988. The number of jobs is expected to rise 28 percent, to 44.2 million, by the year 2000, accounting for almost one-half of all new jobs. Services jobs will be found in small firms as well as in large corporations, at all levels of government, and in industries as diverse as banking, health care, data processing, and management consulting. The two largest industry groups in this division are health services and business services.

Health care will continue to be one of the most important groups of industries in the economy in terms of job creation. Employment in the health services industries is projected to grow from 8.2 million in 1988 to 11.3 million in 2000. New technology and a growing and aging population will increase the demand for health services. Because of the rapid expansion of health care employment, seven of the ten fastest growing occupations between 1988 and 2000 will be health-related. Not all of the health industry sectors will grow at the same rate; outpatient care facilities and offices of practitioners like chiropractors, optometrists, and psychologists will increase the fastest. Hospitals, both private and public, will be growing more slowly than all the other health industries, but faster than the average for all industries. Nonetheless, hospitals will continue to employ the most workers among the health care industries.

Another important industry group that is expected to generate many jobs is business services. These industries employed 5.6 million workers in 1988 and are projected to employ 8.3 million in the year 2000. The largest industry in this group, personnel supply services (which include temporary-help agencies), will add the most new jobs. Business services also include the fastest growing industry in the economy—computer and data-processing services—which is expected to grow five times faster than the average for all industries as a result of a rapidly increasing demand from corporations, government agencies, and individuals. A third industry in business services—research, management, and consulting—is expected to have very rapid growth, although not as rapid as computer and personnel supply services.

Education, in both the private and public sectors, is expected to add 1.2 million jobs by the year 2000 to the 8.9 million employed in 1988. The increase reflects rising enrollments projected for elementary and secondary schools. The elementary school–age population (ages 5–13) will rise by more than 2 million between 1988 and 2000, and the secondary school–age (14–17) by 1.3 million. On the other hand, the traditional college-age population (18–24) has been declining and is projected to continue to decline through the year 2000. (However, rising enrollments of older students, women, foreign students, and part-time students have offset the absolute decline in the 18–24 population.) Not all the increase in employment in education will be for teachers; there are also projected increases in the numbers of teacher aides, counselors, technicians, and administrative staff.

Retail Trade

Nearly 3.8 million jobs will be added in retail trade, which will provide 22.9 million jobs in 2000, up 20 percent from the 1988 level. Restaurants will employ the most workers in the retail trade division and also will be among the fastest growing industries. Substantial increases in retail employment are also anticipated in grocery stores, department stores, and miscellaneous stores.

Government

Between 1988 and 2000, government employment, excluding public education and public hospitals, is expected to increase 7 percent, from 9 million to 9.6 million jobs. Most of the growth will be in state and local government; the federal government is expected to add only 88,000 jobs.

Other Areas of Employment

In finance, insurance, and real estate, employment is expected to increase 16 percent, with 1.1 million jobs added to the 1988 number of 6.7 million by 2000. The fastest growing industry within this division is expected to be security firms and stockbrokers and exchanges, although they will not be growing as fast as in the past. Meanwhile, employment in wholesale trade is expected to rise from 6 million to 6.9 million between 1988 and 2000, an increase of 15 percent.

In the transportation, communications, and public utilities division, overall employment is expected to rise 10 percent from the 1988 level of 5.5 million by 2000. The three fastest growing industries in this division are arrangement of transportation, freight forwarding, and air carriers, each growing at least three times as fast as the division as a whole. Only modest employment growth is expected in the communications industry. Although output will show an increase, new laborsaving technology will deter the creation of new jobs.

Employment in goods-producing industries such as construction, manufacturing, mining, and agriculture has steadily declined in the 1980s and is expected to stay about the same or decline further in the 1990s, according to the BLS.

The Challenges of Workforce/Workplace 2000

We've identified the work force and workplace demographics, as well as where the jobs and the workers will be. What are the other issues we will have to address in order to recruit and retain the best workers in the 1990s?

Specific Groups in Demand

The baby boomers are making their voices heard and their clout felt by corporations all over the United States. In the 1980s, millions of boomers launched their careers and earned (and spent) a great deal of money for the first time in their lives. The 1990s will also be an affluent decade because boomers with a good education and a few years' experience will be in demand in the job market. Most people in their forties and fifties are in their peak earning years, and by the year 2000, nearly 15 million households headed by married people between the ages of 35 and 54 will have incomes of over $50,000. For these people, there are two keys to affluence, which will impact how corporations must deal with these employees. The first key is to be half of a two-income couple. The second is to be flexible. These people must learn more than one job and have more than one vocation. Most people hold an average of ten jobs in their lifetime and change careers at least three times. To keep these workers, corporations must provide them with opportunities (financial and otherwise), or they will have few misgivings about seeking new employment.

Following the baby boomers are the baby busters, the twenty- to thirty-five-year-olds in the work force. They aren't anything like the workaholic baby boomers. The busters have been known to turn down big promotions or quickly acquire money and clout and then give it all up for leisure. Because they are in such short supply, the busters, only 26 million strong, will be in great demand. They will be in a position to make more demands on employers. Unions will have a tough time organizing baby busters, who think for themselves and often do not want a third party interfering with their work relationships.

In the 1990s, companies will have to cast a wide net for workers, and as they do so, they will take a second look at their retired workers, who have a wealth of experience and skills—skills that are desperately needed. The trend to early retirement will be reversed, and more retirees will reenter the work force. Some will work for temporary help agencies that will put them back into their former companies, while some will go back on the company payroll in temporary or part-time positions. There are problems associated with rehiring older workers, but because of the coming labor shortage and the retirees' need for more income, the two forces will get together to help each other through the 1990s.

The Work Force/Workplace Mismatch

One of the fastest growing issues is the mismatch between the types of jobs that go unfilled and the skills of the available workers. The jobs that are open, the ones that employers will be crying to fill in the 1990s, require a high level of technical skill. For example, the United States is in dire need of nurses, but there is a shortage of people with nursing skills and related degrees. The United States is encouraging nurses and other skilled workers to emigrate from Europe, and Asia, and is providing immigration assistance in order to fill the gap. The scramble for people with technical skills may herald a decade of rising salaries and greater job opportunities for anyone trained to handle advanced technologies and complex information.

With fewer technically qualified workers to choose from in the 1990s, the job market will be excellent for anyone with a good education and with above average technical skills and work experience. Jobs for accountants, for example, are expected to increase by 40 percent, to 1.3 million by the year 2000, according to the Bureau of Labor Statistics. Jobs for doctors and teachers are forecast to soar by 3.7 million, or nearly 30 percent. Behind all this good news, however, is a widening gap between what the economy requires and what the new labor force will provide. In the 1990s, it is projected that 75 percent of all the new jobs created will require people with some college education and good technical skills, while only 50 percent or less of all new workers are likely to have gone beyond high school.

The tightening market for skilled labor will help working women. The gap between women's and men's wages, which has been an economic fact of life for over thirty years, has begun to close. From 1985 to 1990, the ratio of women's wages to men's rose from 60 percent to over 65 percent. The Census Bureau reports that working women age 20 to 24 now earn on average only 16 percent less than young men, compared with a 23 percent gap in 1980. That wage gap will close even faster as women are drawn to male-dominated fields. More than 40 percent of new business school students are women, and more women are earning degrees in medicine and law as opposed to degrees in nursing and teaching, which are lower-paying occupations.

Whatever their jobs, more women will take their places in the working world, if only because more women now consider meaningful and well-paid work to be a desirable and achievable goal. The Bureau of Labor Statistics estimates that by 1995, 81 percent of adult women age 25 to 44 will hold jobs.

Training and Retraining the Work Force

The demographics of the workplace show that in this decade there will be a smaller work force that is poorly educated and made up of mostly female, minority, and immigrant workers who lack high-level skills. To make things even more difficult for employers, computerization of the workplace will place millions of today's lower-level jobs out of the reach of the less-skilled computer-illiterate work force. Even low-paying jobs in department stores, discount chains, and fast-food outlets now require computer know-how. The squeeze for new skilled labor is forcing many employers to offer basic skills and computer training and expanded retraining programs to current employees. Indeed, training and retraining is the answer to having the skilled employees that are needed.

Many firms are easing the labor squeeze by expanding on-the-job retraining. At high-tech giants such as Digital Equipment and IBM, thousands of midlevel workers in their thirties are learning new specialties in electrical and chemical engineering. For example, IBM in Boulder, Colorado, is changing its business emphasis from computer manufacturing to software development, and retraining hundreds of workers.

For any one company, the answer to the labor shortage is to find the best people it can, train them, keep them, and retrain them. Because technology is changing so fast, workers will have to be retrained many times during their working life. In fact, the BLS estimates that 75 percent of all U.S. workers currently employed will need retraining by the year 2000.[3]

It has been reported that U.S. companies spend more than $30 billion a year improving the skills of their employees, but is it spent in the wisest way? Corporate executives say that they spend huge sums to educate their workers. They contend that the school system is failing to provide high school graduates with basic skills. However, if you take a closer look at exactly how corporations spend their training dollars, you find that employees with college degrees are 50 percent more likely to receive corporate training than are nongraduates, and executives with postgraduate degrees are twice as likely to get training as those with college degrees. In most corporations, the majority of training dollars are typically spent on employees who need it least.[4]

U.S. corporations have historically been generous to colleges and universities, but starting in 1988, corporate donations decreased significantly. Moreover, only a small percentage of corporate contributions to educational institutions goes to public primary and secondary schools. Of the $2.3 billion that corporations contributed to education in 1990, only $400 million went to public schools, the rest going to colleges and universities. If corporations are to have the trained workers they need by the year 2000, corporate giving to education will have to be earmarked for public primary and secondary schools as well as colleges and universities.

Dealing With Employee Attitudes

Reviving Employee Loyalty

During the 1980s, the wave of takeovers, mergers, and downsizings eliminated more than 2 million jobs in the United States. Experts estimate that 2 million more will be eliminated in the 1990s. Many unemployed workers feel that greed and poor management caused the layoffs of the 1980s. Their bitterness increased when many were forced to take part-time or temporary jobs or jobs at a much lower level than their previous positions. These people are cynical and disillusioned, and they won't easily become loyal, hardworking employees for a new organization. This is one of the most difficult challenges companies face today.

EMPLOYEES AND BUSINESS ETHICS

In the wake of the greedy and sometimes unethical 1980s, companies are hauling out their ethics codes and revising them. The problem with ethics codes is that they are resisted by many people who were laid off in the 1980s or 1990s and saw their companies taken over, merged, or downsized. They regard the codes as window dressing; they look good but aren't expected to affect the realities of the business world today any more than they did in previous years. The senior executives of one large banking corporation drafted their first corporate ethics code in 1990. The executive vice-president said they wanted to "manifest their values." But when they distributed the code among their employees, they got a rude shock. Point by point, the employees disputed the code's precepts. When the company said it believes in open communication, the employees said, "Wrong. Management is very reluctant to be honest with employees." When the company said it believes and carries out the idea of equal employment opportunity, the employees said, "Wrong. Opportunities are manipulated and blocked by higher-ups." Ethics codes will work better if organizations first show through their actions that they are actually doing what they say they want to do. With today's work force, actions must predate written objectives. The best employees want to work for ethical companies. Ethics and retention go hand in hand.

EMPLOYEES AND CORPORATE SOCIAL RESPONSIBILITY

Both employees and consumers seek out socially responsible companies. A growing number of people have made a decision not to work for or buy products from socially irresponsible companies. *Shopping for a Better World,* a book published by the Council on Economic Priorities, lists 138 companies (and 1,300 products), evaluating them on such issues as advancement of women and minorities, protection of the environment, community outreach, and charitable giving. Corporations are taking notice and showing more concern for the environment and for social responsibility. It's a good thing they are, because this is going to be a very big issue in the coming years.

Shifting Patterns of Work and Family Life

Because more than 70 percent of women in the United States now work outside the home, work and family issues are an immediate challenge. The issues of child and elder care assistance, parental leave, flexible work schedules, alternative work arrangements, and family medical benefits will be foremost in employees' minds. These issues will be of primary concern when job seekers look at prospective employers. To underline how important these issues are, some larger organizations—companies like Time Warner, AT&T, Bank of America, Marriott, IBM, and Times Publishing—have even created a new job entitled work/family manager. Work and family concerns are important to attracting and retaining a skilled, effective work force.

Americans Working for Foreign Companies

More Americans are finding themselves working for foreign companies in the United States, something U.S. workers would have found difficult to believe a few years ago. More than 3 million U.S. workers report now to a foreign boss, according to an article entitled "Can We Compete With Japan?" in *American Legion Magazine* (October 1990). "In California, for example, 2,400 subsidiaries of Japanese firms account for $31 billion in investments and about 70,000 jobs. California ships $8 billion worth of exports to Japan, including almost a third of its agricultural output."[5] A Japanese "auto alley" cuts through six states and provides more than 15,000 assembly jobs. Mazdas are made in Michigan, Hondas in Ohio, Toyotas in Kentucky, and Nissans in Tennessee. Mitsubishi has a joint venture with Chrysler in Illinois, and Subaru and Isuzu have both built plants in Indiana.

U.S. workers are flocking to Japanese manufacturing companies for jobs. The style and culture of these foreign corporations varies depending on the company. Some U.S. workers find the management style difficult to live with; others sing praises and have happily adopted the egalitarian spirit of Japanese management. Some American managers working for Japanese companies experience problems.[6] The Japanese run their U.S. subsidiaries not as separate operations but through vertical lines of authority that stretch across the Pacific at every management level. There is little autonomy. All the critical decisions are made in Japan. Every American manager has a Japanese counterpart or shadow who officially serves as the communication liaison with the company in Japan. One study done by the Boston Consulting Group showed that while a formal corporate chain of command includes U.S. executives at the second and third level, the actual decision-making process cuts out Americans altogether. Business is conducted at night on the telephone in Japanese between the Japanese! The shadow system is in place at every Japanese company in the United States. Many U.S. executives who have chosen to work for Japanese companies are having second thoughts. The inequalities in the Japanese system are most evident when business is bad: Only Americans are fired. If the Japanese economy continues to experience problems, more U.S. managers could be looking for jobs. U.S. companies may benefit from this situation in the long run.

American Jobs Moving Out of the Country

Because of the labor shortage and high wages in the United States, many companies are moving outside U.S. borders. The border town of Nogales, Sonora, in Mexico is called the new Hong Kong. There, more than 1,300 U.S.-owned factories with nearly 400,000 workers turn out jeans, hospital gowns, saxophones, radar detectors, file folders, chain saws, false teeth, sunglasses, and garage-door openers. Nogales has become a center for international commerce as well, a base for ITT, IBM, Rockwell, United Technologies, Kodak, Memorex, Kimberly-Clark, and Foster Grant. Smaller operations are also involved. The Chamberlain Group of Chicago built a factory in Nogales to make garage door openers for Sears.

In the last years, factories have closed in the United States in record numbers, and hundreds of thousands of jobs have been lost. U.S. companies have moved their operations across the border to take advantage of cheap labor in order to increase profits. Manufacturers are saving up to $25,000 per worker per year. Some experts say that this low-cost labor is at the heart of the new global economy.

The Global Workplace

As U.S. corporations continue the trend toward globalization of their business operations, the workplace as we know it today will change drastically. The unification of the

European market and China's takeover of Hong Kong are examples of these changes. Probably the most visible example for Americans, with the greatest potential for impact on the U.S. domestic market, is the U.S.-Canada Trade Agreement.

Historically, Canada and the United States have exchanged more goods and services than any other two countries in the world. With the signing of the U.S.-Canada Trade Agreement, trade opportunities and competition will be increased further for both countries. Under the agreement, all bilateral tariffs will be eliminated over a ten-year period (1989–1998). In addition, the agreement facilitates business travel between the two countries and intracompany transfer of employees. Although the agreement creates many new business opportunities for employers, it also presents new challenges. As companies set up or expand operation in both countries, they will encounter many differences in culture, business practices, and legal systems.

Leading Workforce 2000

As the nature of work changes, so does workers' motivation for doing it. And as the U.S. economy has shifted from a manufacturing to a services orientation, some organizations have failed to keep up with the changing desires and values of their employees. The new worker wants clear commitments from management, values autonomy, and wants a say in how his or her job is managed.

As the 1990s progress, we are looking for a new model of leadership. Our current models don't fit the times or the changing American character. We need leaders who are technically competent and who can combine toughmindedness with compassion and empathy—leaders who have a sense of values and an interest in people, as well as a need to get the job done. These leaders must attract and retain the most capable people, and to do so, organizations must create a distinctive culture. They must understand it and be able to communicate it to employees.

The changing business environment, the changing attitudes of workers, and significant advances in technology combine to break down the historical ways in which a business can successfully operate. In addition, there is a significant impact on managing. The culture of a company determines how one should manage. In some companies it is expected that work will get done right away, and a good manager is one who supplies solutions immediately. In other organizations, what's more important is working as a team or delegating work to employees and helping them grow; here, action has a longer time line.

Managers for the 1990s will have to learn to use a variety of managerial styles, depending in part on whom they are managing. They'll learn that:

- Baby boomers like collaboration and teamwork. They share information, and they like to reach a consensus.
- Baby busters like autonomy. They want no restrictions, and they like lots of choices.
- The new diverse work force wants respect and participation.

Managing these groups will require flexibility and skill. In the past, organizations established one cultural norm within the organization. Everyone pretty much fit that culture, and if they didn't fit, they left. To be successful at retaining top performers today, organizations must establish a more open organizational culture and must use a variety of techniques and approaches to communicate and strengthen that culture. The key to recruitment and retention in the 1990s will be the ability of U.S. companies to provide a flexible workplace with a flexible management style.

The way that government, corporations, and nonprofit organizations choose to resolve tough human resources issues in the coming years will have a significant effect on the loyalty and commitment of American workers. Issues like the handling of employees with AIDS and other life-threatening diseases, the accessibility of benefits for same-sex partners, equal pay and promotional opportunities, the accommodation efforts made for disabled applicants and employees, and the management of "big brother" and personal civil rights issues, such as computer surveillance, telephone monitoring, genetic testing, and drug testing, will all tell the story of successful or disastrous employment and retention programs. None of these issues have easy solutions, but all of them must be thoughtfully and honestly addressed.

Notes

1. Howard N. Fullerton, Jr., *Outlook 2000*, U.S. Department of Labor, Bureau of Labor Statistics, 1990.
2. "Tomorrow's Jobs," in *Occupational Outlook Handbook*, U.S. Department of Labor, Bureau of Labor Statistics, 1990.
3. Ibid.
4. Ibid.
5. "Can We Compete With Japan?" *American Legion Magazine*, October 1990.
6. Pat Choate, *Agents of Influence*, Simon & Schuster, 1990.

2

Human Resources Planning

Mary F. Cook
President
Mary Cook & Associates

Human resources executives have long believed that the success of any business depends, at least in part, on effective human resources planning and utilization. Not all executives in other areas agree with that idea. However, there is an increasing awareness in business today that human resources must be managed with the same strategic, future-oriented focus as physical and capital resources. In order for this sort of top-level strategic focus to occur, a critical assessment of the company's strategic plans and its attitudes toward human resources is essential. The HR executive must be able to assess correctly the organization's climate for planning and secure the commitment of the CEO and the other top-level decision makers. An HR plan cannot be successfully implemented without the participation, drive, and commitment of the organization's top people.

Critical Issues in Human Resources Planning

There are at least four critical issues for effective HR planning.

1. There should be an overall corporate strategic plan. The top decision makers should be able to articulate the plan and provide a vision statement for the organization. In that plan there must be a clear statement about the human resource dimensions.
2. The CEO and the functional vice-presidents must establish responsibility and accountability at all levels for the planning and management of human resources.
3. A process is needed in order to implement the plan. That process is the blueprint for moving forward. It includes the linkages among functional areas and the policies and procedures for implementation. The procedures must link human resources planning with the day-to-day business of the organization.
4. The specific elements of the plan include the work force needs, the labor market assessment, the demographics, expected technological innovations, individual assessment and development needs, and the procedures for implementation and control.

Researchers have found that in the most successful organizations, all management positions have a human resources management (HRM) responsibility. Primary accountability for HRM rests with the human resources manager, but operating managers also have a human resources responsibility. The effective management of human resources is dependent on a clear understanding of these joint responsibilities. The organization must establish the proper orientation to support this approach and reinforce it with a variety of techniques to assist both managers. These HR dimensions are enhanced by developing ways of determining and discussing accountability for HRM on an ongoing basis. Effective human resources management, in the context of overall business planning and management, is facilitated to the extent that the organization at all levels establishes and accepts those HR accountabilities.

Brainstorming About HR in Your Organization

As you start the planning process, it's a good idea to try a creative brainstorming activity to expand your horizons and take a look at the big picture. This should be done prior to conducting the situation audit and before you get into the goals and objectives of the actual plan. Bring together a team of managers from several important functional areas of the company. Appoint a group leader and brainstorm, using a flip chart so you can retain your creative and future-oriented thoughts about the HR plan for later use. Put all of your ideas together and make printouts so everyone involved in the planning process will have a copy.

Exhibit 2-1 lists the human and technical issues that you may want to consider before you begin the actual planning. When you start working on the plan, you tend to become rigid and totally objective, and in that linear frame of mind, you may overlook some important issues. List any other issues you or the group thinks will be critical to your organization. After the brainstorming session has been completed, you can move forward to the objective, more formal, structured HR planning process.

Key Elements of an HR Plan

Organization Plan

The human resources plan must be formulated using the assumptions and objectives of the organization's business plans. If the organization does not have a formal plan, key organizational objectives still must be identified. For example, if the organization's objective is to produce $20 million in income during the next twelve months, the organization plan should include specific projects and actions for accomplishing that economic objective, and the human resources plan would identify the numbers and types of people needed and when they would be needed in order to accomplish the plan. Organizational variables might be:

- Structure needed to accomplish plan
- Technology and innovation
- Personality/culture of the organization
- Business objectives
- Jobs and tasks
- Business climate
- Hiring environment
- Changing work ethic
- Global issues

Exhibit 2-1.   Human and technical issues in HR planning.

Human Issues	*Technical Issues*
Acquisitions (proposed)	Action plans on technical issues
Attitudes (worker and management)	Adapting to environment
Benefits costs	Annual plan reviews
Budgets	Assumptions in all areas
Commitment	Audits (internal/external)
Communications	Automation
Comparison with competitors	Competition
Compensation	Components of the plan
Consultants	Control of the plan
Contracts	Cyclical economic downturns
Corporate environment/style	Data analysis
Departmental relationships	Data gathering
Draft or reserve call-up	Employee assessment
Employment agencies	Environmental concerns
Equal employment opportunity	External analysis
Feedback	Global analysis
Health and fitness	Impact analysis
Human resources inventory	Information innovation
Individual development plans	Internal analysis
Line/staff relationships	Inventories
Management development	Locations
Matrix management	Long-range plan
Morale	Market considerations
Objectives	Merger strategies
Obsolescence	Operating plan
Organizational development	Organizational effectiveness
Overseas workers	Organizational objectives
Performance appraisal	Performance analysis
Personnel policies	Productivity analysis
Position descriptions	Staffing forecast
Productivity	Staff inventory
Promotion policies and plans	Skills required
Recruitment	Strategies (to meet objectives)
Relocation	Technology
Safety (workplace)	Trends
Security (workplace)	Work force analysis
Staffing plans	Work environment
Strategies to hire people	Work methods
Succession plan	Workplace 2000
Supervisory training	
Teamwork	
Testing	
Training	
Turnover	
Union concerns	

The effective integration of human resources and business planning is dependent on a company's business strategies. Not only should human resources matters be an integral part of business plans, but the process of reviewing performance against objectives must also include a review of the human resources plans. Executives at all levels must explicitly recognize HR issues and relate them to strategy. This recognition provides the organizational framework for establishing accountability for human resources management. A similar framework for the operating planning process is necessary. The corporate operating plan should include an HR component and an HR orientation that extends throughout the organization. The most effective linkage occurs when each functional area of the organization is accountable for its human resources activities, and those activities are outlined in the business plan.

One of the great failings of human resources plans is the HR planners' ignorance of the organization's direction. In most instances, planners in the HR department must take a business-as-usual approach, while in the boardroom drastic changes in the organization's direction are being discussed. If HR department managers are developing the human resources plan, they must take part in key strategy meetings.

Situation Audit

Many variables can affect your organization. The situation audit is an attempt to itemize all those variables that can or will affect the organization over the next three years. You should classify these elements. Key classifications might be:

1. Outside influences, such as the community, stockholders, customers, and creditors.
2. Inside interests, such as employees, performance of the organization and its workers, adequacy of facilities, and cost of compensation and benefits.
3. Demographics of the work force. An organization's ability to satisfy its future staffing needs depends on the availability of talent. Predicted demographic changes, such as the entry of more women and minorities in the work force, a steadily aging population, and two-career families, will influence the organization's human resources strategies.
4. Technological innovation. How should the company prepare itself for anticipated changes in technology? How might those changes influence the way you should be grooming top management talent?
5. Changing attitudes about work and careers on the part of the work force. For example, organizations are meeting greater resistance to relocation and transfers, more dual-career families have changing benefits needs, and an altered work ethic is changing the way we manage people.

It's important to establish a database through the situation audit that includes past performance, current business situations, forecasts, opportunities and threats, organization strengths and weaknesses, internal and external issues relating to HRM, and any other items that will have an impact on the human resources plan.

Work Force Analysis

The work force analysis details the company's internal strengths and weaknesses and provides crucial information on its present situation. The work force analysis should answer the following questions:

- How many people do we have who can potentially staff positions identified by the forecast of human resources needs?
- How difficult will it be to recruit skilled people from outside the organization to fill forecasted positions if we cannot fill all of the positions from inside the company?
- If the numbers and types of people needed cannot be found either inside or outside the organization, to what extent will the organization's plans and the human resources plan have to be altered, and how will we accomplish our goals?
- Which skill requirements identified in the forecast can be met by training and development that cannot be met through current training and development programs? Where are the necessary training programs going to be found? Will we have to go to the outside for the training? What kind of lead time are we looking at? What are the costs? Are these costs in the budget?

Through systematic evaluation of these questions and others that you will identify as you go through the process, the human resources plan will begin to take shape.

Human Resources Inventory

This is an inventory of all of the people on the payroll, with their skills, abilities, outside experience, education, internal jobs held, and performance levels. The inventory is a critical look at the present work force. It becomes the major HR database and is the profile from which the overall human resources plan is developed. Exhibit 2-2 is an example of a human resources inventory form. Most organizations enter such data into the computer, including it in the human resources information system.

The overall inventory should go beyond a personnel listing to include historical trends and other data. For example, the inventory should indicate the patterns of attrition in the organization, the average retirement age, the projected losses of critical management talent to competitors, and whether the turnover figures reveal patterns and trends that can be projected into the future.

Through careful analysis of current management talent in terms of skills, education, and experience, we can learn about the strengths and weaknesses of the organization's present mix. In what areas is talent abundant? Where is it sparse? Do managers and other professionals have a broad range of experience? If not, how will that affect recruiting plans? Are equal employment opportunity and affirmative action plans being taken into consideration? How is performance determined? Other vital questions can be answered as well.

Human Resources Forecast

Following the internal work force analysis and human resources inventory, future human resources requirements can be forecast through a projection of trends in the economy, trends in demographics developments in your industry, and other important considerations. Then you can make an estimate based on the organization's future business plans. This human resources forecast projects current staffing into the future and compares it with the forecast of requirements to determine the adequacy of the HR capability. Exhibit 2-3 is an example of a form to forecast human resources requirements.

Exhibit 2-2. Human resources inventory form.

Department _____ Date _____ through _____

Name	Title	Performance	Experience	Education	Skills	Jobs Held	Cross-trained	Estimated Annual Cost		
								Salary Cost	Benefit Cost	Total

Exhibit 2-3. Human resources forecast form.

C = Current Staff

F = Forecast Staff

Date _____ through _____

Department		Managers	Professionals	Technicians	Clerical	Estimated Annual		Estimated Total Cost
						Salary Cost	Benefit Cost	
	C							
	F							
	C							
	F							
	C							
	F							
	C							
	F							
	C							
	F							
	C							
	F							
TOTALS	C							
	F							

Labor Market Assessment

The labor market assessment is simply an assessment of the local labor situation—the types and skill levels of the people who are in the market for jobs. If there are large numbers of people to be recruited in more than one area of the country, many sources should be reviewed. The following sources can be used in completing a national labor market assessment:

- U.S. Department of Labor, Bureau of Labor Statistics, Washington, D.C. 20212. Provides national labor statistics.
- *Occupational Outlook Handbook,* published by the U.S. Department of Labor, Bureau of Labor Statistics, Washington, D.C. 20212. Provides information on the outlook for specific job categories.
- *Current Census Statistics,* published by the Bureau of the Census, Washington, D.C. 20212. Census figures give a good idea about the numbers of people available locally and nationally.
- State departments of labor and employment. Provide statistics for particular states.
- Local chambers of commerce. May have labor statistics.
- Local newspapers. Financial pages and want ads reflect the current business and recruiting climate. Check the number of ads each week for the types of jobs you have open or will have open.
- College and university placement offices. Usually provide job candidates.
- Nationwide Advertising Service, Inc., Cleveland, Ohio 44115. Provides information on recruitment, and advertising.
- Other companies in your area that are recruiting for the same types of jobs. Exchange information on the local labor market.
- Your local recruitment network. HR contacts may be one of the most usable sources of information.
- Leaders in the minority community and the church community. Often keep track of the employment climate in their communities and are a good source for diversity hiring programs.
- Mayor's office and governor's office. Provide current labor market information. They sometimes know about changes in the community before they are announced in the newspapers and also occasionally do labor market assessments.

WORK FORCE AND LABOR MARKET ASSESSMENT PROCESS

The work force and labor market assessment process is the roadmap for implementation of the planning and recruiting functions. The process is the same for most organizations. It provides an organized set of procedures to follow from the initial opening of a position through to recruitment and recommendations. See Exhibit 2-4 for an overview of the process.

The labor market assessment should also look at:

- The best employment source by type of position, by location
- Competitiveness of the compensation and benefits package being offered in each recruitment area, as compared to local practice

Exhibit 2-4. Work force and labor market assessment process.

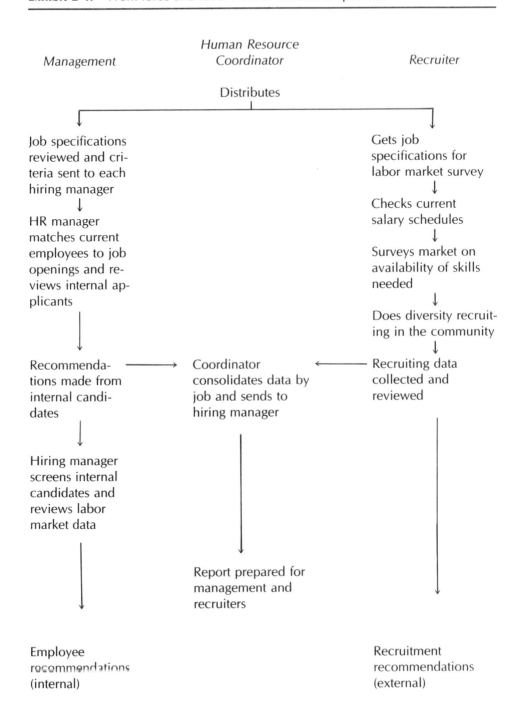

Management

Human Resource
Coordinator

Recruiter

Distributes

Job specifications
reviewed and cri-
teria sent to each
hiring manager

HR manager
matches current
employees to job
openings and re-
views internal ap-
plicants

Recommenda-   →   Coordinator   ←   Recruiting data
tions made from   consolidates data by   collected and
internal candi-   job and sends to   reviewed
dates   hiring manager

Hiring manager
screens internal
candidates and
reviews labor
market data

Gets job
specifications for
labor market survey

Checks current
salary schedules

Surveys market on
availability of skills
needed

Does diversity recruit-
ing in the community

Report prepared for
management and
recruiters

Employee
recommendations
(internal)

Recruitment
recommendations
(external)

- The most common indicators of the availability of qualified people
- Local labor climate and unemployment statistics

Succession Plan

The labor market assessment is the external capability for recruitment. You also need to review the internal capability by completing a succession plan. Succession planning is a procedure for identifying people who can replace key executives, managers, and professionals, and after identifying them, for deciding what development programs are needed to prepare them for moving to higher positions. Succession plans must be reviewed before outside recruiting plans are finalized. There are four key elements of an effective succession plan.

1. The succession plan statement. This is a mission statement that establishes the objectives and commitment of the organization to succession planning.
2. The succession planning backup summary. This lists the key positions and identifies the backup personnel.
3. Individual development plans. After successors have been identified, individual development plans must be made and carried out.
4. Future recruiting plans based on the succession plan.

Succession planning should be done for at least four levels of the organization: president, vice-president, director, and manager. It can be done eventually for all levels, but since the organization is most likely to suffer significant dislocation if someone leaves at the higher levels, it is best to start with these positions. It is also at these levels that development frequently takes place in preparation for promotion. Development here can take a great deal of time, so advance planning is necessary.

Succession planning forces senior executives to think more carefully about what must be done to develop their staff—something that is critical no matter what size the company is. Even smaller companies make a mistake by not developing their employees to move up. If something happens to one of the senior executives, there can be a real problem. With no succession candidates being groomed, there will likely be a lack of continuity and a loss of productivity for a period of time while new people are recruited.

No two companies do succession planning in the same way. Some emphasize only identification of successors, while others put their emphasis on development of younger professionals and managers, with programs to prepare them for greater responsibility. Companies often use some assessment of candidates for promotion to create a fast-track list.

It is important for top management to prepare a key position backup summary for the succession plan. A form for preparing such a summary is shown in Exhibit 2-5. When the key positions have been listed and their backup personnel identified, the individual development plans can be formalized for each backup employee.

Individual Development Plans

The human resources planning process is integrated with individual development through performance appraisals, establishing career paths, and training and development. Appraisals of potential also may determine the possibility of an individual taking on more

Exhibit 2-5. Succession plan backup summary form.

INCUMBENT

Key Position	Dept.	Yrs. in Co.	Yrs. in Position	Performance Level	Current Salary	Salary Range	Comments
						Min.	
Name	Location					Mid.	
						Max.	

BACKUPS

Key Position	Dept.	Yrs. in Co.	Yrs. in Position	Performance Level	Current Salary	Salary Range	Comments
						Min.	
Name	Location	Ready now _____ Years needed for development _____				Mid.	
						Max.	

Key Position	Dept.	Yrs. in Co.	Yrs. in Position	Performance Level	Current Salary	Salary Range	Comments
						Min.	
Name	Location	Ready now _____ Years needed for development _____				Mid.	
						Max.	

responsibility. The plan should be integrated with a program to move people up through the organization as they gain skills and experience. Exhibit 2-6 is a sample form for use in structuring employee individual development plans.

Identifying the High-Potential "Fast Trackers"

Most HR professionals cringe when they hear the term *fast trackers* because in the past the term may have been tied to favoritism. But when it comes to HR planning, it is crucial to identify and develop such high-potential employees. They are the lifeblood of any organization, and to retain them, we must identify them and ensure that they get the development and mentoring they need.

The search for high-potential people, backed by a reliable performance appraisal system, is designed to narrow the field of potential successors to those with the highest probability of reaching the top management ranks. Career planning further limits the possibilities by shedding light on the aspirations of individuals in upper and middle management. The end result should be an objective inventory of the organization's present and future executives.

Most companies put the succession plan, including the fast-track list, on the computer. The career paths of managers and professionals are charted using software that monitors professional and executive talent. The software links people from the succession plan and the affirmative action program into the company's overall human resources plan.

Using Dual-Career Ladders

Many organizations that employ both business and technical or scientific managers have installed dual-career ladders in order to provide promotional opportunities for both types of career professionals. Dual-career ladders will be essential to retention of high-performance technical and scientific employees in the 1990s. One of the most successful organizations using dual-career ladders is Exxon. There, a respected manager can rise to the position of senior vice-president in the management career ladder, while an equally valued scientist with as much seniority and good performance can become a senior scientist in the technical or scientific career ladder. The two jobs carry equal salaries and prestige. Exhibit 2-7 is an example of such a dual-career ladder.

It has been said that technical and scientific people do not necessarily make good managers. They are not always effective in dealing with people in a managerial role on a daily basis. In the past, when companies promoted these employees up through the managerial ranks, some failed at managing. The organization then had only two alternatives: demote them back into their jobs as "individual contributors," or fire them. Many companies, therefore, have adopted the dual-career ladder approach, so the technical and scientific people have opportunities for promotion and can remain successful as they move up. Companies have to find ways to promote these valuable people in order to retain them.

The key to the success of a dual-career ladder is the close attention paid to both management and technical performance in succession planning, and in the ability of management to communicate opportunities to both managerial and technical people. One way to ensure success is to include job opportunities in both career ladders through a computer database. It is important that hiring managers in a far-flung operation consult

Exhibit 2-6. Employee individual development plan form.

Employee _____   Date _____
Department _____   Manager _____
Present Job (No. 1)   Potential Job (No. 2)

Knowledge		Skills	

	Job No. 1	Job No. 2		Job No. 1	Job No. 2
Technical	___	___	Managerial	___	___
General Business	___	___	Technical	___	___
Knowledge of the			Leadership	___	___
Organization	___	___	Problem Solving	___	___
Company Policy	___	___	Decision Making	___	___
Company Procedures	___	___	Administrative	___	___
_____	___	___	Communication:		
_____	___	___	• Oral	___	___
_____	___	___	• Written	___	___
			Organization	___	___
			Planning	___	___
X = fully adequate			Precision	___	___
XX = needs development			Motivation	___	___
			Handling Stress	___	___
			Sensitivity to People	___	___
			Interpersonal Skills	___	___

Training or Experience Needs	How to Accomplish	Date to Be Accomplished
_____	School _____	_____
	Seminar _____	_____
_____	Assignment Shadowing ___	_____
	Experience in position	
_____	Temporary Assignment as _	_____
_____	Special Emphasis on _____	_____
_____	Timing of Promotion for HR plan _____	_____

Exhibit 2-7. Sample dual-career ladder.

Managerial Ladder		Technical/Scientific Ladder	
Title	Salary	Title	Salary
Vice-President, Marketing	$150,000	Research Fellow	$150,000
Director, Marketing	90,000	Senior Research Scientist	90,000
Manager, Marketing	60,000	Research Scientist	60,000
Senior Market Analyst	45,000	Senior Research Analyst	45,000
Market Analyst	30,000	Senior Laboratory Technician	30,000

the database when they are looking for people to fill jobs at higher levels of the organization. Because of the shortage of qualified technical and scientific people in the 1990s, dual-career ladders will play an important role in the retention of a qualified work force, and this approach should be considered in the HR plan.

PERFORMANCE APPRAISAL AND CAREER PLANNING

An objective, workable performance appraisal system lets you evaluate each individual's performance. It provides the opportunity for two-way communication between the employee and the employee's supervisor, and it allows the employee to predict future success on the job. It is an opportunity to provide constructive, valuable feedback. Without a performance dialogue, a company cannot retain its best people. The success of an organization's performance appraisal system is essential in order for any organization to make critical decisions about its future leadership. The performance appraisal process is discussed in detail in Chapter 13.

Employees' career aspirations are crucial considerations in effective human resources planning, as well as in long-term retention. Paying attention to the fit between organizational needs and employee ambitions is more critical today than ever before. Many organizations continue to overlook the possibility of nontraditional aspirations among their talented personnel, but the days are gone when an organization could rely automatically on its ability to dictate an employee's job position, transfer status, and career path.

The ultimate responsibility for career planning rests with the employee. The company's job is to provide the systems, information, and rewards that can influence an employee's personal career decisions. The challenge is to stay attuned to the employee's aspirations and match them to the human resources needs of the organization.

Projecting Recruitment Needs

A review of the work force analysis, succession plan, human resources forecast, and current open positions provides HR planners with a reasonable picture of recruitment needs. In current replacement recruiting, the shortfall is critical. The numbers of open positions are tracked weekly. In long-term recruiting, the process takes on a more leisurely tone. It is still critical, but time frames are less stressful. This type of recruiting frequently targets colleges and universities and relies less on advertising and the use of outside recruitment firms.

A projection of the anticipated recruiting needs should be communicated in detail to the managers of the various departments where any shortfall is being projected as well as to the top executives of the departments that will be impacted. Key managers and top executives can be a resource in the long-term recruiting process.

Approaches to Recruiting

Recruitment is discussed in detail in Chapter 3, but it must be mentioned here because it is a vital part of the HR planning process. Most organizations today use a structured approach to recruiting. There are two elements to a structured recruitment plan. First, there is the need to respond to everyday replacement and turnover problems, and second, there is the need to move people up through the organization. So we do:

- Current replacement recruiting
- Future-oriented succession plan recruiting

Replacement plan recruiting responds to the openings in each department on a daily basis. It is reactive and carries real-time priorities. We need the person now! Succession plan recruiting is future-oriented. Look at the key people in the organization, identify their internal replacements, and make plans for grooming those people to move up in the organization. If there are no replacement possibilities internally, we know there will be holes in the organization, and we establish recruiting goals that become part of the long-range HR plan.

Establishing a Talent Pool

As development and recruitment efforts start to pay off, the organization will begin to form a talent pool, a group of qualified, able individuals. Managing a talent pool is a real challenge, and tough questions inevitably arise. For instance, when positions open up, who should be selected from the pool? What selection criteria will you use? What do you do with talent pool members during the interim between their development and an opening? How much visibility should a talent pool have in the organization? When there are several talented candidates for a new position, does the organization risk losing the "losers" when a successor is selected? These questions have to be addressed early in the human resources planning process, and appropriate policies and procedures must be determined.

Budgeting Recruiting Costs

Top management always wants to know what the bottom line is when it comes to costs. When you complete an HR plan, it's a good idea to show what your actual costs of recruiting and employment are. These costs are easy to compute if you keep track of them as you go along. Exhibit 2-8 provides a sample computation of recruiting and employment costs for twelve professional employees. After you have identified the numbers and types of people you need to recruit, you can project costs by using this sample format.

Exhibit 2-8. Sample computation of approximate costs to the company for recruiting and employing twelve professional employees.

Recruiting Costs

Eight of the employees came through search firms, one was recruited by an employee, and three came through classified advertising.

• Advertising	$4,100.00
• Search firms	
(eight applicants × average salary of $30,000 × 30 percent placement fee)	72,000.00
• Interviewing costs	
— (Recruiter's salary of $28,000 per year, or $13.46 per hour × fourteen hours' interviewing × twelve applicants)	2,261.28
— (Department manager's salary of $50,000 per year, or $24.03 per hour × ten hours' interviewing × twelve applicants)	2,883.60
— Travel expenses to bring applicants in for interviews	3,600.00

Employment Costs

• Relocation	
— Six required to relocate benefits, including help selling old home (six × average cost of $15,000)	90,000.00
— Eight required move of household items (eight × average move of $5,000)	40,000.00
— New employee orientation (twelve × $150 per employee)	1,800.00
Approximate cost of recruiting and employing twelve professional employees	$216,644.88

Note: The costs of new employee training and break-in are not calculated.

Tying It All Together

The human resources plan is a little like a puzzle. Each piece gives you more information and eventually provides a complete picture of your human resources capability.

- The human resources inventory tells you about the people you currently have on your payroll: their skills, abilities, and performance levels.
- The work force analysis tells you which people can be found inside the organization and which positions must be externally recruited.

- The human resources forecast is based on the organization's future business plans so you can forecast your human resources needs.
- The labor market assessment tells you where you will most likely find new recruits to fill your open positions and in which positions you will be short of applicants.
- The succession plan and the individual development plans tell you who the backups are to current key positions, which employees are being groomed to move up, what type of development is needed, and the timing for promotion.

All of this results in an overall human resources plan and provides a complete picture of your organization.

After all the critical elements of the planning process have been reviewed and approved by the CEO and the top executives, it takes from four to six months to actually develop and implement the HR plan.

Evaluating and revising the human resources plan is the final step. Evaluate the plan and the process at least annually so that when there are changes in plans and policies, you can make adjustments quickly. The following should be used in evaluating a plan:

- Number of qualified backups. This one is relatively simple: How many qualified replacements do you have for each key position in the organization?
- Ratio of internal to external successors. Once the planning system is in place, you can expect a drop in the number of positions filled from outside the organization. But you can't aim for the complete elimination of external recruitment. In fact, you need new people coming into the organization so it is constantly revitalized.
- Time needed to fill key positions. If qualified candidates for key job openings can't be found quickly, something is lacking in the development program or askew in the projection of future needs and the external work force analysis.
- Achievement of affirmative action goals by including diversity and disability in the planning effort. The diversity projection and affirmative action plan provide one more way to gauge when the program is a success.

Planning is an ongoing process. Once the plan is completed, it must be reviewed and updated on a regular basis in order to be an effective management tool.

All of the HR data you've gathered in your planning process provides input into the organization's recruiting plan. The recruiting plan then becomes a major piece of the human resources plan. It's also important to provide this information to the managers in the departments so they will have a future orientation to their ongoing development and recruitment activities.

Establishing a Positive Human Resources Climate

The key to the success of the human resources function and HR planning in any organization lies in the quality of the relationship between the CEO and the senior human resources executive. Some aspects of the relationship are professional and task-oriented, while others are more personal and informal. The nature of the relationship between the

CEO and the human resources organization will be a function of at least three dimensions.

1. The degree to which the CEO focuses on the human resources aspects of the business
2. The CEO's regard for the senior human resources executive's capabilities
3. The ability of the two individuals to relate both formally and informally

A clear understanding of the role and responsibilities of the human resources executive as well as the function itself is the basis for an effective working relationship. In addition, HR programs must be operating at high standards. Finally, the function must provide leadership for the organization in terms of change and innovation. With these more formal aspects of the job in place, effective working relationships can be developed and nurtured.

In instances where the relationship extends beyond formal boundaries, the human resources executive enjoys a rather special relationship with the CEO. This could originate from the CEO's personal interest in the field of human resources, or it could happen because the human resources executive acts as a consultant or adviser with respect to the chief executive officer's own performance. This more informal aspect of the relationship tends to be unique, and where it does occur, the overall relationship between the office of the CEO and the human resources function is enhanced.

THE HIRING PROCESS

3

Recruiting

Mary F. Cook
President
Mary Cook & Associates

Even though over the past several years there have been significant numbers of layoffs and downsizings, most organizations are struggling with labor shortages and are looking for new and innovative ways to recruit the workers they need to fill critical positions. Companies in the services industries are having the toughest time, but all organizations—especially those that need teachers, nurses, social workers, trained technicians, and other professionals—are looking for new ways to attract the few workers who are available.

Recruiting today is not like it was only a few years ago. Finding qualified candidates is more difficult because of changing demographics, new work values, the volatile economy, and global competition. All of these factors join together to make recruiting one of the most difficult activities businesspeople face today. Managers find that the old ways of recruiting workers, by running newspaper advertisements and by word-of-mouth, are not very effective. Large company recruiters, small business executives, and the public sector all have to be more creative and innovative and find new, nontraditional ways to locate qualified applicants.

In this chapter we review some basic strategies organizations must consider in order to be successful in their recruiting efforts: designing, implementing, and managing a state-of-the-art recruiting program; reviewing and revitalizing traditional methods; seeking out new labor segments; pursuing individuals who will need to relocate; and finally—and most important—putting an emphasis on and making resources available to the human resources function. Recruitment in light of the Americans with Disabilities Act (ADA) is also discussed. Get your management group together and brainstorm ways to identify and recruit the types of employees you need to fill your open positions. Discuss how workers are changing and how they would impact your organization. Analyze the ways your company may be willing to change its policies to attract these new workers.

Remember when recruiting hard-to-fill jobs that flexibility is the answer. Be open-minded regarding working hours, job sharing, working at home, temporary help, and other alternative working situations. In order to attract the best people, gear company procedures to workers' needs.

Recruitment Methods

The person in the HR department assigned to handle recruiting for an open position can save a great deal of time by sitting down with the department manager and mapping out a recruitment strategy that will work best to fill the open job. There should be a current job description that provides a list of the essential functions of the open position, along with the physical qualifications needed to do the job. The Americans with Disabilities Act requires that employers who are covered by the Act place classified ads and conduct interviews in such a way as to determine if applicants are qualified for employment in the position. Companies must look at the following criteria:

- Job objectives (purposes of the position)
- Essential job functions
- Job standards (minimum qualifications needed to perform essential job functions)
- Job location
- Equipment (that must be used to do the job)

The recruiter can either use the current job description, or a form similar to the one shown in Exhibit 3-1.

There are a number of basic methods used by most organizations today to recruit new employees. Exhibit 3-2 shows these common recruitment methods, indicating which work best for each job category. The methods are discussed in the pages that follow.

Newspaper Advertising

Newspaper advertising can be costly on a per hire basis unless you pay a great deal of attention to it to make it work. Here are six steps to productive newspaper advertising.

1. Know the job. Get all the important details about it before you write the ad. Essential job functions taken from the job description should be included in the ad.

2. Decide where to place the ad in the papers. This depends in part on the timing for filling the job and the level of the job. Most organizations use cheaper classified ads for their lower-level jobs and the more expensive display ads for higher-level executive positions.

3. Develop an exciting vocabulary list that will turn applicants on to your job and your company. You want to entice them to read the entire ad, just as newspaper copy-writers do with their lists of zippy words that describe products.

4. Sell the company's future and its personality as well as the job. Don't oversell, but at least do a good job of describing the best elements of your organization.

5. Determine the tone of the ad. We've all read ads and said, "I'm glad I don't work there." The words you use and the tone of the ad tell a lot about the company. Both the baby boomers and the baby busters who will make up the majority of the work force in the 1990s want to work in a participative work environment and don't respond to autocratic management techniques. Make sure your ad appeals to them.

6. Decide which section of the classifieds the ad will run in. If necessary, run a short cross-reference ad. For example, if you are running an ad for a human resources manager, put a small cross-reference ad under personnel manager.

Pay attention to the smallest details, because it's the missed details that will keep your advertising from being fully effective. At the end of this chapter are sample ads that reflect a participative organizational style and an employee-oriented environment.

Exhibit 3-1. Recruitment worksheet.

Position _____ Department _____

Date Opened _____ Manager _____

Describe the essential functions of the job _____

1. _____
2. _____
3. _____
4. _____
5. _____
6. _____
7. _____
8. _____
9. _____
10. _____
11. _____
12. _____
13. _____
14. _____

Other job related information—Computer skills needed, machines applicant must

be able to use _____

_____

Met with manager and discussed the following methods for recruitment:

_____

_____

Is there a budget for: Advertising _____ Amount _____

                                Agency Fees _____ Amount _____

What is the timeline for filling the job? _____

Has the job been posted within the company? _____ Date _____

Is there an EEO objective for this position? _____

Date position filled _____ Name of person hired _____

Recruiter _____

Exhibit 3-2. Basic recruitment methods.

Recruitment Method	Managers and Executives	Profes- sionals	Technical, Including Data Processing	Admini- strative, Accounting, etc.	Cleri- cal	Laborers and Service Workers
Ads in local newspapers		x	x	x	x	x
Ads in *Wall Street Journal* or other na- tional papers	x	x				
Ads in trade publi- cations and maga- zines	x	x	x			
Ads on TV and ra- dio		x	x	x	x	
Direct mail		x	x	x		
Employment agen- cies	x	x	x	x	x	
Executive search firms	x					
Computerized data- bases	x	x	x	x		
Telerecruiting		x	x			
College recruiting		x	x	x		
Retiree job banks		x	x	x		
Job fairs		x	x	x		
State job services		x	x	x	x	x
Employee referrals		x	x	x	x	x
Internal recruiting		x	x	x	x	x
Walk-in applicants, unsolicited résumés			x	x	x	x

Note: There are times when one of the above methods of filling a job would work better than another, but over time the methods checked should prove most effective.

WHERE TO PLACE ADS

Ads can be placed in both local papers and in national newspapers like the *Wall Street Journal*. Ads in local papers are generally successful unless you are recruiting for hard-to-fill positions or for executive or top professional positions. In these cases, you may want to recruit nationwide, running ads in the *Wall Street Journal,* the *New York Times,* or perhaps the *Los Angeles Times*. Display ads in these newspapers are expensive, but for some positions they can be the most effective recruitment method. See the Resources section at the end of this Handbook for a list of national and leading local newspapers to consider using in your recruitment efforts.

Ads can be placed in both the classified (help wanted) or display sections of the newspaper. Classified ads are cheaper, but display ads may get more attention, and you may find that the quality and quantity of candidates improves. It's a good idea to use a different section of the newspaper than traditionally used: If classifieds have typically been used in the past, try some display ads. Also, no matter what section you advertise in, a good strategy is to group several ads together to gain visibility and decrease total expenditures.

WRITING THE AD

Just as the most successful product marketing campaigns are targeted to a specific market, recruitment advertising is most effective when it speaks to a specific group of candidates. Target the market and use "hot buttons" to reach people. For example, if a company is initiating a recruiting program targeted to the older worker, recruitment messages should be geared to that market. Likewise, if the target audience is experienced computer professionals, the recruitment message should be designed to speak to these candidates and their needs.

When writing an ad, ask yourself: Does the message sell? In today's market, where extensive competition for qualified applicants exists, the recruitment message must be eye-catching, with copy that sells. One strategy is to enlist the help of your marketing or advertising departments in creating powerful ads. Another strategy is to use the services of an outside recruitment advertising agency.

A recruitment ad should prompt qualified candidates to take action. One of the best methods is to include a telephone number (preferably toll-free), and ask candidates to call for more information. Since Sunday help wanted ads are most popular, many companies staff phone lines on Sundays to capitalize on the response the ad may generate on that day. This also encourages those who are working to call at their convenience. The ad should state the hours that the phones will be covered.

Other response methods include requesting applicants to send a résumé and cover letter, to phone to schedule an appointment for an interview, or to drop by the HR department on certain days at specified times. Another strategy is to include in the advertisement a clip-out coupon, which serves as a mini-application form.

If you prefer not to use your company name, you can place a blind ad and give a box number to which applicants can send their résumés. This method eliminates the company's obligation to reply to all applicants. The strategy may save the company a lot of time, especially if the ad is likely to result in a deluge of applications. The blind ad can have other advantages for the employer: The company may not want internal candidates to know that external recruiting is being conducted, or it may want to initiate recruitment activity in anticipation of a vacancy.

The major problem with blind advertising is that many good candidates will not answer blind ads. Some fear that their own employer is running the ad. Some may not answer as a matter of principle: They feel they are releasing confidential information about themselves, and they prefer to know to whom they are sending that information.

If your organization is a government contractor or has an affirmative action program, you must follow certain rules with respect to job advertising.

- State that all qualified applicants will receive consideration for employment without regard to race, color, religion, sex, age, national origin, or handicap.
- Use the phrase *An Equal Opportunity Employer*. At the end of the ad, state ''Equal Opportunity Employer/M/F/H'' (for male, female, and handicapped).
- Remember that under the ADA, essential job functions must be included in recruitment advertising.

PLACING ADS

To place a recruitment ad, call the ad department of a national newspaper or your local paper. (If there is more than one newspaper in your city, pick the one with the highest circulation.) Ask for a classified ad packet, which should contain samples of ads and their prices. You can choose the type of ad you want to use before you call in the ad. Another option is to buy a copy of the paper and browse the ad section. Find an ad you like, one that is the size and type style you want. Then call the classified ad department of the newspaper and tell the ad-taker that you want to place an ad, which you want to look similar to an ad run in that paper on a certain date. The person can find that ad and will have a good idea about what you want. Either process will save time and lengthy discussion. You can use the same process to place a display ad.

Some companies require recruiters to use a help wanted ad form, mainly because they want to retain a record of ads placed, their cost, and the response. A copy of the actual ad can be pasted to the form and retained for future use. See Exhibit 3-3 for an example of such a form.

Trade Publications and Magazines

An effective way to reach professional and technical people in your industry is to run advertisements in the most widely read trade publications. Most professionals read trade publications regularly. Advertising in trade publications, industry journals, and newsletters can also be an excellent way to sell your corporate image. People become familiar with organizations through their advertising, and advertisements that portray the organization in a good light attract people. One problem with running recruitment ads in trade journals, however, is the longer response time, since some journals are published only quarterly.

There are also many specialized magazines that can be effective media for your ads. Refer to the Resources section at the end of the book for a list of such publications.

Exhibit 3-3.   Help wanted advertising form.

Position _____ Requisition No. _____

Department _____

Charge to (Cost Center) _____

Person Requesting Ad _____ Phone _____

>   Note: Ads must be sent to the Human Resources Department by Wednesday
>   at 3 P.M. for Sunday placement.

. . . .

Newspaper(s) _____

_____

Run Ad _____ Days   Dates _____

_____

Under Heading(s) _____

Please insert the actual ad placed for the above position:

Note: Ad copy may be typed on a separate sheet and attached to this form.

. . . .

For HR Department Use Only

Ad Ordered—Date _____ Cost _____ Approved _____

Radio and Television Advertising

Both radio and television have a distinct advantage when recruiting hard-to-find job
candidates: They reach huge numbers of people quickly. Most people watch television
and listen to radio at some time during the day or evening. But such exposure comes at

a price. Television advertising can be expensive, running anywhere from $5,000 per spot all the way up to $200,000. And most experts agree that each spot must be seen anywhere from five to seven times before it's remembered or acted upon. Radio can be more cost-effective than television and offers many opportunities to reach target audiences. Radio ads are most effective when repeated several days running during prime time, when people are driving to and from work.

Radio and television ads should end with a clear request. Ask listeners or viewers to make a telephone call, and have the phones staffed with trained employees who can answer questions about the position and schedule appointments for interviews. Both radio and television can be very effective when paired with newspaper advertising; the radio or TV message should refer to the newspaper ad, which can include a number to call, an address to write to, or even a coupon to complete and mail. Radio and television ads can also be used to invite candidates to job fairs.

Another option companies use is cable television advertising. Usually rates are low, and the recruitment message will still reach a large viewing audience. Companies also may advertise on specific cable television channels, such as MTV. With large, demographically targeted viewing audiences, cable television channels may offer a more favorable advertising rate than other TV channels.

The use of TV for recruiting purposes really depends on your budget and your location. Companies that have many job openings and are located in a large city might find TV ads cost-effective.

Direct Mail

An increasing number of organizations have turned to direct mail as a new nontraditional recruitment method. Direct mail recruiting can target a much larger audience and target it more precisely than the old hit-and-miss recruitment methods. Using direct mail lists from professional associations or other similar organizations, you can speed recruiting efforts to specialized audiences. The cost of direct mail recruitment campaigns is easy to predict and budget for, and the results can be directly measured.

If you are recruiting a large number of people, direct mail recruiting can be cheaper in the long run than running a lot of expensive classified or display ads. Direct mail may not be useful, however, if vacancies must be filled immediately, since responses may not come for several weeks following a mailing. If a first mailing does not generate good results, a second mailing in a specific area beyond the immediate labor market may work. In any event, the best approach in direct mail recruitments is to test a sample of a mailing list, rather than the complete list. A strategy to follow in conducting a direct mail recruiting program follows.

Sample Direct Mail Program

• *Develop a mailing list.* Have a brainstorming session with the people in your organization who can make the best decision on which groups to mail to. After you have decided which groups to target, contact a direct mail company that has those lists. The company can provide mailing labels as well as lists. Direct mail companies are listed in the yellow pages of the phone books in most cities in the United States.

List brokers can also assist in the selection and procurement of a list targeted to certain demographic groups. For the name of a direct mail broker, contact the Mail

Advertising Service Association, 7315 Wisconsin Avenue, Suite 818-E, Bethesda, Maryland 20814, or the Direct Mail Marketing Association, 6 East 43rd Street, New York, New York 10017. Direct mail companies will mail your materials to a specific geographic area. You can choose the area to be targeted. Companies that sell mailing lists can help you target specific age groups, as well as income levels and geographic areas. They will sell you their lists or provide the names and addresses on labels. Mailing lists can also be obtained by contacting recruitment advertising agencies or using your company's advertising agency.

Some professional associations will rent their lists of members. You can also contact employees who may belong to such associations and ask to use their directories.

• *Develop the mailing piece.* The mailing piece can be a personal letter or a flyer describing the job vacancies and career opportunities in the company. The copy should be concise and easy to read. The first paragraph should grab the reader's attention. The more targeted the message, the better. If the company is participating in a job fair, the timing of the mail recruitment program may be scheduled to coincide with that event, and the letter or flyer can be written in the form of an invitation.

Make it easy for any interested recipient of your correspondence to respond. Ask applicants to call for more information about the company or job vacancies or to set up an interview. Indicate the best time for them to call, and make sure the individual responsible for taking the calls will be available. Consider offering evening or weekend hours to make it easier for those who are working. Another option is to include an applicant reply card, with the company's name and address printed on the front of the card. Interested applicants can complete the card and send for more information. The card should explain what recipients can expect if they return it.

• *Time the mailing.* Time your mailing so it doesn't coincide with seasonal vacation times. Don't do a major mailing during or close to national or religious holidays. Spring and fall are good seasons to use direct mail for recruitment.

Employment Agencies and Executive (Retained) Search Firms

For years one of the most traditional methods of recruiting has been the use of employment agencies paid by the company. After all the layoffs and downsizings in the 1980s and early 1990s, some organizations have moved away from the heavy use of employment agencies except when recruiting managers or top executives. Recruitment agencies normally charge a percentage (about 33 percent) of the first year's salary of each person the company hires through an agency. So-called "retained search" companies charge fees plus a retainer to cover their expenses. If you have a position that has been difficult to fill or you think you will have to go out of state to fill a position, you may find the best method is to use an executive search firm. It may be the quickest and most cost-effective method of filling the position, because it's expensive to run ads and keep your recruiters out of state for long periods. A list of executive search firms is included in the Resources section at the end of this book.

Computerized Databases

A recruitment database is a computerized collection of information on potential employment candidates compiled by an executive search firm, an employment agency, or a network of employment agencies. Universities and government employment offices also have computerized databases. Any résumé on the database may be retrieved by users who can search for candidates with the appropriate qualifications of the positions they seek to fill. These qualifications or criteria typically include area of expertise, academic degrees and performance, current salary level, current position, and geographical preferences. Computerized databases become a crucial recruiting tool as companies expand nationwide or overseas.

Telerecruiting

Telerecruiting is one of the newest and most controversial recruitment approaches. It's certainly nontraditional. Many large companies, like Apple Computer, Inc., in Cupertino, California, have telerecruiting departments employing people who spend most of their time on the telephone interviewing and screening candidates for open positions. Their backgrounds include a mix of HR and telemarketing skills.

Telerecruiting expedites the recruitment process. When a company uses an outside recruiting firm, there is a sixty- to ninety-day lag period between an applicant's response to an advertisement and the actual interview. With in-house telerecruiting, applicants are interviewed within two or three days of being contacted. The in-house telerecruiting function has married the technologies of the computer and skills of the telemarketer with the expertise of the HR professional. It provides a much larger database of information on the applicant pool and speeds the recruitment process.

Telerecruiting is controversial; many organizations take offense if they discover their employees are being contacted by other companies at work. A company's top executives should be informed of the decision to use telerecruiting. This will protect the HR person responsible for making the calls should the company's president receive a complaint from an irate competitor. It will also encourage the company to plan a response if a call is received.

Many companies that use telerecruiting hire a third party or use a recruiting agency to make the calls. The third party will not disclose the name of the employer until a candidate indicates genuine interest in the position. By using a third party or an agency, the company eliminates the need to defend itself to a competitor. Also, if the company has inadequate resources to conduct telerecruiting, outside resources can be helpful.

Telerecruiting can be an appealing option, particularly because it entails no cost if in-house resources are used and call lists are not purchased from an outside company. It provides an excellent payback in terms of the number of people recruited for the time and cost invested.

Telerecruiting targets those who are currently employed, which generally ensures a higher quality candidate. It has great appeal because of the variety and types of positions for which it can be used. Personnel who can be targeted for telerecruiting include engineers, designers, finance and accounting professionals, computer programmers, marketing professionals, nurses, and managers at all levels and in all industries. Telerecruiting is an excellent tool if candidates are needed quickly, because it provides one of the fastest turnaround times. A sample telerecruiting program follows.

Sample Telerecruiting Program

• *Develop a recruitment list.* Identify your target recruitment market. If you know where candidates work but don't have their home telephone numbers, your telerecruiter will have to call the person on the job. In the past this activity was frowned on, but today it's become common practice. Ask your department manager to assist your telerecruiter in developing the recruiting list.

• *Develop a script* for the telerecruiter to use. Usually the telerecruiter is more of a marketing person than an HR person. Most marketing people have a more interesting approach. This is important, because you must interest the candidate within the first two or three sentences in order to get a response and sell the candidate. The telerecruiter must quickly gain the ear of the person being called.

• *Design a telerecruiting form* in order to ensure the recruiter gets all the information needed to pursue a candidate further. Have the telerecruiters record any other information they may be able to obtain that will assist in the recruiting process, things like "the candidate is unhappy with current pay" or "candidate wants to leave geographic area." The telerecruiters should also use a rating scale on the form to indicate their opinions of the people called.

• *Establish a special recruitment process* that quickly gets top candidates into the company for an interview. Have your HR interviewers work with the telerecruiters to speed the interviewing along. Set up a selection system that ensures hiring decisions can be made quickly. Some organizations implement excellent recruiting programs, then candidates have to wait weeks or months to be hired. Good people will be picked up quickly by organizations whose hiring processes are speedier and better organized.

College Recruiting

In order to find and hire the young people you need to have in your organization, you will have to make college recruiting a large part of your recruitment process. Increasingly, you will need to be innovative in your college recruiting efforts. To recruit college students, the American Hotel and Motel Association, based in Washington, D.C., distributed over 2,000 copies of its booklet *Answers to Important Questions About Jobs in Hotels and Motels*. The association received over 600 entry-level résumés from college students. Another approach has been taken by Aetna Life, Allstate, CIGNA, Continental, and USF&G. In a program sponsored by the Insurance Scholarship Program in 1990, students from nine colleges were recognized for their award-winning papers on career and recruitment ideas for the insurance industry. The winners each received a $1,500 scholarship and participated in a Career Awareness program in New York City.

SELECTING THE COLLEGES

The companies that are most successful in recruiting the top candidates from college campuses are the ones that develop and implement their programs over time. To develop a quality college recruiting program, most employers are careful not to spread themselves too thin. A good strategy is to develop a strong campus program with only two to four colleges.

To select colleges that meet your needs, review the following criteria:

• *Size*. What is the size of the college or university? Are there enough students enrolled in the programs of interest to support the needs of your company?

• *Location*. Is the college located near company facilities? If not, will students be willing to relocate to the area?

• *Demographics.* Do the demographics of the student population provide for a college recruiting program that will assist the company in meeting its affirmative action needs? What is the profile of the college's student body? One employer selected a local community college for its recruitment efforts because the students attending were mature, were working while attending school (many were paying for their own education), and possessed some valuable work experience that would make them successful on the job.

• *The strength of the college program.* Are there courses offered in areas your company is looking for?

THE COLLEGE RECRUITING PROCESS

In the typical college recruiting procedure, students seeking employment register at the college placement service. This placement service is a labor market exchange providing opportunities for students and employers to meet and discuss potential hiring. During the recruiting season (from about mid-October to mid-March), candidates are advised through student newspapers, mailings, bulletin boards, and so forth, of scheduled company visits. At the placement service, the students schedule preliminary interviews with employers they want to see and are given brochures and other literature about the companies. After the preliminary interviews and before leaving the campus, each recruiter invites the chosen candidates to make a site visit at a later date. Those lower on the list are told they are being considered and are called upon if preferred students decide not to accept employment with the firm.

Students who are invited to the site are given more job information and meet appropriate potential supervisors and other executives. They are entertained and may be given a series of tests as well. The organization bears all expenses. If the organization desires to hire an individual, he or she is given an offer prior to leaving the site or shortly thereafter by mail or phone.

With which companies do the students want to interview? They choose those whose work sounds interesting, whose recruiting program is well done, and whose image on campus is positive. See Exhibit 3-4 for an overview of a typical college recruiting process.

THE EFFECTIVE COLLEGE RECRUITER

In college recruiting, three elements are involved: the organization, the applicant, and the recruiter. The recruiter is the matcher, the one who represents the company and is actually seen by the applicants. The recruiter is viewed as an example of the kind of person the organization employs and wants in the future.

Students tend to prefer recruiters who are under age 55, with the strongest preference being 35–55. They also like it if the recruiter has had work experience in their specialties, has some personal knowledge of the university they are visiting, and supplies good information on the company. Students also have preferences for specific behavior during the recruiting interview. They like recruiters who are friendly, knowledgeable, candid, have a polished style, and take a personal interest in the applicant. Most applicants also appreciate enthusiastic and convincing communicators.

Major flaws students find in typical recruiters are:

Exhibit 3-4. College recruiting process.

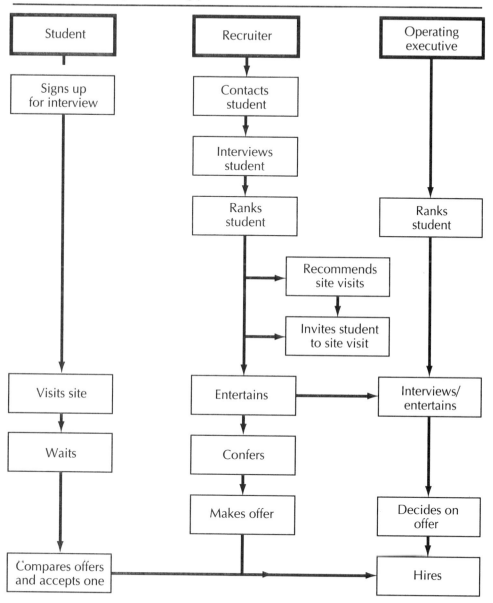

• *Lack of interest in the applicant.* If the recruiter's presentation is mechanical and bureaucratic, students feel there's no genuine interest. One student reported, ''The company might just as well have sent a tape recorder.''

• *Lack of enthusiasm.* If the recruiter seems bored, students feel he or she represents a dull and uninteresting company.

• *Negative or too personal interviews.* Students resent too many personal questions about their social class, their parents, and so on. They want to be evaluated for their own accomplishments. They also unanimously reject negative interviewing styles.

• *Inappropriate time allocation by recruiters.* Students criticize how much time recruiters talk and how much they let applicants talk or ask questions. From the point of view of the applicant, much of the recruiter's time is wasted with a long canned history of the company, number of employees, branches, products, assets, pension plans, and so forth. In addition, many of the questions the recruiter asks applicants are answered on the application blank, so the questions are redundant.

These findings reemphasize the need for a company engaged in college recruiting to train effective recruiters and to have a well-planned visitation schedule. Too many companies do not plan the recruiting interview as well as they do their product sales presentations. The applicant should receive printed material giving company information (such as organization history and details of organization operations). Some companies now produce creative and interesting videos to give applicants this information about the company. These are especially relevant for younger college applicants who've been raised watching TV.

The interview period should be divided about equally between the recruiter and the applicant. Students want to hear about the job itself, the work climate, and the kind of person the organization is trying to hire for the job. Then they would like to be able to discuss how they might fit in and ask other questions. Often, the recruiter talks too long, and almost as an afterthought asks if there are any questions.

Retiree Job Banks

Retiree job banks are growing in popularity as the number of companies using retired employees for temporary and part-time positions grows. According to the February 1990 issue of *Working Age,* the AARP newsletter, the Travelers Companies and Wells Fargo have been joined recently by Digital Equipment Corporation, Hewlett-Packard, CIGNA, and a number of other organizations in responding to issues involving older workers.[1] Retiree job banks enroll retired employees for flexible work assignments and appear to be a promising option as companies lose employees with essential skills.

The Travelers Companies created a job bank in 1981. Ten years later, it listed more than 700 retirees. About half are former Travelers' employees; the other half are recruited from the community. Sixty percent of the Travelers' temporary help requirements are filled by the company's retiree job bank.

If you do not wish to or cannot start your own retiree job bank, another option is to contact nearby companies that have retiree job banks, and ask for retiree referrals.

Job Fairs

A job or career fair involves many companies located within a geographic area. Job fairs are a growing recruitment tool because participation is cost-effective. Advertising and rental costs for the site are shared among employers. According to some published studies, the cost of recruiting a manager or technical employee at a job fair is less than the average cost of running a display in a major newspaper or paying a recruitment agency fee. By attending job fairs, employers can also learn whether their salaries are competitive and can spot employment trends and changes in the labor market.

Job fairs attract many people, including those who are currently employed and might not respond to a newspaper advertisement. Most come with résumés and letters of recommendation, and many candidates can be seen in a short period of time. Some initial screening can be done at the fair, with in-depth interviews scheduled for a later date.

An employer must be willing to make a number of recruiters available for the job fair. If necessary, bring technical people who speak the language of job candidates. They are often in a good position to discuss the company, and prospective employees may feel that a technical employee's view of the company is more realistic than that of a recruiter. In today's highly competitive environment, it's important that recruiters be able to sell the benefits of working for the company.

Employee Referrals

Turning current employees into company recruiters is an excellent way to find job candidates. Employees often know other people in the industry or profession who may be interested in open positions. Studies have also shown that employee referrals are often the best hires, accounting for higher performance ratings and lower turnover rates. In many companies, employee referrals make up 30 percent or more of those recruited.

In some organizations, employees are asked to complete a special employee referral form, which goes to the human resources department. In other companies, employees' names are simply included at the bottom of the referred candidate's application form. The personnel manager then reviews the referred candidate's résumé and arranges an interview. When a referred candidate is selected, the personnel manager should notify and thank the employee who made the referral.

Many companies offer incentives to employees who refer candidates to the company. Incentives can take the form of financial awards or bonus points that can be exchanged for prizes, gifts, or other premiums. The value of the incentive can vary depending on the level of the position and availability of individuals to fill the position. Bonuses can be as low as $25 for entry-level, hourly food-service employees, and as high as $5,000 and up for nurses and technical, professional, and executive managers.

Internal vs. External Recruiting

Internal recruiting is recruiting people already on the payroll to fill openings, as opposed to external recruiting, or hiring people from outside. There are advantages to both internal and external recruiting. (See Exhibit 3-5.) Most organizations feel that a mix of both procedures is necessary to keep a company a vital growing entity.

In order to retain your best employees you need to establish a job posting program so that internal candidates have a procedure to follow when applying for open positions. Exhibit 3-6 is a sample internal job posting policy, which can be revised to fit your company needs. Exhibit 3-7 is a sample job posting application form.

Jobs posted are not necessarily reserved or held exclusively for current employees. The company may concurrently advertise or otherwise recruit qualified persons in the appropriate labor market and may, at its discretion, hire from outside the company. The company reserves the right to hire the most qualified person for the job.

Exhibit 3-5.   Internal vs. external recruiting.

INTERNAL	
Advantages	*Disadvantages*
1. Increased morale of promoted employee	1. Inbreeding
2. Better assessment of abilities	2. Possible morale problems of those not promoted
3. Lower cost for some jobs	3. Political infighting for promotions
4. Motivator for good performance	4. Need strong management development program
5. Causes a succession of promotions	5. Lower-level jobs have frequent turnover
6. Have to hire only at entry level	
EXTERNAL	
Advantages	*Disadvantages*
1. "New blood," new perspectives	1. May not select someone who will "fit"
2. Cheaper than retraining a professional	2. May cause morale problems for those internal candidates not selected
3. No group of political allies in organization already	3. Longer adjustment or orientation time
4. May bring industry insights	4. Outside recruiting is more difficult

Exhibit 3-6.   Sample job posting policy.

The company is generally committed to providing promotional opportunities to employees who have demonstrated exemplary performance and self-motivation. In an attempt to advise employees of job openings, notices will be posted on bulletin boards announcing job vacancies as they occur. All jobs up through manager level will be posted for five working days. Employees who meet the standards and are interested in being considered for posted jobs should contact the human resources manager for an application and further information about the job. Those employees selected for consideration to fill a posted job will be contacted by the human resources manager and will receive an interview.

Walk-in Applicants and Unsolicited Résumés

Human resources departments often receive inquiries from applicants who arrive at the department without first writing or telephoning. In most cases, these individuals are interested in lower-level or entry-level jobs. Such applicants should be allowed to complete application forms. If a member of the HR staff has the time to review the application while the individual is in the office and knows of an open position that the individual seems qualified for, the applicant might be given a first interview on the spot. Otherwise, the applicant should be told that he or she will be contacted at a later date regarding a possible interview.

Many people at all job levels send résumés and accompanying cover letters to

Exhibit 3-7. Job posting application form.

Name _____ Date _____

Current Department _____ Current Job Title _____

Current Supervisor _____

Job Applying for _____ Department _____ Telephone _____

Your qualifications for the job: _____

_____

_____

_____

_____

_____

Other qualifications such as degrees, licenses, etc.: _____

_____

_____

_____

_____

_____

Employee Signature

(continued)

Exhibit 3-7. *Continued.*

. . . .
TO BE COMPLETED BY HR DEPARTMENT

Did employee receive an interview? ——————— yes ——————— no

Date employee was interviewed ———————————————————

Did employee get the job? ——————— yes ——————— no

Why employee did not get the job ——————————————————

———————————————————————————————

Has employee's supervisor been notified? ——————————————

Has employee been notified? ——————————————————————

———————————————————————————————
Human Resources Representative

companies that interest them, in the hope that there is an open position for which they are qualified. Such individuals often state in the cover letter that they will phone the HR department to set up an interview to explore job possibilities. The recruiter has two alternatives: If the résumé and cover letter indicate that the applicant is qualified for an open position, the recruiter can telephone to get further information and possibly arrange an interview. If there is no available position, the recruiter can wait until the applicant phones and then inform him or her of that fact, thanking the applicant for contacting the company and stating that the résumé will be retained and for how long. While an unsolicited résumé can sometimes lead to the hiring of a professional or managerial level employee, in most cases they lead to the hiring of administrative, clerical, or lower-level people.

Recruiting Among Special Groups

Recruiting Employees Who Will Have to Relocate

More and more, companies are hiring executives and professionals nationwide rather than locally and asking these individuals to relocate. Relocation can be extremely expensive for an employer, since relocation policies often include such benefits as paid moving expenses, one month's salary to cover incidental expenses, mortgage interest differentials, and cost-of-living differentials. One rule of thumb is that it costs a corporation one year of an employee's salary to relocate that person. As a result, recruitment among individuals who will have to relocate is often a necessary but weighty matter.

When recruiting applicants who will have to relocate, you need to take extra precautions during the interview process to ascertain how the individual will adjust to the move. You also need to find out if the applicant's spouse will need assistance in finding a job. This is extremely important since dual-career couples will make up a large segment of the work force in the 1990s. If there are children in the family, you should provide information on schools in the area. You should also be prepared to tell the applicant about churches, entertainment, and other activities.

Recruiting From an Immigrant Labor Pool

In an article in the January 1991 *Monthly Labor Review*, William P. O'Hare and Carol J. DeVita discuss the subject of immigrant workers:

> The United States has long regarded itself as a nation of immigrants, but in recent years the number of new immigrants has changed. During the 1950s, about 300,000 legal aliens were admitted each year; now, about twice as many legal immigrants enter the United States on an annual basis. Until the mid-1960s, the vast majority of immigrants to the United States were of European stock. Today, Europeans account for only 11 percent of new entrants. Most legal immigrants are now either from Latin America (38 percent) or Asia (40 percent). And even among these new arrivals, there is a multitude of nationalities and ethnic subgroups, each with its own customs, cultures, traditions, and problems of acculturation.[2]

Immigrants were a traditional labor source in the United States in the early 1900s, but U.S. companies have not deliberately set about to recruit and hire immigrants for many years. Today, however, they are considered a nontraditional but fast-growing source of professional and technical workers. Congress is even addressing the visa problems of professional immigrants to make it easier for companies to bring foreign professionals to the United States.

International search firms can assist in the recruitment and selection of professional immigrants with specific qualifications. See the Resources section at the end of the book for names and addresses of international search firms.

Recruiting Disabled Workers

With the passage of the Americans with Disabilities Act (ADA) of 1990, more organizations have begun to realize that there is a vast untapped labor pool in the disabled community. But to this positive has been added the possible burden of having to comply with the ADA. On July 26, 1992, the employment provisions of the Act became effective. The ADA requires fair treatment of qualified individuals with disabilities. It defines a disabled person as "an individual with a disability, who with or without reasonable accommodation can perform the essential functions of the position the individual holds or desires." As defined by regulations of the EEOC (which is charged with enforcing the Act), a qualified individual with a disability is someone able to perform the "essential functions" of a job with or without reasonable accommodation. To determine if a person is qualified to perform a particular job, the employer must identify in advance the essential and nonessential functions of the job and then determine whether the individual can perform these functions. Employers must determine whether or not an applicant is qualified at the time the hiring decision is made, based on the person's present abilities. The EEOC makes it clear that employers should not make hiring decisions based on speculation about what may happen in the future; nor should they be concerned with the possibility of increased insurance premiums or workers compensation costs.

Determining the ''essential functions'' of a position is critical in evaluating whether or not a disabled person is qualified for the position being applied for. If the individual can perform the essential job functions with or without reasonable accommodations, he or she should be considered qualified for the position. (An employer, however, is not required to eliminate or transfer essential functions to accommodate a disabled applicant or employee who cannot perform them.) The EEOC defines essential functions as ''the fundamental job duties of the position''; marginal duties are not included. It is, therefore, incumbent on employers to determine what employees actually do in their jobs. Position descriptions must be written and kept up to date.

The ADA's definition of disability also bars employers from discriminating against people who have had a disabling condition or are perceived to be disabled. This can happen when a person has been cured of a condition or when a person is falsely rumored to be disabled. An employer cannot base an employment decision on an applicant's history of a disability or disease, such as cancer, because the employer is afraid that the disease will recur. However, an employer may deny employment if it would present a direct threat to the health or safety of the applicant or others in the workplace.

OTHER PREEMPLOYMENT ISSUES

Title I of the ADA prohibits employers from taking certain actions when screening job applicants for employment if these actions could have a discriminatory effect. Generally, these regulations make it illegal for an employer to

- Recruit, advertise, or use job application procedures in a way that discriminates against disabled applicants
- Fail to make reasonable accommodation to the known physical or mental limitations of an otherwise qualified disabled applicant or deny employment to such an applicant based on the need to make reasonable accommodation
- Use qualification standards, employment tests, or other selection criteria that screen out or tend to screen out individuals with disabilities, unless the standard, test, or criterion is job-related and consistent with business necessity
- Fail to select and administer tests to applicants with disabilities who have impaired sensory, manual, or speaking skills in a manner that ensures that the test results accurately reflect the skills, aptitude, or other factors it purports to measure, rather than the disability (unless the test is to measure sensory, manual, or speaking skills)
- In general, make preemployment inquiries about whether an individual has a disability and the nature of severity of such disability

The preemployment prohibitions also apply to applicants who come to an employee indirectly, such as those recruited by an employment referral agency. Employers are barred from making contractual arrangements, including those with an employment agency, union, or collective bargaining group, that have the effect of discriminating against qualified disabled applicants.

ACCESSIBILITY AND TESTING

Disabled applicants must be provided access to application materials and interview sites. This may entail ensuring that the interview site is accessible to an individual with a mobility impairment, such as someone who uses a wheelchair. Accessibility and usability apply to the needs of all qualified individuals with disabilities, including those with visual, hearing, or mental impairments. Accommodations might include putting up signs with larger print, installing ramps, relocating the interview or testing site to a more accessible location, or providing a reader for a visually impaired applicant who wishes to complete the application in the employer's office.

Remember that a qualified individual with a disability is one who with or without reasonable accommodation could perform the essential job tasks. Reasonable accommodation could mean the removal of architectural barriers, but the requirement for accessibility is different from the ADA's requirement that structures be made barrier-free. New structures and new alterations must be barrier-free under the Act, but the requirement for accessibility in the workplace does not mandate removal of each and every barrier in an existing structure.

Regarding testing, under EEOC regulations, an employer is prohibited from selecting or administering any employment test or other criterion that screens out or tends to screen out any class of disabled people, unless it can be shown to be job-related and consistent with business necessity. Accordingly, to be acceptable, an employment test must measure only the skills that are essential for the job in question.

Another factor to consider is whether a disabled applicant can take the test in the usual manner. When administering the test, the employer must provide any reasonable accommodations that the applicant needs to take the test. For instance, applicants with visual impairments might require additional lighting, large type, braille materials, or talking calculators to take a written test. Applicants with hearing impairments might experience similar difficulties with oral testing or instructions and would need to be accommodated with written instructions or even sign-language interpreters. Other accommodations, such as those for people with learning disabilities, might include providing additional time to complete the test, separate testing, or alternative versions of standardized tests.

The EEOC regulations say that employers need only make reasonable accommodations for disabled job applicants whose disabilities are known prior to the administration of the test, and whose disabilities affect manual, sensory, or speaking skills. For example, giving a written test to an applicant known to have dyslexia and difficulty reading is a violation of the ADA. A reasonable accommodation would be to give an oral test.

APPLICATION FORMS AND INTERVIEW QUESTIONS

Preemployment inquiries about disabilities can increase the possibility of discrimination. During its deliberations on the ADA, Congress cited many studies showing that bias based on stereotypes and expected problems with disabled persons often affects the selection process if such information is known. Accordingly, the ADA statute and EEOC regulations prohibit preemployment inquiries that do not relate to the ability of the applicant to perform job-related functions. Job applicants may be asked to describe or demonstrate their ability to perform the essential and marginal elements or tasks of the job, with or without reasonable accommodation. The key point is that the information must be job-related and consistent with the employer's business needs.

Employers may not ask applicants during the preoffer stage if they have a particular disability or disabling condition or inquire about the severity of a disability. Nor may an employer inquire about an applicant's workers compensation history. Likewise, to inquire which organizations an individual belongs to (other than job-related organizations) could be seen as discriminatory, since responses to such questions could lead an employer to make a decision based on an unrelated disability issue.

The main methods used for preemployment inquiries are application forms and interview questions. Employers should review their standard applications and other hiring forms to determine whether any of the solicited responses would provide information that is prohibited. Applications that include questions such as "Do you have or have you ever had [name of a particular disability]?" are illegal unless the employer can show that such inquiry is job-related and consistent with business necessity.

As stated above, an employer is permitted to ask questions about an applicant's ability to perform job-related functions. However, questions must relate to the ability of the candidate to perform the job in question. For example, if driving is a job function, an acceptable question is, "Do you have a driver's license?" The employer cannot, however, ask if the applicant has a visual disability, epilepsy, or any other disability that might preclude the individual from obtaining a driver's license. If a standard application form has such a question, you must recognize the relationship between the question and the job requirements of the position.

Application forms themselves must be accessible to the disabled applicants. If reasonable accommodations are needed by a disabled applicant to complete an application or submit to an interview, then the employer must provide them.

RECRUITMENT ADVERTISING

Recruitment and advertising practices must not discriminate against otherwise qualified disabled applicants. These include activities conducted by the employer itself or by a recruiting or placement firm. The way employers advertise job opportunities affects how many disabled applicants an employer is likely to have. To reach a broader audience that includes disabled people, employers may want to consider nontraditional recruitment outlets. For example, exclusive use of newspaper advertising would create a problem for visually impaired people. In addition to the help wanted ads, an employer can list job openings on a recorded tape operated by a county employment office. Other recruitment sources include disabled student service offices at universities, local advocacy groups, your governor's office, and state vocational rehabilitation agencies.

When you contact the agencies about the services they provide, here are some questions to ask:

- Does the agency evaluate its clients' work potential? If so, how?
- Does the agency provide skills training? If so, what kind?
- Are there financial incentives for hiring the persons the agency represents (e.g.,

targeted jobs tax credits, wage subsidies, and training grants)? How do the incentives work?

- Does the agency provide on-the-job training, coaching, counseling, and follow-
up?
- Does the agency offer awareness training for supervisors and managers?
- What is the agency's placement record, including the number of placements in
specific jobs, retention rates, and so on?

Establishing a Recruitment and Employment Routine

You should establish a recruitment and employment routine within your company. In
doing so, remember that certain procedures and forms are necessary in order to comply
with government regulations. Following are suggested recruitment and employment procedures. (Many of these matters are discussed in detail elsewhere in this book.) A list
of miscellaneous recruiting ideas is also given.

- When an open job cannot be filled within the company, the manager should
complete an employment requisition form describing the job and assisting the
person who has to place the ad to understand the job. In case of a civil rights
suit, it also helps you to remember what jobs have been open and who filled
them. Maintain requisitions in a loose-leaf binder. The requisition also helps you
keep track of the number of open jobs you have.
- Review job descriptions before you place ads and conduct interviews to ensure
you know the job.
- When placing an ad, type it up ahead of time and make a copy. Insist that all
ads be placed through the personnel administrator and that they carry the required
EEO/AAP designation.
- Require all applicants to complete and sign employment applications, even if
they have résumés. The application is a formal document. Be sure it conforms
to state and federal regulations and gives you permission to investigate a prospective employee.
- Set up files on applicants, which should be maintained for one year. Don't accept
applications unless you have jobs available, because you will build a tremendous
backlog of applications.
- Keep an applicant log. It saves a great deal of time when applicants call in to
see if their résumé or application is still on file. The log is a great help if you
are a federal contractor and have a desk audit by the Office of Federal Contract
Compliance and need to furnish applicant data.
- Screen applicants using their applications. This will save hours of your time and
the manager's time in interviewing.
- The interviewing process and interviewing skills are important. The interview
should be planned. You should know the job to be filled and plan the questions
to be asked. Forms can be used to record interview information.
- Reference checking is an important element of the hiring process. No one should
be hired without a reference check. There has been a tremendous rise in negligent
hiring lawsuits in the past few years because people were not properly checked
out before they were hired.

- After a person has been hired, you should pull the employment requisition out of the pending loose-leaf binder and file it in a "filled requisition file," noting the name of the person who filled the job and the hire date.
- Federal contractors should use a "filled position summary form." It greatly simplifies your job in case of a desk audit. (See Chapter 6.)
- When a person is hired, send a new employee confirmation letter, confirming the details under which the person was hired. Always quote salary as a monthly figure. Courts have ruled that when a yearly salary was quoted in an employment letter, it implied the person was guaranteed the job for a year.
- Be sure the new employee receives an employee handbook and is given an orientation to the company and a review of company benefits.
- Establish an employee personnel file in which you file everything to do with hiring, promotion, termination, and benefits. Log all personnel changes in the file and also maintain emergency contact and phone numbers for quick reference. Retain these files for five years after termination. Some companies keep employee personnel files indefinitely.
- Send the payroll information sheet with all the employee information on it to the payroll department to be processed.
- You can purchase a software package that will maintain your entire employee base on the computer. When you get calls about employees all you have to do is call up the data on the screen.

Miscellaneous Recruiting Ideas

- Take advantage of the U.S. Army's Experience for Hire program, designed to place the 150,000 young men and women who complete their tour of duty and return to civilian life each year. These are educated and trained people who can be a valuable new labor source.
- Find and utilize part-time and temporary workers. Perhaps spouses of your current employees may want to work part-time while they raise their families.
- Have a company open house. Advertise the types of jobs you have available, and encourage people in the community to visit your facilities.
- Tap into community-based resources. Network with other recruiters, and exchange information on your open positions. Network with local businesspeople. Create networking committees with similar companies.
- Contact outplacement firms, and give them a list of your open positions so they can send workers let go by other companies.
- Provide cash incentives to lure hard-to-find professionals like nurses into your company for interviews. An ad might say, "We'll pay you $100 to interview us!"
- Design tailor-made recruitment brochures to put out in the community. Tailor the brochure to a target audience.
- Do an employee swap. Form a cooperative relationship with other companies in your community to share hard-to-find employees. Advance Reservations, Inc., of Park City, Utah, and Holland America Line Westours Inc., based in Seattle, Washington, formed a cooperative relationship in hiring reservationists. Although the companies sell different products, they both need workers trained on complex

airline computer systems as well as their individual in-house computer programs, so they share workers.

- Start an employee referral program by having a pizza incentive party or similar gathering. Put together posters and collateral materials and kick it off at a special employee meeting.

Notes

1. *Working Age,* February 1990, published by American Association of Retired People, Washington, D.C.
2. *Monthly Labor Review,* January 1991, published by the U.S. Department of Labor. Written by William P. O'Hare and Carol J. DeVita.

Sample Recruitment Ads

SENIOR SYSTEMS MANAGER
Innovation is the Secret of Our Success

The first step to success is providing talented professionals with the freedom to achieve their goals and then providing them with the best resources, a supportive management, and a stable environment. We've taken these innovative approaches, and now we're at the forefront of the insurance industry, offering an opportunity for a Senior Systems Manager to oversee a large Systems staff developing property/casualty insurance applications in an IBM 9000/620 environment, which includes IBM PS2 MOD 70 Workstations. Microfocus COBOL, CICS, DB2, TSO. Are you:

- A team player with management experience in addition to proven success achieving productivity gains in application development.
- Able to introduce new tools and techniques and to manage large projects successfully.
- Familiar and/or experienced with CASE technology, Metrics, and Programmer Workbenches.
- Experienced with property/casualty insurance applications and STRADIS.

In addition to professional success, you'll enjoy a competitive salary and excellent benefits. For immediate consideration, please send your resume with salary history to:

Box J P417
Wall Street Journal
Equal Opportunity Employer M/F/H

This ad tells applicants that the company gives employees the resources they need to do their job, then steps back and gives them the freedom to take action. Note the words "freedom to achieve their goals," "supportive management," and "stable environment." These are the elements of a job that people are looking for.

PROCUREMENT AGENT

ABC Graphics Printing and Imaging Division in Seattle, Washington, is a leader in color printing technology. Our fast-paced environment has attracted diverse and creative professionals who have brought innovative approaches to problem solving. In response to our current growth, we seek the "best and the brightest" for an opening in our Procurement Department.

Procurement Agent
Electromechanical Commodities

In this key procurement engineering position, you will lead a team of other Procurement Agents with highly focused engineering and supplier teams to cost-reduce unique, state-of-the-art electro-mechanical components. Requires a technical and business degree or equivalent, and experience with meeting product cost objectives for low-cost, high-volume devices (electromechanical preferred). Cost reduction and value analysis techniques essential.

For immediate consideration, please send your resume to: P.O. Box 1000, WS691, MS 63-515, Seattle, Washington 97070.

We Are An Equal Opportunity Employer M/F/H

This ad tells applicants "we're an organization that's looking for self-starters and problem solvers to work in a company that's going places." They want the "best and brightest" people they can find. This is an appealing statement. It also says they welcome a diverse applicant base.

This ad tells applicants that the company feels it is unique and has created a working environment that fosters creativity and personal satisfaction. Most people are looking for this type of work environment and would take a chance that the company has truly created such a workplace.

Secretaries frequently look for jobs that provide a variety of duties and companies that provide personal growth opportunities. Most secretaries also want some autonomy and a chance to be creative in their work. This ad will appeal to that type of secretary.

Most organizations are having a difficult time recruiting nurses. Most nurses are looking for an organization that would provide them with a diversity of duties and present a nursing challenge. They are also looking for an organization that will provide some personal recognition for the job they do. This ad addresses these issues.

This ad says the company has an exciting challenge for the right person, but candidates who apply should have all the necessary credentials. It also says this will not be an easy job and it will take a committed, hard-working leader to succeed.

4

Interviewing

Mary F. Cook
President
Mary Cook & Associates

When you have an open position to fill in your company, you are looking for people who are standouts in five areas:

1. Job-related skills, abilities, and experience
2. Intelligence and aptitudes
3. Education and training
4. Positive social, personal, and behavioral qualities
5. Enthusiastic ''will do'' qualities that emphasize the applicant's motivation to do a good job

An effective interview tells you how the applicant rates in these areas and elicits the information you need to make a successful hiring decision. To conduct such an interview, you have to learn the art of smart interviewing, which saves time and provides the crucial information you need in order to hire the best person.

Before the Interview

Part one of smart interviewing occurs before the first interview is even scheduled. To conduct an effective interview, you need to know exactly what the job entails and what type of person you're looking for. The cost of hiring the wrong person is high, whether the individual stays with the company only a few months and leaves or stays longer, making costly mistakes.

You need to prepare a short, one-page job description that includes the essential job functions, key responsibilities, the principal interactions the employee has on a daily basis, the level of responsibility, the necessary human relations skills, and the job requirements and qualifications. Exhibit 4-1 is a sample job description format. It provides important information that helps an interviewer determine the best questions to ask applicants for the position because it includes the essential functions of the job.

Although nothing in the Americans with Disabilities Act (ADA) specifically says employers have to have job descriptions, it does describe the evidence that the Equal Employment Opportunity Commission (EEOC) will examine to determine whether or not a particular duty of a job in an organization is an essential function. The EEOC will look at evidence of job requirements that, in the employer's judgment, are necessary to do the job. These essential functions should appear in job descriptions, in recruitment advertising, and must be considered when making selection decisions. Accommodation

Exhibit 4-1. Sample job description.

Position/Title: Department:	Date:
Essential Job Functions:	
Physical Requirements of the job:	
Financial Accountabilities:	Interpersonal Skill Requirements:
Principal Interactions:	

(continued)

Exhibit 4-1. *Continued.*

Level of Authority:	Exempt/Nonexempt:
No. People Supervised:	Reports to:
Knowledge/Experience/Education/Requirements	

decisions under the ADA, as well as possible future litigation, could hang on the documentation of essential functions, so the importance of using current job descriptions in the recruitment process becomes evident.

The Employment Application and the Résumé

The employment application is a document that all applicants must complete. It is the formal application for a specific job and requires applicants to provide information about themselves that won't appear on a résumé. In addition, the application contains employment-at-will information and asks the applicant to give permission for the company to check references.

The best method for deciding exactly what to include in your employment application is to obtain some sample applications from local companies. You can also purchase applications already printed from office supply companies. Collect a number of blank applications and review them to see what information they contain and what style they use. After drafting your own application, make sure that it is legally sound by having your company attorney review it. Exhibit 4-2 is a sample employment application.

You will often have a résumé (and cover letter) submitted by the applicant to review as well as an application. Many times, in fact, you will have the résumé before the applicant arrives for the interview and completes the application. You should by all means review résumés if you have them, but realize that their value is limited because it is the applicant who decides which facts to include and which to omit. You also cannot rely on the accuracy of a résumé. Still, they do provide some data and can be examined for breaks in employment, neatness, typographical and spelling errors (an indication of carelessness), and so on—as can the cover letter that may have accompanied the résumé.

Screening the application and résumé can save a great deal of interviewing time. You should look for certain things on an application and résumé.

- Look for breaks in employment. If the applicant is qualified for a job and gets an interview, the interviewer should ask what the applicant was doing during those times.

(*text continued on page 72*)

Exhibit 4-2. Sample employment application.

	AN EQUAL OPPORTUNITY EMPLOYER—MALE/FEMALE/HANDICAP We do not discriminate on the basis of race, religion, national origin, color, sex, age, or handicap. It is our intention that all applicants be given equal opportunity and that selection decisions be based on job-related factors.
Instructions	Please answer each question fully and accurately. No action can be taken on this application unless all questions have been answered. Use blank paper if you do not have enough room on this application. **PLEASE PRINT,** except for the signature on back of the application. All information you give on this application will be held in strict confidence.
Personal Data	Last name First name Middle name Telephone number Street address City State Zip code Job applied for _____ Today's date _____ Are you seeking: Full-time ☐ Part-time ☐ Temporary ☐ employment? Are you between 18 and 70 years of age? Yes ☐ No ☐ Date of birth _____ (for jobs with minimum age requirements) If you are applying for a job with minimum age requirements, you may be required to submit proof of age. Social Security number _____ Are you a citizen of the United States or do you have a valid work permit? Yes ☐ No ☐
Military	Military status: Active duty service from _____ to _____ Branch of service _____ Service duties _____ Are you a member of a reserve organization? Yes ☐ No ☐
General	Were you ever employed by this company? Yes ☐ No ☐ If so, when? _____ Have you ever applied to this company before? Yes ☐ No ☐ If so, when? _____ Have you ever been convicted of any violation of the law (except a minor traffic violation)? Yes ☐ No ☐ If yes, give particulars _____ Have you missed any work during the past six months? Yes ☐ No ☐ If yes, how much? _____ Are you now or do you expect to be engaged in any other business or employment? Yes ☐ No ☐ If yes, explain _____ For driving jobs only: Do you have a valid driver's license? Yes ☐ No ☐ Driver's license number _____

(continued)

Exhibit 4-2. *Continued.*

		Highest Grade Completed	Did You Graduate?	Date of Leaving
Education	Name, address and location of High School: _____ College or University: _____ College major _____ Degree: _____			
	Additional educational and/or vocational or technical training information:	Courses taken	Courses completed	Date of leaving
	Name, address and location of school _____			
Health	Do you have any physical limitations which would adversely affect performance of the job for which you are applying? Yes ☐ No ☐ If yes, explain _____ Would you take a physical examination, if required? Yes ☐ No ☐			

	Give three references (not relatives)			
References	Name Address	Telephone		Company
	1. _____			
	2. _____			
	3. _____			

	List names of employers in consecutive order with present or last employer listed first. Account for all periods of time including military service and any periods of unemployment. If self-employed, give company name and supply business references. **PLEASE GIVE MONTH AND YEAR**					
Work History	Name of Employer	Employed	Pay	Title and Duties	Reason for Leaving	Name of Last Supervisor
	Address	From	Start			
	City, State, Zip code	To	Final			
	Telephone					
	Name of Employer	Employed	Pay	Title and Duties	Reason for Leaving	Name of Last Supervisor
	Address	From	Start			
	City, State, Zip code	To	Final			
	Telephone					

Name of Employer	Employed	Pay	Title and Duties	Reason for Leaving	Name of Last Supervisor
Address	From	Start			
City, State, Zip code	To	Final			
Telephone					

Is any additional information relative to change of name, use of assumed name, or nickname necessary to enable us to check your work record? Yes ☐ No ☐
Are you currently employed? Yes ☐ No ☐
If yes, may we contact your present employer? Yes ☐ No ☐

Special Skills

If you are an experienced operator of any business machines or equipment, please list
_____

If you are an experienced operator of any plant machines or equipment, please list
_____

Do you type? Yes ☐ No ☐ Words per minute _____
Do you take shorthand? Yes ☐ No ☐ Words per minute _____
List computer skills and languages _____

Consent to Investigate Report

As part of the hiring process, you should know that we will be checking your references. We may contact those persons whom you have identified to us as potential references. In addition, we may also contact other friends, acquaintances, business associates, or anyone who knows you. When we contact a reference, we may ask a series of questions. They could be about your personal background, education, work experience, character, or personality. We may use an outside company to check references. If we do, under the federal Fair Credit Reporting Act we are required, upon your written request, to provide you with the name and address of the company that is checking your references so that you may contact them for further information.

I have read and fully understand the foregoing. I hereby voluntarily consent to allow the company, or any of its employees or designees, to check my references by contacting any person whom they deem to be an appropriate reference. The company representatives may ask any questions which they consider relative to their hiring decision, including questions about my personal background, education, work experience, character, and personality.

Signature _____ Date _____

(*continued*)

Exhibit 4-2. *Continued.*

<table>
<tr><td rowspan="2">Affidavit</td><td>I certify that the answers given by me to the foregoing questions and statements are true and correct without consequential omissions of any kind whatsoever. I agree that the company shall not be liable in any respect if my employment is terminated because of falsity of statements, answers, or omissions made by me in this question-naire. I also authorize the companies, schools, or persons named above to give any information regarding my employment, character, and qualifications. I hereby re-lease said companies, schools, or persons from all liability for any damage for issuing this information. I certify that all statements and answers to questions about my health are true and were made by me without any reservation. I understand that any mis-leading or incorrect statements may render this application void, and if employed, would be cause for termination. I understand that if employed I have been hired at the will of the employer and that my employment may be terminated at will, at any time, and with or without cause, the employer's only obligation being to pay salary or wages due and owing at the time of the termination.</td></tr>
<tr><td>Signature _____ Date _____</td></tr>
<tr><td>Company Use Only</td><td>Disposition _____ Date Employed _____ Starting Rate _____
Job Classification _____ Department _____ Clock No. _____
Interviewed by _____Interviewer's remarks and recommendations _____
_____
_____
Application information checked by: Name _____ Date _____</td></tr>
</table>

- Verify that the applicant has experience in the type of job being applied for.
- Check the applicant's course of study. Did the individual take courses that provided the technical expertise needed to do the job being applied for?
- Check to see if the applicant has been convicted of a crime. You cannot deny someone a job because he or she has been charged with a crime, but you can, in certain circumstances, if there has been a conviction. (For example, if a person has been convicted of stealing money, you could refuse to hire that person for a job that required handling of large sums of money.)
- Look at the overall appearance of the completed application and résumé (spelling, neatness, etc.).

Set up your own screening indices based on your company needs and the requirements of the job. Your screening process should be tailored to your specific informational needs.

The Interview

There are usually two interviews, sometimes more. The first interview is generally conducted in the human resources department by a recruiter or personnel interviewer. The second interview is done in the functional department by the supervisor or manager. As the applicant progresses through the interview process, more interviews may take place. In addition to the standard two interviews, some organizations add a group interview, where the applicant's peers in the department have an opportunity to meet the candidate and ask pertinent questions.

Types of Interviews

Various types of interviews can be conducted. Depending on the level of the job and the personal qualities needed in the position, make a decision on what type of interview is best suited to provide the most information. The types of interviews are as follows:

• *Structured interview.* This is a standardized, systematic, structured approach to interviewing. It includes specific, preidentified questions, making efficient use of time and helping the interviewer obtain a great deal of information. Be careful that this type of interview doesn't become too impersonal. A good structured interview provides time for interaction between the interviewer and the applicant.

• *Comprehensive interview.* An employment interview of this type follows a plan, but it encourages the interviewer to deviate from the plan and pursue important points in detail. It is less structured than the structured interview, but it too includes specific, preidentified questions.

• *Conversational interview.* This is basically an unplanned, open-ended, often haphazard discussion between the employer and the applicant. Many such interviews are conducted every day, but generally little more than rapport is established between the two parties. This nondirective type of interview can be useful in a counseling situation, but time pressures make it inefficient for employment purposes. The conversational approach does not provide the comprehensive information required for an objective selection.

• *Stress interview.* In this approach, the employer deliberately subjects the applicant to pressure and observes how well he or she is able to handle it. Many applicants feel a great deal of stress in an ordinary interview. A stress interview is not positive and can violate the dignity of the applicant. Stress interviews are therefore not often used.

• *Group interview.* Today companies that have a more participative management style are using group interviews to improve their selection decision-making capability. The group interview shows how well an applicant gets along with people under pressure. It also provides the staff members who will be the new employee's peers with a chance to evaluate final candidates before they are hired. Group interviews are normally conducted in a structured format with each interviewer given time to ask one or two questions regarding the applicant's qualifications or career aspirations.

Some companies tell the applicant ahead of time what type of interview will be used. Others prefer not to forewarn the candidate. Most companies use a combination of a structured and comprehensive interview, perhaps followed by a group interview.

The best interviews for most organizations is either the structured or the comprehensive interview, a systematic approach that illicits a great deal of information while at the same time giving the interviewer an opportunity to observe how applicants handle themselves. If you are going to conduct a structured interview—or a comprehensive interview—you simply write out the questions you feel will allow you to obtain the

most important information you can from the applicant. Then allow the applicant time
to ask questions, creating a two-way dialog.

The Question Roadmap

The first questions you should always ask are the ones which are job-related. You want
to find out if the applicant has the necessary skills and experience to perform the essential functions of the job. The interview then progresses to career and behavioral issues.
Using the structured or comprehensive interview format, construct a question roadmap—a list of questions you want to ask the applicant in order to get the information
you'll need to make the best hiring decision. To do this, ask yourself some questions
first then decide what you will ask the applicant.

Ask Yourself	*Ask the Applicant*
Work-related issues:	
• What are the essential job functions?	• Here's a list of the essential job functions. Can you perform these functions? Please elaborate.
• Would accommodations be required for this applicant to do the job?	• What accommodations, if any, would be needed to assist you in performing the job?
• What level of problem-solving skills does the applicant have?	• Describe your methods for solving difficult work problems.
• Can the applicant describe an effective work environment, one in which he or she is comfortable and has been successful?	• What type of work environment makes you most comfortable? What level of personal supervision suits you best?
• Will the applicant enjoy the work, the job, the environment in this company?	• What was your most rewarding job? Explain.
• Has the applicant had positive work experiences that he or she can describe?	• Describe one of your most rewarding work experiences.
• Can the applicant openly identify and discuss a major problem he or she has had at work? Did the applicant handle it effectively?	• Discuss a major problem you've encountered on a job. How did you handle it?
Career objectives:	
• Does the applicant have specific career objectives?	• What are your long-range career objectives?
• Does the applicant have a plan for attaining those objectives?	• How do you plan to achieve your objectives?
• Is the applicant realistic about personal strengths and weaknesses?	• What do you consider your personal strengths and weaknesses? What do you feel your development needs are—if any?

- Is the applicant realistic about success on the job?

Relationships:

- Can the applicant describe an effective work relationship?

- Can the applicant handle hostile situations effectively?

Initiative and follow-through:

- Does the applicant complete his or her own tasks? Follow through on job assignments?

- Can the applicant work independently, or does he or she need close supervision?

Attitude:

- How flexible is the applicant? How does he or she handle uncertainties?
- Does applicant have a balanced company/self-interest?
- Explore the applicant's loyalty level.

- Does the applicant take pride in doing a good job?

- Explore indications of the applicant's cooperativeness.

- Is the candidate enthusiastic about work?

Stability:

- Is this person excitable or even-tempered?
- Is the applicant impatient, or understanding?

- How do you evaluate job success?

- Describe the relationship that should exist between a supervisor and a subordinate.
- Tell me about a situation where a fellow employee or supervisor disagreed with you and perhaps was hostile toward you. How did you handle the situation?

- Do you like to work alone? How do you feel when you complete a project on your own? What do you do if you find you can't finish an assignment on time?
- Describe your most positive supervisor/subordinate work relationship. Why did it work well? Was there close supervision?

- Have you ever been uncertain about a job? How do you handle adversity?

- How do you feel about business demands versus personal time demands?
- Who was your best and worst boss? Describe them. Describe the best and worst companies you've worked for.
- What duties did you like most in your last job? Least? Describe a situation where you were proud of the job you did.
- What skills do you use in working with other employees? How important is teamwork in getting a job done?
- What turns you on about a job?

- What things disturb you most in a job? Why?
- How do you get along with people you dislike? What skills do you use?

- Does the applicant show likes and dislikes freely?

- Is the candidate poised, or impulsive; controlled, or erratic?

- Is the applicant career-happy?

- What actions irritate you? What do you do about it? What were your most unpleasant work experiences? Describe.
- Describe your most pleasant work experiences. When did you enjoy a job the most?
- How did you get into this career field? Would you change careers if you could?

Insight:

- Is the applicant realistic in self-appraisal?
- Does the applicant desire self-improvement?

- How does the applicant take constructive criticism?

- Tell me about your strengths and weaknesses.
- Are your weaknesses important enough to do something about them? Why or why not? What have you done about your weaknesses?
- What is the most useful and useless criticism you've received? How did you feel? How did you respond?

Be creative in developing questions. Review the job description and pick issues pertinent to the specific position as you develop the questions for the applicants for that job. These questions will provide insight into an applicant's behavioral style at work as well as provide information directly relevant to the job. Be sure to ask the same questions of each applicant. You must ensure that you have not discriminated against any applicant by asking easier questions of one than another.

In order to ensure that you will be asking the most pertinent questions—and the same questions—of each applicant, it's a good idea to use an interview guide form. Exhibit 4-3 is a sample. Write the questions you plan to ask for a job opening on the form, and then use it for each interview for that job. When you've developed an interview guide that works well for a specific job, retain it and use it each time the job comes open, adjusting the form as the job changes.

It's more comfortable for both you and the applicant if you take only short notes during the interview and complete the evaluation portion of the form after the applicant has gone. Taking lengthy notes during the interview is disruptive and may annoy or upset the applicant.

Interviewing Techniques

When questioning an applicant, don't just accept the first answer and let it go at that: You need to probe further. To do so, listen attentively to each answer, and ask follow-up questions. Don't try to demonstrate equal or superior knowledge even if you possess it. Realize that the best responses are given freely. Those which are guarded or tentative because an applicant doesn't have the level of expertise needed to do the job will be obvious.

To elicit honest, thoughtful answers from applicants, do the following during interviews.

Exhibit 4-3. Interview guide form.

Applicant's Name ———————— Position ———————— Interviewer's Name ———————— Date of Interview ————————

Selection Considerations/Job Qualifications	Questions to Ask	Information Obtained	Evaluation
			☐ Outstanding ☐ Acceptable ☐ Questionable ☐ Unacceptable
			☐ Outstanding ☐ Acceptable ☐ Questionable ☐ Unacceptable
			☐ Outstanding ☐ Acceptable ☐ Questionable ☐ Unacceptable
			☐ Outstanding ☐ Acceptable ☐ Questionable ☐ Unacceptable
			☐ Outstanding ☐ Acceptable ☐ Questionable ☐ Unacceptable

• *Ask specific job-related questions first.* Review the job description and ask the applicant questions that relate to the essential functions of the open position. Be specific and probe for details about how the applicant would go about performing the job.

• *Stimulate value judgments.* You can get insights into a person's value system if you ask how he or she feels about punctuality, personal commitment to a job or company, or relationships with previous coworkers. This information is more valuable than an interviewer's assumptions about an applicant's value system. The candidate's values and past behavior are the best predictor of future behavior. Each specific example that a candidate describes will help you to predict how the person might handle situations with your company.

• *Probe choice decisions.* In examining choice decisions, you are attempting to discover why an applicant selected one course of action over another—for example, why he or she majored in business instead of marketing. Listening to why a decision was made can provide insights into the individual's reasoning and value system. This technique is more valuable than asking what an applicant would do in hypothetical situations. It allows the interviewer to look at the applicant's choices in past work situations.

• *Use silence.* Some interviewers are uncomfortable using silence, but silence provides time to think (which is often what the applicant is doing). Interviewers who encourage applicants to take their time before responding will learn more than those who don't. An applicant will often provide more pertinent information than anticipated when the interviewer does not respond immediately after an answer is given.

• *Use reflective statements.* A good interviewing technique is reflecting comments back to an applicant. It shows you were listening and wish to stimulate more discussion of an answer. Do this in a natural way that shows interest or concern. Use expressions like "did I understand you to say" and "let me see if I understood you."

The job interview takes into consideration the fact that most applicants today are educated and experienced in the art of interviewing. Dozens of books are published every year on the subject. Most applicants are turned off by the games some interviewers play. If you want to hire the best people, it's important that you develop a process and a personal interviewing style that is credible and saves both you and the applicant valuable time. Your personal interviewing style should be structured, thoughtful, and relaxed.

Twenty-Three Pointers for Developing a Positive Interviewing Style

1. *Prepare for the interview.* Study the application, the résumé, and any other information about the applicant before the interview. In this way you can explore those areas that require special attention (such as lapses in employment history) and skip over points already covered. This early review helps structure the interview, saves valuable time, and gives you credibility as an interviewer. Be sure to review the current job description.

2. *Set the stage.* It's important that the interview be conducted in quiet surroundings with a minimum of distractions. A private office should be used and interruptions, like telephone calls, avoided. The interview setting tells the applicant something about the class and the culture of the company.

3. *Establish rapport with the applicant.* Open with small talk that eases tension and makes the applicant feel comfortable. A word of caution, however: Some interviewers go beyond the bounds of rapport and become too friendly. Objectivity is then biased by personal considerations. While it's all right to discuss skiing, for example, you don't want to let the fact that the person is or isn't a skier bias your thinking about the individual's job qualifications.

4. *Conduct a structured or comprehensive interview.* A good interview progresses from nonthreatening, job-related questions to more personal subjective and/or behavioral issues. A good interviewer learns to probe in a variety of areas, obtaining more than just superficial information. By using a structured or comprehensive interview and an interview guide form, you can be sure to ask the questions necessary to get all the information you can from the applicant.

5. *Encourage the applicant to talk.* In the fact-finding stages of the interview, it's the applicant who has the facts and the interviewer who wants the information. So the applicant should be encouraged to talk and the interviewer should listen at least 75 percent of the time.

6. *Ask open-ended questions.* You don't get much good information by asking questions that can be answered with a yes or no. Use phrases like "please explain," "tell me about," "please describe," and so on.

7. *Avoid leading questions.* A leading question gives the applicant a cue to what you expect to hear. Questions should be asked in such a way that the applicant has to provide a narrative answer without previous cues from the interviewer.

8. *Use a conversational style.* While the interview should follow a plan and questions should be prepared in advance, specific questions should be phrased in a natural, conversational way. Sometimes, there are good reasons for varying the sequence of the interview. As applicants vary in knowledge and experience, it stands to reason that the interview approach will also vary to meet changing circumstances. The interviewer should, however, remain in control; it is dangerous to let an applicant run away with the interview and, much like in the résumé, present only his or her story. Use direct questions in conversation as necessary to pinpoint the specific reasons underlying such common generalities as "no opportunity for advancement," which is often given as the reason for leaving a previous job.

9. *Follow up on hunches or unusual statements.* If an applicant says, "Well, he was that kind of guy and I just don't get along with that kind of guy," probe further. You want to find out if the comment is just hot air or a potential problem in attitude. In a way, you need to play detective when you interview. Pursue unusual comments and ask nonjudgmental questions. Probe for more information than is initially given. Say things like "Yes, can you explain further?" or "What do you mean by that?"

10. *Listen with the third ear.* The best interviewers listen to what is really being communicated, not just what is being said. It's estimated that a person can think seven times as fast as normal speech; an alert interviewer will use that time to analyze in depth what the applicant is saying. Listening is an active, not a passive, process, You can be extremely perceptive in the interview by listening to the undertones of the conversation.

11. *Avoid moral judgments.* Interviewers have to suppress personal feelings about the morals and standards of applicants. You have to be careful not to discriminate based on personal prejudices.

12. *Watch body language.* If a person tenses on a question, that might indicate that some hedging is included in the answer, and you should pursue with further questioning. Physical responses provide almost as much information as verbal ones if you pay attention to them.

13. *Reveal aspects of yourself during the interview.* Don't monopolize the interview talking about yourself, but when you share one or two things, you develop rapport and warmth. If you can open up, you will be more likely to open up the applicant. There is a positive psychological aspect to one-on-one exchanges.

14. *Show energy and enthusiasm.* A job candidate looks at your enthusiasm and style and judges the company according to your attitude. A terse, formal style will not make an applicant comfortable. It will not elicit open responses, and it will give the applicant a negative feeling about the organization.

15. *Assess general attitudes and personality.* Encourage discussion about previous jobs and what the applicant liked and disliked about them. Ask questions about frustrations, failures, and successes in previous jobs in order to get a feel for the applicant's attitudes about work and companies in general.

16. *Emphasize what is important.* While a significant portion of the employment interview should focus on work history and experience, part of the interview time should also be devoted to education.

17. *Discuss the job.* The interview is a two-way street. After the interviewer has the necessary information from the applicant, it's appropriate to discuss the job and the organization. It's best to hold this discussion at the end of the interview to avoid the applicant's slanting answers to meet the qualifications of the job. There's another reason: If you are convinced that an applicant is highly desirable, you should make every effort to interest the individual in joining the organization. If, on the other hand, you believe the applicant is not qualified, then you shouldn't try to "sell" the candidate.

18. *Assess organizational culture.* As a credible interviewer you must be able to match the applicant to the organization. You can do that only if you understand the organizational culture in which you work and can identify the personality profiles that can perform effectively in your environment. This is one of the most important factors in retention of employees.

19. *Treat each applicant in the same manner.* Ask the same questions of all applicants for a specific job in order to avoid charges of discrimination. You can't be easier on one applicant than another.

20. *Train to interview diverse applicants.* In the 1990s there will be a more diverse applicant base for most open positions. Although you must treat all applicants in the same manner and ask the same questions of each candidate for a specific job, interviewing minorities, people from other cultures, and people with disabilities requires an understanding of diverse interviewing techniques. It's cost-effective to have someone qualified train you and your managers in the techniques of diversity interviewing. In order to comply with ADA guidelines, it's also necessary to know the essential job functions of a position in order to conduct a thorough interview.

21. *Take notes.* It's necessary to take some notes if the interview is to be evaluated later. Not only does this help you analyze the data after the applicant has gone, but it also helps in being thorough and systematic in covering important aspects of the appli-

cant's background. Note taking, however, should be limited so you can maintain as much eye contact as possible and listen closely to what is being said.

22. *Use adequate time.* It takes time to conduct a thorough interview. At least an hour is needed to review the background of a managerial applicant. (An inexperienced clerical applicant, on the other hand, might be interviewed in twenty minutes.) The rule in all cases is to take whatever time is needed to get all the facts required for making a good decision.

23. *Conclude the interview.* After sufficient data are exchanged, discuss the next step in the selection process. Tell the candidate when he or she will be contacted next, whether to schedule another interview or to inform the applicant of your hiring decision.

If you are interviewing to fill a particularly important or sensitive management position, you may want to engage the services of a behavioral consultant. Behavioral issues are difficult for the average human resources professional or departmental vice-president to spot, but they are absolutely critical to performance in management positions.

Inappropriate Interview Questions

There are certain questions that should not be asked during an employment interview. (Legal hiring issues are discussed in detail in Chapter 18.) Questions seeking the following information can be construed as discriminatory and illegal and cannot be asked of applicants before they are hired:

- Date of birth
- Maiden name
- Previous married name
- Marital status
- Spouse's name
- Spouse's occupation and length of time on the job
- Spouse's place of employment
- Number of children and their ages
- Child care arrangements
- Arrest record (you can ask about convictions, but you cannot refuse employment because an applicant has been convicted unless the conviction relates to an applicant's ability to perform the job)
- Disability status
- Ancestry
- National origin (color)
- Age
- Sex
- Religion
- Affiliations with Communist party or union
- Garnishment of wages
- Reasons that would prevent an applicant from maintaining employment

Much of the above information is necessary for personnel records and employee benefits programs. Once the individual is employed, you can use a postemployment form to obtain the information. A sample postemployment form is provided in Chapter 6.

Errors Commonly Made by Interviewers

Interviewers commonly make a number of errors that can lead to failure to hire the right people. They include:

- Asking leading questions
- Making decisions too early in the interview
- Following a stereotyped pattern of investigation without recognition of individual differences
- Asking discriminatory questions about disabilities or life-styles
- Lacking knowledge of essential job functions
- Letting pressure of duties shorten interview time
- Doing more talking than they should
- Failing to direct the interview and wasting time
- Becoming overly enthusiastic about a person during the initial interview
- Not knowing what to look for
- Tending to be overly influenced by individual factors, rather than considering the applicant as a whole
- Lacking skill in asking questions, in motivating applicant responses, and in recording interview data

Among other criticisms made of interviewers and selection decisions are the following:

- Allowing one undesirable factor to influence judgment
- Not preparing for the interview
- Under the pressure to fill a job, deciding on an applicant before all the facts are in
- Being too routine in interviewing instead of adapting each interview to the individual and being creative in questioning
- Being interviewed by the candidate instead of controlling the interview
- Dragging the interview on too long
- Not making a hiring decision in a reasonable time frame, keeping the applicant hanging
- Not thoroughly checking references before hiring an applicant

A major issue with some applicants is that all too frequently interviewers fail to give them time to ask questions in order to ascertain whether or not there is a fit between the person and the organization. It's important to ensure that the applicants feel there is a fit and that they feel they were given the time and the courtesy to ask questions they feel are important.

Interviewing Candidates With Disabilities

Interviewing skills need to extend to nontraditional applicants, including those who are physically and/or mentally challenged. When a job opens and a person with a disability applies, look on the person as any other job applicant; the only difference is that the applicant has a physical or mental disability. Most people with disabilities won't apply for a job they don't think they can perform. However, as an interviewer, it's your responsibility to determine if the applicant is qualified. You should do it in the same way you'd handle any other applicant. Here are some tips that can help you feel at ease when interviewing a disabled applicant.

• *Greeting the applicant.* Greet the person as you would any applicant. When in doubt about helping individuals around the limitations caused by their disability, the questions "May I be of assistance?" or "Is there anything I can do to make your interview more pleasant?" will allow applicants to tell you what, if anything, is needed?

If the applicant has a visual limitation, identify yourself, shake hands, and, if you're moving to another location, offer the applicant the option of taking your arm for direction. Let the applicant feel the back of the chair where he or she is to sit. If the applicant brings a guide dog, allow the dog to do its job.

If the applicant has a hearing limitation and you have no experience in sign language, look at the individual, speak in your regular tone of voice, and be prepared to exchange information in writing. Have note pads and pencils handy. If the applicant is accompanied by an interpreter, ask the interpreter to sit next to you to better handle the exchange, but look at the applicant—not the interpreter.

If the applicant has mental limitations, greet the person as you would any other applicant and use the vocabulary common to the job. In a few minutes, you'll have a good understanding of the level at which the individual can communicate.

• *Handling the application.* Follow your company's regular procedures. If the applicant's disability prevents him or her from filling out an application, offer assistance or allow the person to take it home, stating a specific time to return it. This is a reasonable accommodation to your regular procedures.

• *Discussing reasonable accommodation.* During the interview, you'll discuss tasks performed by the applicant on previous jobs and the tasks to be done in the new job. This is the time to ask if there are accommodations that need to be made in order to enable the person to perform the job effectively. The question of accommodation should be raised after the individual has been determined to be qualified for the position.

It's a good idea to review the Americans with Disabilities Act (ADA) of 1990 to get a better feeling about reasonable accommodation issues. The Legal Center, an advocacy organization for persons with disabilities and older persons, located at 455 Sherman Street, Suite 130, Denver, Colorado 80203-4403, can provide more in-depth information about the ADA. The Center has a supervisor's training manual, a video, and other materials to help organizations comply with the ADA.

After the Interview

Immediately after the interview, take the time you need to complete an applicant appraisal form. This is an important detail in finalizing the interview and preparing critical data for the selection process. Be sure to include all of the information obtained from the interview so the best hiring decision can be made. Exhibit 4-4 is a sample form.

Exhibit 4-4.   Applicant appraisal form.

Interview Date _____

Name of Applicant _____   Position _____

This rating form will become a part of the applicant's personnel record which may be made available to governmental compliance agencies upon request.

DO NOT FILL OUT IN THE PRESENCE OF APPLICANT Review the current job description and rate the candidate in all categories below. Comment in each section.	Outstanding	Above Average	Average	Below Average
1. *ESSENTIAL JOB FUNC-TIONS*—Can the applicant perform the essential functions of this job?				
2. *EXPERIENCE*—How does previous experience relate to current opening? Review in light of the essential functions of the job.				
3. *MENTAL CAPABILITY*—Verbal ability, judgment, analytical skills, logic, decisiveness, etc.				
4. *PHYSICAL CAPABILITY*—Can the applicant perform the physical requirements of the job as defined in the job description?				
5. *EDUCATION/SKILLS*—Degree(s), professional licenses, registration, certifications, languages, equipment, computer skills.				
6. *GOALS AND AMBITION*—Initiative, persistence, drive, goals are well defined (as they relate to predicting success on this job).				

General comments: _____

_____

For additional comments use back of form.

Overall Appraisal:

   Outstanding _____ Above Average _____ Average _____ Below Average _____
Recommend employment for current opening: Yes _____ No _____
Future consideration: Yes _____ No _____ If yes, for _____ position
Recommendation based upon:

     Application Review _____ Interview _____
     Telephone Contact _____ References _____

Signature of Interviewer:	Date Completed:

5

Testing

Diane Arthur
President
Arthur Associates Management Consultants, Ltd.

Preemployment and employment tests may be defined as procedures for determining job suitability. This is accomplished by examining the skills, knowledge, mental or physical capabilities of applicants or employees according to a predetermined set of objective guidelines. The results are assessed in relation to the requirements and responsibilities of a given position, and conclusions are drawn as to the appropriateness of the applicant's qualifications. The issue of testing often evokes more controversy than any other area of employment. Ask any manager or human resources specialist about preemployment and employment testing and you are likely to elicit one of the following responses:

> "I'm all for it! An employer needs to know as much as possible about a person before extending a job offer. Testing can provide the kind of information you could never get from just asking questions during an interview. In fact, I won't even conduct a face-to-face interview for most jobs without first administering a series of tests and assessing the results."

> "I'm in favor of tests overall and, generally speaking, believe in their predictive abilities concerning job success. But how do I know if I'm administering the right test or even if I should be testing at all? I'm always afraid that I may be violating someone's civil rights and that my company will end up being sued."

> "I don't like the idea of relying on tests to help me decide if someone is right for a job or not. In fact, I don't believe any selection device can tell an employer absolutely that someone will either do well or perform poorly on the job. Basically, then, I'd have to say that I disapprove of tests and have very little faith in test results overall. I'd go so far as to say that I consider some tests to be dangerous in that they may result in inaccurate, inappropriate, or incomplete conclusions. I'd rather conduct a series of in-depth interviews to determine job suitability."

What is interesting about these three typical responses is that they all make sense: Tests can indeed be valid indicators of job success, if they are carefully selected and measured against the parameters of a specific job. However, it is also true that there are legal ramifications for incorrectly administering tests or using tests that are not proven

Portions of this chapter appeared in slightly different form in Diane Arthur, *Recruiting, Interviewing, Selecting, and Orienting New Employees*, 2d ed. (New York: AMACOM, 1991).

indicators of job success—unvalidated tests. In addition, the tendency to overrely on testing to predict job suitability can result in individuals being inappropriately placed (an act likely to result in morale or disciplinary problems) or qualified applicants being turned away because of low test scores.

Regardless of one's personal views, tests may be considered a valid part of the recruitment and selection process if there is first a careful and objective analysis of testing, in terms of its characteristics, guidelines for validation, scoring, and relationship to discrimination. Various types of tests should be reviewed for applicability to specific jobs. Numerous classifications exist, including intelligence, personality, physical ability, honesty, and drug use. Indeed, knowing what tests are most suitable for a given job can be a challenge in and of itself.

Uniform Guidelines on Employee Selection

In 1978 the Equal Employment Opportunity Commission, the Department of Labor's Office of Federal Contract Compliance Programs, the Civil Service Commission (since renamed the Office of Personnel Management), the Department of Justice, and the Department of the Treasury together issued a set of *Uniform Guidelines on Employee Selection Procedures*. These *Guidelines* were designed to pilot employers through the testing process by providing a framework for determining the proper use of both preemployment tests relative to referral or hiring decisions, and employment tests pertaining to promotions, demotions, transfers, training, retention, and any other employment decisions. It is significant to note that the *Uniform Guidelines* also cover selection procedures other than tests, including interviews, application forms, references, and performance appraisals. Hence, the more encompassing expression "selection procedure" is preferred over the term "test."

The *Uniform Guidelines* apply to private employers with fifteen or more employees, state and local governments, most employment agencies, labor organizations, and contractors and subcontractors of the federal government.

Validation

Validation refers to the demonstration of the job relatedness of any test or other selection procedure. The *Uniform Guidelines* help to ensure job relatedness by requiring that all selection procedures not have an adverse impact on the employment opportunities of individuals of a particular race, sex, religion, or national origin. Adverse impact is defined by the *Uniform Guidelines* as "a substantially different rate of selection in hiring, promotion, or other employment decision which works to the disadvantage of members of a race, sex, or ethnic group." A selection rate for any race, sex, religion, or national origin that is less than four-fifths, or 80 percent, of the selection rate for the group with the highest selection rate is considered a substantially different rate of selection. Accordingly, employers are required to conduct validity studies of tests where adverse impact has occurred and, in general, are advised to use only valid tests, even if adverse impact has not been shown.

In broad terms, validation begins with a thorough job analysis to identify the requirements of the job. The next step entails identifying selection devices and standards that will isolate those applicants or employees meeting the job requirements. Testing current employees and applicants without using the test scores to influence any employment-related decisions can help measure the effectiveness of the selection device being tested. This process should take place over a long period of time and be applied to a large sample population to make more credible the validity of the results. The last phase involves preparing a detailed validation report that outlines and documents the steps taken.

Three different methods of determining validity are recognized by the *Uniform Guidelines*. The first is *criterion-related validity*, a statistical demonstration of a relationship between scores on a selection procedure and the job performance of a sample of workers. The second method is *content validity*, a demonstration that the content of a selection procedure is representative of important aspects of performance on the job. The final method is *construct validity*, a demonstration that a selection procedure measures something believed to be an underlying human trait or characteristic, e.g., honesty, and that this trait or characteristic is important for successful job performance.

While all three validation methods are recognized by the *Uniform Guidelines,* most employers rely on content validation, believing that it most accurately predicts job success. It is also generally agreed that the criterion-related process, while effective, can be a long and expensive procedure to administer. Construct validity has been the source of much debate, in that the soundness of any trait claimed to support successful job performance is difficult to establish.

Many employers turn to industrial and personnel psychologists with expertise in validation research for help with the validation of their selection procedures. These trained psychologists may be faculty members in colleges and universities, independent consultants, or members of consulting organizations. Additional information regarding individuals qualified to conduct validation studies may be obtained from the American Psychological Association, 1200 17th Street, NW, Washington, D.C. 20036.

In addition to test validation, other areas for which trained professionals should be consulted are the creation of employment tests or the tailoring of existing tests to better meet the needs of a specific business. ''Homemade'' tests developed by nonprofessionals place employers at greater risk of liability since such tests are harder to validate than professionally developed and researched tests. Tests developed by professionals are also considered more likely to be good predictors of job performances than homemade tests.

Purchasing a prepackaged test from vendors, including expert psychologists, can have its drawbacks, however. The credentials and reputation of any vendor should be checked carefully. Beware of vendors who use terms such as ''valid,'' ''reliable,'' and ''court defensible'' without substantial supporting documentation. In addition, the vendor's publication record should be reviewed. Most importantly, a test's relevance to your objectives should be determined. This may be accomplished by examining the test's underlying research, then bypassing those tests for which little or no validation research exists or which claim validity for use with occupational groups unlike those in your organization.

Purchasing or using a test that does not have a sound base can only increase your potential liability; furthermore, it will do little to ensure that you have hired those candidates with the best chance for success on the job. Employers who choose to continue using a test with an adverse impact may be found to be engaged in discriminatory practices and hence be held liable for various penalties, including back pay awards, plaintiff's attorney fees, and the loss of government contracts. If, however, an employer has substantial evidence of validity or has a study under way that is designed to document the evidence required by the *Uniform Guidelines* within a reasonable time, an employer may continue to use a test that is not yet fully validated for statistical purposes. In such instances, however, employers are discouraged from making hiring decisions based on unvalidated test results and are instead urged to explore alternative selection procedures.

Legal Aspects of Testing

Employment tests are governed by both federal and state laws covering fair employment practices. This is important to note, since many state laws allow discrimination claims to be tried by juries that may award punitive damages in addition to back pay.

One of the first cases to focus on employment testing discrimination was *Myart* v. *Motorola* in Illinois in 1966. Leon Myart, a black applicant for a job at a Motorola factory, alleged that the hiring practices at Motorola were racially discriminatory in that he had been asked to take a qualifying test containing questions requiring familiarity with a predominantly white, middle-class culture. A hearing examiner for the Illinois Fair Employment Practices Commission agreed that this was discriminatory, but the Illinois Supreme Court overturned the examiner's ruling. Nevertheless, news of this case alerted the public to the issue of testing and discrimination.

Griggs v. *Duke Power Co.* attracted even greater attention to the issue of testing and discrimination with its landmark ruling in 1971. Up until the passage of Title VII of the Civil Rights Act of 1964 (making it illegal to discriminate against any individual with respect to any term or condition of employment, on the basis of race, color, religion, sex, or national origin), Duke Power openly practiced racial discrimination by employing black workers only in the labor department, where they were paid less than workers in other, all-white departments. Once Title VII rendered such practice illegal, the company opened up job opportunities to blacks in all departments, but it established a new set of hiring requirements. These requirements included a high school diploma and satisfactory scores on two aptitude tests, the Wonderlic Personnel Test and the Bennett Mechanical Aptitude Test. Blacks argued that the tests and diploma requirements had an adverse effect, were arbitrary, and were not job-related. The trial court ruled that the tests did not violate Title VII because Duke Power did not have a discriminatory intent. The U.S. Supreme Court disagreed, stating that Title VII was concerned with the consequences of employment practices, not motivation. The Court thus drew an important distinction between intent and effect. The Court further criticized employment testing in general, and while *Griggs* v. *Duke Power Co.* left companies free to use tests, it limited the use of tests having an adverse impact on minorities by its holding that "Congress has forbidden giving [testing or measuring procedures] controlling force unless they are demonstrably a reasonable measure of job performance."

Another landmark case dealing with testing and discrimination is *Albemarle Paper Co.* v. *Moody,* decided by the U.S. Supreme Court in 1975. While this case also involved employment requirements of a high school diploma and two tests, what made it particularly significant was that Albemarle had hired a psychologist who found a significant correlation between the test scores for current employees and their performance evaluations. The Supreme Court was not impressed and stipulated that having a psychologist claim that the tests were a valid indicator of job success did not provide a sufficient basis for their use.

In 1982, *Connecticut* v. *Teal* focused on yet another aspect of testing and discrimination. This case concerned an employer who required employees to pass a written test in order to qualify for promotion. The written test had not been validated, and the proportion of blacks passing the test was only 68 percent of the proportion of whites. However, not everyone who passed the test was promoted, and the percentage of blacks who were promoted was actually higher than that of whites. This, however, did not influence the U.S. Supreme Court's ruling that tests still had to be validated. The high percentage of blacks who were promoted did not compensate for the possibility that the test had discriminated against those blacks who failed it.

One final case involving testing and discrimination is offered: *Watson* v. *Fort Worth Bank & Trust*. In 1988, Clara Watson, a black woman, was denied a promotion on the basis of the evaluation of her work by white supervisors. She sued and offered evidence that, on the average, black workers received lower performance ratings and fewer promotions than did whites. The U.S. Supreme Court agreed with Watson, ruling that subjective employment practices are subject to the same standards as are objective criteria, such as tests, used to make hiring decisions.

These examples of testing and discrimination clearly support the importance of strict adherence to the *Uniform Guidelines on Employee Selection* and their validation requirements. Employers are urged to consult with an attorney specializing in employment law for advice regarding the use of specific tests. Chapter 18 of this Handbook also discusses the legal aspects of testing, and the Resources section at the end of the book provides names of some testing services.

Testing Advantages and Disadvantages

By the time most of us start working, we probably have been subjected to twenty or more years of testing, beginning as early as preschool. The process continues at work, as tests are given to screen out, evaluate, classify, predict, and promote. We may also be asked to take tests to determine if we are strong enough, smart enough, or healthy enough, and then there are honesty tests, drug tests, and personality tests. It is doubtful that many of us have ever stopped to think about how many tests we have taken so far in our lives, but if we did, the resulting number would undoubtedly be startling.

Because testing is such an integral part of our lives—especially the time we spend at work—it is helpful to examine the various advantages and disadvantages of testing.

Testing Advantages

Many tests evaluate a job candidate's achievements, thereby measuring current skill level. Others focus on aptitude, or a person's potential ability. Tests may also help determine how motivated a person is likely to be in a certain type of job and/or work environment. In addition, tests may be used to screen out individuals with certain undesirable traits, such as job-related physical disabilities or drug use.

In this regard, job-related, validated tests certainly seem to be useful recruitment and selection tools. They can help employers select employees who are more capable, better motivated, and less likely to bring certain unacceptable qualities to the job. Also, tests can help distinguish among otherwise similarly qualified candidates. Relevant, too, is the widespread belief that the objective nature of testing can help employers make unbiased employment decisions. This lends itself to another benefit of testing: When tests are fair representations of the skills and knowledge needed to perform a given job, employers are more likely to be portrayed as impartial. This in turn may serve to enhance the overall image of the organization.

Testing Disadvantages

Naturally, there are also disadvantages associated with employment testing. A tendency to overrely on tests for screening or hiring purposes is one of the greatest concerns expressed by opponents. Even if a test is well designed and properly used, the results can only indicate which individuals are most *likely* to do well. No test can point with certainty to those people who *will* do well. Hence, employers are cautioned against using test scores exclusively to make employment decisions; tests should instead be viewed as one of many factors contributing to selection.

While there are several multipurpose tests, many tests are designed to emphasize and therefore seek out individuals who possess specific skills or knowledge. This can screen out candidates who might otherwise make good employees. In some instances, the qualities being sought via testing may be acquired through a minimal amount of on-the-job training or education.

Opponents of testing also point out that many people react negatively to the mere idea of a test; others, who may in fact be qualified, simply do not do well on tests. This can result in a distorted or incomplete picture of a candidate if too much emphasis is placed on test scores.

Types of Tests

Any manager or human resources specialist who has been exposed to employment testing knows that there is a myriad of tests from which to choose. In an attempt to diminish any confusion over the vast array of tests available, two primary test classifications are offered: (1) physical and security-related tests, and (2) achievement and aptitude tests.

Physical and Security-Related Tests

Physical and security-related tests are intended to ensure a work force of individuals who are physically able to perform the essential functions of their jobs, do not threaten the healthy or safety of others, have been honest in the representation of their skills and background, and may be trusted in their daily dealings on the job.

Toward this end, the five most commonly used physical and security-related tests are:

1. Polygraph tests
2. Written honesty tests
3. Preemployment physical examinations
4. Drug tests
5. AIDS tests

POLYGRAPH TESTS

Polygraph tests, or mechanical lie detector tests, have been all but banned from use by private sector employers as a result of the Employee Polygraph Protection Act of 1988. The greatest implication of this federal statute is that employers are no longer permitted to use lie detectors as screening devices for job applicants. Violaters of the Employee Polygraph Protection Act may be fined up to $10,000 per test; may be required to hire, reinstate, or promote the employee or applicant; and/or may have to pay lost wages and benefits, as well as attorney's fees. Employers are required to post conspicuously a notice of this act where all applicants and employees may see it.

Some states have polygraph laws that are even more restrictive than the federal statute. These state laws will not be preempted by federal law unless the state provisions conflict with the federal act. Employers who use polygraph tests unlawfully risk not only violation of federal and state statutes but also legal liability on the basis of defamation and invasion of privacy.

In spite of the Employee Polygraph Protection Act and any prevailing state laws, however, controversy over the use of polygraph tests continues. This is because of the fact that there remain certain exceptions where polygraph testing is permitted. It is allowed, for example, when employers hire workers for security-sensitive jobs and pharmaceutical work, and when employers are involved in manufacturing, distributing, or dispensing controlled substances. In addition, the Employee Polygraph Protection Act does not apply to the federal, state, or local governments or industries with national defense or national security contracts. Moreover, businesses with access to highly classified information may continue to use polygraph tests. However, although these employers are exempt, they may not use the results of the polygraphs as the sole basis for making an employment-related decision.

Use of polygraph tests is also permitted to investigate employees reasonably suspected of stealing or committing other infractions. Access to stolen property alone, however, is not considered a reasonable basis for suspicion. An employee believed to have committed an infraction must first receive a written notice that identifies the loss being investigated, states the employer's basis for suspicion, and explains the employee's statutory rights under the federal act. Employees must also be advised of their right to consult with counsel before and during the examination.

Employees and applicants may refuse to take the polygraph test or may terminate it at any time. No test is allowed to last longer than ninety minutes. In addition, upon learning the test results, employees and applicants may request a second test and/or hire an independent examiner for a second opinion.

Test takers must not be asked degrading or intrusive questions or questions about sexual behavior, union activities, or religious, racial, or political beliefs. They must be given advance notice relative to testing conditions, and, before the test begins, they must be permitted to review all questions. Afterward, they must receive a written copy of the test questions, their responses, and any opinions based on the test results.

Employers may test according to these exceptions and guidelines only if they utilize the services of licensed, bonded examiners.

WRITTEN HONESTY TESTS

The use of written honesty tests, also known as integrity or paper and pencil tests, has grown tremendously since the passage of the Employee Polygraph Protection Act.

In fact, approximately 5 million written honesty tests are currently given each year, representing a 20 percent annual increase since 1988. With employee theft estimated at $40 billion a year nationwide, according to the U.S. Chamber of Commerce, employers are legitimately concerned over finding a means for spotting applicants who are likely to steal.

Written honesty tests generally take about twenty minutes to complete and are scored by computer in seconds. The cost ranges from seven to fifteen dollars per exam.

Supporters of written honesty tests believe that they are an effective means of reducing employee theft. They are generally considered less intimidating than polygraphs, and test publishers argue that their written honesty tests are highly accurate and based on extensive research.

However, opponents argue that written honesty tests result in misclassifying many test takers as dishonest when in fact they never do behave in any of the ways predicted by the test. In addition, there is concern over relying on such test results to determine job suitability. There are many pros and cons surrounding the use of paper and pencil honesty tests. If you are thinking of using these tests it would be a good idea to contact a testing consultant—for example, the American Psychological Association or the Association of Personnel Test Publishers—for more information. Refer to the resource section on the back of this book for testing consultants.

PREEMPLOYMENT PHYSICAL EXAMINATIONS

Preemployment physical exams can help identify individuals who are physically unable to perform the essential functions of a given job in a safe and effective manner. More specifically, they may disclose a person's past and present state of health, prior exposure to harmful substances or an injurious environment, family health history, and genetic composition. (It should be noted that proponents of genetic testing maintain that such tests can identify certain job applicants or employees predisposed to specific types of occupational illness. Opponents, however, argue that genetic testing is not routinely warranted for employment purposes and could unfairly exclude qualified workers.) Predictive screening can also assess an applicant's susceptibility to future injury.

Employers are advised to ascertain their state's specific guidelines and requirements regarding prevailing preemployment physical restrictions before beginning or continuing with physical exams. This can usually be accomplished by examining state fair employment acts or civil rights acts or by consulting with an attorney knowledgeable in this area.

The restrictions and guidelines generally include requiring the employer to pay for the entire cost of the examination, providing the employee with a copy of the test results, and maintaining the confidentiality of the results. State regulations may also control the timing of tests and who may or may not be tested. Some states restrict preemployment physicals to only those applicants who have been extended an offer of employment. In these instances, employment is generally conditioned on the successful completion of the medical exam. Other jurisdictions stipulate that preemployment medical exams must be given to all applicants, including applicants with prevailing disabilities. Depending on the test results, accommodation for those with physical or other impairments may be required, barring undue hardship to the employer. It is also important to note the stipulation in the Americans with Disabilities Act (ADA) of 1990 that disabled individuals cannot be singled out for physical exams. The ADA also places limits on the types of preemployment medical inquiries and exams that employers may use and affects employers' ability to conduct medical exams of current employees.

Increasing numbers of employers are asking applicants and employees to sign waivers acknowledging that the company does not guarantee the accuracy of its physician's conclusions. This sort of waiver is an attempt to limit the employer's liability for negligence if the employee later suffers an on-the-job injury as a result of a condition that was not detected during the preemployment physical.

Preemployment physical exams can be significant in their detective and evaluative abilities, assuming the physician administering the exam is familiar with those tasks that are essential to the performance of each job applied for, and evaluation is limited to the candidate's ability to perform those tasks. Test results are not always accurate, however, and offer limited predictive qualities. Consequently, physicals are best used as one of several selection devices, or not done at all.

DRUG TESTS

Drug testing is one of the most controversial areas of testing confronting employers today. And yet every year more employers institute testing programs.

Random testing programs are slowly gaining support from the courts. For example, in May 1990, New York State's highest court upheld random drug testing for prison guards in New York City. This decision, say legal experts, is likely to prompt an increase in the random testing of whole classes of workers throughout the state, as well as influence the decisions of other state courts in upcoming cases. Lower courts in other states have also upheld random drug testing. For example, prison guards in Iowa are subject to random testing, as are policy officers and firefighters in Annapolis, Maryland.

Other surveys indicate that the majority of employers in the United States favor some form of drug testing. This is exemplified by a 1989 survey conducted by the Gallup Organization for the U.S. Chamber of Commerce. It revealed that of the more than 1,000 employers surveyed nationwide, 97 percent feel that drug testing in the workplace is appropriate, at least under some circumstances, and 55 percent believe periodic drug testing is warranted.

Proponents of preemployment and employment drug testing cite the escalation of drug use in the workplace as the primary reason for their support. Such an increase has resulted in numerous problems, including increased absenteeism, more on-the-job accidents, a higher incidence of theft, and greater medical costs. In addition, the passage of the Drug-Free Workplace Act of 1988 (which requires all grant recipients and private sector businesses with federal contracts in excess of $25,000 to certify that they will maintain a drug-free workplace) has prompted many employers to implement drug testing programs, even though this is not mandated by the Act.

Opponents object to drug testing because of potential legal liability. (For instance, across-the-board drug testing as part of a "zero tolerance" policy designed to deter drug use off the job as well as on the job has been criticized by some courts as an unwarranted invasion of privacy.) Opponents also point to excessive costs for properly conducted drug testing programs, an adverse effect on employee morale, and the possibility of erroneous results.

Concern over the possibility of erroneous results is grounded in the technique most commonly used for drug detection: *urine testing*. The two categories of urine tests, screening and confirmatory, can both result in false positives; screening tests are less accurate than confirmatory tests. Screening tests cost less to conduct—from six to eleven dollars each, as opposed to between sixty and one hundred dollars per sample for confirmatory tests—and they are easier to administer. They are therefore often the tests of choice for many employers. Accordingly, there is a great deal of concern over non-drug-using applicants and employees being falsely accused of drug use. When positive screening test results occur, employers are advised to conduct a second, confirmatory test. If the second test reveals drug use, employers may deny applicants employment or may terminate an employee after ample opportunity is provided for treatment or cessation of drug abuse.

This course of action has legal ramifications in the form of suits filed by applicants and employees claiming they have been falsely accused of drug use. One common reason for such lawsuits is the allegation that positive test results may not prove any act of wrongdoing. Urine can retain traces of drugs for anywhere from a few days, in the case of cocaine and amphetamines, to a month, as with the drug classification cannabinoids. Consequently, while a urine test may indicate use of an illegal drug, it cannot establish with certainty that the drug was used during working hours, impaired the employee's ability to perform his or her work, interfered with the work of others, or endangered the safety of others.

Other lawsuits stem from false positive test results caused by the use of legitimate over-the-counter drugs. This is most likely to occur when screening tests are used, since they frequently report "drug detected" without distinguishing which drug is involved. To reduce this possibility, it is advisable to ask test takers to identify all drug products used in the weeks prior to the test, including legal medications.

Because positive urine tests do not tie in directly with any allegations of wrongdoing and since these tests often detect common drugstore items, some employers are seeking alternatives to urine tests. One option is a *blood test*. Alternative nonmedical drug tests, such as *balance and reflex performance checks,* may also be considered as substitutes for urine tests. As with blood tests, the results of nonmedical tests can indicate on-the-job impairment.

Another nonmedical drug test that has recently been introduced to the workplace is the *critical tracking test*. This test is intended to assess on-the-spot employee fitness by measuring fine hand-eye coordination and quick reaction time. In addition to detecting drug impairment, it is also designed to detect alcohol use, lack of sleep, emotional stress, and illness. It is considered most appropriate for workers in jobs where safety is a critical factor.

The test takes approximately one minute to administer. Workers are asked to keep an electronic pointer centered on a computer screen; since the pointer continuously moves, test takers must manipulate a knob to return it to the center of the screen. The longer employees are able to control the pointer, the higher their psychomotor performance rating. Performance on any given day is measured by the computer against the worker's previously established normal performance. Some employers who administer the test to groups of workers, like drivers, do so each day before they begin their shift. Anyone who fails the test is temporarily assigned to other duties.

Supporters of the critical tracking test applaud the fact that it focuses on job-related impairment and provides immediate results. Opponents express concern over possible inappropriate reactions by employers toward employees who fail the test. They also question the applicability of the test to positions requiring the performance of complex tasks and decision making.

In addition to blood tests and various nonmedical drug tests, other alternatives to urine tests are being utilized. One such test, which is highly controversial, is *hair analysis*. In this process, hair samples are examined using radioimmunoassay, then confirmed by gas chromatography or mass spectrometry. (This is the same technique used to test urine samples.) The premise of the hair analysis test is that chemicals in the bloodstream, both legal and illegal, are left in hair follicles and subsequently trapped as the hair grows, thereby providing a record of past drug use. Types of drugs, as well as frequency and duration of use, can all be determined. Supporters of hair analysis maintain that it is a valid drug test accepted by courts in criminal trials; however, there have been few court cases involving hair analysis in an employment context. Proponents also contend that the test provides a detailed record of drug use and is less embarrassing than urinalysis. Opponents claim that the process is highly invasive in that it provides information about an individual's drug-use history, instead of determining whether or not he or she is able to function safely on the job.

Another alternative to urine testing is the *pupillary-reaction test*. Here, an individual's eyes are examined by a trained professional who determines how the pupils react when shined on with a flashlight. The premise is that the pupils of subjects under the influence of drugs or alcohol will react differently to light. Urine tests are usually required to confirm the results of the pupillary-reaction test. Supporters maintain that the test is noninvasive. Opponents argue that certain medical conditions may give a false positive reading and that follow-up tests are necessary. In addition, a trained professional is needed to administer the test.

Employers who plan to utilize any form of drug testing should develop and implement a set of well-defined, written guidelines, available to all employees. These guidelines should include a description of the purpose of drug testing, who is to be tested, what method of testing will be used, where and when testing will take place, who will administer the test, and how the test will be administered. If urine tests are to be conducted, the guidelines should include a description of the manner in which specimens will be collected (privacy and dignity should be preserved without compromising test security or hampering test results). In addition, all applicants and employees being tested should be asked to sign a consent form, agreeing to the drug test and to the release of the results to the employer.

State laws on drug testing vary and should be checked carefully by employers. In addition, employers should consult with an attorney before implementing a drug testing program of any kind.

AIDS TESTS

Basing employment decisions on factors related to acquired immune deficiency syndrome (AIDS) is considered discriminatory, so there is little justification for employers to implement an AIDS testing program. In addition, there is no direct test for AIDS itself. Current tests can show only whether a person has developed antibodies in response to the presence of the AIDS virus. The presence of antibodies, or of the AIDS virus itself, does not mean for certain that the person will develop AIDS. Perhaps more significantly, it does not mean the person can infect someone else through casual contact. According to a Surgeon General's report on AIDS, "Everyday living does not present any risk of infection. You cannot get AIDS from casual social contact. . . . Nor has AIDS been contracted from . . . eating in restaurants (even if a restaurant worker has AIDS or carries the AIDS virus). You cannot get AIDS from toilets, door-knobs, telephones . . . [or] office machinery.'' The Surgeon General's conclusions regarding AIDS have led courts to declare that there is no risk to coworkers from AIDS virus carriers or AIDS-infected individuals. In addition, the Americans with Disabilities Act defines people with AIDS as being disabled and grants them protection under the Civil Rights Act of 1964.

The Centers for Disease Control (CDC) has issued recommendations for preventing the transmission of AIDS in the workplace. According to the CDC, AIDS has not been proven to be spread by casual contact, nor is it known to be transmitted through the preparation or serving of food. Hence, routine AIDS antibody screening is not recom-mended for people providing personal services and those preparing and serving food and beverages. The CDC does, however, recommend that testing be made available to health care workers and others who wish to know their AIDS status.

In those rare instances when an employer feels justified in testing an applicant or employee for AIDS, prior consent should be obtained from the individuals, and that person should be informed of test results. Employers would be wise to review the ADA before establishing testing guidelines or revising their preemployment policies.

Achievement and Aptitude Tests

Achievement and aptitude tests are often categorized together, although they are not the same: *achievement tests* measure current skills and indicate a person's existing abilities, while *aptitude tests* measure a person's potential to perform a given task.

Five of the most frequently used achievement and aptitude tests are:

1. Intelligence tests
2. Tests of job knowledge
3. Physical ability and psychomotor tests
4. Personality tests
5. Work samples

INTELLIGENCE TESTS

While research has shown that intelligence is a fine indicator of future work suc-cess, particularly in the absence of a verifiable work history, experts do not seem to be able to agree as to just what intelligence is. Some experts maintain that there is an intelligence quotient (IQ) that measures a person's ability to perform all cognitive or thinking tasks. Others believe that intelligence is multidimensional, that is, it consists of separate mental abilities that cannot be averaged out to equal one level. Still others contend that intelligence consists of many cognitive abilities that together result in an overall mental ability.

Two experts in the field, Professor John Hunter of Michigan State University and Frank Schmidt of the U.S. Office of Personnel Management and George Washington University, have developed a process called *validity generalization,* which uses a tech-nique called meta-analysis. This technique is supposed to assess the true relationship that exists between intelligence test scores and job performance.

However disagreement over the specific means for measuring intelligence contin-ues. Some believe in using general intelligence tests that concentrate on abstract functions involving the use of verbal or numerical reasoning. Tests currently available for use in business include the Personnel Tests for Industry (available from The Psychological Corporation, San Antonio, Texas), which include a five-minute verbal test and a twenty-minute numerical test, and the Thurstone Test of Mental Alertness (Science Research Associates, Inc., Chicago, Illinois), a twenty-minute test of more than one hundred questions relating to word meaning, definitions, and arithmetic reasoning.

Many employers choose instead to use aptitude tests that evaluate more practical abilities. A number of such tests are available for measuring clerical, mechanical, and computer-related abilities. Examples include the Minnesota Clerical Test, the Bennett Mechanical Comprehension Test (both distributed by The Psychological Corporation), and the Computer Programmer Aptitude Battery (distributed by Science Research Associates).

There are also several multiple-aptitude tests that measure a variety of job-related aptitudes. The General Aptitude Test Battery (GATB), developed by the U.S. Employment Service, for example, consists of twelve tests and includes measurements of verbal, numerical, and spatial abilities. Widely used by private employers and state job services across the United States, the GATB is facing discontinuance by the federal government. The Department of Labor is conducting an investigation of the test's "within-group" scoring method, whereby separate scoring scales for different racial groups are permitted in order to avoid adverse impact on minority groups. The result, according to the Labor Department, may be reverse discrimination. If the reevaluation of this test results in its permanent discontinuance, other tests are likely to be challenged as well.

Another multiple-aptitude test is the Flanagan Aptitude Classification Test. It measures aptitude for sixteen different job skills, including basic arithmetic, knowledge of correct English grammar, sentence structure, problem solving, and the ability to use good judgment in practical situations.

Published intelligence tests cost an average of three to five dollars per person; multiple-aptitude tests cost more. Volume discounts are generally available. Employers who want to purchase intelligence tests should ask for proven evidence that the test is valid relative to the type of job for which it will be used. Multiple-aptitude tests usually have a higher validity rate than do single tests. Additional information regarding an intelligence test's validity may also be found in such test directories as the *Mental Measurements Yearbook*.

Intelligence tests are most effective when used to select applicants who have a level of cognitive ability that closely matches specific job requirements. This in turn can lead to greater job satisfaction and hence a higher rate of productivity.

TESTS OF JOB KNOWLEDGE

Job knowledge or trade tests require applicants to demonstrate their degree of existing knowledge regarding how a given job is performed. In other words, job knowledge tests screen prospective employees to ensure they have the experience claimed. These tests are based on the belief that the more closely a test resembles a given job and the more it measures performance against actual examples of tasks typically performed, the better it will be able to predict actual job performance.

Most job knowledge tests are developed according to the content-validation method and are considered to have fairly high validity. Some companies prefer to develop and validate their own tests. Others favor purchasing commercially prepared and validated tests. Before doing this, however, employers are urged to conduct a thorough job analysis to determine the appropriateness of the purchased test. Information regarding commercially developed job knowledge tests can be obtained from Employers' Tests and Services Associates, in Chambersburg, Pennsylvania; the National Business Education Association, in Reston, Virginia; The Psychological Corporation; and Purdue University, in West Lafayette, Indiana.

Job knowledge tests can be written or oral. Oral tests may consist of a series of questions asked by a test administrator or may be more structured, with a panel asking job applicants a preselected set of questions. A structured scoring system determines the results. Oral tests generally take less time to administer than do written tests, but they are not easily standardized, making a challenge more likely. Written tests of job knowledge are most common and are generally scored as "pass" or "fail." They are more easily administered and standardized and more comprehensive than most oral exams. They may, however, be costly to develop and, since they are written, tend to emphasize literacy. This could pose a problem if literacy skills are not job-related.

The majority of companies that conduct job knowledge tests require them of clerical and other office positions, production and service jobs, and technical work. Tests may include office math, office procedures, general clerical ability, stenographic skills, secretarial procedures, mechanical familiarity and knowledge, accounting procedures, typing, and word processing.

PHYSICAL ABILITY AND PSYCHOMOTOR TESTS

Physical ability tests, also known as strength and endurance tests, are often used as preemployment selection devices for positions requiring physical performance. Since it is extremely difficult, if not impossible, to judge a person's strength and level of endurance on the basis of body size and appearance, physical ability tests allow employers to determine which applicants or employees are most physically capable of performing the essential functions of a given job. These tests are also a means for reducing many on-the-job injuries that can occur when tasks require more strength and endurance than an employee can exert without excessive stress. These injuries in turn can lead to increased absenteeism and turnover, as well as workers compensation and health insurance claims.

The preferred validation method for physical ability tests is content validity. This means that a thorough job analysis has determined that a given test accurately reflects the primary duties and responsibilities of a specific job. Many employers contact private agencies or clinics for assistance with physical ability testing. The cost per person is generally in the range of twenty to thirty dollars.

Psychomotor tests are used primarily for semiskilled, repetitive work, such as packing and certain forms of inspection, and generally measure such abilities as manual dexterity, motor ability, and hand-eye coordination. Most psychomotor tests are simulation tests, although written tests are used in some instances. The most valid psychomotor tests call for the use of the same muscle groups as the job requires. Custom-made tests that reproduce the combination of motor abilities required have been shown to have fair validity. Several prepared psychomotor tests are available, including the Purdue Pegboard, the Hand-Tool Dexterity Test, the Crawford Small Parts Dexterity Test, and the O'Connor Finger Dexterity Test. Although these tests may be based on validity studies, local validation is still recommended.

PERSONALITY TESTS

There is a great deal of controversy surrounding the use of personality tests. Supporters maintain that an objective personality test, coupled with other traditional selection devices, can provide a clear picture of a person's abilities, interests, and potential. This in turn may result in lower turnover rates and increased productivity. Proponents also maintain that personality tests gather information in such a way that the people taking these tests are unaware of exactly what they are revealing. Hence, there is little chance of charges of discrimination and resulting lawsuits.

Not everyone agrees, however. Opponents of personality tests as a preemployment and employment assessment tool argue that personality is extremely difficult to measure. Even if tests could perfectly measure an individual's personality, there is no reason to assume that this would result in more productive work. In addition, there is concern over the apparent inherent assumption that personalities do not change, thereby implying that matches deemed appropriate or inappropriate via testing will remain so. Furthermore, there is doubt as to the validity of personality tests that fail to take into account the role of motivation: An unmotivated employee is not apt to perform well on the job, even with the desired personality traits.

There are several different types of personality tests, all of which focus on a variety of psychological characteristics. There are, for example, tests that measure a person's emotional stability; ability to work under pressure; and susceptibility to depression, paranoia, hysteria, and schizophrenia. Drug abuse and eating disorders may also be identified through the use of such tests as the Minnesota Multiphasic Personality Inventory, which was recently updated to reflect more accurately today's language, concerns, and culture.

These and other personality tests are usually designed by psychologists with expertise in human behavior and statistical analysis. Test publishers generally sell personality tests only to those trained in psychological testing. For example, the *1990 Personnel and Career Assessment Catalog,* published by The Psychological Corporation, provides a lengthy description of rules and qualifications governing the sale of testing materials. In addition, it maintains the right to require evidence of the purchaser's qualifications. Likewise, the *1989 CPP Catalog of Tests and Materials for Business* (Consulting Psychologists Press, Inc., Palo Alto, California) clearly states:

> Psychological tests have potential to benefit humankind when they are properly used. Improperly used, they are at best of little value, at worst dangerous. For this reason, the Committee on Ethical Standards of the American Psychological Association requires that distributors of certain restricted tests limit their sale to persons whose education and experience should enable them to use tests appropriately.

The message goes on to define the qualifications for various levels of testing.

Information regarding the services of industrial psychologists who might assist your organization with the development and/or implementation of validated psychological tests can be obtained from the American Psychological Association.

One form of personality test that is just beginning to capture the attention of employers is based on *color psychology.* It is called the Lüscher personality or color test, named after its originator, Dr. Max Lüscher, a Swiss psychologist. Originally used by psychologists and physicians as an aid in diagnosing conditions of strain or psychosomatic illness, it also revealed personality characteristics. The Lüscher color test has since been modified for use in business.

Assessments are based on the test taker's preference for various shades of color and combinations of colors. The underlying premise of the test is that people will choose colors that reflect their physical and psychological needs. These needs in turn reflect a person's psychological and physical condition. The test takes approximately five minutes to complete, and no questions are asked.

Supporters of the Lüscher color test maintain that the test is appropriate for all individuals, regardless of education or cultural background. It is further claimed that normal types of color blindness have no bearing on the validity of the test. Employers should note that the soundness and validity of this test as an employment selection device is questionable and not yet adequately proven. The simplicity of the test should not lull employers into attempting self-administration. Lüscher color test administrators should have formal training in its use, proper credentials, and practical experience. Samples of their work and references from other employers who have used the test should be ascertained as well.

Another form of personality test gaining in popularity is *graphology,* or handwriting analysis. Supporters of this method claim that a person's handwriting reveals information about emotional stability, impulsiveness, vulnerability to stress, assertiveness, social skills, integrity, and a host of other characteristics. It is further maintained that handwriting cannot be faked; therefore, it is concluded, graphology is likely to provide a clear picture of a person's strengths and shortcomings.

Not everyone agrees that the size, slant, loops, space between letters, pressure, and rhythm of someone's handwriting can reveal job-related personality traits. There is little empirical evidence supporting the validity of graphology as a preemployment or employment selection device.

Employers who opt to use graphology as a selection device are cautioned against relying on it as the primary or exclusive means for determining job suitability. Other, more reliable measures of past experience, ability, and predictors of potential should be focused on, with graphology used only as a possible means of either acquiring additional information or confirming known information.

Employers who use the Lüscher color test, graphology, or any other personality test that is relatively new and undocumented should collect their own validity data and proceed with caution.

Work Samples

Work sample tests require applicants to demonstrate the level of skill they possess. There are two basic types of work samples: verbal and motor. Common verbal work samples include in-basket tests for managers and tests of ability to write business letters. Motor work samples might include programming tests for computer operators and stenographic tests for secretaries. Both verbal and motor work samples are considered to be highly valid predictors of job success.

Because of this and the fact that they are generally well accepted by job applicants and employers alike, work sample tests are growing in popularity. They may be used with actual job-related equipment, such as a typing test, or performed on simulated equipment, as with a repair simulation test. Since work samples evaluate an existing level of achievement, they are best used to select experienced workers who already have a degree of proficiency in a given area. Hence, they are often used in making promotion decisions.

Work sample tests may be developed after conducting a complete and thorough job analysis. Many companies choose to contact qualified outside professionals for assistance, such as the Educational Testing Service, in Princeton, New Jersey; National Computer Systems Professional Assessment Services, in Minneapolis, Minnesota; and QUIZ, Inc., in Atlanta, Georgia. These are but a few of the suppliers who will either help an organization custom-develop work sample tests or provide prepared samples. It should be noted that work sample tests are time-consuming to administer.

Testing Guidelines

Any employer conducting preemployment and employment tests should have testing guidelines prepared in writing. These guidelines should clearly state the primary objectives of the organization's testing program and describe how various tests are administered, evaluated, and interpreted. These guidelines should be made available to all those directly involved in the testing process.

Guidelines for test administration should also be established. These guidelines should include the following:

- Tests should be given only when job-related criteria indicate a direct correlation between test results and job performance.
- The testing environment should be the same each time a test is given.
- The same tools or materials should be distributed in exactly the same order and manner each time a test is given.
- The language used to describe the purpose of the test should be identical each time the test is administered.
- Oral instructions should be recited at the same rate of speech using the same tone of voice and at the same pitch and volume.
- The same amount of time should be allotted for the test each time it is given.
- Every effort should be made to eliminate known anxiety-producing factors, such as uncomfortable seating or excessive noise.
- The number of people with access to test scores or answer sheets should be limited.
- Tests should be scored by experts with proper training.

Computer-administered tests are increasingly being used to help ensure the uniformity of test administration. Instructions and questions appear on a computer monitor, and test takers record their responses with a light pen, used directly on the screen; a computer mouse, which controls the cursor on the screen; or a keyboard, upon which answers are typed.

Proponents of computer-administered tests assert that this method eliminates the possibility of administrator bias. Opponents maintain that test scores can be adversely affected if users are not comfortable with computers. All computer-administered tests are subject to the same standards and requirements for selection procedures outlined by the *Uniform Guidelines on Employee Selection Procedures.*

Disabled test takers may require special accommodations. For example, visually impaired applicants may be given more time to complete a test or have tests presented via cassette tapes, with the assistance of a reader, or written in large print or braille. Hearing-impaired test takers may require written instructions or sign language to substitute for spoken directions. Test takers with motor disabilities may require special access to test sites, specially adapted equipment, or personal assistance. Under certain circumstances, it may be deemed appropriate to waive the test altogether and permit some alternative demonstration of job ability instead.

With the passage of the Americans with Disabilities Act, there are new issues of accommodation for persons with disabilities applying for jobs. The ADA takes effect in 1992. Employers must become familiar with its requirements before that time.

Summary

Employers who are concerned with preemployment and employment testing must weigh a number of factors, such as what constitutes a test, validation, the legal aspects of testing, the advantages and disadvantages of testing, the differences between certain types of tests, and when certain tests are appropriate. Employers should establish reasonable and equitable testing guidelines.

6

Selection

Mary F. Cook
President
Mary Cook & Associates
with David C. McClelland, Ph.D.
Chairman of the Board
McBer and Company
Professor of Psychology Emeritus
Harvard University
and
Lyle M. Spencer, Jr., Ph.D.
President and CEO
McBer and Company

The employee selection process is one of the most critical human resources functions. In addition to matching qualified people to jobs, the selection process has an important public relations impact. Discriminatory hiring practices, impolite interviewers, unnecessarily long waits, inappropriate testing procedures, and lengthy decision-making processes produce unfavorable impressions of an organization. Poorly handled selection can considerably damage the image all departments have worked hard to build. If qualified, high-performing applicants are directed to the human resources department and, once there, receive less than top-quality service, the best people—the people you want and need most in your organization—will go elsewhere, and eventually the company's reputation will suffer.

When an organization has an open position, an assumption is made that somewhere there is a qualified person to fill that job—an individual who is not just technically and experientially qualified, but mature and motivated enough to come into the organization and become a top performer. When a person applies for a job, that individual brings many expectations, desires, and emotions to the situation. Selection is a very important concern because its objective is to match the person to the job and to the organization in a manner that promotes positive feelings and long-term success for both the company and the employee.

Selecting the Right Person for the Job

The final selection decision must match the "whole person" with the "whole job." This requires a thorough analysis of both the person and the job; only then can an intelligent decision be made as to how well the two will fit together. You must weigh all the facts intelligently and come to a sound conclusion. This element of judgment is of critical importance. Up to this point the selection system—recruitment, interviewing, and so on—will have helped gather data in a systematic fashion, but how this information is evaluated depends upon the judgment of the evaluator. The ultimate decision about who will be hired is generally made with two factors in mind: the applicant's qualifications for a given job opening, and the person's potential for future promotion. These two factors should be kept separate, and stress should be placed on matching an applicant to a specific position. Looking into the future and trying to determine what a person's potential may be five or ten years from now is difficult; nevertheless, this may have an important bearing on the employment decision. Still, your goal should be selecting the best person for the job that is currently available.

A person's intelligence, education, training, experience, skills, aptitudes, and so on, are fairly obvious from the résumé, application, and interview. But it is the personal "will do" characteristics—drive, determination, stability, maturity, and so on—that determine whether or not the person will put those basic abilities to good use.

Unskilled interviewers often pay more attention to the applicant's more obvious abilities than the personal "will do" qualities because the former are easier to evaluate. But many employees fail because they lack those critical "will do" characteristics. In essence, as an interviewer, you want to discover and hire an achiever: a person who is not only technically qualified, but who performs on the job and gets the work done, or gets it done through others. What the person will do in the future is best determined by what he or she has done in the past. This emphasis on "will do" characteristics is based on a number of principles:

- Actual behavior is largely determined by a person's habits and character traits, such as initiative, and perseverance.
- These traits develop early in life and become so conditioned that they seldom change.
- Future behavior can be determined from a detailed analysis of past behavior.

The interview and reference checks provide the basic data on applicant's "will do" attributes. The interview also measures the applicant's technical abilities. Taken together, they provide a good picture of the whole person and help you hire the right person for the job.

Be advised that the individual and the organization are not the only factors involved in deciding who will be hired. Decisions are also affected by such things as the labor market, government regulations, and a company's affirmative action needs. Ultimately, though, it is the applicant and his or her traits and abilities that have the greatest influence on a hiring decision.

Using Assessment Centers

Management expert Douglas Bray, thought to be the father of the assessment center concept, once said, "It's easier to increase skill in someone already skilled than in a klutz." One way to find out if a person is skilled is through the use of an assessment center, which many organizations use in their selection process. There are approximately 2,000 corporate assessment centers in the United States, and 75 percent are used to evaluate three types of positions: (1) first-line supervisors in industrial settings, (2) sales managers, and (3) office supervisors and managers. Assessment centers are also being used in police and fire departments and sports organizations.

Organizations use assessment centers in a variety of ways, depending on the application they have in mind. However, most assessment centers have several similar characteristics:

- They use multiple assessment techniques, including at least one job-related simulation exercise (group problem solving, in-basket exercise, interview simulation, etc.).
- They use multiple assessors, who receive prior training.
- Judgments are based on pooled information from these multiple assessors and techniques.
- There is a separation in time between the behavioral observation and the overall evaluation.
- Dimensions of performance have been identified by a job analysis.
- Exercises are designed to provide information on these dimensions.

A traditional assessment center normally operates as follows: A group of six to twelve candidates are sequestered with three or more assessors who have been trained to observe and evaluate behavior. (Assessors may be line managers, members of the personnel staff, or psychologists; managers who act as assessors are usually two or more levels above the participants in the organization, but do not supervise the participant.) The assessors observe the participants' behavior in management games, leaderless group discussions, role-playing exercises, and other activities. Some organizations also combine simulation techniques with background interviews and tests, and some combine personality, general interest, or intelligence tests with simulation exercises and actual job tryouts.

The idea is to use behavior or performance to predict behavior or performance, and the exercises are organized around dimensions that are related to job success in a particular job—typing, assembling, delegating, planning, decision making, managing, etc. In order to ensure that assessments are objective, a company should take steps to ensure that the essential job functions are properly described. If not, the elements developed from the description won't accurately reflect what's expected of the applicant.

Exhibit 6-1 provides an idea of the different types of assessments that might be used in the selection of a professional baseball player and a business manager. A typical assessment may take from three days to a week, depending on the number of candidates being assessed.

There are many independent assessment consultants throughout the United States.

Using a Selection Inventory

A selection inventory is a useful tool in making hiring decisions. This is a list of the most critical skills an applicant must have in order to be successful in your organization. (Naturally, applicants must have all of the technical and educational requirements of a position, but after those have been verified, you must address other important issues.) Once you construct a selection inventory, you can use it again and again with your applicants.

Exhibit 6-1. Types of assessment used in selection decisions.

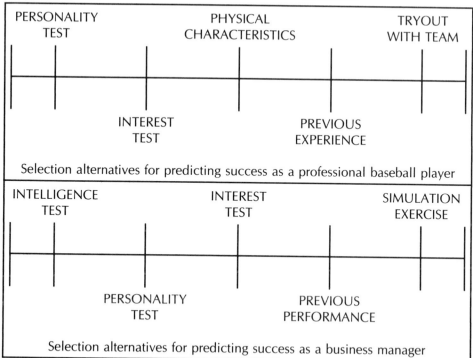

Selection alternatives for predicting success as a professional baseball player

Selection alternatives for predicting success as a business manager

Exhibit 6-2 is a sample selection inventory form for one organization. You should develop your own inventory form based on essential job functions and the traits and skills important to success in your company. In addition, the form should be adapted to fit specific jobs; you would not use the same criteria for a clerical job and a management position. The information you include on this form should be coordinated with the questions asked in the interview, so you will have all the data needed to make the right selection decision.

Using Work Sampling

Many organizations today are moving to work sampling as a method of competency assessment. The main reason is that, as a result of the 1971 case *Griggs* v. *Duke Power Co.*, the use of any test is considered illegal if it has an adverse impact on a protected class, unless it can be shown to be job-related. Work sample tests present an applicant with a structured representation of the actual work to be performed and thus *are* job-related. A good example of a work sample is a properly structured, timed, and scored typing test used to select typists. Work sampling usually has a high degree of content validity: The content of the test is representative of actual performance on the job.

Work sampling is generally thought to be a good alternative to written aptitude tests. There are several reasons for their growing use in employee selection.

(text continued on page 111)

Exhibit 6-2.   Sample selection inventory form.

Place a plus in front of each item where the applicant stands out.

JOB SKILLS

People who will be most successful in our company:

_____   Have the skills and abilities to perform the job
_____   Have past experience in this type of position
_____   Can describe effectively ways and means to accomplish the essential functions of the job
_____   Can identify the qualifications needed to do the job and specific actions that must be taken
_____   Have experience in using the necessary machines, computer programs, and/or software to adequately perform job functions

MANAGERIAL SKILLS

People who will be most successful in our company:

_____   Are conscious of priorities, and focus on the tasks most important to the organization
_____   Know how to delegate responsibility to people who are capable of handling it
_____   Have a record of hiring and training successful employees
_____   Use careful planning to avoid crises and anticipate future company needs
_____   Work effectively in high-pressure situations
_____   Set clear, measurable goals, and use them to judge their own performance as well as that of the company and its workers
_____   Balance attention to detail with a broad perspective
_____   Take the time to analyze their own mistakes and learn how to avoid them in the future

INTERPERSONAL SKILLS

People who will be most successful in our company:

_____   Must be able to work effectively with others
_____   Gain the loyalty and confidence of their superiors, their peers, and the people who work for them
_____   Encourage others to succeed, and do not feel threatened by their success
_____   Listen to comments with an open mind
_____   Have a record of working successfully with people from marketing, production, finance, sales, and other specialized areas
_____   Have a record of maintaining high morale in the units they have supervised

_____ Motivate others by their example
_____ Willingly give credit to others for their contributions, while accepting responsibility for failures of subordinates

ANALYTICAL SKILLS

People who will be most successful in our company:

_____ Get the necessary facts before making decisions
_____ Consider the overall impact of their business decisions
_____ Make business decisions, not emotional decisions
_____ Keep up to date on technical developments and competitors' activities, and pay attention to ways the company can benefit from new developments
_____ Evaluate the risks and rewards of alternatives
_____ Recognize the key features of complex problems, and don't get lost in details
_____ Are aware of deficiencies in their technical backgrounds, and seek competent assistance when necessary

PROBLEM-SOLVING SKILLS

People who will be most successful in our company:

_____ Can define and isolate the _real_ problems
_____ Will discover new ways of looking at problems
_____ Can decide on the best alternatives
_____ Minimize barriers within their work environment
_____ Take reasonable action to implement decisions
_____ Can convince others to accept decisions

TEAM SKILLS

People who will be most successful in our company:

_____ Work with others as part of a team effort
_____ Can differentiate management styles and their characteristics
_____ Understand the motivations and needs of others
_____ Can apply motivational theories to work situations
_____ Get cooperation from peers as well as supervisors
_____ Can analyze causes of interpersonal conflict
_____ Know how to apply transactional analysis for understanding and resolving conflict

PERFORMANCE SKILLS

People who will be most successful in our company:

_____ Turn a job into a growth experience
_____ Identify their own performance profiles

(continued)

Exhibit 6-2. *Continued.*

   _____ Maximize assets and strengthen weaknesses
   _____ Assume more responsibility as proficiency expands
   _____ Make their abilities known to superiors
   _____ Practice self-motivation, and create their own reward systems to increase self-confidence
   _____ Develop their own career action plans

COMMUNICATIONS SKILLS

People who will be most successful in our company:

   _____ Know how to build communication links
   _____ Can remove barriers to communication
   _____ Have good listening skills
   _____ Use feedback effectively
   _____ Get their ideas across in a professional manner
   _____ Understand how nonverbal communication affects their interactions

PERSONAL ATTITUDES

People who will be most successful in our company:

   _____ Regard their work as a challenge and an opportunity for gaining personal satisfaction, not merely as a source of income
   _____ Have a reputation for honesty, reliability, and trustworthiness
   _____ Are willing to take positions that are not necessarily in agreement with those of their superiors
   _____ Initiate action: propose goals, define problems, find alternative solutions
   _____ Accept added responsibility, and handle new situations well
   _____ Rarely make excuses for not performing to standard
   _____ Face up to the facts of a situation even when the facts are not to their advantage
   _____ Work for organizational results, not personal glory

Selection Inventory Summary

Applicant Name _____

Department _____

Date _____

Job Skills
Total Plus Points _____

Managerial Skills
Total Plus Points _____

Interpersonal Skills
Total Plus Points _____

Analytical Skills
Total Plus Points _____

Problem-Solving Skills
Total Plus Points _____

Team Skills
Total Plus Points _____

Performance Skills
Total Plus Points _____

Communications Skills
Total Plus Points _____

Personal Attitudes
Total Plus Points _____

Grand Total _____

• *High content validity.* Because work samples are a sample of the actual work performed on a job, they have high content validity, which is important should they be challenged on an adverse impact claim. They are valuable because they have a direct and logical relationship to job behavior and provide applicants with an idea of their potential suitability for a job.

• *Accurate predictor of job performance.* Work samples are a more accurate predictor of job performance than pen and paper psychological tests because it is more difficult for an applicant to "fake" job proficiency on a work sample than on an aptitude test. This means that work samples are generally more accurate than other types of employment selection devices.

• *Absence of adverse impact.* Work samples are not as subject to court challenges as pen and paper psychological tests are. Research on work samples has shown that as a selection device they conform easily to EEOC standards for test fairness and adverse impact.

• *High employee acceptance.* Most applicants prefer the performance activity over a written test because it is less difficult and more fair. Applicants tend to be motivated to do well when doing a work sample that appears on its face to be valid, because they understand that the tasks they are being asked to perform relate to the job and provide a fair method of assessing job success. Also, most applicants do not view work samples as an invasion of their privacy, as they often do with background checks and personality tests. Job applicants also can assess their own chances for success in a job.

• *Reduced turnover*. Some HR people feel that turnover rates may be reduced by using work samples to select job applicants. In fact, studies in work sample tests have shown a marked decrease in turnover.

Work samples do have drawbacks, however, which may cause companies to forego their use.

• *Difficulty of implementation and administration*. Work samples can be difficult to implement and administer. Often they must be given individually to a single job candidate. Occasionally, however, work samples may be given to several candidates at once if the HR administrator is able to track the actions of all applicants at one time.
• *High cost*. Work samples can be costly since they require supervision and monitoring. This is true if a large number of job applicants are involved. Work samples must also be developed and implemented, and for a large pool of job applicants, this may be more costly than purchasing a written aptitude test.
• *Length of time*. Work samples can be time-consuming. They often require individual supervision and may take more than an hour to complete. If you track the cost of designing, implementing, and administering the work samples in your cost-to-hire calculations, they will escalate considerably.

Further information on work sampling and other means of employee assessment can be found in Chapter 5.

Competency Assessment Methods

As organizations in the United States grow, merge, and change through constant reorganization, human resources professionals—charged with the responsibility of finding and retaining the best people—are being forced to become more proficient in the selection methods they use. One method that is growing in popularity is the competency assessment method. The following discussion of competency assessment methods is contributed by two of the top consultants in this field, Dr. David C. McClelland and Dr. Lyle M. Spencer, Jr.

Definition of a Competency

A competency is defined as "an underlying characteristic of an individual which is causally related to effective or superior performance in a job." [1] By differentiating between competencies, you distinguish superior from average performers. Threshold, or essential, competencies are required for minimally adequate or average performance. Differentiating competencies are required for superior performance. The threshold and differentiating competencies for a given job provide a template for personnel selection, succession planning, performance appraisal, and development.

Competencies can be motives, traits, self-concepts (attitudes or values), content knowledge, or cognitive and behavioral skills—any individual characteristics that can be measured or counted reliably and that can be shown to differentiate significantly between superior and average performers, or between effective and ineffective performers. The competencies are:

- *Motives,* which are the underlying need or thought pattern that drives, directs, and selects an individual's behavior, e.g., the need for achievement.

- *Traits,* which are a general disposition to behave or respond in a certain way, such as having self-confidence, self-control, stress resistance, or "hardiness." [2]

- *Self-concepts* (attitudes or values), measured by respondent tests that ask people what they value, think they do, or are interested in doing. Such tests include occupational preference inventories like the Strong-Campbell Vocational Inventory or psychological tests like the California Personality Inventory.

- *Content knowledge* of facts or procedures, either technical (how to troubleshoot a defective computer) or interpersonal (the five rules of effective feedback), as measured by respondent tests. Content knowledge by itself rarely distinguishes superior from average performers.

- *Cognitive and behavioral skills,* either covert (deductive or inductive reasoning) or observable (e.g., "active listening") skills.

Competencies can be related to job performance in a simple causal flow model, which indicates that motive, trait, self-concept, and knowledge competencies aroused by a situation predict skilled behaviors, which in turn predict job performance. (See Exhibit 6-3.) Competencies include an intention, action, and outcome. For example, Exhibit 6-3 shows the competency of achievement motivation, which is a strong concern with doing better against an internal standard of excellence, and a concern for unique accomplishment. This predicts entrepreneurial behaviors: goal setting, taking personal responsibility for outcomes, and calculated risk taking. In organizations, these behaviors lead to continuous improvement in quality, productivity, sales, and other economic results, and to innovation in the development of new products and services. Causal models like this one provide managers with a simple way to do "risk assessment" in evaluating candidates for a job. The risk of hiring a person without achievement motivation, in this example, is less improvement in performance, less entrepreneurial behavior, and fewer ideas for new products or services.

Competencies differ in the extent to which they can be taught. Content knowledge and behavioral skills are easiest to teach; altering attitudes and values is harder. While changing motives and traits is possible,[3] the process is lengthy, difficult, and expensive. From a cost-effectiveness standpoint, the rule is to hire applicants with core motivation and trait characteristics and then develop their knowledge and skills. Most organizations do the reverse: They hire on the basis of educational credentials (like MBAs from good schools) and assume that candidates come with or can be indoctrinated with the appropriate motives and traits. It is more cost-effective to hire people with the "right stuff" (motives and traits) and train them in the knowledge and skills needed to do specific jobs. Or, in the words of one personnel manager, "You can teach a turkey to climb a tree, but it's easier to hire a squirrel."

Competencies and Competency Clusters

Twenty competencies are most often found to predict success in technical/professional, managerial, and executive jobs. These are shown in Exhibit 6-4 in six clusters: (1)

Exhibit 6-3. Competencies as related to job performance.

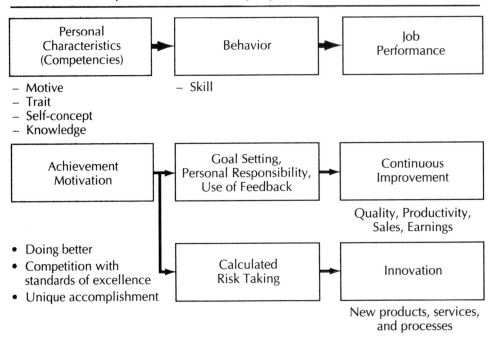

Achievement, (2) Helping/Service, (3) Influence, (4) Management, (5) Cognitive, and (6) Personal Effectiveness.

Competencies in the Achievement cluster include Achievement Orientation, Concern for Order or Quality, and Initiative. Achievement Orientation is defined as taking steps to improve one's performance or the performance of others. One strives to accomplish specific challenging objectives or to compete against a standard of excellence. Concern for Order or Quality involves monitoring and following to be sure tasks are organized efficiently and completed to standards. This is a lower level of achievement, essentially a high standard of excellence combined with high fear of failure. It leads to the obsessive "checking up" characteristic of good auditors, quality control inspectors, or nuclear reactor operators. Initiative is defined as doing more than a job requires (discretionary effort) and/or acting before being asked or forced to by events (anticipation). While initiative can be taken for objectives other than achieving goals (e.g., influence), initiative consistently factors with the Achievement cluster, because entrepreneurial and innovative behavior usually also involves initiative.

Achievement competencies are most important in entrepreneurial, sales, and technical/professional individual contributor jobs—programmers, engineers, planners—where work requires taking individual initiative and personal responsibility for task accomplishment to a standard of excellence (efficiency, quality) and/or innovation.

There are two Helping/Service competencies. The first is Interpersonal Understanding, which includes the attending and responding competencies (nonpossessive warmth, accurate empathy, genuineness) found in effective counselors.[4] The second competency

(text continued on page 118)

Exhibit 6-4. Competencies that predict success in technical/professional, managerial, and executive jobs.

I. Achievement Cluster	Technical Professional	Executive	Managerial
1. Achievement Orientation Acting to improve performance, do a task better (faster, more efficiently, at lower cost, etc.) by committing oneself to accomplishing challenging objectives, or competing against a self-defined standard of excellence. This standard of excellence may be one's own past performance (striving for improvement), an objective measure (results orientation), the performance of others (competitiveness), goals one has set, a unique accomplishment (an entrepreneurial new venture promoting a new product, service, procedure, etc.), or doing something new (innovation).	X	X	X
2. Concern for Order, Quality Acting to minimize errors and maintain high standards of quality by checking or monitoring data and work and by developing and maintaining systems for organizing work and information.	X	X	
3. Initiative Taking self-directed or self-motivated initiative to do more than is expected or required in the job, act before being required to by events, improve job performance, avoid problems, or find or create new opportunities.	X	X	X

II. Helping/Service Cluster

	Technical Professional	Executive	Managerial
4. Interpersonal Understanding Understanding, interpreting, and responding to others' concerns, motives, feelings, and behaviors; accurately recognizing strengths and limitations in others.	X	X	X
5. Customer - Service Orientation Being concerned with helping or serving others; making efforts (including initiative and tenacity) to discover and act to meet the customer's or client's needs. Clients may include internal staff (such as a boss or downstream department), students, or actual external customers.	X	X	

(continued)

Exhibit 6-4. *Continued.*

	Technical Professional	Executive	Managerial

III. Influence Cluster

	Technical Professional	Executive	Managerial
6. Impact and Influence Acting to have an impact on others (individuals or organizations), to influence or persuade others. (Specific intents to develop others' abilities or to meet others' needs are scored on the Developing Others and Customer Service scales. Use of positional power to influence others' behavior with little concern to persuade them to agree or comply willingly is scored on the Directiveness scale. Impact and Influence covers all other types of impact.)		*X*	*X*
7. Organizational Awareness Showing the ability to learn and understand the power relationships in one's own or other organizations (customers, suppliers, etc.). This includes the ability to identify the real decision makers and the individuals who can influence them and to predict how new events or situations will affect individuals and groups within the organization.			*X*
8. Relationship Building (Networking) Acting to develop and maintain a network of contacts, both inside and outside one's own organization, with people who may be able to supply information, assistance, or support for work-related goals. This includes efforts to build or maintain friendly relationships with people who are or might someday be useful in achieving work-related goals.		*X*	*X*

IV. Management Cluster

	Technical Professional	Executive	Managerial
9. Directiveness: Assertiveness and Use of Positional Power Using personal power or the power of one's position in an effective and appropriate way, to set expectations, enforce rules, confront others about performance problems, set boundaries for others' behavior, and tell others what they must do. This relates to behavior in both supervisory roles and nonsupervisory roles (e.g., a secretary making arrangements with a hotel or supplier, a salesperson asking assertively for an order of a specific size).		*X*	
10. Developing Others Acting to teach, train, develop, or otherwise improve the skills of others by providing clear, behaviorally specific, and helpful performance feedback, by effective coaching and mentoring, and by providing helpful developmental experiences and opportunities.		*X*	

	Technical	Professional	Executive	Managerial
11. Teamwork and Cooperation Acting to develop cooperation and teamwork within a group or team by cooperating, seeking the input of group members, encouraging their participation, keeping them informed, finding ways to reduce conflict within the group, and finding solutions that may benefit all involved parties.	X			
12. Team Leadership Acting as the leader of a group or team, usually from a position of formal power. Takes on the responsibilities and roles of the leader—takes care of and inspires the group. May be combined with the Teamwork and Cooperation scale.			X	X

V. Cognitive Cluster

	Technical	Professional	Executive	Managerial
13. Technical/Professional/Managerial Expertise Acquiring, using, and communicating technical expertise (*depth* of knowledge in terms of education or experience) and/or managerial expertise (*breadth* in terms of numbers of people or size of organization impacted).	X		X	X
14. Information Seeking Collecting and using information relevant to work-based problems or opportunities: getting several opinions or inputs or investigating issues and known facts before making decisions.	X			
15. Analytical Thinking Breaking complex problems, processes, or projects into component parts and considering or organizing the parts in a systematic way, e.g., making systematic comparisons of different features or aspects, setting priorities on a rational basis, identifying time sequences, or identifying causal (if → then) relationships.	X	X		
16. Conceptual Thinking Seeing patterns or connections between situations that are not obviously related, identifying key or underlying issues in complex situations, or using creative, conceptual, or inductive reasoning to develop novel concepts.	X	X		X

VI. Personal Effectiveness Cluster

	Technical	Professional	Executive	Managerial
17. Self-Control, Stress Resistance Acting to keep one's emotions under control and restrain negative behaviors when provoked, faced with opposition or hostility from others, or working under conditions of stress.	X	X	X	

Exhibit 6-4. *Continued.*

	Technical Professional	Executive	Managerial
18. Self-Confidence Expressing belief in one's ability to accomplish a task and select an effective approach to a task or problem. This includes confidence in one's own ability in increasingly challenging circumstances, confidence in one's own decisions or opinions, and the ability to handle failures constructively.	X		
19. Organizational Commitment, "Business-Mindedness" Acting to align one's behavior with the needs, priorities, and goals of the organization; putting the organization's needs before one's own; acting in ways that promote organizational goals or meet organizational needs.	X	X	X
20. Flexibility Acting to adapt to and work effectively with a variety of situations, individuals, or groups. The ability to understand and appreciate different and opposing perspectives on an issue, adapt one's approach as the requirements of a situation change, and change or easily accept changes in one's own organization or job requirements.		X	X

is Customer Service Orientation: acting to understand and meet the needs of others, motivated by feeling rewarded by helping someone else.

Helping/Service competencies predict success in helping and human services work: teachers, counselors, therapists, consultants, social workers, nurses, day care and nursing home care givers, and customer service representatives.

Influence competencies are driven by concern for personal impact, or "socialized" power motivation: the ability to influence others in order to serve ends greater than oneself, such as the common good.[5] Socialized power is distinguished from personalized power motivation, or power used for self-aggrandizement. The three Influence competencies—Impact and Influence, Organizational Awareness, and Relationship Building—include direct one-on-one persuasion and organizational influence skills: knowing whom to influence, networking, and assembling the political coalitions needed to operate large organizations.

Influence competencies are required in all managerial positions, sales, and high-level staff individual contributor positions (strategic planners, human resources executives, other internal consultants), where effectiveness depends on the staffer's ability to influence senior line managers.

Management competencies are a specialized subset of the influence competencies and include Directiveness (assertively giving direct orders in a way that gets compliance), Developing Others (coaching subordinates to develop their skills), Teamwork and Cooperation (facilitating collaborative group processes), and Team Leadership (ranging from being able to run a meeting well to being able to give charismatic speeches that arouse motivation and commitment in all of an organization's members). Managerial competencies predict performance in supervisory and leadership positions, plus teaching, police, and political roles.

Cognitive competencies include Technical/Professional/Managerial Expertise, Information Seeking, Analytical Thinking, and Conceptual Thinking. Technical Expertise is knowledge actually used to solve problems. At higher levels of technical expertise, superior performers act not just as experts but as missionaries actively offering help and promoting new technology. Information Seeking is the collection and use of relevant information prior to making decisions. Analytical/Thinking is the ability to "systems analyze" complex information and to array data by cause-and-effect inferences (if X happens, then Y is likely to happen), by priorities (A is more important than B), and by time sequences (do N at time 1 in order to be able to do M at time 2). Conceptual Thinking ranges from the use of learned concepts to the creation of new concepts, in order to make sense of new, unorganized data.

These competencies are important in technical/professional and lower-level managerial jobs. Higher order conceptual skills predict success in senior professional and managerial jobs requiring strategic thinking and planning.

Personal Effectiveness competencies include traits such as Self-Control, Self-Confidence, Organizational Commitment, and Flexibility. These do not factor with the other clusters but do predict superior performance in a wide variety of jobs. They are qualities generally associated with personal maturity.

With the exception of the Personal Effectiveness cluster, competencies are grouped by intention, rather than behavioral description. Intention can be a single motive or several motives acting together in different proportions. For instance, Developing Others is defined by the intention to assist others to develop their knowledge or skill or personal characteristics; Impact and Influence, by the intent to influence, persuade, or have an impact on others; and Achievement Orientation, by the intent to do things in a better way.

Exhibiting a given behavior indicates an increased likelihood of exhibiting more behavior with a very similar intent, but not necessarily more behavior that is similar in structure but has a different underlying intent. For example, delegating is not a competency because delegating behaviors occur in a number of competencies, depending on the intention involved: One can delegate for the sake of efficiency (Achievement Orientation), to establish oneself as the leader (Team Leadership), to enable others to develop their abilities (Developing Others), etc. Delegating in order to develop the other person's abilities is more likely to predict other Developing Others behaviors (like giving feedback to support another's development of abilities) than it is to predict, say, delegating in order to get the job done most efficiently, which is driven by Achievement Orientation.

Procedure for Conducting a Competency Research Study

There are five steps to follow in conducting a competency research study.

1. DEFINE PERFORMANCE EFFECTIVENESS CRITERIA

The first and very important step is to define the criteria for superior performance: How do you know a superstar when you see one? If the wrong criteria are chosen, all subsequent research is biased. The best criterion is usually a composite of hard performance data, e.g., sales, profits, or productivity measures (where these exist for a job), plus nominations by managers, peers, subordinates, and knowledgeable observers (clients or human resources professionals who know the job).

2. DEFINE A CRITERION SAMPLE

The research sample consists of a clear group of superior performers (defined as those performing one standard deviation above the average on the performance effectiveness criteria, or the top 10 percent) and a comparison group of average performers in the target job. One standard deviation is chosen because of its demonstrable economic value to an organization. It has been shown that, depending on the complexity of the job, one standard deviation above the mean is worth between 19 percent and 48 percent of output for nonsales jobs and between 48 percent and 120 percent for sales jobs.[6] A recent survey of forty-four companies in the Southeast found that for salespeople earning an average of $41,777, superior performers sold on average $6.7 million, and typical performers sold on average $3 million. Superior salespeople sold 123 percent more than average salespeople, a difference worth approximately eighty times salary.[6] These data suggest the practical economic value of a competency model. Helping a firm find even one additional superior salesperson would yield $3.7 million, which is a benefit that can cost-justify a considerable investment in competency research.

3. COLLECT DATA

Data is collected on superior and average performers in the criterion sample using several methods: expert panels, surveys, an expert system database, behavioral event interviews, and observation.

• *Expert panel* methods involve asking observers who know the job what competencies they think are required for adequate or average performance (threshold competencies) and which characteristics distinguish superior performers (differentiating competencies). Experience indicates that about 50 percent of the competencies identified by expert panels are validated by a full competency study.*

• *Surveys* ask observers who know the job to indicate the extent to which average and superior performers exhibit specific behaviors that define competencies. So-called 360° ratings (i.e., superiors, peers, subordinates, and clients, who are "all around" the job incumbents) provide the best data. For example, superior managers consistently produce significantly higher morale, as measured by employee satisfaction and organizational climate surveys completed by their subordinates.

• An *expert system database* containing data from some 650 competency models can be queried and asked to infer competencies likely to predict superior performance in a job given certain requirements of the job. For example, an expert system will ask to what extent "continuous efficiency and productivity improvements" or "developing new products and services" is required by the job. High responses on these items will

---

*Expert panels err in two ways. They identify "motherhood" or "folklore" competencies, e.g., integrity or command presence, that are not validated by other data collection methods. They also miss competencies, such as achievement motivation or eliciting visual and tactile imagery, for which they lack a psychological vocabulary.

raise achievement motivation as a competency required for effective performance in this job, because previous studies of superior performers in jobs requiring performance improvement and innovation have found achievement motivation to be a differentiating competency.

• The *behavioral event interview* (BEI) provides detailed narrative accounts of how superior and average performers have thought about and acted in their most critical success and failure job experiences. Transcripts of these interviews can be analyzed for the presence, level, and strength of motive, trait, self-concept, cognitive, and skill competencies that differentiate superior from average performers.

• *Observation* can be done of superior and average performers in actual or simulated (assessment center) work situations, and their behavior can be coded for competencies related to job performance. Observation methods have the disadvantage of being very expensive; properly done BEIs can substitute for observation.

4. Analyze Data and Develop a "Competency Model" for the Job

Data from the expert panels, surveys, expert system, BEIs, and observation are content-anaylyzed to identify behaviors and personality characteristics that (1) distinguish superior from average job incumbents, or (2) are demonstrated by all incumbents adequately performing the job.

BEI transcripts are first coded for known competencies, then subjected to "thematic analysis" to identify new or unique competencies. All examples of "uniques" are then coded. Competency coding criteria are refined until they can be recognized with acceptable inter-rater reliability. A detailed competency dictionary and coding manual is prepared to guide empirical coding of interview, assessment center, or other operant data from job incumbents or candidates. This dictionary and coding manual provides the competency model for the job.

Traditionally, competency models were presented as a list of competencies with associated behavioral indicators, examples, and discussion. In the newest models, competencies are scaled in intervals that permit precise definition of job competency requirements for both average and superior performance—and assessment of individuals—at any level in a job family.

5. Validation

Criterion and predictive validity of the competency model is tested by determining the extent to which competencies, coded from BEI transcripts and/or assessed using psychometric tests or assessment center ratings, correctly identify known superior versus average performers in a second criterion sample, or correctly predict adequate and superior performance of new hires. (It is worth noting that the behavioral event interview, initially used as a hypothesis generation method in constructing the model, can also be used as a psychometric assessment method if properly conducted.)

Human Resources Applications of Competency Assessment Data

Job competency anlayses provide valuable information for many HR functions: recruitment, selection, placement, performance appraisal, training and development, career pathing, succession/human resources planning, competency-based pay, and retention. In a competency-based HR system, all HR functions are based on the congruence, or match, between job competency requirements and person competencies.

In terms of selection, the fundamental proposition is that the better the fit between the requirements of a job and the competencies of a person, the higher will be the person's job performance and job satisfaction. High job performance and satisfaction in turn predict retention because (1) good performers need not be fired, and (2) satisfied employees are less likely to quit.[7]

For example, Exhibit 6-5 shows the fit between the competencies of a technical professional and the competency requirements of his first job (industrial chemist) and fourth job (manager of an oil refinery). This person can be seen to be a good match for his first job, which largely required individual contributor competencies: achievement motivation, technical expertise, and cognitive skills. However, he is not a good match for his fourth job: His individual contributor skills exceed the managerial job's requirements, and he lacks the interpersonal and organizational influence skills needed to succeed in upper management.

In the job competency approach, analysis starts with the person in the job, makes no prior assumptions as to what characteristics are needed to perform the job well, and determines from open-ended behavioral event interviews which human characteristics are associated with job success. The method emphasizes criterion validity: what actually causes superior performance in a job, not what factors most reliably describe all the characteristics of a person in the hope that some of them will relate to job performance.

The Reference Check

After you've devised your interviewing plan, chosen the best type of interviews, actually interviewed all the candidates for the job, and arrived at the best method for assessing job competency, you've come to the point where a decision must be made: Whom will you hire? There is one last but very critical element of the selection process: the reference check.

It is necessary to conduct reference checks in order to verify basic information given by the applicant and to obtain additional information about the applicant's qualifications. The HR manager or the interviewer usually makes these contacts by telephone or by letter. At least one or two reference checks should be completed on every applicant you are considering hiring. However, you should be aware that a rejection decision cannot be based on a reference check. If the individual has all of the qualifications, experience, and/or skills that the position requires, he or she must be considered for the job despite a negative reference.

Normally, a reference check consists of the verification of the applicant's job title as well as dates of hire and termination. If possible, further information can be obtained concerning performance. All information received through a reference check is of a confidential nature and should not be given to an applicant or referred to during the course of an interview. It's difficult to obtain reference information via the telephone today because in recent years lawsuits have been won by applicants who found that their previous employers were giving derogatory job references to companies who were checking on them. Companies have other reasons for wanting references. Some companies have

Exhibit 6-5. The job-person-fit profile.

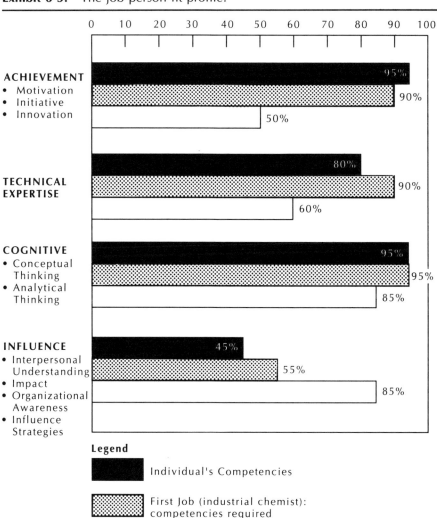

been hit with penalties by courts for crimes their employees committed—even when the crimes were committed off the job. The courts say that employers should have known more about the people they hired. The problem is that it's tough to learn about the work habits of applicants, let alone their potential for criminal conduct.

Legal Aspects of Reference Checking

Under the Privacy Act of 1974, reference checking invades an applicant's privacy if it is "unreasonable." In deciding whether the reference checking is reasonable or unreasonable, a court will consider a variety of factors, including:

Exhibit 6-6. Sample form for obtaining consent to a reference check.

As part of the hiring process, you should know that we will be checking your references. We may contact those persons whom you have identified to us as potential references. In addition, we may also contact other friends, acquaintances, business associates, or anyone who knows you. When we contact a reference, we may ask a series of questions. They could be about your personal background, education, work experience, character, personality, or personal habits. We may use an outside firm to check references. If we do, under the feredal Fair Credit Reporting Act, we are required, upon your written request, to provide you with the name and address of the firm that is checking your references so that you may contact them for further information.

AGREEMENT

I have read and fully understand the foregoing. I hereby voluntarily consent to allow ABC Company, or any of its officers, employees, agents, or designees, to check my references by contacting any person whom they deem to be an appropriate reference. The ABC Company representatives may ask any questions they consider relevant to their hiring decision, including questions about my personal background, education, work experience, character, personality, and personal habits.

Signed _____ Date _____

- The type of information the prospective employer gathers.
- The number of contacts the employer makes in order to check references.
- Whether the prospective employer had a legitimate need for the particular information that it obtained. In other words, was it job related?

Before checking references, always obtain the written consent of the applicant. In any suit for invasion of privacy, the single most important factor that the court will consider is whether or not the applicant consented to a reference check. An applicant who did consent probably would not be successful in claiming that the reference check invaded his or her privacy. Exhibit 6-6 provides sample language for obtaining an applicant's consent to a reference check. Some companies include this consent as part of their application form.

You should review your reference checking procedures to make sure that the criteria used in reaching employment decisions is relevant but not discriminatory. Here are some questions you might ask yourself before completing a reference check.

- Are you being consistent? Are you sure job standards are applied evenly in all job classifications? If an item is grounds for denying a job to one applicant, it should be the same for another.

- Do you use a telephone interview checklist? Using a standard format will keep you from digressing into areas not relevant to the job.
- Is job data collected relevant? Be sure information obtained from reference checks and used for employment decisions is job related.
- Are you keeping written documentation? Be prepared to back up your hire or no-hire decision with written proof verifying that the decision was based on relevant job information.

See Chapter 18 for additional information on the legal aspects of reference checking.

Successful Telephone Reference Checking

Telephone reference checking is one of the best strategies you can use to screen job applicants. Although it's sometimes difficult to get the answers because companies are wary of giving out information on former employees, it's worth an attempt, because telephone reference checking is immediate, provides a considerable amount of useful knowledge, and is relatively inexpensive.

Keep the telephone interview on track by using a reference check form such as the one that appears in Exhibit 6-7. (You may wish to add questions to it that are relevant to the job.) There are many advantages to working from a prepared and structured telephone reference check form. The main one is that it enables you to ask all the important questions in rapid and sequential order—a strategy that almost always results

Exhibit 6-7. Telephone reference check form.

Applicant's Name ————————————— Department ————————————

Company Contacted ————————————— Telephone ——————————

Individual Contacted ————————————— Title ——————————————

    When did the applicant work for your company? From ———— To ————

    What was the applicant's position/title? ————————————————

    What information can you give us concerning the following?

        Performance ————————————————————————

        ———————————————————————————————

        Attendance ————————————————————————

        ———————————————————————————————

        Reason for termination ——————————————————

    Is the person eligible for rehire with your company? Yes ———— No ————

        If not, why? ————————————————————————

        ———————————————————————————————

Additional Comments ———————————————————————

———————————————————————————————————

in getting the facts. This is because the technique does not give the respondent sufficient time to make up answers, even if he or she wanted to.

When you call, ask the questions in the order in which they appear on the form, but be flexible because the telephone reference check is really an interview. As such, it requires you to be adaptable. For example, you may wish to ask a question that does not appear on the form in order to have the respondent elaborate on a statement.

What if the person says it's against company policy to give references over the phone, or all he or she will give you is the applicant's job title and dates of employment? You must be personally convinced that the information you seek is vital in order for you to make a fair, accurate, and objective hiring decision and, furthermore, that you have every right to obtain this information. Consequently, you should feel no reluctance or hesitation in asking for this information. Indeed, if you are confident, you are very likely to be successful in overcoming resistance. Stress confidentiality at the outset of the conversation. This makes it easier for the other person to respond to your questions.

If the HR staff member or former supervisor is still unwilling to give you the information, be politely insistent, emphasizing that you need the information in order to give the applicant fair consideration. If the person still insists that it is against company policy to furnish such information ask if you can send a written reference form for written completion. Offer to reciprocate with reference information when they are hiring. Make sure you tell the person that the job applicant has authorized you, in writing, to check references. This will protect the former employer from a suit brought by the applicant.

Companies can be hired to do reference and background checking. A list of some of these groups is included in the Resources section at the end of the book.

Evaluating Reference Information

It is obviously important not only to obtain reference information but also to assess and evaluate it properly. Be particularly sensitive to how the respondent talks about his or her former employee. Does the person speak positively, enthusiastically, or even glowingly of the supplicant? Or is he or she curt, brief, or relatively guarded in the comments expressed? Take into consideration the fact that some people are by nature placid, unenthusiastic, or excessively critical and would not be particularly positive about anyone or anything.

It is also possible that a job applicant may not receive a favorable reference from one particular employer. The candidate should not automatically be rejected. As you know, failure in one position does not always forecast failure in another. Check with more than one employer to get a well-rounded view of the applicant. In fact, each significant employer should be checked before making a final selection.

Hiring the New Employee

Confirming the Agreement

After you have interviewed and selected the best candidate for the job and made a verbal offer that has been accepted, draft a letter of confirmation of your agreement with the applicant. The letter should state your agreement in terms of pay and perks and welcome

Exhibit 6-8. Sample new hire letter.

Date

Mr. John Q. Smith
34900 Youngstown Drive
Youngstown, Pennsylvania 10446

Dear John:

We are pleased to confirm our offer to you of employment as an accountant in our finance department at the monthly salary of $3,000, effective on your first day of employment, which is to be July 15, 19xx. Our company has a ninety-day evaluation period for all employees. That period will be from July 15, 19xx to October 15, 19xx.

We feel your abilities and experience will provide much needed expertise in our accounting department, and in turn, we hope the company can provide you with opportunities and professional growth commensurate with your personal performance in the job. Of course, there are never any guarantees of long-term employment in today's business environment, but we all hope that our company will prosper and that our positions will remain viable.

On your first day on the job, you will go through an orientation program. Company benefits will be explained to you at that time.

We are happy that you are joining our organization and hope that you will contact us if there is anything we can do to assist you in the first few days on the job.

Welcome to the XYZ Company!

Sincerely,

Laurence J. Coaveles
Human Resources Manager

---

the new employee to the company. Salary should always be stated as a monthly figure. Courts have ruled that when a yearly salary was quoted in an employment letter, it implied the person was guaranteed the job for a year. If you so desire, the letter can also reinforce the fact that you are an ''at will'' employer. (Employment-at-will means that the employer has the right to terminate the employment relationship for any reason, or no reason, at any time.) Some organizations feel that the ''at will'' statement is too negative to put in a new hire letter, while others feel it is necessary to reinforce the employers right to hire and fire at will from the beginning of the relationship.

All applicants should be notified in writing once you have reached your hiring decision. Exhibit 6-8 is a sample new hire letter, and Exhibit 6-9 is a sample rejection letter.

Exhibit 6-9.   Sample rejection letter.

Date

Ms. Sheila Smith
5362 Utica
Denver, Colorado 80017

Dear Ms. Smith:

This letter will acknowledge receipt of your inquiry regarding employment opportunities with Rocky Mountain Cable Company.

We have carefully reviewed your credentials together with those of other applicants
and have selected, for further consideration, an applicant whose background is
more closely related to the needs of our current job requirements.

We will have another opening in about thirty days, and your experience in financial planning would make you a qualified candidate for that position. As soon as
that position has been approved and we commence our recruiting activities, we
will give you a call.

Your interest in Rocky Mountain Cable Company is appreciated, and we hope that
you will keep in touch with us.

Sincerely,

Mary Brown
Director
Human Resources Department

Confidentiality Agreements

Today many companies are requiring confidentiality agreements from people filling executive positions. This new emphasis on confidentiality is because of laid-off or downsized executives who may have compromised competitive information. In addition, many
executives who leave companies voluntarily and go into business for themselves take
technology and/or client information with them. Therefore, more companies are using
confidentiality agreements. The sample agreement in Exhibit 6-10 can be adjusted to fit
your specific situation and should work in most instances. The agreement does not
guarantee that the employee will abide by the promises of confidentiality he or she
signs. It does, however, give the employer a little more clout legally if the employee
does compromise competitive proprietary information.

Exhibit 6-10. Sample confidentiality agreement.

The nature of products and services provided by the ABC Company requires that information be handled in a private, confidential manner.

Information about our business or our employees or clients will not be released to people or agencies outside the company without our written consent; the only exceptions to this policy will be to follow legal or regulatory guidelines. All memoranda, notes, reports, or other documents will remain part of the company's confidential records.

Personal or identifying information about our clients or our employees (such as names, addresses, telephone numbers, or salaries) will not be released to people not authorized by the nature of their duties to receive such information, without the consent of management or the employee.

The undersigned individual agrees to abide by this confidentiality agreement.

_____

Name

_____

Witness

_____

Date

Postemployment Form

A great deal of information that cannot be asked in an employment interview is needed after the employee is hired in order to comply with EEO reporting requirements and to ensure the employee's benefits are properly computed. Exhibit 6-11 is a sample form that can be used after the person has been hired to obtain all the necessary personal information.

Selection Record Keeping

If your company is ever charged with discrimination in hiring practices, you will be asked to provide the EEOC or your state civil rights commission with a list of all your open positions for a specific period of time, the names and background information on the applicants for those open positions, and the name of the person who was actually hired. If you don't have a record of this information on each job, you may spend hours trying to pull it together for a hearing or a court case.

Exhibit 6-11. Sample postemployment form.

Please complete this questionnaire, which provides information for personnel and benefits records.

EMPLOYEE NAME _____
    Address _____ Home Telephone _____
    Date of Birth _____ Social Security Number _____
    Marital Status _____ Date of Marriage _____
    Previous Married Name _____
    Dates of Military Service: from _____ to _____
NAME OF EMPLOYEE'S SPOUSE _____
    Date of Birth _____ Social Security Number _____
    Address if Different _____
    Home Telephone _____ Business Telephone _____
    Employed by _____
    Occupation _____
DEPENDENTS CLAIMED AND RELATIONSHIP

_____
_____
_____

IMMIGRATION FORM I-9 _____ yes _____ no
Our affirmative action program and governmental reporting requirements require the following information:
Sex: _____ M _____ F
Ethnic Group: _____ Caucasian _____ Black _____ Asian-American
        _____ Spanish Heritage _____ American Indian
Disability: _____ yes _____ no
    If yes, describe _____
Disabled Veteran: _____ yes _____ no
    If yes, are your receiving disability pay? _____
Vietnam Veteran: _____ yes _____ no
U.S. Citizen: _____ yes _____ no
Name of person to be notified in emergency _____
    Home Telephone _____ Business Telephone _____

Exhibit 6-12 is a filled position summary form. This form can be a real time-saver and an essential part of the selection records. Be sure the form is completed on every open position.

Notes

1. R. E. Boyatzis, *The Competent Manager: A Model for Effective Performance* (New York: Wiley-Interscience, 1982).

Exhibit 6-12. Filled position summary form.

Position/Title	Department	Date Job Opened	Date Received	Hiring Manager	Telephone

Salary Range	Job Group Code	Compensation Approved/Name

EEO/AAP Status	Transfers, Promotions

Post Job? ☐ Yes ☐ No	Date Posted	Posted Until	Reason for Not Posting

	Yes/No	Contact Person	Date	Number of Responses	Results
External Recruiting					
Applicants on File					
Minority/Female/Handicap Files Searched					
State Employment Contacted					
Minority/Female/Handicap Agencies Notified					
Advertising					
Used a Search Firm					
Name of Firm					

Applicant's Name	Phone Number	Race/Sex/H	Source	Recruiter	Date	Referred	Manager Disposition	Final Disposition	Date of Notification

Hire Date: Date _____ Offer Made to _____ Source _____

Salary _____ Race/Sex _____ Start Date _____ Recruiter's Signature _____

2. S. C. Kobasa, S. R. Maddi, and S. Kahn, "Hardiness and Health: A Prospective Study," *Journal of Personality and Social Psychology* 42 (1982): 168–177.
3. D. C. McClelland and D. Winter, *Motivating Economic Achievement* (New York: Free Press, 1971).
4. R. R. Carkuff, *Helping and Human Relations,* vols. 1 and 2 (New York: Holt, Rinehart and Winston, 1969).
5. D. C. McClelland, "A Competency Model for Human Resource Management Specialists to Be Used in the Delivery of the Human Resource Management Cycle," McBer & Co. (Boston: 1975).
6. S. Sloan and L. M. Spencer, "Participant Survey Results," paper presented at Hay Salesforce Effectiveness Seminar (Atlanta: February 28, 1991).
7. E. A. Locke, "The Nature and Causes of Job Satisfaction," in Marvin Dunette, ed., *Handbook of Industrial and Organizational Psychology* (Chicago: Rand McNally, 1976), pp. 1328–1330; R. T. Mowday, L. W. Porter, and R. M. Steers, *Employee-Organization Linkages: The Psychology of Commitment, Absenteeism, and Turnover* (New York: Academic Press, 1982); and D. F. Caldwell, "Soft Skills, Hard Numbers: Issues in Person-Job/Person-Organization Fit," paper presented at Personnel Testing Conference of Southern California spring conference (Ontario, California: April 12, 1991).

7

Orientation

Mary F. Cook
President
Mary Cook & Associates

Orientation is the planned introduction of new employees to their jobs, their coworkers, and the policies, processes, and culture of the organization. The new employee orientation has four main purposes:

1. *To create an initial favorable impression of the organization,* its work, and its culture and to give the new employee information about the company and its products. Many executives and human resources managers feel that the lack of an effective orientation program for new employees may be responsible for high turnover during the first few months of employment.

2. *To introduce the new employee to coworkers, peers, and subordinates.* This positive initial introduction goes a long way toward enhancing interpersonal acceptance in a work group. Meeting new people and trying to fit into the existing work environment creates stress and anxiety for a new employee. Also, it's important to introduce new employees to the social mores of their work group and to the culture of the organization.

3. *To give new employees a complete overview of the benefits they will receive* as employees of the company, including the timing of the benefits (waiting periods). New hires are also given a thorough review of personnel policies and procedures. Copies of any employee handbooks and manuals should be given to new employees when they report to work or within the first week on the job.

4. *To provide a solid introduction to the specific job the employee will be filling.* The person should be given a job description, pertinent procedural manuals, and any other materials that would provide a quick review of the quality and productivity requirements of the position.

Establishing an Orientation System

To establish an orientation system, you must set objectives regarding what to cover. The information should be brief and to the point but should include all of the areas that the employee needs to know about in order to get up to speed quickly. The overriding question guiding the establishment of an orientation system is: What does the new employee need to know *now*? Often new employees receive a large amount of information they do not immediately need, but they fail to get vital information they do need during the first few days on the job.

Here are a few things you should cover in the orientation:

- Company history and objectives
- Company products
- Company status: where it operates, how large it is, and how many employees it has
- Company vision statements and organizational culture
- Affirmative action and diversity programs
- Management practices and norms
- Human resources policies and procedures
- Employee relations practices
- Compensation programs and how they work
- Benefits programs, what they cover, and how to use them
- Training and development opportunities
- Safety and health programs
- Employee assistance program (EAP), if you have one
- Government regulations pertaining to the company or to employees
- Delegation of authority for management-level employees
- Performance appraisal program
- Disciplinary policies and procedures
- Grievance procedures
- Termination procedures
- Union contracts, if applicable

The orientation objectives suggest two-way communication. Be sure to provide time for new employees to ask questions, and take the time you need to answer them fully. In fact, if there are no questions either during or after the orientation, something is wrong. You may not have established the climate for open dialogue. To ensure that discussion does occur, ask for questions, and generate discussion after each specific area of the orientation is covered.

It's important that new employees feel at the outset that they belong in the company and that they are important, valuable, and wanted. Both the department manager and the human resources representative should be prepared to welcome the employee and participate in the orientation. Also, coworkers need to be aware that a new employee is arriving. This is especially important if the new employee will be assuming duties previously done by an employee who is still in the department or by a well-liked individual who recently left. You don't want the new employee to feel like an interloper. The manager should prepare the other employees by discussing the new worker and going over the purpose and the job that the new person is expected to do. These discussions should be positive and honest.

In a large organization, it is especially important that the manager and the human resources representative coordinate all the information for the new employee. This coordination is a further indication of the importance of the whole idea behind an orientation. In a small organization the manager decides what is to be explained; in larger companies the HR department may handle the entire orientation. Most organizations systematize this process by developing an orientation checklist, which lists the items to be covered by the HR department and the new employee's manager. A team effort makes the system more successful. Exhibit 7-1 depicts the responsibilities of the HR staff and department manager and shows how managers can work effectively with HR people in orienting a new employee.

Exhibit 7-1. Orientation responsibilities of HR staff and department manager.

Human Resources Department	*Department Manager*
Recruits and hires employee for the manager	Makes final hire decision
Places employee on payroll and HR information system	Participated in orientation
Designs and coordinates formal orientation program, including orientation checklist	Prepares coworkers for new employee
Explains benefits and company organization	Introduces new employee to coworkers
Evaluates and updates orientation activities	Provides overview of job and work rules
	Follows through to mentor and train new employee

An effective orientation system will reduce the new person's adjustment problems by creating a sense of security, confidence, and belonging. It will sustain or build a new employee's self-confidence. Research suggests that new employees are concerned that they may not perform immediately and are anxious in front of experienced coworkers. The orientation can aid in minimizing these problems.

Topics to Cover

Exhibit 7-2 is a sample checklist for a new-employee orientation. It should be revised to suit your specific needs. New employees are apt to have many questions that go beyond the material included on the checklist. They look to the human resources representative as a prime source of information about the company and working conditions. Here is a list of fifty-eight questions the HR representative or person conducting the orientation should be able to answer.

The Job

1. How long is the new-employee evaluation period?
2. When and how should an employee report an absence? How long can an employee be absent without notice before being subject to discharge?
3. On what basis is an employee penalized for being late?
4. What is the company's system of warnings and penalties when rules are broken?
5. Is promotion determined by merit or seniority? How can an employee find out about jobs that are open?
6. How does the seniority system work? Is it companywide or departmental?
7. How is an employee's performance appraised? How frequently are performance appraisals done?
8. How does the grievance procedure work?

Exhibit 7-2. Sample checklist for new employee orientation.

Name of Employee _____

Department _____ Date _____

The items on this checklist should be reviewed on the new employee's first day of work. When all of the items on this checklist have been reviewed, the immediate supervisor should sign the form and return it to the human resources department to be filed in the employee's personnel file.

☐ Extend a warm welcome to new employee.

☐ Give new employee a tour of the entire facility and provide an overview of the company, its history, and its products.

☐ Introduce new employee to supervisor and fellow workers.

☐ Explain department function and organization briefly:
  • Purpose of department work
  • Relation to other departments
  • Organization of the department

☐ Explain and show department layout:
  • Location of work area
  • Location of coat closet, water fountain, cafeteria, restrooms, and fire exits (with review of office security measures)

☐ Review new employee's job:
  • Go over the job description and the essential job functions
  • Explain briefly the purpose of the job
  • Stress the confidential nature of work (where appropriate)
  • Explain training periods

☐ Give new employee the name of his/her supervisor and supervisor's telephone extension.

☐ Follow personnel policies:
  • Give employee the company handbook, and review important personnel policies
  • Discuss evaluation period
  • Have employee complete postemployment forms; be sure to obtain emergency phone numbers and contacts.

☐ Explain departmental procedures:
  • Overtime
  • Progress reports and performance reviews
  • Telephone procedures
  • Reporting absences

☐ Discuss employee compensation:
  • Paydays
  • Salary raises

☐ Discuss employee benefits:
  • Medical
  • Life insurance
  • Pension
  • Savings (e.g., 401(k) plan)
  • Vacations, holidays, and time off
  • Waiting periods for benefits
☐ Cover hours of work:
  • Starting and quitting time
  • Flexible work schedules (if applicable)
  • Lunch and break periods
  • Work schedules
☐ Other items to be covered

The above orientation was completed by _____

Department Manager/Supervisor _____

Human Resources Representative _____

Note: The supervisor and the HR person can split the responsibility for covering all the items on the orientation checklist. Personnel policies, benefits, compensation, and hours of work are usually handled by the HR representative.

9. What is the policy on layoffs or terminations?
10. Are there physical examinations? Is an employee's health checked periodically or after an illness?
11. Do you check for drugs? If so, how often?
12. How long are lunch periods, and is the employee paid for them?
13. What eating facilities are available?
14. When and how long are rest or break periods?
15. When, where, and under what conditions can an employee smoke?
16. How can an employee make a personal telephone call or receive a call?
17. Is an employee obliged to join a union as a condition of employment?
18. How much cleanup time is a worker permitted (for workers on machines or on a production line)?

The Pay

19. When, where, and how is an employee paid?
20. What are the company's overtime policies? Is there a meal allowance when overtime goes into three or four hours?
21. Does an employee get premium pay for working afternoon or night shifts?
22. Is there an incentive system? How does it work?

23. If an employee reports for work and none is available, is he or she entitled to call-in pay? How much?
24. If an employee is injured on the job and sent home, is he paid for a full day, a half day, or what?
25. What is the policy on severance pay?
26. Is an employee given paid time to vote?
27. Does the company pay employees who are on jury duty?
28. What is the policy on military leave when the employee is called up for active duty or if the employee is in the National Guard? Does the company pay for time spent in the service?
29. How is vacation pay computed?
30. What is company policy on pay increases?
31. Does the company give bonuses?

The Benefits

32. What is the company's sick leave and medical program? Is sick leave paid?
33. What is the company's leave-of-absence policy?
34. When does an employee become eligible for pension benefits? Life insurance? Medical insurance?
35. When does a new employee become eligible for vacation?
36. How long are vacations? Are longer vacations granted as length of service increases?
37. Can you carry over vacation time from one year to another?
38. What holidays are given during the year?
39. Does the company make loans to employees?
40. Is there a credit union? How does it operate?
41. Is there a company training program?
42. Does the company sponsor educational courses? If an employee wants to take an outside course, will the company pay part or all of the cost?
43. Is there an employee stock purchase plan or a 401(k) plan? If so, how does it work?
44. Is there a contributory insurance program? How much does the employee pay?
45. What's provided in the company pension plan? What are the eligibility requirements?
46. When can an employee retire?
47. What will an employee's pension income be, based on present earnings?

Miscellaneous

48. How big is the company, what does it make, and what are its annual sales? Briefly, what is its history?
49. What is the company's reputation in the community and as a corporate citizen?
50. What is the organizational culture?
51. Is there an employee counseling service or an EAP? How do you use it?
52. What employee clubs or groups are there?
53. Is there a suggestion system? How does it operate?
54. How does an employee get news into company publications?
55. How do you use the bulletin boards?

56. Where do employees get supplies?
57. Where are the restrooms, mailroom, and so on?
58. What is the general style of dress and personality of the organization?

The human resources professional conducting the orientation is also responsible for covering and explaining the company's position on equal opportunity employment, affirmative action, and managing diversity. The sample policy statement in Exhibit 7-3 should be part of the employee handbook. If you don't have an employee handbook, it is a good idea to include the statement as part of the packet of material handed out to new employees during the orientation. (The notice should also be posted on your bulletin boards. It should be checked by your company attorney prior to distribution.)

Making Orientation Interesting

As previously stated, you don't want to give new employees too much information or confuse them the first day or week they are on the job, nor do you want to bore them when they are anxious to get to work. One way of making sure the new employee is entertained, challenged, and informed is to vary the type of media you use in the orientation. Use personal presentations, videos, and written materials. Many companies also now provide part of their orientation on computer.

The orientation should rely on technology, graphics, interesting personal presentations, and the participation of the new employee. When you conduct orientation meetings, be sure the guidelines are straightforward. Select presenters from various departments who are enthusiastic about their work and are entertaining. Work with presenters to help them separate "need to know" from "nice to know" information. Encourage them to practice and improve their presentations. Ask them to use vivid anecdotes that illustrate the points they want to make. Set time limits and impose them. Invite employees to serve on panels, and feature those whose enthusiasm for their job is infectious. Stimulate questions from the audience. Ask for feedback on the effectiveness of the event and for additional ways that the organization can support new people.

You might consider having the orientation go on over a period of time, not just one event on the first day on the job. You may also change your orientation as you see it evolve. Like any major process, a successful orientation depends on establishing a system to ensure adequate resources, planning, communications, development, testing, revision, update, and maintenance.

The Employee Handbook

Most HR people feel it's important to have an informative and up-to-date employee handbook. The handbook is an employee's road map. It should tell employees about the company, its rules, and their benefits. Exhibit 7-4 is a sample table of contents for an employee handbook.

Some labor attorneys do not like employee handbooks because courts have ruled in certain cases that they were considered to be employment contracts. You therefore need to have various disclaimers in the handbook. Exhibit 7-5 is a sample statement explaining that the handbook provides guidelines and is not a legal document or em-

Exhibit 7-3.   Sample affirmative action statement of policy.

THE XYZ COMPANY
EQUAL EMPLOYMENT OPPORTUNITY
AFFIRMATIVE ACTION PROGRAM

STATEMENT OF POLICY

The XYZ Company is and always has been an equal opportunity employer. The company observes and complies with Title VII of the Civil Rights Act of 1964, the Age Discrimination in Employment Act of 1967, the Americans with Disabilities Act of 1990, the Civil Rights Act of 1991, and all other federal acts.

These acts prohibit discrimination because of race, color, religion, sex, national origin, age, or disability in hiring, promotion, transfer or demotion, recruiting, advertising, compensation, layoff or termination, and other benefits, or conditions of employment.

Our affirmative action program also states that we will not retaliate against anyone who has opposed our employment practices or who has testified or participated in any proceedings under the federal acts.

To reaffirm and supplement the long-standing and continuing commitment of the XYZ Company to equal employment opportunity, a specific affirmative action program sets forth the actions being taken and to be taken by officials and employees of the company to meet its moral and legal responsibilities concerning equal employment opportunity. Periodic analyses of all personnel actions will be conducted to ensure that all departments are complying with our affirmative action program.

The director of equal employment opportunity is primarily responsible for implementing and monitoring the affirmative action program and the equal employment opportunity function, but it is also the responsibility of all managers and supervisors. The XYZ Company is committed to our affirmative action program in all of our operations.

President
XYZ Company

---

ployment contract. Exhibits 7-6 and 7-7 are different samples of acknowledgment forms that employees should sign, stating their understanding that the handbook is not a legal document. Both exhibits also state the concept of employment-at-will. The signed acknowledgment forms should be placed in the employee's personnel file. These disclaimers might be helpful in the event of future litigation. You should have your company attorney review your handbook and its disclaimers before it is published.

Exhibit 7-4. Sample table of contents for an employee handbook.

EMPLOYEE GUIDELINES

INTRODUCTION

ALL ABOUT THE COMPANY

EMPLOYEE RELATIONS POLICY

INTERNAL AND EXTERNAL COMMUNICATIONS
Employee Newsletter
Suggestion System
Bulletin Boards

YOUR JOB
Evaluation Period
Work Hours and Days Off
Attendance: Who to Call If Absence Is Necessary
Civic Duties: Jury Duty, Voting
Leaves of Absence
Military Leave of Absence
National Guard
Maternity Leave
Funeral Leave
Personal Leave of Absence

YOUR PAY
Pay Periods
Wage Rate
Raises
Overtime

YOUR BENEFITS
Benefits and Services
How to Use Your Benefits
Holiday Pay
Vacation Pay

THE RULES WE WORK BY
Work Rules
Solicitation and Distribution
Termination Procedures

SAFETY
Safety Procedures
Reporting a Work Injury

EMPLOYEE ACKNOWLEDGMENT FORMS

Exhibit 7-5.   Sample statement of the employee handbook as providing guidelines.

This handbook provides guidelines related to appropriate handling of matters concerning company personnel. These guidelines should not be interpreted as a legal document or an employment contract. Questions regarding the guidelines should be directed to your immediate supervisor.

The company reserves the right to alter, change, add to, or delete any of these policies, procedures, or guidelines at any time with or without notice.

Orientation for Specific Types of Employees

Orienting Management Employees

There is much additional critical information that should be passed on to new management-level employees in their first few weeks on the job. You should prepare a separate checklist to be used when orienting management- or executive-level employees. It's costly to bring on new, highly paid executives and then leave them abruptly to learn

Exhibit 7-6.   Employee acknowledgment form to be included in employee handbook: Sample 1.

NOTICE TO ALL EMPLOYEES:

This employee handbook is a guideline and describes only the highlights of company personnel policies and procedures. In all instances the official personnel policy manual, benefits plan texts, trust agreements, and master contracts as appropriate are the governing documents. The employee handbook is not to be interpreted as a legal document or an employment contract. Employment with the company is at the sole discretion of management and may be terminated at any time for any reason with or without cause.

Nothing in this handbook constitutes an express or implied contract or assurance of continued employment or states that just cause is required for dismissal.

I have read and understand the handbook and this notice to employees.

_____

Employee Signature

_____

Date

Exhibit 7-7. Employee acknowledgment form to be included in employee handbook: Sample 2.

I have received a copy of the XYZ Company employee handbook and understand that I am to become familiar with its contents. If I have questions, I am encouraged to talk with my supervisor.

While the company hopes to be able to maintain all of the benefits, policies, and practices described herein, the company must retain the right to change, modify, suspend, interpret, or cancel any of the benefits, policies, and practices without advance notice.

It is also understood that this handbook does not constitute an express or implied contract of employment. Only the president of XYZ Company has the authority to enter into any agreement of employment for a specific term, including "lifetime" employment. Such an agreement will be valid and binding on the company only when the agreement is set forth in a written document and signed by both the employee and the president.

I also acknowledge that I have the right to terminate my employment relationship with XYZ Company at any time, with or without advance notice or cause consistent with the concept of employment-at-will, and the company has that same right.

Witness:

_____

Employee Signature

_____

_____

Date

important procedures by chance, on their own, over an extended period of time. These are some of the issues you should cover in the management orientation:

- Delegation of authority
- Key management responsibilities
- Executive group culture and modus operandi
- Additional benefits and perks
- Corporate social responsibility: goals and objectives
- Board of directors information (if applicable)
- Current customer or stockholder issues that will impact the new executive
- Succession plan
- Special travel commitments or proposed business trips
- Calendar of current and ongoing corporate events
- Organization chart

- Current corporate strategic long-range and short-range plans
- Current corporate budgets and budgets for the manager's or executive's own department
- Human resources policies and procedures, including affirmative action responsibilities
- Purchasing procedures for the manager's or executive's department
- Overview and chart of the people in the manager's department, with performance information.
- Current list of assignments and specific responsibilities delegated to the manager
- Calendar of events for the manager's or executive's first week on the job, including dates and times to meet with the boss and key peers

The first item on the list, delegation of authority, is an important one. Most new executives struggle to understand exactly what level of authority they have in a new job, and organizations often don't have anything in writing that establishes levels of authority. You don't need a complicated policy, but a written policy will save everyone a great deal of time and lost productivity and will eliminate undue stress for new management-level employees. Exhibit 7-8 is a sample policy explaining a company's delegation of authority.

Exhibit 7-8 refers to set expenditure authority levels for approving business transactions and contractual agreements. Exhibit 7-9 is a chart showing one company's delegation of authority and approval for such transactions. Such a chart, which should be distributed to all new management-level employees, provides important information in a clear, easy to understand manner.

Orienting Disabled Employees

When you hire a person with a disability, you should find out what type of special accommodations are needed. You should also provide people with disabilities with a special orientation that should include areas especially equipped for persons with disabilities; bathrooms, lunchrooms, exits, entrances, and so on. It's also a good idea to assign someone in the department or in the HR department to act as a "buddy" the first week on the job. Some companies do this for all new employees, but it is especially helpful for the disabled.

Orienting Immigrant Employees Who Are New to the Community

More and more companies are hiring immigrants. Many are technical and professional people who know the technical aspects of the job, but they have other special needs when it comes to being oriented to the company and the community. Here again, the buddy system is a good idea because it will provide a friend who can be called upon when the employee has questions or runs into problems either at work or in a new home.

You may also need to provide an in-house workshop on English for immigrant workers. Such language workshops go a long way toward helping them understand the job and the company and toward making friends in their new environment.

(text continued on page 147)

Exhibit 7-8.   Sample policy on delegation of authority.

From: The President

To: All Vice-Presidents, Directors, and Managers

Subject: Delegation of Authority

The purpose of this memorandum is to provide for delegation of the president's authority to approve and authorize projects, contractual agreements, and general business transactions to ensure the orderly conduct of company business.

Objectives and Expectations

The company is committed to ambitious and demanding performance expectations of its management-level employees as stated in our current business plans. In order to meet these expectations, it is essential that decisions be both effective and expeditious in order to achieve a balance of highly professional and reasoned judgments and demanding time schedules. It's also important for the process of decision making and control to support and encourage the development of effective managers.

Important decisions are to be made thoughtfully with the involvement of individuals most qualified to make judgments, and once the decisions are made, authority and responsibility is delegated to the persons most knowledgeable about implementing those decisions. This judgment is based on the premise that vice-presidents, directors, managers, and supervisors will commit company resources in a responsible and professional manner, including, but not limited to, the following:

- Persons whose expertise relates in an important way or who will be affected by the contemplated action should be involved.
- Commitments of resources will not be made until proper approvals have been obtained.
- Persons responsible for commitments will bring superiors and others affected up to date on the progress of authorized programs or projects.

Control systems and other formal procedures are important to monitor actions and highlight progress. In support of this policy, the following plans and processes should be followed with regard to:

- *Long-Range or Strategic Plans.* The general directions and objectives that the company will follow for each of its major lines of business. Operating targets and financial projections for projects shall be determined, as well as major business strategy alternatives.
- *Annual Operating Plans and Financial Budgets.* Specific projects and work that will be accomplished during the current year toward planned achievement of the long-range plan, including organization and staffing needs and planned expenditures for both regular operations and capital projects. It is a principle of this system that budgets be thoughtfully prepared and presented by operating managers and once the components are approved, that authority to act be expeditiously delegated.

(continued)

Exhibit 7-8.   *Continued.*

- *Personnel and Salary Budgets, Reviews, and Procedures.* Human resources needs are identified and implemented through procedures designed by the human resources department, including human resources plans and budgets, recruiting, hiring and terminations, performance reviews, merit and promotional increases, and development programs.
- *Authority for Expenditures.* Authority covers specific capital projects or programs for acquisition or disposition of: (1) assets (purchase or lease), and (2) contractual services (consulting, environmental, feasibility, services and studies, etc.).
- *General Policies and Procedures.* Specific instructions and directions on how the company will operate in key administrative areas.
- *Contractual Agreements.* Contractual agreements, in response to a particular need, are prepared for the company by the law department, which should be involved early in the process to ensure that agreements protect company interests and are operationally workable. The finance department and the cognizant operating department will review and approve contracts prior to final execution.
- *Management Reports and Reviews.* Specific monthly reports (capital projects, financial statements) that help executive management to review results and manage by exception. In addition, progress reports on projects will be reviewed by appropriate management as needed.
- *Audits.* As documents related to commitment of funds are processed, they are reviewed by key administrative staff (purchasing, legal, accounting, personnel, and treasury) for propriety and correctness. In addition, special reviews and annual audits are performed by the internal audit function. Any irregularity or questionable transaction or practice is brought to the attention of the appropriate vice-president or the president.

Policy on Delegation of Authority

The president hereby delegates authority as follows:

- *Capital Projects.* Capital projects include construction of facilities and equipment, purchase or lease of buildings and equipment, disposition of property, release of land holdings, programs for development, feasiblility and other studies, etc.
- All capital projects in excess of $2,500, or lease commitments of more than two years, require an authority for expenditure (AFE) request.
- Authority to approve capital projects for less than $2,500 is delegated to the president or appropriate vice-president, director, manager, or supervisor.
- Authority to approve capital projects in excess of $2,500, which were included in the current annual budget and which do not exceed company authority level, is delegated to the president or appropriate vice-president.
- All capital projects of a magnitude that exceed set authority levels and that are included in the current year capital budget, along with any capital projects exceeding $2,500 that are not included in the budget, must be approved

by the president. After these projects have been approved, authority is hereby delegated to the appropriate vice-president. The vice-president may delegate to managers reporting to him or her the authority to initiate commitments by providing a written copy of such delegation to the chief financial officer.

- *General Business Transactions.* General business transactions include requests for disbursements; requests for materials, supplies, repairs, etc.; payroll time reports; invoices from outside vendors; and petty cash vouchers. Authority is hereby delegated, in accordance with set expenditure levels, for approval of general business transactions that were reasonably contemplated in the current year budget and operating plan to managers and supervisors in their areas of responsibility. If required expenditures exceed or were not contemplated in the current year budget, they must be approved by the appropriate vice-president.
- *Contractual Agreements.* All contractual agreements and commitments in excess of $25,000 or of two-year time periods for services, leases, land acquisition, rentals, equipment purchases/leases, etc., must be reviewed and approved by the law and finance departments prior to final approval. Contracts of less than $25,000 and a two-year time period, which are the subject of standard forms prepared by the law department, will be handled through purchasing.
- *Other Business Transactions.* Approval for travel expenses and transactions such as new hire salaries and salary increases is hereby delegated in accordance with set expenditure authority levels.

Orienting Older Workers

Older people reentering the work force may need a special orientation and retraining. During orientation you should make sure to cover benefits and procedures relating to an older group of workers, such as special medical or pension regulations, safety, and so on.

As you plan your new employee orientation program, you will think of other things to include. Give your new employees the same emphasis and time commitment you give your most valued customers. When you have spent thousands of dollars recruiting, interviewing, and selecting valuable employees, it's important and cost-effective to provide the best orientation program you can put together and to use the best people available in your organization to carry it out. You have recruited and hired these people—now you want to develop and retain them.

Exhibit 7-9. Sample delegation of authority and approval for general business transactions.

Transactions	Approval Level				
	President	Vice-Presidents	Directors	Managers	Supervisors
Petty cash vouchers	X	X	X	X	X
Payroll time reports	X	X	X	X	X
Salary increases over $1,000 per employee per year	X	X			
Invoices from outside vendors below $1,000	X	X	X	X	X
Request for disbursements	X	X	to $5,000	to $2,500	to $2,500
Request for materials, supplies, repairs, etc.	X	X	to $5,000	to $2,500	to $2,500
Capital expenditures Less than $2,500	X	X	X	X	X
More than $2,500	X	X			

X denotes authority to approve transaction.

PART III

COMPENSATION AND BENEFITS

8

Basic Compensation

Robert M. James
Vice-President
Hay Management Consultants

This chapter addresses the subject of base salaries for all types and levels of employees. It discusses the basics of existing and emerging compensation practices, from definitions and basic structures through implementation, analysis, and strategies for change. Because base salaries cannot be considered in a vacuum, references are made to other areas such as benefits plans, incentive programs, hourly wage practices, and performance appraisal.

Like all professionals in our increasingly technical and specialized world, compensation people and salary administration practitioners have developed a jargon all their own. The following terms, along with definitions and examples, will be a useful guide in understanding and moving through this chapter.

Basic Definitions of Compensation Terms

Area differential is a specifically identified and communicated dollar or percentage of salary amount added to the pay of an employee working in a geographic area that requires some premium above and beyond an organization's normal pay practice.

Banding is grouping a generally broader than normal collection of similar jobs into a "super salary grade" to provide broad flexibility in administering salaries, often in combination with similar incentive compensation opportunities.

Compa-ratio is the relationship of actual salaries to the midpoint of the salary range established for the job within the salary administration system or salary grade structure. For example, if an employee in Grade Four has a salary of $14,000 and the Grade Four midpoint is $16,000, the employee would have a compa-ratio of 87.5 percent ($14,000 ÷ $16,000). Compa-ratios can be calculated for individual employees, groups of employees, or business units, or on a companywide basis.

Compression occurs when the salaries or hourly wage rates of a lower-ranked, or -rated, group of employees are higher than or too close to the salaries provided to higher-ranked, or -rated, employees. A union settlement that raises the wages of production workers up to the salary paid to their foreman is an example of compression. Compression is always caused by forces external to a well-designed salary administration program, which should be structured to avoid this problem.

A *cost-of-living increase or adjustment* is a salary increase unrelated to individual or corporate performance and simply added to maintain an employee's standard of living or purchasing power due to changes in area cost of living. Cost-of-living increases are nearly always the products of specific mathematical formulas, usually applied on common dates each year, and are often the result of bargaining unit settlements being extended to nonunion employees. Cost-of-living increases are infrequently used today.

Equity adjustment is a special salary increase, permanently added to an individual's salary, because analysis has shown that the individual's salary, salary range, or grade was too low relative to comparable positions. Merit or cost of living is not a factor. The increase is simply a demonstration of the organization's willingness to implement its value system of internal ranking and equity. Extensive audits of a salary system or structure usually result in some equity adjustments, and if they are substantial or numerous they may be spread over two or three separate increases within a short time frame (e.g., three to nine months).

Exempt refers to an employee or group of employees who are "exempt" from (not covered by) the overtime requirements of the Fair Labor Standards Act. Exempt employees are not paid overtime for working more than forty hours in a week. However, to avoid compression, first-line supervisors are often paid overtime (perhaps at straight time as opposed to time-and-one-half or double time) even though they are exempt from the overtime requirement.

Functional pricing means using a special, usually higher, salary level for a special function or job family in response to market pressure.

A *green circle* is used to indicate an individual who is paid below the minimum of the salary range or grade set for the job. On a chart plotting jobs in relation to salary range, such an individual would traditionally be circled in green to highlight the problem. (See *Scattergram.*)

Knowledge-based pay refers to a system that pays specific amounts for each skill required for the job or area and provides increases to employees as they acquire new skills. This is not related to annual merit increases for overall performance. Such a system can establish and pay for needed skills.

Lump sum merit increases are merit increases provided in the form of onetime lump sum payments that do not increase base pay. Lump sum merit increases, once very rare, have been used fairly extensively in recent years to avoid permanent increases in fixed costs. As Exhibit 8-1 indicates, they are not popular with employees because they do not increase base pay or related benefits, including pensions, life insurance, disability plans, and so on.

Market pricing relates to the setting of salaries or salary ranges on the basis of market pressures or surveys, usually by functional or job family areas, with limited or no regard for any system of internal ranking or internal equity. Market pricing is often used on a limited, highly selective basis for special functional areas where a severe skill shortage exists. Market pricing requires the willingness to decrease as well as increase salaries in response to market conditions if unnecessary fixed costs are to be avoided.

Merit budget is the pool of money set aside to provide merit increases during a year and is usually expressed in terms of dollars on a company, unit, or departmentwide basis.

Merit increase is a salary increase based on individual performance, or merit. An across-the-board increase, an equity adjustment, a promotional increase, a cost-of-living increase, or an area differential are not merit increases and would not generally be used to reduce a merit increase otherwise payable. Merit increases are normally given once a year either on a common annual date applicable to all employees or on individually determined dates tied to the anniversary of employment (anniversary date).

Merit pool is the same as *merit budget*. Both terms are often expressed as a per-

Exhibit 8-1. Lump sum merit increases, 1988–1989.

Firms using lump sum merit increases	15%
Employee reaction to use:	
Negative	31%
Neutral	29%
Positive	40%

Source: Hay Survey of 600 Compensation Conference Firms.

centage of payroll and used to describe the level of overall payroll change the company intends to provide for the coming year.

Nonexempt refers to an employee who is not exempt from the provisions of the Fair Labor Standards Act and who therefore must be paid overtime for working more than forty hours in a week or on a designated holiday. Great care should be exercised in accurately determining the nonexempt and exempt personnel within an organization. Nonexempt employees who are denied overtime have recourse to legal action, and penalties can involve significant sums for retroactive violations of overtime rules.

Performance appraisal is the judgment of individual employee performance by superiors and is usually done in anticipation of determining an annual salary increase. Elaborate systems, complete with self-rating forms, sign-off procedures, and extensive supervisory training, are often used for performance appraisal—and with good reason. Inequitable, inconsistent, or arbitrary performance appraisal, whether actual or merely perceived, can destroy the best-conceived system of internal equity and motivation ever constructed for a salary program.

Performance rating is a classification or differentiation of employees by a superior on some scale used for salary increases and often other purposes, such as promotion potential. Scales can be numeric or semantic and typically have five steps to permit gradations of judgment, although three-step scales are gaining converts. Common performance scales are illustrated in Exhibit 8-2.

On a semantic scale the definition used for the 3 rating, where most employees are expected to be rated, is an important decision. Employees will be more likely to accept a rating of "good" or "solid" than the more commonly used "competent," "satisfactory," or "average." Many systems use bell curves to control performance ratings, either as standards or guidelines, with only about 5–10 percent of the population expected to be rated in the top category, as a 5 (or 1); 5–10 percent expected to be rated in the bottom category, as a 1 (or 5); and about 60–70 percent typically expected to fall in the middle category.

Performance review is the meeting at which the superior discusses the performance rating with the employee. This is most often done at the same time the annual salary increase is disclosed. Many psychologists and other professionals argue that this is a mistake as the level of the salary increase will overshadow all other discussion, which might otherwise be a positive experience with sustained advantages for all parties.

Exhibit 8-2. Common performance scales.

Semantic Descriptions		Numeric Descriptions		Definition
Outstanding	Excellent	5	1	Significantly exceeds expectations
Superior	Very Good	4	2	Exceeds expectations
Competent	Average	3	3	Meets expectations
Adequate	Developing	2	4	Does not meet expectations
Marginal	Inadequate	1	5	Significantly under expectations

Piecework is a variable pay system that provides a specific dollar reward for a specific unit of work successfully completed—for example, ten cents for every widget assembled. Piecework pay systems are usually limited to high-volume, relatively low-skilled assembly functions. With adequate quality control procedures, a piecework system can effectively function as a built-in supervisor, as it is an individually controlled and self-monitoring incentive plan linking compensation costs to value produced. In their most basic mode, sales commission programs are essentially piecework programs.

Point factor system is a system of ranking jobs within an organization on the basis of some consistently applied criteria that result in "points" being assigned to each job. Such a system is highly useful in establishing internally equitable salary ranges or grades within an organization. Gross differences in job content are easy to identify and for employees to accept (e.g., the president's job is universally accepted as bigger than the janitor's). More subtle differences, especially when diverse areas are compared (such as accounting and marketing), are far more difficult to rank. A well-documented, consistently applied, and well-communicated point factor system can establish a job rating system that produces acceptable internal rankings on which salary ranges or grades can be based. Companies using identical point factor systems usually subscribe to a club survey that reports participants' salary practices on the basis of job content (expressed in point factor ratings), permitting accurate market pricing that is unrelated to unique differences in titles, revenue size, or organizational reporting relationships. The Hay Guide Chart-Profile Method of job evaluation is the most widely used and well-known point factor system, but many other such systems exist. Under various guises and in various forms, all systems use criteria that can be applied across all job families, such as:

- *Know-how* or *knowledge* required for the job, whether technical, professional, managerial, or relative to interpersonal skills.
- *Problem-solving* skills required in terms of both the range and complexity of problems addressed.

- *Accountability* or *responsibility* for end results. This is basically a recognition of the role and ability of the position to affect an organization's operations and/or success levels, such as revenue or profits. This factor also recognizes the type of impact (direct, primary, shared, contributory, etc.) as well as its magnitude in terms of dollars controlled or produced.

Some systems add specific educational degrees or professional requirements obtained, and for certain types of jobs, working conditions are used to add extra value. One key to all such systems is clear documentation of job requirements through a *position description* and/or *accountability statement* because it is always the position (job) that is rated, not the individual incumbent. Since such systems are, by design, blind to race, age, religion, sex, and national origin, they are frequently cited as useful tools in defending against charges of discrimination within a salary system. Point factor systems do not determine individual pay, just salary ranges or grades within an organization. Individual performance, as determined by performance ratings, determines individual pay within the ranges or grades established. And, as necessary, the market will ultimately determine individual pay even outside of established ranges or within special, higher ranges developed by functional pricing for scarce skills.

Alternatives to point factor systems include market pricing for high-population positions and then a slotting of other jobs around this benchmark sample on a judgmental basis; structuring grades or ratings on the bases of organizational or reporting relationships (e.g., steps down from the president); and combinations of both approaches.

Recovery means that in any stable organization of at least several hundred employees, total salaries will go down by about 1 percent every year in the absence of any merit increases. This is true because there is a constant flow of employees leaving or being promoted and having their jobs taken by employees who are new to the job and, therefore, paid at a lower rate (lower in the range), with the organization saving, or "recovering," this difference. The actual percentage figure varies from organization to organization, influenced by such things as turnover, number of new hires, and similar factors. Because of recovery, regardless of whether it is 0.5 percent or 1.0 percent, actual average merit increases can be higher than the merit budget and still have total payroll only increase by the size of the merit budget. For example, assuming an organization is willing to increase payroll by 5 percent, it could establish a 5 percent merit budget. Assuming a 1 percent recovery, it could issue merit increase guidelines permitting an average increase of 6 percent and have this result:

Total payroll 1/1/91:	$1,000,000
Average merit increase (6 percent):	60,000
Recovery (1 percent):	(10,000)
Total payroll 1/1/92:	$1,050,000 (5 percent higher)

A *red circle* is used to indicate an individual whose salary is above the maximum of the salary range set for the job. On a chart depicting company pay practices, such an individual would traditionally be circled in red to highlight the situation. (See *Scattergram.*)

Salary grade is a pay level (usually a salary range, not an individual amount) established for a grouping of similar jobs. For example, all jobs with a rating of 200 to 249 on a point factor system would be placed in a single salary grade. The alternative to salary grades would be individual salary ranges for every job with a different rating.

Salary range is a band or spread of salary opportunity set for every job or by salary grade. Every range has three key points as illustrated below for a typical exempt employee salary range:

Maximum	$24,000	120 percent of midpoint
Midpoint	$20,000	100 percent of midpoint
Minimum	$16,000	80 percent of midpoint

This is often called a 50 percent range because the maximum ($24,000) is 50 percent larger than the minimum ($16,000). For nonexempt employees, ranges are normally more narrow (85 percent–100 percent–115 percent), since performance distinctions are more difficult to determine and the need to move employees more quickly to midpoint exists. Salaries and salary increases for both exempt and nonexempt employees are then communicated and administered within this range to recognize the fact that employees' experience and performance will vary and to provide motivation through salary growth opportunities without requiring promotion. The midpoint of the range is often called the market rate because organizations set their midpoints at the competitive, marketplace, level they choose to use for their jobs. This is the optimum mix between possibly conflicting objectives—what they can reasonably afford, and what they have to pay to attract and retain needed talent. For scarce skills in a given job family (e.g., engineering), the midpoint (and therefore the entire range) could be higher under a functional pricing approach.

Scattergram is an analysis tool used to determine the internal equity and salary administration effectiveness of a program. The key elements of a scattergram are: plots for each job in the organization (or a benchmark sample) placed on the chart where pay levels and job size (rankings) intersect; a line of central tendency (CT) that reflects the overall pay practice of the individuals plotted; and two "tolerance lines" plotted at 120 percent and 80 percent of the central tendency to reflect a typical exempt salary range. Red circles (those above maximum) and green circles (those below minimum) would then be identified. A typical scattergram might look like Exhibit 8-3. The program represented by this scattergram looks pretty good. Pay increases as jobs get bigger or more important, and only four positions fall outside of a normal tolerance range. Given this situation, three key decisions would face the organization:

1. Is the central tendency an appropriate salary range or grade midpoint for the organization?
   - Can the company afford the salary range?
   - Is it competitive enough to permit the company to attract and retain needed talent?
2. Why do the two red circles exist, and should action be taken to correct this seeming inequity relative to other employees?
   - Do the red circles represent critical skill personnel holding jobs with clear market premiums?

Exhibit 8-3. Typical scattergram.

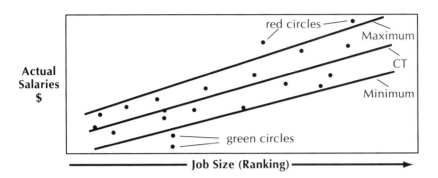

• Are they outstanding performers clearly worth this premium, even though it is above the normal parameters for the ranges?
• Are they employees who have been demoted but the company elected not to cut their pay?
Action: Probably no action should be taken for the first two situations since an organization must ultimately pay what is necessary to attract and retain critical skills and outstanding performers. Probably a salary freeze should be declared for the third situation, until the ranges move up over time and the individuals' pay falls within tolerance again.
3. Why do the two green circles exist, and what action is appropriate?
• Do the green circles represent new hires?
• Are they recent promotions who received a promotional increase but it wasn't enough to bring them into the range?
• Are they marginal performers?
Action: An immediate or rapidly scheduled series of equipment adjustments is indicated for the first two situations if the internal equity communicated for the program is to have any meaning. Alternatively, if an organization is following a pure market pricing strategy and the new hires have the necessary skills and were able to be hired at the existing rate, the salaries should be maintained. For the third situation, the marginal performers, an aggressive and well-documented program of counseling, training, and monitoring is indicated, leading to either discharge or improved performance, which permits pay at the range minimum.

Basic Purposes and Perspectives on Base Salaries

The Employer's Perspective

From the employer's perspective, the entire compensation structure represents cost to the organization (probably the single largest cost to a services sector firm) and should be structured and utilized to maximize the "return on compensation." This return can be measured against two basic criteria:

1. The ability to attract and retain needed talent.
   - For the bulk of the work force, a certain level of skill, experience, and continuity is important to maintain everyday operations.
   - Historically, the compensation system for this population has had this approximate mix of elements for every one dollar of total compensation:
     (a) Base salaries: 65–70 cents
     (b) Benefits package: 20–25 cents
     (c) Incentive pay: 0–10 cents
   - As base salary composes the great bulk of this package, salary rates must be kept at reasonably competitive levels, or attraction and retention will be impossible. Similarly, the base salary system must be perceived as internally equitable and reasonably motivational, or morale will suffer and turnover or productivity will become intolerable problems.
   - In recent years many organizations are varying this compensation mix significantly by offering multiple forms of incentive compensation such as gain-sharing, cash profit sharing, group or unit incentives, and individual bonus award programs. Such programs tend to attract and retain a different, more risk-tolerant, group of employees and reduce the need for both external competitiveness and precise structures to ensure internal equity and salary increase processes within a base salary program.
   - For unique individuals with critical skills, the issue of attraction and retention is a simple one: You simply pay whatever it takes to attract and retain this critical skill.
   - Ideally, any individually tailored packages will contain large elements of incentive pay to link the extra cost to demonstrated value received.
2. The ability to motivate employees to perform at superior levels and deliver quality results to every assignment.
   - For base salaries, the use of salary ranges and a thorough, consistently administered performance appraisal program can provide some of the needed motivation. The two key requirements are:
     (a) Supervisors willing to make tough decisions with monitoring procedures to maintain reasonable consistency.
     (b) Flexibility within the program to permit exceptions when justified by real business needs.
   - This is difficult to achieve with total merit budgets in the 4–6 percent range that has been recent practice in the United States. The tendency has been to spread this limited amount of money around the entire population, as indicated in Exhibit 8-4. This differential, only about 3 percent from the middle range (satisfactory performer) to the superstar, is clearly not very motivational.
   - Two alternatives to these traditional merit actions are gaining favor. First, retain multistep ratings but be far more aggressive in merit differences. Second, revise the whole concept of salary use: Adopt incentive or spot bonus plans as the motivational element, and use salaries primarily for maintenance of living standards, with most employees brought to range or grade midpoints

Exhibit 8-4. Percentages of average merit increases.

Industrials—1990	Performance Rating	Financials—1990
8.0%	Highest	8.7%
6.7%	Next Highest	7.0%
5.2%	Satisfactory	5.3%
3.3%	Lowest Eligible	3.2%

Source: Hay Compensation Conferences, Participant Practices.

and kept there. Merit action under these two alternatives is illustrated in Exhibit 8-5.

The Employee's Perspective

From the employee's perspective, his or her compensation is probably the single most critical factor in the whole employment relationship. Exhibit 8-6, which reflects responses from thousands of employees nationwide, supports this statement.

Although the availability of acceptable alternative employment opportunities obviously tempers their thinking, most employees expect the following from their organi-

Exhibit 8-5. Alternatives to traditional merit increase methods.

Aggressive Use of Traditional Multistep Ratings	
Rating	Average Merit Increase
Outstanding	9–10%
Superior	6–7%
Satisfactory	3–4%
Developing	0–2%
New, Marginal	0%

Change to Maintenance Mode	
Rating/Situation and % Population	Salary Increase to Group
Superior, Low in Range (10–15%)	9–10%
Most (70–80%)	4%
New, Marginal (10–15%)	0%

Exhibit 8-6.   Ranking of work force values.

Rank	Middle Manager	Professional	Clerical
1	Pay/Benefits	Pay/Benefits	Pay/Benefits
2	Challenge	Challenge	Respect
3	Advancement	Advancement	Advancement
4	Authority	New Skills	New Skills
5	Supervision	Respect	Supervision
6	Accomplishment	Supervision	Challenge

Source: Hay research for management database.

zation's compensation program (these expectations are primarily directed at the base salary system):

- Their compensation should be externally competitive relative to alternative opportunities.
- Their compensation should be internally equitable relative to their peers within the organization, which means:
  —Compensation opportunities for similar-size jobs should be the same.
  —If their performance is better, they should receive more money.
- Their individual performance should be recognized, which means:
  —Their performance ratings are reasonably consistent with their own perceptions.
  —Their compensation increases reflect what they as individuals accomplished.
- If some form of incentive is added as a perceived substitute for base salary, it should be a reasonable trade, which means:
  —Total opportunity for at-risk gain should be at least two times the loss.
  —A solid—perhaps 50/50—chance should exist for doing slightly better.
  —They should feel that their individual or departmental efforts will impact performance against the incentive goals in some meaningful way.

Employees also have growing concerns regarding the effectiveness of their take-home pay in light of increasing taxes and other deductions, such as exploding employee costs for group health care. The importance of this last issue is often overlooked when gauging employee reactions to proposed salary actions, but it is very real. The impact of average required charges for family medical coverage for a lower-paid position is illustrated in Exhibit 8-7. Is it any surprise that reduced salary increase budgets or salary freezes can cause considerable anguish? In short, all successful total compensation, and especially salary programs, should be developed, structured, communicated, and administered with a high degree of empathy for basic perceptions.

Exhibit 8-7. Average employee premiums for family
medical coverage.

Year	Annual Amount	As percent of $9,900 Take-Home Pay
1985	$259	2.6%
1990	$594	6.0%

Source: Hay/Huggins Benefit Survey of 1,000 Firms.

Establishing a Salary Program

In establishing a salary program, three basic issues must be addressed. This section discusses these issues and the various methods of addressing them.

Determining the Level of Compensation

The first issue is determining the optimum competitive level and mix of compensation for the organization. This involves answering several key questions:

- What compensation market is the company in?
- What level of talent does the company need or want for various segments of its business?
- What can the company afford to pay, and how?
- How tight is the market for needed skills?
- Does the company offer opportunities, working conditions, a location, an image, or other intangibles that will require (or permit) it to pay more (or less) than market rate for needed talent?
- If the company is already established, what does its turnover rate and open job list indicate about current compensation levels and, perhaps, compensation mix?
- Does the company or the area have active bargaining units that should influence decisions on pay levels or mix relative to comprehension or unionization?

With respect to the compensation marketplace, the following is true for the majority of jobs, and the action indicated is typical:

1. For nonexempt employees, the local marketplace is the ruling yardstick, and for most employers cash compensation will consist solely of base salary. Barring unique, industry-specific, skills, most nonexempt employees will be recruited locally and will seek alternate employment in the immediate area. The following suggestions or comments will help in setting nonexempt practice.
   - Participate in one or more local surveys such as are offered by local personnel associations or, in major cities, by national consulting firms.

Exhibit 8-8. Development of salary ranges.

Job Ranking (in Points)	Individually Constructed Salary Ranges	Graded Structure With Ranges	
400	$21,914–19,056–16,198	$21,275	
389	$21,563–18,750–15,938	$18,500	Grade 3
360	$20,637–17,945–15,253	$15,725	
316	$19,230–16,722–14,214	$18,515	
305	$18,880–16,417–13,954	$16,100	Grade 2
280	$18,080–15,722–13,364	$13,685	
228	$16,420–14,278–12,136	$16,100	
219	$16,132–14,028–11,924	$14,000	Grade 1
208	$15,780–13,722–11,664	$11,900	
Judgmental or point factor rating.	Note that ranges go from 115 percent of midpoint at maximum to 85 percent at minimum.	Note that ranges overlap with about a 15 percent difference.	

- Select several high-population jobs with representative, generic descriptions, and compare your practices to similar jobs in the area.
- Slot remaining jobs around these benchmark samples using some consistently applied and understood system of ranking.
- Construct ranges for each job or, as is common for nonexempt positions, group several similarly ranked jobs into grades, and develop a salary range for each job. These two alternatives are illustrated in Exhibit 8-8.
- The midpoint of the individual ranges or grades should be your market rate, that is, the competitive salary level you are willing to pay for each job, assuming solid, experienced performance.
- New hires with little or no experience should be hired at or near the range or grade minimum.
- Experienced employees with solid performance should be paid at or near midpoint.
- Experienced employees who are outstanding performers should be paid at or near maximum.

2. For exempt, professional, and technical employees, the marketplace is more regional than local, and for highly specialized, industry-unique skills, it may well be national or even global. The following suggestions or comments will be helpful in setting exempt salaries.
   - Participate in one or more surveys that reflect your industry and the types and levels of jobs you need in this category.
   - Be extremely careful in matching your jobs in these surveys. Since titles can be very misleading, surveys that require participants to report jobs on a consistently applied basis (e.g., a common point factor system, a constant formula reflecting revenue size or reporting level, or a reference to common

position descriptions) should be used whenever possible. National consulting firms, industry associations, and professional organizations all provide such surveys.

- Once solid market pay levels have been determined for matched jobs, the remaining positions can be ranked or slotted in relation to the matched jobs and salary ranges or grades established.

- As for nonexempt positions, range or grade midpoint should represent your market rate, with individual pay rates determined in a similar manner within each range.

- Unlike the situation with nonexempt employees, selecting this market rate level will probably involve a review of competitive practices with respect to incentive plans as well as base salaries, with the issue of cash compensation mix (salary versus incentive) being a factor in your decision regarding base salary midpoints.

3. For managerial and executive positions, the marketplace is clearly national, and for many positions it is very industry-specific as well. The following suggestions or comments will be helpful in setting salaries at this level.

- Use at least two surveys. Club surveys with industry-specific comparisons and very careful comparisons are especially critical here.

- For very senior officers, competitive firms' proxy statements can also be reviewed, as the compensation of the five highest paid executives must be reported annually by all publicly traded companies in the United States.

- For officers it is often also important to determine the group of companies that the board (or compensation committee of the board) considers most important in establishing compensation practices each year. A recommendation that doesn't display data from this "magic list" is likely to be unacceptable.

- For officers and executives the compensation marketplace is clearly not just a base salary marketplace. Annual and long-term incentive opportunities, including stock plans such as options, must be integrated into any decision regarding market rate and, therefore, salary range midpoints. Compensation mix and the vehicles involved are critically important and should be clearly understood and considered before salary ranges are set.

- Once a market rate and salary range midpoint is determined, the ranges themselves and the placement of individual salaries within ranges is normally the same as for other employees. However, broad banding and even identical salary amounts are sometimes used at officer levels to further emphasize the incentive portions of compensation.

Administering the Program

The second issue is administering the program once it is set up. Successful administration involves answering these key questions:

- How frequently does the company change salary ranges?
- How frequently does the company provide salary increases?
- How does the company determine salary increases?
- Who approves salary increases, and using what process?

- How does the company determine a promotion, and what should a promotional increase be?
- What should the company communicate to employees?

CHANGING SALARY RANGES

With respect to changing salary ranges, it is typical practice to audit a program's competitiveness every year and take this action:

1. If past decisions on the desired competitive level (e.g., average) are still appropriate, all salary ranges can simply be adjusted upward to reflect market movement. "Market" may, of course, be different for different segments of the organization's work force, as might the decision on pricing appropriateness. Assuming a decision is made to preserve past practice and all survey analysis indicates that the "market" is increasing by 5 percent, then the salary range action would be as follows:
   - Multiply existing range midpoints by 1.05.
   - For range maximums, multiply by 1.20 for exempt employees and by 1.15 for nonexempt employees.
   - For range minimums, multiply the new midpoint by 0.80 for exempt employees and by 0.85 for nonexempt employees.
   - Many programs would round all figures to the nearest fifty or one hundred dollars, but this can distort ranges for lower pay levels.
2. The ultimate range or grade structure should look graphically like Exhibit 8-9, with overlaps of about 15 percent between grades.
3. If business conditions, turnover, recruiting conditions, or a revised need for talent indicate a change in market pricing—up or down—the action would be as follows:
   - Select a new, appropriate, competitive position.
   - Set midpoints at this new level.
   - Construct ranges, maximums, and minimums, as shown in Exhibit 8-9. To the extent a decline in past market pricing were desired, a simple action of "no change" in existing ranges could accomplish a downward revision equal to the market change with a minimum of administrative effort.
4. A similar freeze of past salary ranges may be indicated if an analysis of compa-ratios indicates that the organization is not in reality implementing its existing and communicated policy of salary practice in the marketplace.

This last situation requires further explanation. Assume an organization announced that it intended to be an "average payer" in the market and set salary range or grade midpoints at the average of the market. So far, so good. However, assume that merit budgets were set too low or available funds were not spent, so that very few employees were actually paid anywhere near midpoint. In this case, overall compa-ratios (actual salaries divided by midpoints) would be well under 100 percent, and in terms of real pay, the organization would clearly not be an average payer. It is important to remember that it's real salary, not midpoints, that employees take to the grocery store. Exhibit

Exhibit 8-9. Salary range or grade structure.

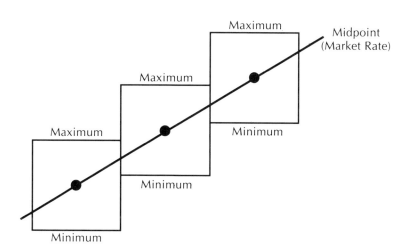

8-10 gives a general feel for typical compa-ratios. The exhibit is generally applicable across all sectors.

There is a strong message here on the use of salary ranges in most programs. At the clerical/support level, the compa-ratio is low because turnover and promotion activity is high. Therefore, many jobs are held by new, inexperienced personnel who are accordingly and appropriately paid at the bottom of the job's salary range (a compa-ratio of 85 percent). At the senior executive level, turnover is low and promotion opportunities are very limited. Therefore, jobs are held for extended periods of time, experience is solid, and performance is normally strong, so that salaries are paid above the midpoint (compa-ratio over 100 percent).

Exhibit 8-10. Median compa-ratios nationwide for industrial companies.

Type of Employee	Average Compa-Ratio
Clerical/Support (Nonexempt)	92–94%
Professional/Technical (Exempt)	96–98%
Middle Management	98–100%
Senior Executives	102–105%

Source: 1990 Hay Compensation Survey.

SALARY INCREASES

With respect to salary increases, practice in the last three decades has been to provide salary reviews and usually increases on an annual basis. Several key issues and typical actions are involved:

1. One of two approaches is normally used for timing: All eligible employees receive an increase on a common date each year, or increases are made on anniversary dates throughout the year. Neither approach is right or wrong, but they do have different impacts.
   - A common date approach is easier to price out since all increases will, barring turnover, apply for eleven months if all increases are effective on, for example, February 1. In addition, this method telescopes all performance reviews into a single time frame that requires a concentrated effort, but arguably provides more consistency and is easier to monitor and control.
   - Anniversary date action spreads the burden of review and action throughout the year, arguably permitting a more extensive and effective result. In a one-year analysis, the cash flow cost of increases is less since salary changes are spread over the entire year; but over a series of years the cash flow cost is the same under both methods. However, the anniversary date method does permit a consistent action for new hires because the first merit opportunity will be one year from date of hire for everyone. The common date approach requires proration for the first "common date" occurring after date of hire since it could occur anywhere from one to twelve months after the hire date.
2. The controlling factor in the amount of increase is, of course, the merit budget established for the organization, or its subunits or various employee groups. Beyond this commonality there are probably as many approaches as there are organizations if all the subtleties of various actions are considered. However, about three general approaches are followed as described below.
   - *Compa-Ratio/Performance Grid Method.* This is the most sophisticated and complex approach and, if exceptions aren't tolerated, can be the most rigid. The concept is to match individual performance to position in range (compa-ratio) and provide staggered increases to move everyone eventually to the "correct" position in the range (compa-ratio), which has been defined and communicated as shown in Exhibit 8-11 (exempt employees shown).

     To accomplish this, an annual salary increase guide is provided to each department, which indicates the increases that can be provided to employees based on a dual match of: (1) the individual's performance rating, and (2) the individual's compa-ratio. Once a merit budget is approved for the year, this guide can be prepared by the human resources department by determining existing compa-ratios, and either: (1) assuming a guideline bell curve for performance ratings, or (2) analyzing performance ratings submitted and approved in advance. The salary increase guide would look like the sample shown in Exhibit 8-12. The compa-ratios are existing salaries divided by the midpoint of the new, higher, salary range adopted for the upcoming year. The sample guide would spend about 5 percent of payroll assuming typical compa-ratio and performance ratings.

     As indicated in Exhibit 8-12, an outstanding performer uses the entire range

Exhibit 8-11. Compa-ratio/performance grid method of salary increases.

Experience	Performance	Correct Compa-Ratio
Extensive	Outstanding	113–120%
Broad	Superior	105–112%
Good	Solid	97–104%
Developing	Acceptable	89–96%
Little	Marginal	80–88%

with larger amounts than the norm (4–5 percent) if existing compa-ratio is lower than desired (113–120 percent). This permits such people to move quickly through the range, assuming outstanding performance continues, but doesn't provide a relatively new hire with a huge increase to get immediately to a 113–120 percent compa-ratio. Similarly, marginal performers or new hires who are supposed to be paid in the 80–88 percent compa-ratio area could receive modest increases if they're already there, but no increase if their compa-ratio is over this level.

• *Total Budget/Limited Control Method.* This is perhaps the most flexible approach, but it can lead to inequities and inconsistencies. Basically, each department or area is given a total budget to spend as they see fit with only very limited controls and guidelines, such as:

(a) Salary range maximums for each employee that cannot be exceeded without special approval.

(b) Guidelines on suggested distribution bell curves based on performance.

(c) Set minimum and maximum individual increase amounts that cannot be deviated from without special permission.

Exhibit 8-12. Sample salary increase guide.

	Compa-Ratio in New Range				
	80–88%	89–96%	97–104%	105–112%	113–120%
Rating	Salary Increase Permitted				
Outstanding	10–11%	9–10%	7–9%	6–8%	4–5%
Superior	9–10%	7–9%	6–8%	4–5%	0%
Solid	6–8%	5–7%	4–5%	0%	0%
Acceptable	4–5%	3–5%	0%	0%	0%
Marginal	2–3%	0%	0%	0%	0%

Organizations that follow this approach frequently require a central submission of contemplated actions so some measure of overall consistency can be imposed, at least by discussion and persuasion if not actual dictates.
  • *Control/Flexibility Method.* This is a hybrid that provides the bulk of the merit budget funds to departments to be used by following either of the two methods discussed above, and then provides "extra" funds for lump sum merit action. Such extras could be in any of the following forms:
    (a) A common amount, or pool, to each department of something like 0.5–1.0 percent of payroll.
    (b) A "CEO pool" of 0.5–1.0 percent of total payroll that can be requested by departments.
    (c) varied unit/division pools with the amount dictated by unit/division performance each year.
  Pool funds can then be used with broad discretion for special lump sum merit awards to recognize outstanding individual or unit performance, provide money to individuals at the top of or over their salary ranges, or similar circumstances where the "allowed" salary increase is considered inadequate.

Any of these methods or the multitude of variances in between can work. Administrative concerns, the perceived need for control and internal consistency, and the faith in performance judgments are all obvious issues to be considered in selecting the "correct" approach for any organization. In addition, the existence and use of incentive plans, the viability of the salary program as a tool to attract and retain needed talent, and employees' perceptions of external competitiveness and internal equity are all key factors to be considered.

GENERAL SIZE OF INCREASES

With respect to the general size of increases, several rules of thumb are worth considering:

  • Merit budgets must be at least equal to the change in salary ranges every year, or overall compa-ratios will decline.
  • An increase of less than at least 2 percent will generally be demotivational, and an increase of less than the much-published national inflation rate figure will generate a negative employee reaction. A zero increase provides a stronger message, and a zero followed by a 4–5 percent increase once performance improves provides an even stronger message.
  • Too large a onetime merit increase (e.g., 15–20 percent) creates expectations that cannot be fulfilled. A series of 8–10 percent increases over short time frames (e.g., four to six months) probably has more lasting motivational value.
  • Extraordinary onetime actions are better rewarded with lump sum bonus payments than special salary adjustments that are permanently built into the base rate.
  • Timing as well as amount can be used to differentiate between performance. All increases don't have to be annual; in fact, annual salary increases were unheard of until the last thirty years or so.

- Salary increases impact benefits costs very directly for salaried personnel. For every dollar salaries are increased, about thirty-five cents of benefits cost is incurred for a typical organization.
- Salaries represent fixed and significant costs, and for most employees salary increases are probably the single most powerful motivational and behavior modification tool in an organization's arsenal. They simply *must* be intelligently applied if any reasonable return on compensation is to be realized.

PROMOTIONS

With respect to promotions, any change from one grade to another or, under a point factor system, a job size increase of at least 15 percent, is generally considered a promotion. Promotional increases are typically granted at the time of the promotion, and these practices are followed:

- An average increase is about 10 percent.
- Increases over 20 percent are generally spread over two or three segments separated by three to six months.
- Promotional increases are not normally used to reduce merit increases, but if the normal "merit time" closely follows the promotion, a larger, combined, increase is often given.
- In some systems a combined increase would always be given (probably 15–17 percent, not 10 percent), and a new anniversary date would be created effective with the date of promotion.
- If the promotional increase doesn't bring the salary up to the minimum of the new job's salary range (an unusual situation), normal action would be a scheduled series of increases over three to nine months to raise salary to minimum.

COMMUNICATION ABOUT COMPENSATION

Regarding communication about compensation with employees, a lot is rarely enough. Considering the size of corporate payrolls, it is abysmal how little is typically spent on communicating an organization's philosophy, competitiveness, salary opportunities, and the advantages and equity provided by salary administration procedures. Most organizations should shy away from communicating individual salaries or, in point factor systems, individual job size points. Everything else should be communicated as often and as well as possible if maximum value is to be received from a salary program. For maximum value, employees should know and understand all of the following:

- How competitive their pay levels are, and why.
- How much is spent each year on salaries and other compensation items.
- How salary ranges or grades are constructed, and why.
- How salary increases are determined, what opportunity an individual has, and how it can be realized.
- What the pay opportunities are for open jobs, and what skills and duties such jobs require.

- How any incentive plans apply to their work, what influences performance, how they can impact such things, and what progress is being made throughout the measurement period for eventual payout.
- What their individual salary range or grade is, where they are in the range, and what type of experience, performance, or skill is required to move up. This latter information, along with facts concerning the last two or three increases, is sometimes incorporated in an annual benefits statement.

Handling Exceptions

The third and final issue is handling exceptions. This involves answering these knotty questions:

- Should salary policies and procedures be different for different business units or locations?
- Should practices be different for different job levels or functional skills?
- Should unique packages be used for special skills or key individuals?
- Should special actions be considered for special circumstances or events?
- If salary ranges or grades are used, should out-of-range situations be permitted?

The answer to all of these questions is an emphatic yes—provided there are rational reasons for the difference. In this age of computers, "administrative reasons" are unacceptable explanations for denying a justified exception to standard practice. Moreover, as demographic changes bring in multitudes of new employee needs and concerns to the workplace (such as job sharing, flexible hours, and work-at-home schedules) the old-fashioned monolithic salary structure with fixed, rigid rules will simply not work. Similarly, global competition and the need for excellence and quality at all levels of any organization require the maximum amount of flexibility and creativity for an organization's single most powerful tool—compensation. Most of the innovative responses to these new realities are addressed elsewhere in this Handbook. However, the salary program does have a role to play.

VARIANCES BY BUSINESS UNIT

With respect to variances by business unit, some key distinctions could make separate salary policy or action very appropriate. If the business units are operating in different sectors of the economy (e.g., retail and petroleum), a clear difference in competitive market rates and practices probably exists and must be addressed. Exhibit 8-13 reflects average compensation practices by various segments of the economy at two job levels in relation to an index of 100, which represents average all-industrial practice.

Obviously, broad differences exist. An organization operating in two diverse economic sectors simply must adjust its philosophy, strategy, and administration to address the realities of each marketplace. A total compensation, not just salary, analysis is very important here.

Geographic differences can also require varying pay practices even if the economic sector is the same between locations. This is particularly true for nonexempt personnel who will be recruited locally and are unlikely to transfer. Clearly identified geographic differences may, however, be best addressed by an area differential rather than by to-

Exhibit 8-13. Average compensation practices by various segments of the economy.

Sector	Professional/Technical	Middle Management
Banking	96	96
Insurance	92	94
Not-for-Profit	97	92
Blue Cross/Blue Shield	89	84
Consumer Products	100	107
Chemical/Pharmaceutical	103	107
High Technology	102	102
Metals/Mining	104	108
Heavy Manufacturing	97	99
Light Manufacturing	97	99
Petrochemical/Energy	119	120
Food/Tobacco	97	100
Paper Products	101	103
Transportation	103	103
Utilities	109	103
Telecommunications	115	119
Retail Sales	101	110

Compensation Averages vs. Index of 100

Note: For professional/technical, only base salary is used. For middle management, base salary plus 1990 annual incentive or bonus awards are used.
Source: 1990 Hay Compensation Survey.

tally different systems. If a special, clearly identified, "premium" is applied as opposed to just a different salary level, the premium can be most easily removed should an employee transfer from, say, the Los Angeles branch to corporate headquarters in Lawson, Missouri. In some cases, such area differentials are applied in decreasing stages and are related to housing costs when an employee is transferred to an area with an excessively high real estate market.

VARIANCES BY DEPARTMENTS OR WORK AREAS

When looking at departments or work areas, salary practices should vary to the extent market practices or, most particularly, incentive practices are significantly different from one to another. As the use of work force incentives expands, organizations are adopting multiple salary practices depending upon the type and intensity of incentive opportunity adopted by a department or area. Obviously, such a practice requires careful communication and reasonably equivalent chances of receiving incentive awards at all levels from one department or area to the next.

VARIANCES BY FUNCTIONAL AREAS

With respect to functional areas, it must be recognized that the real world doesn't value all skills equally, and the laws of supply and demand—not cost of living or need—govern the market rate of pay. At any given time some functional skills will be scarce, and unless a salary program is flexible enough to develop and use responsive premiums, any hope of achieving the attraction and retention objectives will be frustrated. Two basic methods are commonly used to provide such premiums.

1. A separate, higher salary range or grade is developed for all impacted positions, and normal salary administration guidelines are then applied.
2. Alternatively, regularly ranges or grades are used along with normal guidelines, and a separately developed and communicated "premium" is then simply added on top.

The latter method will highlight the distinction more dramatically, which could cause more internal problems, but would also be easier to change or discontinue as supply catches up to demand—and it will. For a multiple job function (e.g., data processing), it is critical to identify any supposed premium by various distinct jobs. This is true because as supply begins to catch up with demand it will catch up first at the entry level. This is reflected by the experience of most firms with respect to data processing premiums. In the late 1980s, 8–12 percent premiums for the entire function were common. Today, little or no premiums are being paid for entry level positions, only modest premiums for programmers, and significant premiums only at the systems design and senior manager level. One other key point should be made for functional pricing: Watch your survey use. Multiple surveys should be used rather than a single survey put out by the professional association of the function under consideration.

UNIQUE PACKAGES OF TOTAL COMPENSATION

Unique packages of total compensation, including special base salary treatment, are sometimes both necessary and desirable for individual employees who have particular value for an organization. Rigid adherence to any system or administrative guidelines at the cost of losing special talent or extinguishing the drive for creative value creation is patently absurd. Exceptions should of course be made with care, or all pretense of internal equity, accurate market pricing, predictability, cost control and the creation of a solid foundation of base salaries will be lost. A creative, motivating, and possibly open-end system of incentive compensation is often the best way to reward special talent and make the necessary exceptions to a reasonably consistent program of base salaries. However, should circumstances so dictate, the base salary of a "must have" individual must simply be whatever it takes if the basic objective of attract and retain is to be obtained.

In any program out-of-range situations are going to exist. These are the red circle and green circle people on a salary analysis, or scattergram, display. If a salary system using salary ranges or grades is to have meaning, the objective should be to pay all employees within the range or grade limits. Discussion follows of specific cases regarding to out-of-range situations.

1. The midpoint salaries are by definition the market value established by the organization for the job or skill level represented by the position. Therefore, most employees should be paid close to that level: That's what the jobs are worth and what the organization has decided it can afford to pay for them.

2. Paying employees below minimum, even if they are willing to join for such rates, basically says the organization has been something less than honest in communicating its ranges or grades and their use. The minimum is already only 80 percent of the midpoint, or market rate (85 percent for nonexempt, usually), and this spread has been communicated as "enough" to recognize differences in experience and performance. Therefore, employees under minimum should be brought up to minimum as quickly as possible and certainly within a year or two. If this minimum is proved to be well over what is needed in the marketplace to attract and even retain needed talent, then the midpoints are probably too high and the entire range or grade structure should be lowered.

3. A below minimum "hiring rate" approach is used by some organizations, especially for high turnover, high population, functions. Under this approach the salary sequence is typically handled along these lines:
- Initial salary levels are set at a special "hiring rate" that is below range or grade minimum. About 70 percent of midpoint is typical.
- Then, carefully documented progress reviews are held on a set schedule for every new hire with increases, if earned, every three months or so to bring the individual's salary up to midpoint in three or four steps during the first year of employment.
- This approach has three advantages, assuming the hiring rate is sufficient to attract employees in the first place.
  (a) It lowers the salary cost for a new, unknown quantity.
  (b) It forces close monitoring of new hires and recognizes or denies progress in a very meaningful way.
  (c) It does take a successful new hire into the range or grade after a year or less, preserving the validity of the organization's communicated pay philosophy.

4. An above maximum situation is a more difficult problem. Two reasons are usually responsible for above maximum salaries.
- One possibility is the proven existence of special, unique talent that has a market value to the organization in excess of established norms.
- The second, more frequently experienced, possibility is the existence of an employee who has been demoted to a lower rated or ranked position or who holds a job that, for whatever reason, is no longer of as much value to the organization as it once was.

In the first situation, no action is warranted other than frequent monitoring to ensure that the identified premium is still valid. If it is, continue salary increases and/or develop appropriate incentive programs to pay whatever it takes to retain and motivate this unique talent.

In the second instance, two possible actions are indicated. If there is serious nonperformance or a clear indication that no further need exists for this employee or position, some form of termination or reassignment at a lower or frozen salary level is probably indicated. If, however, the situation is unrelated to personal performance, most organizations would not cut pay. Typical action would be clear communication of the situation to the employee, and then a diminution of increases and/or a prolongation of time periods for subsequent salary adjustments. As salary ranges or grades are normally increased annually, such salary action will eventually bring the individual's salary back to the range or grade maximum. Since the maximum is, by definition, 120 percent (or 115 percent for nonexempt) above the market rate (midpoint) for the job, the lower/prolonged salary increase strategy may well need to be continued beyond the point when the maximum is reached.

Special Issues in Salary Policy and Administration

As a conclusion to this discussion of base salary programs and their administration, a few special issues should be addressed.

Salary Surveys

Salary surveys come in many forms, and careful use is critical. First, a selection must be made from among a multitude of available surveys. Because surveys are the universally accepted means of determining and communicating market rates, your surveys must be carefully selected and consistently used. Too many surveys can be confusing, but using a single survey can be misleading. Most organizations use the following approach:

1. A single survey is used consistently every year to establish the norm or annual standard. Such a survey should be demonstrated to be one where all of the following is true;
   - Clear, solid job matches exist for your key and/or high population positions.
   - Your market, whether defined by industry, location, size, or talent needs, is represented by data collected and displayed.
   - The methodology of displaying data is well understood and accepted by your organization, so that as new jobs are created they can be slotted and compared to survey data.
   - The market rates reflected by the survey have been demonstrated to reflect your actual experience with respect to attraction and retention.
   - The data displayed captures all needed information (such as salaries and incentive or other compensation data deemed necessary) and is expected to do so for many years to come.

   The "single survey" may well be different for different segments of an organization's work force, but such a primary source is highly desirable for all groups.
2. Perhaps three or four other surveys are then used to check the primary source each year. These are frequently "specialty surveys" related to special markets,

specific areas, or certain aspects of total compensation not covered by the primary source. (For instance, a benefits survey may be used to augment the cash compensation reflected by the primary survey.)

3. For specific functional areas, special surveys are also commonly used when the potential need for functional pricing appears to exist. Examples are data processing, engineering, investment jobs, actuaries, and sales positions.

Establishing your own club survey may be desirable, but care is needed here as well. If competing organizations exchange raw data on compensation, they can be in violation of antitrust legislation. Therefore, an independent third party is needed to collect the raw data and then feed back practices in terms of quartiles or similar statistical rankings not identified by individual firms. The club can, and should, set the parameters of the ultimate display, agree on the positions to be surveyed, and establish the position descriptions or other framework needed to assure valid comparisons, but they can't exchange raw data.

You must be able to interpret and explain survey data. As most surveys display data in terms of percentile lines to reflect competitive practice, a brief definition of the meaning of percentile line labels may be helpful.

- *P90 (or the ninetieth percentile)* means the level where 90 percent of the positions or individuals are paid less than this point and only 10 percent are paid more.
- *P75 (or third quartile, or the seventy-fifth percentile)* means the level where 75 percent of the positions or individuals are paid less than this point and only 25 percent are paid more.
- *P50 (or median)* means the rate that divides rankings of pay for positions or individuals exactly in half—half above and half below.
- *Average (or mean)* means the average pay practice for the positions or individuals surveyed. A clear indication of the spread of practices encompassed by the survey can be quickly obtained by comparing the median and average figures. If they are close, the spread is reasonably narrow, with few "high flyers" or "very low payers." If they are widely different (e.g., 20 percent or more), it is a clear indication that a broad range of varied pay practices exists, probably involving some significant highs and lows. This may mean that the job match or description being used is not very good. It may also mean that unique skills are involved and/or some functional pricing exists or is beginning to surface.
- *P25 (or first quartile, or the twenty-fifth percentile)* means the level where 25 percent of the positions or individuals are paid less than this point and 75 percent are paid more.
- *P10 (or the tenth percentile)* means the level where 10 percent of the positions or individuals are paid less than this point and 90 percent are paid more.

Setting salary levels against a survey is a critical and usually annual challenge. The single overriding fact to keep in mind is that there is no right place to be against a survey. Key questions are:

- *What can you afford?* Being super-competitive, attracting and retaining anyone you want, and going bankrupt is not very appealing to anyone.

• *What do you need to pay?* Attraction and retention problems and realities will guide you here, but it is also true that subaverage pay will, over time, attract subaverage talent, absent some overwhelming differences in less critical areas. It may be necessary to pay more or differently in the future to attract a better or different type and level of talent than you now have. Attracting and retaining the wrong level or kind of talent is of little value.

• *How are you paying?* Setting salaries solely on the basis of other organizations' salary practices is frankly stupid. This is especially true for officer-level personnel where incentive compensation, in both annual and long-term forms, is common practice and often produces far more significant dollar opportunities than salaries alone. As incentive use spreads downward in most organizations, salary policy and pricing decisions will be more and more determined by total cash (salary plus incentive) practices and opportunities. (See Chapter 9.)

Collective Bargaining Situations

Wages in collective bargaining situations are beyond the scope of this chapter with respect to actual bargaining strategy and the complex body of labor law and regulation that governs such action. One aspect of collective bargaining is important relative to salary programs, especially for nonexempt personnel and first-line supervision. This issue is compression. At some point, negotiated wage rates and job sizes will meld into and probably overlap practices for nonunionized personnel. In addition, front-line supervisors will be in constant contact with such wage earners, and, moreover, the source of many such front-line supervisors will be the pool of wage-earning employees. Therefore, hourly wages paid in the bargaining unit will clearly influence salary policy. A promotion to supervision needs to carry with it an increase in earnings even if this requires some special "supervisor differential" (e.g., 10–15 percent) not otherwise available under the range or grade structure adopted. This extra pay will then impact the salaries of the next higher-rated job, and the next if promotion opportunities are to be valid in terms of pay opportunity. Typical practice is to decrease slowly, or feather out, this differential as salary levels increase, so the full amount is not simply carried throughout the system. In addition, incentive opportunities can be added, either from the initial point or higher up the job rating scale, to offset or decrease the base salary differential.

Final Thoughts

Compensation is the single most important bullet in an organization's arsenal of attraction and retention ammunition. A good base salary program is the basic ingredient in this compensation equation, and a good program should have all of these characteristics:

• It should be rational in terms of business strategy, affordability, and human resources needs.
• It should be understood by employees and ideally perceived by all personnel as rational, internally equitable, externally competitive, and consistently administered.

- It should be established within the carefully conceived context of a total remuneration strategy and policy that addresses these fundamental questions:
—What are you trying to do?
—What type and level of personnel will your total program attract and retain?
- It should be sufficiently structured to permit constant and consistent administration, pricing, and communication on an ongoing basis.
- It should be infinitely flexible to permit those special actions needed to address special situations, but clear identification and justification of special actions is needed to avoid upgrading an entire program (and its costs) in response to a unique situation or a temporary functional pricing problem.
- It should feel good when you're done. Simple, visceral reactions are often as valid as an infinite amount of statistical analysis. If it doesn't feel good, it probably isn't.
- If it is working, you should be able to attract and retain the level and type of personnel you need. Probably in conjunction with one or more incentive plans, you should also be able to motivate, recognize, and reward those innovative actions that enhance the levels of productivity and quality critical for survival in an increasingly competitive and global marketplace.

As you can see, fair and competitive compensation is one of the most important elements in long-term retention of employees.

9

Executive and Alternative Compensation

Robert C. Ochsner
Director of Compensation
Hay Management Consultants
and Steven E. Gross
Managing Director
Workforce Variable Compensation Practice
Hay Management Consultants

Chapter 8 covered basic salary compensation. However, there are a number of kinds of compensation beyond salary, and they are discussed in this chapter. Since they were applied first to executives, they have generally been known as "executive compensation." In the 1980s, nonsalary compensation began to be offered fairly widely to non-executives as well. Terms like "alternative" and "nontraditional" compensation are applied to many of these offerings. Three points will help set the stage for our discussion of rewarding employees with a compensation package, rather than by fixed salary only:

1. It is more difficult to measure external market competitiveness of packages than it is to measure fixed salaries, for the following reasons: Every package is different; data are much harder to acquire and handle; and variable compensation plan values are imprecise because they must be estimated.

2. The process of packaging compensation creates the art of compensation architecture. Designing a package mix that is most appropriate for the strategy and culture of an organization is an extremely complex process and uses knowledge and process skills that are not needed in regular salary administration.

3. The purpose behind packaging nonsalary compensation with salary is to provide pay for performance. Thus, package design must address fundamental questions of fairness—specific to each organization—between employees (executives or not) and shareholders (or other stakeholders). As a result, there are no standard packages, and line management is much more involved with executive and alternative compensation than it is with regular salary and benefits.

Executive Compensation

The years since World War II were an era when U.S. business prospered, then had to adapt to being just one of several major players in an increasingly interrelated global economy. Executive compensation emerged as a fact of U.S. business life over that same period. Recently, it has become a frequent cause of criticism and discontent. Executive compensation has become very complex, and executive pay has grown so fast that we often feel it is out of control. Fascination with the amounts top executives make has turned the subject into grist for the mills of newsmagazines and newspapers. Most of these discussions create the impression that executive compensation is badly flawed; in fact, some of the discussions work very hard at creating that impression.

Executives still have to be paid—and, more than ever, management and boards of directors need guidance in how pay can attract, retain, and motivate capable executives. This section of this chapter does not ignore the criticisms, and it is not an apology for weak management. It is intended to be a practical and factual primer on this important subject.

Purposes of Executive Compensation

There are many legitimate purposes for an organization's executive compensation program. Fundamentally, three purposes are common to almost all programs:

1. They provide an appropriate mix of pay, including performance incentives for maximizing shareholder values.
2. Pay is competitive with opportunities outside the organization and equitable for management responsibilities inside the organization.
3. Having a specific program for executives convinces them that they are needed and valued.

The last factor is never cited as a purpose, but nearly every organization treats executives differently. This must mean that some degree of special executive treatment has become a corporate value out of competitive necessity.

Some programs have purposes that are inconsistent. This can arise from the built-in conflict between the need for retention and motivation in every compensation program, or it can result from a real-world conflict between the short- and long-term goals of the organization. In either case, what is needed is balance, with any tilt dictated by long-term strategy.

Purposes are sometimes found that are counterproductive or simply unworkable. A favorite is paying high—or with insufficient performance leverage—across the board to offset an undesirable organization environment. While this is legal, it is very expensive and undermines the performance-based management style that is needed to succeed today.

Much of the mystique associated with executive compensation in the United States comes from its technical complexity, most of which is real (although tax simplification and other changes tend to reduce the complexity somewhat). The multiyear nature of incentive and retirement contracts, the presence of securities law issues (which most corporate managers do not confront otherwise), and the differing accounting and tax treatment of deferred compensation still add up to an irreducible core of complexity.

Our discussion of executive compensation focuses on business realities and does not attempt to deal with technical issues, which can easily fill a whole book by themselves. This is consistent with today's environment, where economic issues of value largely eclipse procedural and technical ones. We concentrate on what managers need to know to develop objectives for their compensation programs and to design strategies to achieve those objectives. It should be remembered, however, that the actual implementation of executive compensation plans requires proper attention to detail and competent professional help to avoid serious problems.

Components and Elements

Executive compensation can be divided into five areas, or elements. These elements represent the major functions of an executive compensation program: salary, annual incentive or bonus, long-term incentive, benefits, and perquisites. No organization actually has all of these plans, with most having less than half. Some components are present in only a small percent of organizations. Exhibit 9-1 indicates the prevalence of these plans among groups of executives.

Salary

The material on basic compensation in Chapter 8 is equally applicable to executive salaries, but there are several important additions and amplifications. It is more common to survey executive salaries by specific job match or even title. This is most pronounced for corporate positions that have a single incumbent and are common to many organizations. The chief executive officer, chief operating officer, heads of functions like finance, human resources, and law, and their direct reports fall into this category.

Surveys by job title usually incorporate a size dimension, having the effect of ranking the organizations surveyed in terms of their scope. It is therefore assumed that the larger the organization is, the larger a given position in its top management will be. This is generally accepted, although the relationship is more logarithmic than linear. Common measures of size are revenues, assets, and numbers of employees. They best fit the industrial, financial, and services sectors, respectively. For cross-sectoral surveys, a "market basket" of several measures may be needed. If data on the desired positions

Exhibit 9-1. Prevalence of executive compensation plans.

Executive Group	Base Salary	Annual Bonus	Projected Present Value of Long-Term Award	Benefits	Perquisites	Average Total $000/Year
CEO	35%	22%	29%	12%	2%	$1,483.1
COO	36%	21%	27%	14%	2%	882.4
CFO	38%	18%	28%	15%	2%	574.7
Senior Executives	37%	19%	26%	16%	2%	586.8
Line Executives	41%	18%	21%	17%	3%	386.8
Staff Executives	41%	17%	21%	18%	3%	366.2

Source: Hay Management Consultants, Executive Compensation Report—Industrial Management, 1990.

are available for a reasonable number of similar companies of comparable size (i.e., within 50 percent above or below), it may be possible to eliminate the size dimension from the explicit comparisons. As with any compensation survey, while convenience samples are the norm, it is necessary to guard against bias in selecting the sample.

Most but by no means all companies use salary ranges for executive positions if they use them for other managers. There is frequently more latitude, however, in the executive ranges. The range may be wider (75 percent or 100 percent instead of 50 percent), or there may be a midpoint but no explicit boundaries. Several positions that share a common title (executive vice-president, senior vice-president, vice-president) but are not closely equal may be combined in a double- or triplewide range to promote teamwork, or even to create a horse race for succession.

Year-to-year administration of executive salaries differs from that of other managers. Prior to the 1970s, executive salaries were not reviewed every year. In the inflationary 1970s, annual reviews became the norm, and they still are. However, full external surveys are not always done every year, so interim increases may reflect general pay market movement rather than specific industry or position data. Executive jobs may be grouped for increase purposes (for instance, all vice-presidents get 6 percent except Ralph, who is in trouble). Many companies have a common increase date for executives even though other increases are spread over the year and may involve variable timing. Position in range gets less weight with executives than with other managers, especially when the incumbent is high in the range and no promotion is available. In general, companies apply salary freezes and reductions to executives in a manner comparable to other managerial employees.

It should be apparent that executive salaries are more flexible and individualized, less governed by rules and formulas, and administered with more care than those of other managers. While this is a generalization, it reflects the purpose of an executive compensation program cited above: to tell executives that they are needed and valued. As we go through the other elements of executive compensation, this will be even more apparent.

Having said all this about executive salaries, it probably appears that they are administered in a vacuum. Nothing could be further from the truth. The real marketplace for executive pay is based on the combination of salary and annual incentive, or bonus. Almost every survey covers this combination (usually labeled total cash, or something similar) as well as salary. An important source of market information, the compensation tables of proxy statements, is not required to separate salary and bonus, and most reporting companies do not show them separately. As a result, the annual media blitz on executive pay tends to report as "salary" the combination of salary and bonus. Since the highest and most-publicized figures are caused by above-average bonuses, the public's perception of executive compensation is tainted in the process.

Annual Incentive

Three major aspects of today's annual incentive plans deserve coverage in a general business discussion like this:

1. Design (structure, eligibility, and terms)
2. Size of awards
3. Survey issues

INCENTIVE PLAN DESIGN

Incentive plan designs come from four different heritages. Most plans contain a mixture of principles from several of these heritages. Blending them into a single plan takes thought, because they are somewhat contradictory.

The oldest heritage is the true bonus plan. (The word *bonus* is often used for any incentive or contingent payment.) Awards, and sometimes even eligibility to receive an award, are determined after the fact, based on superiors' evaluation of the degree of deservedness and the organization's ability to pay. Essentially, awards are discretionary and will probably be viewed as subjective. This can work fairly well in smaller, owner-managed companies, but effectiveness declines as size increases and ownership is more distant. From an executive viewpoint, the perceived risk of true bonus plans is high, and therefore potential awards must be larger to compete in the pay marketplace. Given the company's greater discretion under these plans, however, it well may be willing to pay more when circumstances warrant.

True executive bonus plans are relatively uncommon today, except in smaller companies. (In any company where major stockholders are also executives, this kind of plan can lead to disguised dividend problems with the IRS.) The main reasons for their decline were: (1) desire on the part of executives and boards to set up formulas and rules, and (2) development of behavioral theory in the 1950s and 1960s stating that incentives alter executive behavior and produce improved results only if the results and rewards are spelled out in advance.

And so organizations began to marry financial rewards to organization performance, with behavior as a sort of catalyst. There have been millions of incentive plans designed to do this, but there are only three main types: pools, budget-based, and MBO-driven (in increasing order of complexity).

Pool plans are designed to share some percentage of financial results among the management group. The most common type is a profit-sharing pool (e.g., the pool receives 5 percent of each year's pretax profit). Where capital is a material factor, this is usually modified to provide some minimum return on capital that is not shared (e.g., 5 percent of pretax profit in excess of 6 percent of average capital). The pool is split among participants in some established manner; it generally is more than proportionate to salaries, with higher-paid executives receiving greater percentages of salary. Pools can continue from year to year with little modification. They are relatively simple and really represent a formalization of the way most owners approach the design of a true bonus. In the postwar United States, industrial companies began to establish formal executive incentives, and most of them were of this type.

Certain problems tend to arise with pool plans. They are insensitive to short-term conditions and even to the current business plan. They are linked to behaviors only through the organizationwide bottom line, which is relatively distant to most staff executives, as well as to many line executives. They can become a comfortable entitlement, and the participants resist change. They may provide an incentive not to invest in the future of the company.

Companies began to experiment to find ways to correct these problems. Some pools were divisionalized, to bring the formula closer to participating executives' responsibilities. The biggest change was development of budget-based incentives. Their formula changes each year, using the budget or business plan as a target. Awards are thought of

Exhibit 9-2. Budget-based incentive.

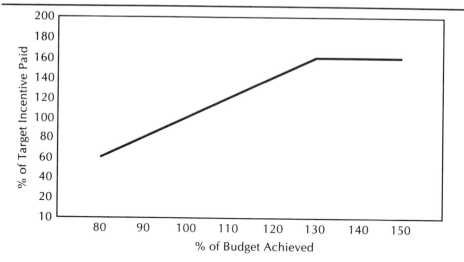

as a percentage of a target amount. The percentage of the target amount the participant actually receives depends on the percentage of the business target that is achieved (see Exhibit 9-2).

Budget-based incentives have remained popular. Most of them now include components for both company and division goals. There is a built-in problem of tying compensation directly to business plans, since it leads to "sandbagging" plans. In this instance "sandbagging" relates to the possibility that a CEO might establish a business plan that he could easily attain in order to get a large raise or bonus. The best way to avoid this is to create a two-step process. First, a business plan is developed and approved, and then the incentive targets are finalized. They may be the same as the numbers in the plan, but they can be higher or lower to recognize that the plan is relatively easy or relatively ambitious, respectively.

The 1970s saw the development of management-by-objectives (MBO) incentives, coinciding with the growth of MBO systems. In practice, this usually meant that specific (often nonfinancial) goals were introduced as a component, or as a multiplier, in budget-based incentive plans. This met two real needs: The resulting plan fit staff jobs much better, and it allowed companies to introduce strategic milestones, to balance the emphasis on short-term results that is found in budgets.

MBO incentives take many shapes: Since conceptually they can include corporate, unit, and individual goals and measures, there is opportunity for a great deal of complexity. Exhibit 9-3 shows a sample of an MBO plan. Although the opportunity to tailor a different plan for each participant each year is inviting, it must be balanced against the time needed to do it and the difficulty of correctly selecting so many goals and measures, for without them an MBO plan breeds disunity and charges of favoritism. Unless the MBO plan is clearly advantageous—or management wants to change to a

Exhibit 9-3. Sample MBO plan.

INCENTIVE PLAN
Fiscal 1993
Award Calculation Matrix

				Division:	Specialty Chemicals
				Incumbent:	Steve Green
				Position:	VP Marketing
				Base Salary:	$118,000
				Target Inc:	35.0%

Component	% Weight	Threshold	Competent	Target	Outstanding	Maximum
Division Profit Contribution (millions)	25	64 6,195	72 8,260	80 10,325	88 11,358	96 12,390
Sales Volumes (millions)	40	750 9,912	800 13,216	850 16,520	900 18,172	950 19,824
Percent of Sales in High-Value Products	25	35 6,195	37.5 8,260	40 10,325	42.5 11,358	45 12,390
Personal Development (as evaluated by president)	10	2,478	3,304	4,130	4,542	4,956
TOTAL INCENTIVE	100	24,780	33,040	41,300	45,430	49,560

Signature _____

Date _____

more positive and energetic culture to renew the business—a simpler level of incentives may be a better starting point.

SIZE OF AWARDS

The size of annual incentives is rarely designed or surveyed in absolute dollar terms. Most designs focus on the incentive as a percentage of the executive's annual salary. These percentages are usually under 100, but they have grown substantially since 1970 and may compare favorably with a year's salary. Most executive incentive plans use the concepts of minimum, target, and maximum levels (again, expressed as a percentage of the participant's salary) or at least have two of the three concepts. It is also normal for these percentages to increase with job level. Exhibit 9-4 illustrates this, showing 1990 levels for these percentages, across a range of typical executive jobs.

The other reality about annual incentives is that they are more often surveyed as part of total annual cash compensation than alone. An executive's incentive can be evaluated only in combination with salary; it does not have much significance by itself.

SURVEY ISSUES

Annual incentive surveys, therefore, are part of executive total cash surveys. While attention is paid to prevailing salary levels by themselves (although incentive levels alone do not draw comparable interest), there are almost no pay surveys today of executive jobs that do not include both. A major problem with surveys is their focus on the quantitative (how much?) and their lack of information about the qualitative (what are the terms and conditions?).

Thus, it is relatively easy to determine the distribution of incentives last year in a group of comparable companies, often down to individual positions. At the same time, it is extremely difficult to determine what was done to earn them, how much the payouts would have differed if company results had been higher or lower, whether the payments are made in cash, deferred, or otherwise contingent, and a multitude of similar questions.

We can see that not only design but even surveying of executive compensation needs art as well as science. Once annual incentive is packaged with salary, complexities and subtleties affect all related activities. These same things that give executive compensation its elusive quality and its resulting power refuse to let us deal with it in a narrow or mechanical way.

There are a few characteristic problems for the manager in interpreting surveys of executive total cash. First, the sample of companies can easily be biased or simply too small to be statistically significant. Be particularly wary of sample sizes under fifteen or twenty companies. Also, make sure that the companies either are truly comparable in size and complexity or else that the results are portrayed or adjusted to put the relationships in perspective. The range of executive total cash, like many other real-world distributions, has a "long right tail." As a result, the average may considerably exceed the median. In this environment, it is easy to select survey companies so as to increase subtly the apparent "market" by as much as 25 percent above the median (or statistical midpoint) of the broad market. Another survey issue is the matching of individual positions across companies. There is considerable variation in the degree of responsibility and authority that attach to a given title, as a result of the differing patterns of organization and ownership that different companies have. For example, although the CEO position is closely comparable in most companies, where it is the fountainhead of power, it is less authoritative (by up to about 25 percent) in certain circumstances, which seem to be more common than they used to be:

- When there is an active, separate chairman of the board
- When there is significant institutional ownership

Exhibit 9-4.   Characteristics of annual incentives for executives, 1990.

Position	Sales Exceeding $1.5 Billion				Sales Less Than $1.5 Billion			
	Percent Eligible	Median Target Incentive (% of Base Salary)	Percent Receiving Incentive	Median Actual Incentive (% of Base Salary)	Percent Eligible	Median Target Incentive (% of Base Salary)	Percent Receiving Incentive	Median Actual Incentive (% of Base Salary)
Chief Executive Officer	90%	57%	95%	62%	90%	46%	79%	41%
Chief Operating Officer	90%	54%	96%	56%	90%	39%	78%	40%
Chief Administrative Officer	88%	38%	95%	41%	92%	30%	84%	28%
Chief Financial Officer	93%	41%	98%	44%	89%	30%	79%	31%
Head of Finance (Treasurer)	87%	35%	94%	38%	89%	21%	85%	21%
Head of Accounting (Controller)	90%	35%	95%	34%	88%	21%	84%	22%
Head of Tax	91%	30%	94%	29%	92%	20%	93%	15%
Head of Internal Audit	86%	26%	88%	29%	92%	17%	85%	19%
Head of Information Systems and Data Processing	87%	29%	92%	28%	85%	20%	87%	19%
Head of Engineering	83%	29%	97%	33%	79%	20%	86%	21%
Head of Law	93%	39%	96%	40%	87%	31%	84%	31%
Head of Human Resources	91%	37%	97%	36%	86%	26%	80%	26%
Head of External Relations	85%	35%	96%	33%	70%	17%	89%	29%
Head of Research and Development	93%	38%	93%	39%	98%	27%	77%	22%
Head of Corporate Planning	93%	35%	98%	34%	89%	30%	91%	20%
Head of Operations	93%	35%	95%	42%	89%	30%	81%	33%
Head of Marketing and/or Sales	91%	37%	94%	35%	90%	25%	82%	25%
Group, Subsidiary, Division Positions	*Sales Exceeding $500 Million*				*Sales Less Than $500 Million*			
Group Head	100%	51%	100%	65%	96%	39%	82%	38%
Subsidiary Head	90%	37%	98%	43%	91%	32%	93%	34%
	Sales Exceeding $150 Million				*Sales Less Than $150 Million*			
Division General Manager	95%	38%	93%	40%	89%	30%	84%	31%
Operating Unit Head	95%	40%	94%	44%	91%	30%	82%	31%

Source: Hay Management Consultants, Executive Compensation Report—Industrial Management, 1990.

- When a family ownership exercises effective control
- When the company is a wholly- or majority-owned subsidiary

In short, the comparative size of the CEO position is affected by relationships above it. On the other hand, positions below the CEO are affected most by the way the company is organized internally. For example, the controller position will vary depending on whether it is responsible for the management information system and internal audit, as well as whether it has solid or dotted-line reporting relationships to the business unit controllers. Similarly, some heads of sales have responsibility for some or all of the classic marketing function, while in other companies marketing incorporates some sales functions, such as sales forecasting. Examples like this can be given for every executive position.

There are two points that are important to emphasize about executive surveying. First, the size of an executive job is not a "numbers game" driven by factors like the number of employees reporting to the position or the sales volume produced below it. The kinds of things those employees do, the skills needed to coordinate their efforts, and the complexity of designing, making, and selling the products and services that the sales dollars represent are the things that make an executive job. An executive pay survey can be termed a "market comparison" only if it matches jobs that are similar in these respects.

Second, all surveys provide data. If they are thoughtfully done, they provide more than data: They provide information for decision support. But they cannot provide the decisions themselves. Only management, acting with the board of directors, can decide what forms and levels of executive pay are right. They have the right—directors even have the duty—to be informed before deciding. Information may make the decision process easier and make it easier to reach consensus, but it cannot transfer responsibility away from officers and directors. For every company that has tried to ignore the market because it is "different," there is one that has tried to abdicate responsibility for executives' pay by blindly following reported market levels. Neither approach is legally proper, and neither will provide the desired attraction, motivation, and retention.

Long-Term Incentive

The third element of executive compensation is a family of plans that are grouped as long-term incentive (LTI). They have in common a long-term (i.e., multiyear) focus and the presence of some degree of contingency that is aimed at providing incentive. Exhibit 9-5 summarizes the main types of LTI, along with a brief description of each one. There are myriad variations and combinations of these, and there is no standardized terminology, which can easily result in confusion. Some companies adopt plans with labels that are quite misleading, in an apparent effort to make the plan seem more mainstream than it really is. Most medium and large companies today offer several kinds of LTI. There is a trend to "omnibus" LTI plans, in which as many as eight or ten types of grants are authorized, and discretion as to their use is left to the board compensation committee, composed of outside directors.

Many types of LTI involve the company's securities or options on them. It is important to remember that both federal and state securities laws apply to them. Although certain exemptions are applied to executive transactions, there are also additional executive pitfalls, such as Sections 10 (insider trading) and 16 (short-swing transactions)

(text continued on page 190)

Exhibit 9-5. Summary of main types of long-term incentive plans.

Stock Option Plans

Plans in which awards offer the right to purchase a specified number of shares of the corporation's stock at a specified price during a specified period of time. Generally, the plans are either "tax-qualified" (ISO) or "nonqualified" (NQSO) and often include alternate rights or are offered in tandem with other incentive opportunities.

1. Incentive Stock Options (ISO)

    Briefly, an incentive stock option that qualifies for favorable tax treatment under Section 422A of the Internal Revenue Code. Some of the major requirements of this section are:

    ☐ Option term cannot exceed ten years
    ☐ Option price must be at least 100 percent of fair market value at time of grant
    ☐ Plan with specified requirements must be approved by shareholders
    ☐ Vesting is limited to $100,000 aggregate fair market value during any calendar year

2. Nonqualified Stock Options (NQSO)

    Sometimes referred to as "nonstatutory stock options," a nonqualified option is an option that does not meet all the requirements of Section 422A of the Internal Revenue Code for incentive options. Nonqualified options usually have a ten-year option term and are usually priced at 100 percent of market value at time of grant.

3. Stock Appreciation Rights (SAR)

    A stock appreciation right (SAR) may provide an executive with an election (generally subject to the approval of the administrative committee) to receive an amount of cash or stock equal to the difference between current market value of company stock and the option price in lieu of exercising an underlying stock option. This allows the executive to receive an amount equal to the appreciation in the stock's value without raising the money that would be needed to exercise the stock option.

Performance Share/Performance Unit Plan

1. Performance Share Plan (PSP)

    A performance share plan is a phantom stock asset plan that contingently grants stock units to an executive. These grants entitle him/her to actual shares of stock or their cash equivalent at time of payment (e.g., unit value may appreciate or decline between the initial award and the payment date) if predetermined objectives are achieved. The number of units that become payable, if any, depends on the extent to which the objectives are achieved.

Performance share plans generally start with a basic award stated in artificial shares, but payment is contingent upon the achievement of a predetermined performance objective during the award period. If the performance objectives are achieved, the award will be payable in full in shares of company stock equal to the number of artifical shares initially awarded or in their cash equivalency at the time of payment. The plan may provide for payment of half the number of artificial shares awarded or some other percentage of payment if performance falls short of the objectives required for full payment but does, nevertheless, meet lesser objectives.

2. Performance Unit Plan (PUP)

A performance unit plan is a phantom asset plan that contingently grants units to an executive that entitle him/her to cash payments or their equivalent in stock value at the time of the award (unit value remains constant) if predetermined objectives are achieved. A performance unit plan is similar in most respects to a performance share plan except that the value the executive receives relates to the value placed upon a share or unit at the time of grant; the value of the original units does not appreciate or decline.

Restricted Stock Plan

A plan in which awards are made in the form of shares of company stock. Actual shares of stock are currently transferred to the employee but carry restrictions such as prohibitions against disposition or rights of first refusal, and may be subject to substantial risk of forfeiture; e.g., termination of employment. Examples are restricted stock, letter stock, and Section 83 stock.

Miscellaneous Stock Equivalent Plans

1. Book Value/Asset Appreciation Plan

A book value asset plan is the same as a performance share plan except that the value of stock units is determined according to nonmarket measurements such as book value of stock. A book value appreciation plan is similar in all respects to a phantom stock option plan except that the payout value is determined according to book value of company stock or some other nonmarket evaluation.

2. Phantom Stock Plan

A phantom stock option is a phantom stock appreciation plan that grants a number of units to an executive. Each option creates rights to a payment equal to any appreciation that occurs in the market value of a share of company stock between the date of grant and some future date. It is often accompanied by dividend equivalent payments. It differs from other stock incentive plans in that no stock is actually transferred to a participating executive.

(continued)

Exhibit 9-5. *Continued.*

   3. Dividend Equivalent Plan

     A dividend equivalent plan is a phantom stock income plan that grants a number of units to an executive, each of which creates rights to a payment equal to any dividends paid on a share of the company's stock. Dividend equivalent plans are similar in format to phantom stock option plans, except that payment is limited to dividend equivalents and does not include any appreciation, as do phantom stock option plans. In most instances, dividend equivalent payments will be connected with another long-term plan.

---

of the Internal Revenue Code, which must be carefully observed, as well as special reporting requirements. The accounting and tax treatments of an LTI plan are almost always different, and neither seems logical to nonspecialists.

Design of these plans takes into account factors not found in other areas of pay, such as earnings dilution and potential effects on percentages of ownership. For example, a 51 percent or 81 percent majority owner can be expected to oppose an LTI stock plan because it could reduce ownership below the voting control or tax consolidation threshold, respectively. Non-U.S. owners frequently opposed any LTI plan because these plans are uncommon in their home country, and superiors of the U.S. executives do not receive them.

Eligibility for an LTI is usually more restrictive than for annual incentive. Rules of thumb include: the top two or three levels of management, executives with base salaries over $90,000 per year, those with annual incentive targets above 25 percent of base, and so on. The number of executives in the plan tends to be larger for stock option plans (which usually do not involve compensation expense from an accounting viewpoint) than for other types of plans. As a practical matter, executives must be able to meet current expenses comfortably out of current income before being asked to take part of their compensation in the form of LTI, which is deferred for a number of years and inherently riskier than current cash.

Developing standards and targets for the size of LTI awards is easily the most difficult task discussed in this chapter. There are a number of reasons for this.

   • LTI can be measured either at the time of grant or at the time of payout, but neither is really accurate. Value at grant is simply an educated guess about the net present value of a deferred, contingent promise. Value at payout is mathematically precise but fails to capture the value of awards that are forfeited before they vest, and it is subject to "heaping" of payouts in high years of business and stock market cycles.

   • Data on competitive practices are especially difficult to obtain and to interpret, and the amounts of both awards and payouts fluctuate wildly from year to year. It can be hard to gain a picture of a "market level" in the same way that is done for salary and annual incentives.

   • Types of plans and even conditions of awards within a type vary so much that they are difficult to compare. While they can all be reduced to common scales of economic (dollar) value, they have very different time frames, risk levels, and effects on executive motivation and retention.

In addition, the size of LTI awards must be evaluated two ways: as individual awards, and in the aggregate as a transfer of a percentage of the value of the company from shareholders to management. As individual awards, criteria of appropriateness include in the short term the relation of LTI to current cash compensation. It is typical today to have LTI awards whose value is the annual equivalent of 40–60 percent of annual cash for a CEO, ranging downward to 10 or 20 percent of annual cash for the lowest-ranking participants. In the longer term, it is common to have a target for the cumulative value of LTI, expressed as a multiple of annual cash (for example, ten to twenty times for the CEO, three to five times for the lowest rank) or as a percentage of net worth (e.g., 30–40 percent of net worth for the CEO, 10–20 percent for the lowest rank). Parenthetically, it is important to correlate these longer-term LTI targets with retirement plan targets. If the company targets ten to twenty years' pay in LTI for the CEO, it should probably not also provide a supplemental executive retirement plan (SERP) to guarantee a total lifetime pension of 70 percent of final average annual cash compensation, a value equal to another eight to ten years' pay.

The timing of plan cycles and the measures of performance used in the LTI plan must be considered in conjunction with the terms of any annual incentive offered to the LTI participants. Not that it is wrong for them to be different—a more common problem is that they are too much alike. A favorite LTI plan is "performance units" or "performance shares" payable on three-year measurement cycles, with a new cycle starting each year. The measure of performance is often an increase in EPS or return on equity, which can even be self-calibrating (e.g., based on the prior three years' actual result), whether or not the company is returning its cost of capital. To participants, this plan, with an annual payout and the "cushioned ride" of generally makable goals, feels too much like an annual plan. It is just a short step from becoming another entitlement for occupants of the executive suite.

Benefits

With rare exceptions, generally when an executive does not want a given benefit and has bargained for something else instead, executives receive all the benefits the company provides for other salaried employees. The role of executive compensation in benefits, therefore, is to deal with two areas of supplemental benefits.

1. Restoration of benefits above any maximums in the regular plans.
2. Providing additional types of benefits not enjoyed by other, nonexecutive employees.

Maximums may result from: (1) limitations imposed by law, as in pension and 401(k) savings plans; (2) limitations imposed by insurers, as in group life and disability plans; or (3) limitations imposed by company policy, as in major medical and vacation plans. Restorations of the first two kinds are usually explained as a matter of "equity," although the restoration often does not extend to affected employees who are not in the executive group. Restoring limitations of the third kind really amounts to creating more benefits.

The most common type of executive benefit is the supplemental executive retirement plan. Since the Employee Retirement Income Security Act (ERISA) introduced limitations on the amount of benefits that can be paid from a qualified retirement plan, SERPs have been used to circumvent the limitation by paying the difference directly from the company. Often, separate "funding" arrangements are made. Since they cannot increase executive security very much and frequently provide less investment return than just leaving the money in the company, they do provide a good living for the agents and brokers who specialize in designing them. Another tendency of SERPs is to increase benefits for the covered executives beyond those the law took away. The percentage of benefit can be higher, the service required can be less, bonus and other additional compensation can be added to the formula, and survivor benefits can be added. Coupled with the inexact nature of cost estimates in a small pension plan, there are in effect no cost controls on many SERPs.

Another common area of supplemental executive benefits is reimbursement of uninsured health costs. In effect, the regular health plan is extended to 100 percent of actual charges from the first dollar, including mental and nervous illness and other areas that in regular plans are either excluded or limited and covered at 50 percent or less. Supplementing life and disability insurance are also popular executive benefits. Waiting periods are often waived for life and health plans, especially when an executive was recruited from another company and would otherwise be uninsured for one to three months. Executive vacation schedules are very commonly better (although executives are expected to make themselves available throughout their vacations if needed). Of particular note is that vacations are much less sensitive to company seniority and more to the executive's amount of career seniority. Therefore, minimum vacation is frequently set at three or four weeks, but the schedule increases only to five or six weeks after thirty years.

Perquisites

This is the final element of executive compensation, and in many ways it is the strangest. Perquisites, or "perks," are closely related to benefits. They include anything (1) currently furnished to an executive in kind, not cash, that (2) has economic value, and (3) is not classified elsewhere. The most common examples are company cars and club memberships.

Perquisites grew up in the 1950s, stimulated by the fact that they represented tax-free income to executives in an era of high tax rates. Also, executive compensation packages then were less complete than they are today. Over the following thirty years, the IRS began to look closely at corporations' deduction of perquisite costs, from hunting lodges to the fabled three-martini lunch, to see if they were really "ordinary and necessary" business expenses. Income tax rates fell over the years, and the culture changed so that hunting trips and long lunches had less value to executives. Perquisites became more work-centered; the latest hot perk is a cellular telephone for the company car.

Alternative Compensation

The last few years have seen dramatic shifts in the way leading organizations in the United States and Pacific Rim countries pay their employees. Alternative, or variable,

Exhibit 9-6.   Integrated business strategy to achieve results.

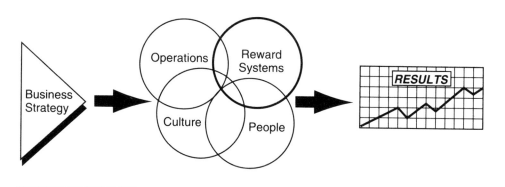

Source: Hay Group.

compensation, once the exclusive domain of executives and salespeople, is now being applied to the entire work force—from hourly workers to senior executives. This 1990s approach introduces a contingent element to the total compensation package by linking a portion of pay to the achievement of specified individual or unit goals. When added to base salaries or wages, variable compensation typically offers greater total compensation opportunities than plans that offer only fixed wages, even though fixed salaries in the variable program may actually be lower.

Need for New Approaches

While reward systems must support business strategy, so must the operations, culture, and people. Reward systems (pay) are only one of four interrelated elements that must work together to drive business results, as shown in Exhibit 9-6. The adoption of variable pay programs is recognition that current pay systems are not likely to work in the 1990s and that innovative approaches are crucial. The cumulative effect of a number of forces within the business environment is causing companies to rethink their pay philosophies with their employees. These forces include:

- Heightened short-term performance expectations from shareholders and the investment community
- Unrelenting government regulation
- Shift in employment from industrial to services sector
- Globalization of the economy
- Intensifying competition, both domestically and internationally
- Introduction of major new technologies
- Shifting demographic patterns
- Changing employee attitudes

Because of these factors, neither employers nor employees can live up to the tenets of the traditional ''employment contract.'' Implicit in that contract was a pledge from the organization to provide job security, a regular increase in pay, a relatively risk-free

Exhibit 9-7. Employees' perception of linkage of pay to performance.

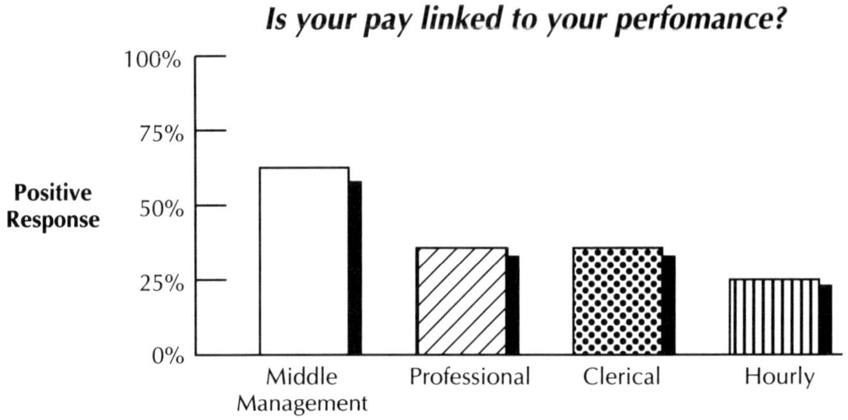

Is your pay linked to your perfomance?

Source: Hay Group.

environment, and opportunities for promotion to employees who did their jobs well. In return, employees would deliver performance of required tasks, loyalty, long service, and patience.

Today, the Hay Group's employee attitude surveys show a continuing decline in workers' confidence, commitment, and loyalty to their corporate management. Generally, employees do not perceive their pay as linked to their performance, as indicated in Exhibit 9-7. With these attitudes comes a declining level of employee commitment and loyalty to the company.

Employees are clearly responding to the fact that recessions, globalization, and heightened competition have reduced companies' ability to provide long-term commitments to their workers. Many organizations—including some of the world's largest and most successful companies—have radically changed the nature and makeup of their work force through staff reductions, early retirements, and increasing use of temporary or contract workers. The result is that companies are no longer building up the staffs that they once did, and they are therefore unable to make or live up to the same implicit promises about long-term rewards for loyal and steady performance. At the same time, employees are placing a greater premium on individual fulfillment. This is especially true among younger workers, who are placing more emphasis on opportunities through which they can gain greater control over their lives. This quest can include a desire to ''own'' the jobs they perform as well as a desire to own—at least partially—the companies for which they work.

As Exhibit 9-8 illustrates, the declining attitudes among employees are particularly prevalent among professionals, who are one-third less likely than management or hourly workers to say that they plan to remain with their company for the next five years. Motivation and commitment among this key employee group is now linked more to their chosen professions than to the companies that employ them. It is not uncommon,

Exhibit 9-8. Employees' plans to remain with current employers.

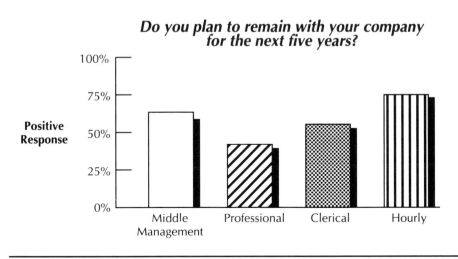

**Do you plan to remain with your company
for the next five years?**

Source: Hay Group.

for example, for computer or data-processing professionals to be more loyal to a particular type of hardware or software than to the company that employs them to operate that particular system.

All this leads to a fundamental reworking of the employment "contract," now more appropriately called the "working arrangement." In this relationship, employees expect the following:

- Effective leadership
- Greater participation in decision making
- A balance between the risk and reward associated with their pay
- An opportunity for enrichment and self-fulfillment
- Stimulating job content

At the same time, employers expect employees to:

- Make a value-added contribution
- Be responsive to changes in the work environment
- Develop an orientation toward quality and customer, be it the external customer for the employer's products and services or internal customers for the employee's particular services
- Make a commitment to the work unit
- Accept a pay program that is linked to business results

This change in the employer-employee relationship is fundamental. And, while it entails a new set of greater challenges for employers in the future, successful implementation of the new working arrangement can lead to a more motivated and productive work force, and therefore significant competitive advantage for the companies that wholeheartedly embrace its principles. Our research in the United States has shown that organizations with a highly participative environment in which innovation is encouraged perform at substantially higher levels than counterpart companies that do not foster those cultural aspects.

In the United States, a key to making the working arrangement actually work is variable pay, or alternative compensation. Specifically, variable pay allows an organization to support the participative culture that leads to improved financial results. Variable pay arrangements align compensation with business results and encourage the employee to be a stakeholder in those results. When employees share a portion of the risk, they become more involved, demand more financial information about the organization, and operate in a true partnership environment. Variable pay arrangements also help break down the entitlement mentality of many workers, so they will come to understand that there is more to earning greater rewards than merely staying on the payroll for another year. These variable pay arrangements help organizations attract and retain the best workers.

Lastly, and probably most important, variable pay helps communicate companies' values to employees, by defining the range of reward opportunities for specific employees or work units and by defining the ways in which performance will be measured. This is noteworthy because people tend to behave as they are measured.

Variable Pay Options

There are many types of variable pay programs available to organizations. These include approaches designed for both individuals and groups of employees. Here are some of the more common contingent compensation plans.

- *Gainsharing.* These plans typically provide production workers with a share of the value gained from increased productivity. This gain is calculated using a predetermined formula. The most commonly used measures are direct labor hours or labor costs as input and production units as output. Improvement is shared with the employees on some percentage basis, commonly 25 percent, 50 percent, or more.

- *Profit Sharing.* These plans provide a broad group of employees with a share of a pool created by the profits of the organization. The payout is usually provided through a prearranged formula. It can take the form of a percentage of all profits or a percentage of profits above an identified standard, such as return on the equity or capital invested in the business.

- *Group Incentives.* These are variable arrangements for a group of employees, small or large (but typically less than the entire company or unit). Through the plan, eligible employees receive a variable award based on increased performance against targets. These plans could be applied to settings such as a work unit, a manufacturing site, or a sales department.

- *Individual Incentives.* Most commonly, these are management-by-objective incentives, individualized for highly skilled technicians, professionals, managers, and other individual contributors. These incentives work best when the participant has the discretion to establish his or her schedule on a day-to-day basis. They are used in situations where management seeks to direct the discretionary behavior and activities of a subset of employees.

• *Lump-Sum Payments.* These are periodic (often annual) payments made in lieu of part or all of normal base pay increases. In the United States they have been used most commonly as a substitute for annual increases to hourly wages for production workers. Under a typical arrangement, an employee would receive a percentage of pay equal to a normal pay increase. But that percentage would not go into the base wages for future increases or be included when determining the value of any benefits programs based on pay.

• *Pay for Knowledge/Skill.* Through these programs, a "ladder" is created within a job family that employees can climb at their own pace. As they acquire additional skills, their compensation is adjusted accordingly. These plans work best in situations where a team performs a number of activities associated with one product or process, and the acquisition of additional skills by any member of the team keeps down the unit's size and makes it more efficient.

• *Key Contributor Programs.* These are usually onetime award plans to provide incentives for a small group of key employees in an organization—typically 2 to 5 percent of the work force—based on successful completion of a project, program, or product. They can also be used to help retain employees who are particularly valuable to the organization and would be difficult and expensive to replace.

• *Job Rates.* Job rates replace a merit pay system with a standard rate or midpoint for a job after a period of time on the job. Typically, an employee would reach this midpoint or standard rate after three to five years. Future increases would then come only from range adjustments. These programs are often used in conjunction with other incentive programs.

• *Long-Term Programs.* These are tied to measurement periods that are longer than one year. They include both cash and stock award programs.

All of these types of plans are being tried in varying degrees throughout the United States and the rest of the world. A recent Hay-sponsored survey revealed a great deal of experimentation with and consideration of the different plan types (see Exhibit 9-9). Currently, individual incentives and key contributor programs have the highest prevalence, with profit sharing and lump-sum payments close behind. The experimentation is occurring at all levels, most likely in larger companies at the business unit and division level, as well as at plant sites and in smaller groups or individual departments rather than the entire corporation. Over the next few years, we expect to find that most leading organizations in the United States have experimented with one or more of these kinds of plans as part of an integrated incentive compensation strategy.

Pay plan types can generally be categorized as encouraging either individual/group performance or cost control. Group incentives, profit sharing, gainsharing, and long-term programs support group performance. Pay for knowledge/skill, key contributor programs, and individual incentives support individual performance. Lump-sum payments, base pay freezes, separate pay hikes, and job rates encourage cost control.

Designing and Implementing a Variable Pay Program

In the typical company that has not used these methods, a disciplined approach is required to design and implement a successful variable pay program. Based on our consulting experiences with several multinational organizations in the United States, we have identified thirteen steps crucial to implementation, as shown in Exhibit 9-10. While

Exhibit 9-9. Prevalence of variable pay programs.

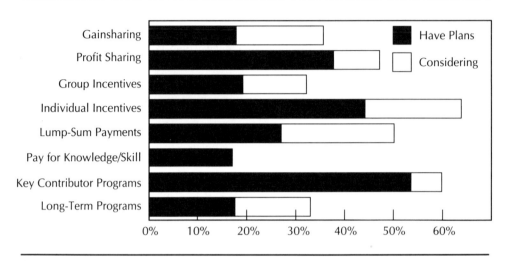

Source: Hay Group.

Exhibit 9-10. Methodology for implementing a variable pay program.

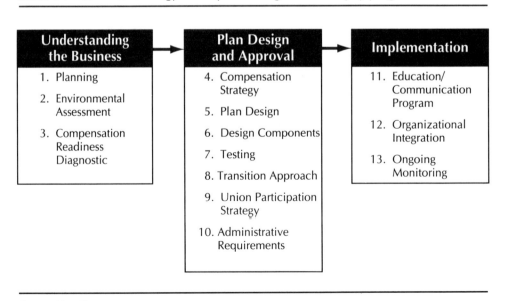

Source: Hay Group.

some steps can be completed concurrently, the completion of all steps is necessary for successful implementation.

1. *Planning.* First, a task force must be formed. The task force membership should include staff and line management, personnel from headquarters and the field, and possibly hourly and union employees. Their initial assignment is to create a task force charter/mission statement. It is critical to the success of the plan to create linkage with a plan sponsor/champion who can provide constant guidance and leadership to the team and help with the formulation of the team's charter.

2. *Environmental Assessment.* This step includes a review of: the business strategy; place in life cycle; all existing human resources systems, processes, and initiatives; evaluation of economic/industry issues; review of evaluation of business measurement/reporting systems; determination of both current and desired pay competitiveness; assessment of business leverage factors; and, most importantly, determination of what employees will be expected to do differently as a result of the variable pay program. Exhibit 9-11 outlines the primary focus of employees at different levels in the organization and sample goals that could be tied to their incentive plans.

3. *Compensation Readiness Diagnostic.* During this step, baseline data are gathered on employees' perceptions of current reward processes, including: the organization's focus (is it individually or group oriented?); its clarity of direction; how demanding it is; the degree of pressure for performance; the degree to which employees are encouraged to provide initiative in their jobs; employees' ability to bring about change in their jobs or organization; the level of trust, commitment, and desire to achieve that exists within the organization; the ability of the firm's management systems to support performance planning and measurement; and the level of satisfaction with current compensation, both in terms of performance measurement and levels of pay. This diagnostic typically entails both a quantitative measure through completion of an employee survey

Exhibit 9-11. Primary focus and goals of implementing a variable pay program.

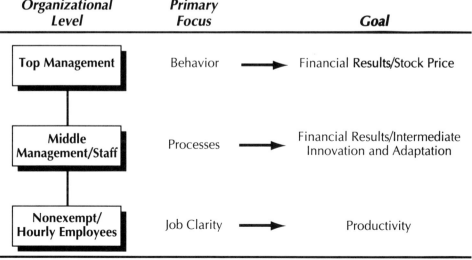

Organizational Level	Primary Focus	Goal
Top Management	Behavior →	Financial **Results/Stock Price**
Middle Management/Staff	Processes →	Financial Results/Intermediate Innovation and Adaptation
Nonexempt/Hourly Employees	Job Clarity →	Productivity

Source: Hay Group.

Exhibit 9-12. Correlation of dynamics in corporate culture with successful/unsuccessful implementation of variable pay plans.

	Successful Plans	Troubled Plans
Group Orientation	43%	30%
Clarity of Direction	45	39
Pressure for Performance	67	50
Encouragement of Initiative	48	22
Trust/Commitment	52	22
Achievement Motivation	28	55
Performance Measurement	72	39
Compensation	31	20

Percentages indicate fovorable responses of employees.

Source: Hay Group

and a qualitative assessment through focus groups that can provide insight to the findings produced by the survey.

A survey conducted by Hay revealed that certain existing dynamics in a corporate culture correlate with the successful or unsuccessful implementation of variable pay plans (see Exhibit 9-12). The results showed, for example, that employees working for companies with successful incentive plans have greater "trust and commitment" (52 percent favorable) than employees in companies with troubled plans (22 percent favorable).

4. *Compensation Strategy.* This step requires a company to formulate a set of philosophies, beliefs, principles, and plans for the organization. The objective is to define the specific characteristics of the performance/reward structure that will serve as a framework for making compensation decisions. This step should conclude with specific actions that the organization will follow to implement the strategy on a prioritized time-phase basis.

- *Sample Beliefs.* These are several specific "truisms" about what the pay program is intended to accomplish in the organization. Typical objectives could include: attracting and retaining high-quality employees who contribute to the organization's success, encouraging individual and team achievement of corporate business strategy and performance goals, and providing pay in a simple and understandable matter.
- *Sample Principles.* These are the parameters through which the beliefs will be pursued. Typical principles could include such statements as: compensation will

be composed of a base and variable element for all employees (hourly workers to senior executives); total cash compensation (base pay plus variable element) should range from below average to substantially above average, based on achievement of incentive goals; and base pay levels will be below average when compared to appropriate industries and job markets in which we compete for talent.

An approach to begin developing beliefs and principles is to document the current corporate environment and visualize beliefs and principles as the future ideal state, recognizing that any differences between the two will be the starting point for compensation plan design.

5. *Plan Design.* This step answers specific design questions, such as: Will employees have compensation at risk? Will existing pay be directed into a fixed and variable element, or will a variable plan be offered in addition to fixed pay arrangements (the "new money" approach)? The mix of pay needs to be specified for each eligible group, both in terms of the ratio of fixed to variable pay and in terms of how specific amounts of pay will be determined (award levels, plan goals, etc.). Finally, the company's compensation competitiveness must be determined as well as whether it is in the position desired.

6. *Design Components.* Specific design components should include: basic assumptions and constraints; measurement criteria for the various company, unit, group, or individual performance levels; specific performance goals and payouts; measurement periods; eligibility criteria; type of payout (immediate or deferred, cash and/or stock impact on current programs); degree of employee involvement in its design; and how the plan will be administered.

7. *Testing.* Methods plans should be created to test the various plan designs during development with employee focus groups throughout the organization. This testing process will help to ensure that the participants will buy into the design process and accept the plan once it is implemented. Cost models should also be used to determine payout at various levels of performance.

8. *Transition Approach.* The compensation plan must be integrated with existing award systems. Its impact on future base pay increases and on the organization's overall base salary/wage program design and administration will have to be addressed, and the timing of the plan implementation must be determined. Will it be immediately or gradually phased in? It is important that the plan design(s) be tested at pilot locations before attempting to install the plan on a full-scale basis.

9. *Union Participation Strategy.* Create a strategy to win long-term union support for the plan's success. Determine the rationale for union acceptance as well as the timing of the plan's implementation: Will it be at contract renewal time, or will it require a midterm negotiation? Finally, consider how the plan should be communicated to union membership—specifically, will there be a union/nonunion distinction?

10. *Administrative Requirements.* Administrative requirements need to be identified and minimized during the design process to prevent them from becoming burdensome. The administrative plan should include items such as goal measurement, pay definition, impact on benefits, participant eligibility, record keeping, and payout issues.

11. *Education/Communication Program.* In this step, a communications strategy is developed that will bring about an immediate level of understanding of the new plan by all employees and, more importantly, create an atmosphere for acceptance of the program. Specific strategies to introduce the plan in a consistent manner might include the development of videos and brochures and the creation of communication seminars to help managers learn how to convey details about the program to their own employees. Our experience is that the conveyance of the plan is most successful when line management talks directly to employees. It is crucial that the plan be communicated continuously.

12. *Organizational Integration.* Probably the most important aspect of the implementation process, it is during this process that management and employee initiatives are identified and developed in order to link reward programs to business strategy and employee involvement programs. Training and development needs of managers are identified, employee and managerial roles are redefined, while managerial/supervisory capabilities and motivational skills are upgraded.

13. *Ongoing Monitoring.* Once the plan is implemented, periodic testing of the program and its acceptance must be conducted, and corrective action must be taken when necessary. To encourage ongoing support of the plan, methodology to allow for employee feedback should be developed. Over the long term, it becomes critical to assess how well the plan supports the desired culture, produces the anticipated financial results, and creates the operating efficiencies and employee attitudes that are needed to pursue the company's strategic goals.

Actual Applications

Variable compensation plans have been installed in a wide range of organizations in the United States over the last several years. These organizations represent every stage in the business life cycle, from entrepreneurial and growth to maturity. The following case examples illustrate how U.S. industry is responding to the challenges of the 1990s. The compensation strategy adopted by AT&T establishes and reinforces a start-up culture based on quality orientation as leading to business success. The Union Carbide example relates how a once highly profitable, now struggling enterprise is dealing with its revitalization efforts to restore its former profitability.

AT&T Universal Card Services

During spring 1990, when the industry appeared saturated and no new entries were possible into the market, AT&T formed a consumer credit subsidiary, Universal Card Services (UCS), to issue VISA and Mastercards in direct competition with major credit card issuers such as Citibank, Chase, and American Express. To gain entry into the crowded market, UCS offered its customers a credit card with a lifetime of no annual fees (with some restrictions) and excellent customer service. The public response to the offering was overwhelming: By the end of 1990, UCS was the sixth largest issuer of credit cards in the United States, having issued more than 4 million cards.

UCS created an all-employee group incentive plan to establish and reinforce a culture focused on quality customer service and to meld the rapidly growing employee population, which grew from a few hundred employees in February to almost 3,000 by

December 1990. The strategy used by UCS tied employees' compensation to the organization's success, measured in terms of productivity and quality of service. The use of quality as an incentive plan measure is both innovative and an extension of a total quality management trend that continues to change the way U.S. business will operate in the future.

After a cross-functional senior management team was formed, the design process began with the establishment of a compensation strategy identifying plan objectives. Employees were involved in the development of employee measures and goals. With this foundation established, various plan alternatives, funding formulas, and plan mechanics were tested by simulating them against anticipated performance until the right combination was realized.

The Excellence Award Program measures eighty-one specific quality standards for the five semiautonomous sections within UCS operations and customer service. Opportunity exists for employees to earn two different awards based on the achievement of companywide or departmental objectives. Performance relative to these quality objectives is typically measured on a daily basis, so that when each day's objectives are met, a sum of money is added to the company pool and/or the department/individual pool. If both overall company and department objectives are achieved for the quarter, it is conceivable that employees can earn a maximum of 12 percent times their quarterly base pay. During the first two quarters of 1990, employees achieved a 75 percent success rate on attaining their quality objectives, resulting in an 80 percent of payout potential. It is anticipated that as the business grows, so will the Excellence Award Program. Future considerations include tying an employee's award to individual performance and utilizing financial measure of success.

UCAR CARBON COMPANY

UCAR Carbon Company is a subsidiary of Union Carbide that manufactures graphite electrodes for the steel industry. Having once been the industry leader, UCAR's position and profitability eroded over the latter half of the 1980s as a result of increased competition and overcapacity of the industry. After experiencing several layoffs, management concluded that improving quality and increasing productivity along with expense reductions was the only road back to desired profitability.

As part of UCAR's revitalization, compensation needed to reinforce this new culture and clearly indicate to all employees that prior business practices had to change. UCAR established a design team composed of staff and line managers to review the company's approach to compensation. One of the team's first tasks was to solicit employee opinions via focus groups conducted throughout the company's facilities. The resulting information provided reassurance to the design team that an all-employee variable compensation program based on financial results was crucial to the long-term viability of UCAR.

Opportunity Sharing, a financially oriented incentive program for all salaried, hourly, and union employees, began in 1989. Division profits are shared through a payout (up to 18 percent of straight-time base pay) once a threshold of profitability level is achieved. When performance exceeds prior years' results or UCAR's cost of capital, the funding formula pays out 20 percent of the profit above threshold.

Extensive communication and training programs were established to encourage both employee understanding and acceptance. Since the Opportunity Sharing plan measures overall financial results, line managers identified how each individual employee's efforts could have impact on profitability. Although there was no payout by the plan for 1989 because of depressed demand during the second two quarters, there was a modest payout for 1990. UCAR learned from the program that culture change is a long-term process requiring consistent action, one in which immediate results are not always possible, and success is frequently measured in incremental improvements.

WHAT WORKS?

Our experience with Union Carbide, AT&T, and other companies indicates that the following is crucial for program success:

- A simple plan design that employees understand and accept
- A program that supports business strategy and encourages the accomplishment of stated business goals
- Plan goals that become aligned with results
- Training, provided to all participants, that encourages them to become involved and perform jobs differently in order to accomplish plan goals
- An ongoing communications program to reinforce plan objectives and to help establish reasonable payout expectations

Summary

In today's business reality, offering variable pay to only those who head the business is no longer enough. The successful enterprises of the 1990s that will be global in perspective and compete on all continents must provide opportunities to all of those who contribute to business operations. This trend is moving from the Far East and the United States to other parts of the world, as other countries face the same kinds of changing business conditions and shifts in attitudes and demographic patterns.

We are definitely at the beginning of a new era in compensation—one in which more employees at all levels will begin to participate as a partner with their employers to manage the business, improve productivity, enhance quality, and share in the business results through participation in all types of variable pay programs. The most forward-thinking organizations will incorporate this "partnership" mentality in their compensation planning in order to attract and retain top-level, high-performing employees at all levels of the company.

10

Standard Benefits

Carol Benjamin
Consultant
The Wyatt Company

In the early part of this century, employers began providing benefits to employees as part of their total compensation package. The "traditional" benefits package has evolved over time, just as employees' attitudes and corporate philosophies have evolved. The changes in business and social culture from the 1950s, when many benefits programs were designed, to the 1990s, when employers are developing benefits packages for the work force of the future, are significant. Some of the differences that impact benefits programs are outlined in Exhibit 10-1.

In addition, as U.S. businesses become positioned for the twenty-first century, there are many new and critical human resources issues to address. Employers are grappling with how to alter their compensation and benefits programs to meet the changes necessitated by these issues. If benefits programs are going to assist employers in attracting and retaining the best workers, those programs must be responsive to employees' needs. At the same time, employers are faced with rising benefits costs that are the result of increased legislation, insurer insolvency, the cost of advanced technologies, hospital costs and doctors fees, and the aging work force.

This chapter outlines some of these issues and how employers are addressing them through their standard benefits programs.

Exhibit 10-1. Changes over time affecting benefits programs.

Then	Now
• Nuclear families of working male with female and 2.3 children at home	• Double-income families with and without children, and single-head families
• White male–dominated work force	• Multicultural work force
• Cradle-to-grave expectations	• Portability issues
• Paternalistic employer	• Shared responsibility
• Entitlement perception of benefits	• Benefits as part of total compensation
• Low cost of benefits	• Benefits costs escalating faster than consumer price index and an employers' ability to pay.
• Protection for illness	• Promotion of wellness

Benefits Philosophy

Every employer has some sort of philosophy governing its benefits program, which is implicit in the design of the existing benefits program. However, many employers are unable to articulate or outline specifically their benefits philosophy. When they attempt to do so, they find that their existing benefits program is not necessarily compatible with the philosophy.

Often, employee benefits programs have been the product of evolution, rather than the result of a careful, thought-out, proactive strategy. Consequently, components have often been added or modified in a vacuum, without overall direction or control. The development of any cohesive, integrated employee benefits program can best be accomplished when the employer's benefits philosophy and objectives are explicitly defined and used as a basis for the evaluation and design of the program.

Employers should periodically pause to examine management's philosophy for providing benefits in order to better position their organizations for the coming years. Issues that should be discussed include the role and purpose of benefits, responsibility for providing benefits, how the benefits program should be funded, and existing and desired employee and employer perceptions about benefits.

When addressing future benefits needs, five questions come to mind.

1. What is management's "desired state" for the benefits philosophy. In other words, what does the organization hope to achieve with the benefits program?
2. What are the various benefits components that exist now? What should be the interrelationship of the various components?
3. How well do the existing benefits components support management's philosophy?
4. What changes are necessary and appropriate to adapt existing benefits components to support management's philosophy?
5. What are the cost implications of those changes? What can the company afford?

Another way of asking these questions is: Where do you want to be? Where are you now? How do you get where you want to be? What is the cost? Can you afford it?

There are several approaches to addressing and answering these questions. Typically, management begins by identifying its employee benefits philosophy and objectives. Examples of issues that are often considered include:

- What does management want to achieve through the benefits program?
- Are benefits considered a unique form of compensation, or should they be treated similarly to other forms of compensation?
- Should management be sensitive to the level of benefits provided by other employers? If so, at what level should benefits be positioned relative to those other employers? Should they be equal? Less? More?
- What is the employer's perceived responsibility to provide benefits?
- What is the most appropriate emphasis among the various components of benefits? Are there subsidiaries, divisions, or employee groups for which the mix of benefits should differ?
- To what extent will management listen to the employees when restructuring the benefits program?

- What message does the organization want to send its employees through the design of the benefits program? Are benefits programs used as a means to attract and retain good employees?
- Should employees have the ability to control the form of their benefits? How much control? Total? Partial?
- How should the various components of benefits be funded? To what extent should the employees share in the cost of the program? Should the program be dependent upon profitability or productivity?
- Should internal administration and communication capabilities dictate benefits design?

Following the initial process of discussing these and other philosophical issues, a benefits policy statement should be drafted to reflect the conclusions reached. Once finalized, the benefits policy statement is used to develop an action plan and a blueprint for designing appropriate benefits plans.

The Benefits Program

Based on the employer's objectives, the following may be part of the benefits program:

- Medical coverage
- Dental coverage
- Life insurance (including dependent life insurance)
- Accidental death and dismemberment (AD&D) insurance
- Disability insurance (short-term and/or long-term)
- Vision and hearing care
- Prescription drug coverage
- Health promotion and wellness
- Retirement (defined contribution savings vehicle and/or defined benefit pension plan)
- Vacation time and holidays
- Sick pay
- Educational assistance
- Relocation

The employer may or may not pay the cost of all or part of these plans—again, depending on management's philosophy and objectives. Based on whether an employer pays for all or a portion of the benefit, the plan will be called a noncontributory or a contributory plan. A plan is noncontributory when the employer pays the full cost. A plan is contributory when employees must pay a portion or all of the cost for coverage. In addition to the organization's philosophy, such things as competitive factors and affordability of the plans influence whether or not the plans are noncontributory or contributory.

When designing benefits plans, an employer will decide which benefits programs will be included; if the plan is to be contributory or noncontributory; and which employees will be allowed to participate. Often, there are coverage restrictions. Issues to be addressed include:

- Whether or not certain groups of employees should be excluded
- What types of discrimination issues may be generated
- How part-time and temporary employees should be included
- Whether or not there should be a waiting period for coverage based on an employee's length of service
- Whether or not there should be a waiting period for preexisting conditions if they are to be covered.

When providing benefits programs for employees, most employers must abide by both state and federal laws. Federal laws provide an opportunity for employers to provide benefits to employees on a nontaxable basis. The employer also receives a tax deduction for providing certain benefits. In exchange for this favorable tax treatment for both the employee and employer, there are laws and regulations employers must follow that:

- Prohibit age discrimination in benefits
- Prohibit mandatory retirement
- Control the amount of nontaxable benefits that can be provided to highly paid versus non–highly paid employees
- Ensure that pregnancy is treated as any other illness
- Ensure that broad participation is encouraged
- Ensure that a certain percentage of employees are covered
- Ensure that plans are communicated to employees
- Ensure that certain benefits may be continued by employees upon termination

There are various laws that cover the many different types of benefits programs. Before developing an actual plan design, an employer must become knowledgeable about the laws and regulations governing each particular benefits area being considered. In addition, there are reporting requirements, including the need to file documents and annual reports with the government and to distribute certain mandatory materials to employees.

The Legislative Environment

Since the 1970s, employers have been inundated with legislation impacting their employee benefits programs. Some of this legislation has caused employers to make changes in their benefits; some has caused them to take a completely new benefits direction. This legislation has not always resulted in providing better benefits for employees. Some employers have chosen to discontinue plans, rather than deal with extensive and costly compliance issues. Often, legislative changes do not provide a clear direction for employers but offer them a real challenge in redesigning benefit programs. The following is a short overview of eight key regulations pertaining to employee benefits

1. *Health Maintenance Organization Act of 1973 (HMOA).* Requires employers to offer local health maintenance organization (HMO) coverage to employees if approached by a qualified HMO.
2. *Employee Retirement Income Security Act of 1974 (ERISA).* Establishes federal

reporting and disclosure requirements and fiduciary standards for employee benefits plans. Provides substantial revisions to the Internal Revenue Code regarding standards for employers' funding and vesting of employee retirement plans.

3. *Tax Equity and Fiscal Responsibility Act of 1982 (TEFRA).* Lowers permissible retirement benefits, provides parity between corporate and self-employed retirement plans, and restricts tax benefits for highly paid employees.
4. *Retirement Equity Act of 1984 (REA).* Provides enhanced protection for spouse's retirement benefits.
5. *Consolidated Omnibus Budget Reconciliation Act of 1986 (COBRA).* Provides continuation of health and dental insurance benefits to employees and their dependents at group rates upon the employees' termination from an employer, if employees pay premiums. Also includes the *Single Employer Pension Plan Amendments Act of 1986 (SEPPA),* which revises funding requirements for pension plans.
6. *Tax Reform Act of 1986.* Revises all aspects of U.S. tax law. Changes the way benefits are taxed and the levels at which workers and employers are taxed. The Act contains substantial changes to the compensation and benefits provisions of the Internal Revenue Code.
7. *Technical Corrections and Miscellaneous Revenue Act of 1988.* Provides corrections and changes to the Tax Reform Act of 1986. Contains numerous changes to compensation and benefits provisions of the Internal Revenue Code. Reduces the penalty for violation of COBRA, among other things. There are revisions in the area of health care, cafeteria plans, dependent care, and educational assistance.
8. *HMO Act of 1988.* The first significant amendments to the HMO Act of 1973, affecting employer-HMO relationships. These amendments, affecting only federally qualified HMOs, include nondiscriminatory employer contributions, a new rate-setting method, disclosure of calculations, a self-referral option, and repeal of dual choice in 1995 (so that employers will no longer have to offer employees both an indemnity and an HMO plan).

There are other federal and state laws that pertain to employee benefits, but these have had the most significant impact on employers' benefits plans.

Types of Benefits

Medical Coverage

U.S. consumers' expectations for health care coverage present interesting challenges for employers who design, maintain, and implement benefits programs. Society demands immediate access to health care. The U.S. consumer often expects to be cared for by specialists and seeks new approaches to terminal illnesses at any cost. These factors all contribute to rising health care costs, as do the following:

- New medical technologies
- Inappropriate use of medical services
- Oversupply of facilities

- High malpractice rates
- Inflation
- Lack of cost-sharing
- Aging population

Rising health care costs are prompting continuous study by employers of their health plans. Employers have learned that the total cost and use of health care services must be managed because shifting part of the cost to employees is not enough.

The following section discusses various types of medical plans, with information on new approaches in dealing with rising health care costs. Before types of health care plans are described, it is important to understand some key terms.

- *Deductible.* A specific dollar amount that an individual must pay before reimbursement for expenses begins. The purpose of the deductible is to encourage only necessary care by requiring the individual to pay for some of the up-front expenses.

- *Coinsurance.* The amount of charges the insured and insurer share once the deductible has been met. The most common coinsurance arrangement is for the employer to pay 80 percent of covered expenses after the deductible and the individual to pay 20 percent.

- *Copayment.* The out-of-pocket amount the covered individual pays for each service. Most health plans have either a copayment or a coinsurance provision.

- *Maximum out-of-pocket limit.* The maximum amount of covered expenses that an individual will have to pay in a plan year. Generally, there is an out-of-pocket limit for an insured individual as well as for the insured dependents.

- *Reasonable and customary charge.* The maximum amount that an insurer will consider eligible for reimbursement. Charges above the reasonable and customary amount are higher than allowed under the plan and therefore not covered.

- *Lifetime limits.* The maximum amount that the plan will pay in an insured's lifetime, frequently $1 million. Many plans do not have such limits.

- *Adverse selection.* The tendency of an individual to select the plan that is most favorable to his or her particular health status when choosing an option offered by a specific insurance plan. This tendency may result in more cost to the plan if it is not adequately addressed in the plan design and cost structure. Adverse selection, which is also called antiselection, also refers to a situation caused when a person with existing or pending health care needs applies for insurance coverage that is financially favorable to the individual but costly for the insurance plan.

As employers have struggled with rising health care costs, new approaches have been developed to providing group medical coverage for employees. Various designs and approaches are discussed below.

BASE PLUS PLAN

Although these plans are not as popular as they were in the 1970s and early 1980s, nearly one-third of U.S. employers continue to sponsor them. They are called base plus plans or first-dollar plans because the plan usually pays hospital expenses at 100 percent, with an employee paying nothing. These hospital expenses are considered the "base" and, therefore, are paid at 100 percent from the first dollar of expense incurred. Other health care expenses, such as office visits, are subject to a deductible paid by the insured, who then shares additional expenses with the insurer, according to the coinsurance schedule dictated by the plan. These plans provide few opportunities for managing health care costs and therefore are declining.

COMPREHENSIVE PLAN DESIGN

With a comprehensive plan, the insured *first* pays a deductible before any expenses are reimbursed by the plan. Once the deductible has been met, the insured and the insurer pay their respective portions of the coinsurance until the out-of-pocket limit is met. Once the out-of-pocket limit is met, the plan pays 100 percent up to the annual lifetime maximum amount. Since the insured must pay the deductible before the plan begins to pay, the comprehensive plan encourages more cost-effective care than a base plus plan.

MANAGED HEALTH CARE APPROACHES

In order to better manage health care expenses, two types of health care approaches are becoming increasingly popular:

1. Health maintenance organizations.
2. Point-of-service plans, both preferred provider organizations (PPOs) and point-of-service HMOs.

There are some key differences among the types of managed care programs, including:

- Provider choice: How much choice will the insured have in selecting health care providers?
- Benefits design: How will benefits be provided to employees?
- Claims processing: Who will be responsible for processing and paying claims?
- Providers' risk sharing: Will providers share in the cost of health care with the plan and the covered group? If so, how?
- Employer's financial arrangement: Will the plan be fully insured, partially insured, or self-insured by the employer?

Managed care plans differ from the traditional indemnity arrangement in various ways. The different types of plans and the factors affecting them are discussed below.

Indemnity Plans Indemnity describes the traditional arrangement for medical, dental, vision, and hearing plans offered by employers. The employer develops the plan design and provides a uniform benefit to all employees. The design of most indemnity health plans is either a base plus or comprehensive, as described above. Employees are allowed to select any care provider they wish to obtain services from. Employers determine how these plans will be funded. Plans can be fully insured, partially insured, or self-insured.

More and more, a utilization review (UR) feature is added to these plans in order to manage health care costs better. There are several types of utilization review, including the following:

- *Individual case management:* Designed to facilitate cost-effective treatment and care. Attempts to identify and coordinate the resources needed to offer the patient quality options and maximize the effectiveness of the care provided.
- *Preadmission certification:* Certification of medical necessity that is required before an employee can be admitted to the hospital for surgery or other treatment.
- *Second opinions:* Opinions provided by independent physicians that surgery or other treatment is necessary.
- *Discharge planning:* Involves arrangements, once a patient is discharged from the hospital, for continued care at home or in an extended-care facility.
- *Retrospective review and audit:* Provides a backward audit of costs and charges to provide better future management of health care costs. It will also provide a record of provider pricing practices.
- *Specialized review:* May be required for expenses such as mental and chiropractic care.

The UR organization evaluates the appropriateness, necessity, and quality of the health care being provided. It offers some control over providers' decisions on what care to give. Employers can obtain UR services through a UR organization, a third-party administrator, or an insurer.

Health Maintenance Organizations HMOs may have the greatest opportunity for controlling health care costs. They are structured to reward providers for the efficient delivery of quality health care. HMOs provide a comprehensive range of health care services for a predetermined price. The HMO maintains contracts with hospitals, clinics, physicians, dentists, and other providers. The contracts specify the amounts the providers may charge for their services. Employees who choose the HMO must utilize only the providers who contract with the HMO.

The annual percentage of increases in HMO premiums has generally been lower than increases in indemnity plan costs. If cost were the only consideration in sponsoring benefits, employers might only offer their employees the choice of an HMO. However, most employers are not willing to restrict employee choice to this extent. Therefore, those employers offering an HMO generally also include an indemnity plan option in their programs. Both types of plans should be offered if you want to attract and retain workers. Some employees, especially executives, will not opt for an HMO.

Many employers have experienced adverse selection against their indemnity plans because the healthier, younger employees tend to select HMOs. HMOs typically cover wellness expenses such as physicals, well-baby care, and immunizations, which are generally not covered in traditional indemnity plans. Employees pay small copayments each time they obtain services, rather than having to pay a deductible first. These features tend to be attractive to the healthier, younger population. Individuals who are not healthy tend to favor the indemnity plan where they can select their providers of care from the entire universe of providers. The HMO option may not be available in small communities.

Preferred Provider Organizations In a typical PPO arrangement, employers or insurers contract with providers (physicians, dentists, hospitals, etc.) who have agreed to discount their services in return for anticipated increased volume. Through its plan design, the employer encourages employees to use these providers by providing more generous benefits when the PPO is utilized. Employees like PPOs because they can decide whether or not to use a preferred provider each time they seek care, even though their benefits will be less when they choose to use an out-of-network provider.

Although PPOs can help manage costs, unless the participating providers have a financial stake in controlling utilization, they may encourage patient usage in an effort to maintain fee levels, thereby reducing potential cost savings. The employer's plan design is also critical to maintaining costs. More generous benefits provided when employees use a PPO can be greater than the fee discounts negotiated from the preferred providers if the plan design is not appropriate.

Managed Care Networks It appears that in order to meet the employer's objectives of managing health care costs and still maintaining a plan that is attractive to employees, managed care networks (or point-of-service networks) will become more popular. Such plans are designed to combine the cost-control potential of an HMO with the point-of-service choice of a PPO.

In a managed care network arrangement, an insurance carrier or an HMO assumes administrative and financial responsibility for an employer's health care plan services. The insurance carrier or the HMO establishes a network of physicians and hospitals by using its purchasing power to secure contractual arrangements designed to encourage the delivery of cost-effective quality services.

Each employee selects a primary care physician, who manages the patient and has access to specialty and referral care by providers within the network. As with a PPO arrangement, employees can choose between network and nonnetwork providers each time they seek care, but benefits are much greater when they go to the network providers. It is important that the in-network benefits are greater so as to encourage employees to use these contracted providers.

SOLVING THE COST PROBLEM

Some of the factors contributing to rapidly increasing health care costs are manageable, while others are not. Prior to an employer's attempting to develop solutions to manage health care costs, health care data should be collected in order to analyze specific problems that may be causing costs to rise. The employer should collect data such as the following before attempting to solve its problems:

- Several years of claims experience in order to identify utilization patterns, unusual claims, etc.
- Charges and allowed payments
- Expenses by diagnosis and provider

Such data typically can be furnished by the insurance carrier or third-party administrator. The information will assist the employer in determining cost-management approaches that will be most effective.

In addition to trying some of the plan designs and approaches described above, employers are developing programs to encourage employees to improve their health and educating employees on the prudent use of health care providers.

A new and controversial practice in the 1990s is when employers charge an added monthly premium to employees who choose to continue unhealthy behaviors, such as smoking and maintaining obesity. There have been discussions and even some court suits about this policy. Some companies prefer to put a more positive spin on the issue. They pay employees for practicing healthy habits. For example, they pay employees to take nonsmoking courses and to quit smoking. In addition, they may pay them a small monthly bonus for a certain number of months after they quit smoking. They may pay employees a small bonus each time they use the exercise center and so on. It's hard to tell whether any of these novel practices will make any difference in health care costs over the long run.

Dental Coverage

Dental plans became popular in the 1970s and remain so today. The types of services that are typically covered under a dental plan are:

- Diagnostic
- Preventive
- Restorative (crowns and dentures)
- Prosthodontics and periodontics

In addition, orthodontics are covered frequently, but usually only for 50–75 percent of the cost. Orthodontia also typically has a lifetime benefits limit. Cosmetic services are typically excluded from dental plans.

Most dental plans are designed with an emphasis on prevention. They typically have a deductible that is paid by the insured and a coinsurance with an annual out-of-pocket limit.

Life Insurance and Accidental Death and Dismemberment Insurance

Most employers provide a group life insurance plan for employees. Group life insurance plans pay a lump-sum benefit to a designated beneficiary if an employee dies while employed. Most frequently, the benefit is tied to the employee's pay since its purpose is to ease the financial loss for the beneficiaries when the employee dies. The employer may provide up to $50,000 of life insurance to the employee tax-free. The cost of amounts greater than $50,000 are imputed as taxable income to the employee. Some companies let employees purchase greater amounts of insurance at their own expense.

Accidental death and dismemberment (AD&D) insurance provides benefits if, as the result of an accident, an employee dies or suffers the loss of limbs or sight.

Disability Insurance

Employers often offer short-term and long-term disability plans to provide benefits to employees who are unable to work because of accident, injury, or illness. Short-term disability (STD) plans are usually designed to provide benefits based on the amount of service an employee has with the employer. The plan may be a self-insured sick leave plan (where the employer bears the entire cost), an insured plan (where an insurance carrier is involved), or a combination of the two. STD plans frequently replace 100 percent of the employee's pay for a stipulated period of time. Short-term benefits generally terminate after six months of disability.

Long-term disability (LTD) plans generally begin benefits payments after the employee has been disabled for at least six months. The purpose is to replace a portion of the employee's income during an extended illness or injury. LTD benefits vary in terms of the amounts and payment periods. However, the most common plans provide benefits equal to 50–70 percent of an employee's pay, less Social Security and workers compensation benefits. The benefit generally continues until the employee recovers or reaches retirement age.

If an employer provides noncontributory disability plans, the benefits made to the employees are generally taxable, unless employees pay for the disability plans with after-tax dollars. Disability plans must be managed effectively by the employer and/or the insurer to promote rehabilitation and return the employee to work. Most employers are required to provide workers compensation benefits as mandated by the laws of each state.

Vision and Hearing Care

Both vision and hearing benefits are relatively new. Most of these plans provide benefits on a scheduled basis. Fixed-dollar amounts are reimbursed to the employee for exams, lenses, frames, contacts, and hearing aids. Since both vision and hearing expenses are very predictable, these plans are less common and must be carefully designed and priced to prevent adverse selection.

Prescription Drug Coverage

Prescription drugs may be covered under the standard medical plan or designed as a freestanding plan. The freestanding plans work much like an HMO, where the employee will utilize a specific provider and pay a small copayment for each prescription. If prescription drugs are covered under the standard medical plan, the employee usually must meet the deductible first and then share the remaining expenses with the employer under a coinsurance schedule.

Health Promotion and Wellness

The most current benefits trend is to promote and reward employees' good health and wellness. Plan designs and incentives are used to encourage behavioral modification to encourage healthier employee life-styles. Some of the items being addressed are.

- Smoking cessation
- Stress management
- Exercise
- Weight control
- Proper nutrition

Employers may install corporate fitness centers, sponsor classes and programs, and offer healthful meals in the company cafeteria. By promoting wellness, employers hope to improve morale and reduce absenteeism, benefits costs, and turnover.

Employers are also beginning to encourage preventive care by covering routine checkups, immunizations, Pap tests, etc., at time intervals based on age and sex. Many employers provide an incentive or additional benefits to healthy employees. These incentives might take the form of lower premiums for health coverage, lower deductible and coinsurance amounts, or additional days off.

Retirement Plans

There are many types of retirement plans. Before the best type of plan for a particular organization can be determined, management's retirement income objectives must be identified. Below are some of the issues to address when identifying an organization's retirement income objectives:

• *Provide security.* Security may be defined as identifying the amount of pay replacement an employee will need at retirement and then determining the organization's responsibility toward providing it. Future security also may be addressed by determining the extent of the organization's commitment to protect employees against inflation.

• *Generate high perceived value.* It is important for the organization to determine how important the "perceived value" is versus the actual value of the plan. Often, a retirement plan that is easy to understand has higher employee-perceived value than a more complicated plan that may actually provide a better benefit. Whatever the case, a plan is most valuable to a company when it allows you to attract and retain the best workers; therefore the value of the plan must be effectively communicated to all employees.

• *Motivate employee performance.* The organization must determine whether or not it wants to use its retirement plan to motivate and reward performance.

• *Ensure competitiveness.* The degree to which the retirement plan will help an employer recruit and retain key personnel must be considered. It also may be important to provide a certain type of retirement plan to ensure that employees perceive the program as competitive. Another issue to consider is the image of the organization as an employer in the community based on the benefits employees receive upon retirement.

• *Promote employee concern for the success of the organization.* An employer must determine if the retirement plan benefits should be based on the success of the organization.

• *Determine the predictability of the benefit.* An employer must decide to what extent employees need to be able to predict the benefits amounts they will receive upon retirement.

• *Determine who should bear the investment risk.* Whether the employer or the employee assumes the investment risk—gains and losses—will influence the type of plan selected.

• *Determine the target population.* Some types of plans benefit older employees with longer service, while others benefit younger employees with shorter service. Therefore, it is important to consider the organization's work force and determine what employee groups should be targeted when developing a retirement plan.

Exhibit 10-2. Differences between defined contribution plan and defined benefit plan.

Feature	Defined Contribution Plan	Defined Benefit Plan
Plan Defines	Employer's and employee's contributions	Benefits employer must pay
Distribution of Money	Most to people below the age of 55	Most to people above the age of 55
Investment Risk	With employee	With employer
Size of "Severance Benefit" for Short Service	Large severance benefit	Small severance benefit
Understandability	Less difficult to understand	More difficult to understand
Flexibility to Solve New Retirement Problems	Little or no flexibility	Substantial flexibility
Vesting	Faster vesting	Slower vesting
Administration	Less complex to administer	More complex to administer
Federal Regulations	Less complex	More complex

Note: Vesting refers to the time at which an employee is entitled to all or some accrued pension funds prior to retirement.

• *Determine the portability of the benefit.* Should a short-service employee be able to leave with a significant benefit prior to retirement age?

• *Decide on the level of employee involvement.* Whether or not employees may contribute to the plan or whether or not they are required to contribute are critical factors in determining the type of retirement plan.

Once these issues and other objectives are identified, it becomes easier to determine what type of retirement plan is appropriate for the organization.

For years the most common type of pension plan was the defined benefit plan. It is funded by the company and provides a given dollar amount of monthly pension benefits for life beginning at retirement. In contrast, a defined contribution plan promises no set benefit. In a defined contribution plan the employee decides how much to contribute. The most popular defined contribution plan is a 401(k) profit-sharing type of plan. Typically employees do not receive as much benefit from a defined contribution plan because the company is not required to maintain a particular level of funding. Contributions may vary depending on the company profits. Exhibit 10-2 shows the major differences between defined benefit plans and defined contribution plans. Exhibit 10-

Exhibit 10-3. Employee groups favored under retirement plans.

Defined Contribution Plan	Defined Benefit Plan
Younger employees	Older employees
Employees with long periods of potential service	Employees with long periods of past service
Employees who terminate, die, or become disabled	Employees who stay with the company until retirement

3 outlines the employee groups who are favored for a certain level of contribution by the employer under the two types of plans.

TYPES OF RETIREMENT PLANS

There are many types of retirement plans. Four will be discussed here.

Defined Benefit Plans Just as the words state, the defined benefit plan defines the benefit the employee will receive at retirement. Although benefits may be payable upon separation from service, most typically they are payable upon retirement. The employer's contribution to a defined benefit plan varies, and the employer bears all of the investment risk.

The defined benefit plan has a benefits formula that is developed as a result of the employer's retirement income objectives. Some of the key questions in determining the formula include:

- What level of retirement income should be provided? If the level is to be based on pay, the definition of pay must be determined. If the level is to be based on service, the employer must determine how service will be counted or calculated.
- When should this targeted level of benefits be provided?
- What is retirement age?
- Will the target income level include Social Security?
- How many years of service should be required for an employee to have earned the targeted level of benefit?

As with any type of benefits plan, there are advantages and disadvantages to defined benefit plans. The advantages are as follows:

- The plan appeals to older employees and those with longer service.
- Control of plan investments remains with the employer.
- The plan makes it possible for employers to provide early retirement incentives to employees.
- Employers can provide ad hoc benefit increases to current retirees.
- The plan guarantees a specific lifetime benefit to employees.

Exhibit 10-4. Types of defined contribution plans.

	Profit Sharing	Money Purchase	Savings/Thrift	ESOP
Company Contributions	Based directly or indirectly on profits	Based on formula regardless of profits	Usually based on employee contributions	Based on formula regardless of profits
Employee Contributions	May or may not be required	May or may not be required	Usually required	May or may not be required

- Employees' retirement income objectives can be set and met.
- Past service benefits can be provided.
- There is funding flexibility even though there are some limitations.

The disadvantages are as follows:

- Employees with shorter service who terminate employment are left with a very small benefit, if any.
- The plan is difficult to understand.
- Employer's liability is not known precisely, and there is potential for unfunded liabilities.
- The investment risk remains with employer.
- Pension Benefit Guarantee Corporation (PBGC) premiums are due each year. (This is an organization similar to the FDIC. It is a government agency that insures pension plans.)
- Compliance with changing laws and regulations can be difficult.

The significance of each advantage and disadvantage must be measured against the employer's objectives in order to determine their relative significance.

Defined Contribution Plans Again, as the name indicates, with a defined contribution plan the employer defines the amount of the contribution to be made on behalf of the employees. With a defined contribution plan, employees have individual accounts. The benefits are variable based on the amount of the employer's contributions, the investment experience, and, possibly, forfeitures. Benefits are payable upon death, disability, termination, or retirement. There are several variations of defined contribution plans, which are summarized in Exhibit 10-4.

Under the *profit-sharing* plan, the employer makes available money according to the company's profits. Profit-sharing plans may apply to all employees, limited groups of employees, or only executives. Under the *money-purchase* plan, the employer's contribution is based on a fixed percentage of annual compensation, regardless of company profits. Under the *savings or thrift* plan, employees are given the option of saving a designated portion of their regular pay through payroll deductions; the money is invested in a vehicle chosen by the employee and usually matched by the employer. The 401(k) plan is one common example. Under the *ESOP,* or employee stock-ownership plan, employees are given company stock as an incentive; once they become vested, employees can redeem the stock when they leave the company.

The advantages of defined contribution plans are as follows:

- The plan appeals to younger employees and those with shorter service.
- The plan is easy to understand.
- The employer can shift the choice of investment responsibility to the plan participants.
- Qualified plans eliminate the need for actuarial services.
- The plan eliminates unfunded pension liabilities. The employer's liability is limited to the annual contribution.
- The plan provides a visible accumulation for the employee's retirement.
- The plan is more accessible to and portable for the employee than a defined benefit plan.
- Regulatory compliance is generally easier than with defined benefit plans.
- Funding flexibility can be provided in profit-sharing plans.
- It is possible to link the employer's financial performance with profit-sharing plans.

The disadvantages are as follows:

- The plan may not appeal to older employees and those with longer service.
- The plan makes it difficult for the employee to meet specific retirement income objectives.
- The retirement benefit is heavily influenced by investment performance.
- Administrative expenses can be high.
- Under the plan the employer cannot provide early retirement incentives to employees.
- Employers cannot increase benefits to current retirees when benefits become small as a result of high inflation.
- Past service benefits cannot be provided.
- The employee bears responsibility for managing retirement benefits before and during retirement.

Cash Balance Plans A cash balance plan, a relatively new type of plan, combines some of the features of defined benefit and defined contribution plans. Cash balance plans look like defined contribution plans but are qualified as defined benefit plans. The employee has an individual account, like in a defined contribution plan. The account increases each year by a set contribution based on the employee's pay and by a guaranteed investment return. Thus, the employer assumes all of the investment risk. The funding of a cash balance plan is more flexible than a defined contribution plan because the employer is funding the underlying benefit and not the actual contribution to the account.

When employees terminate or retire, they can receive the account balance either as a lump sum or as an annuity. Like a typical defined contribution plan, a larger portion of the employer contribution goes to younger employees who terminate than to the older, long-service employees.

The advantages of cash balance plans are as follows:

- The plan appeals to younger employees and those with shorter service.
- The plan is easy to understand.
- Control of plan investments remains with the employer.
- It is possible for the employer to provide early retirement incentives to employees.
- Past service benefits can be provided.
- The plan provides a visible accumulation for retirement.
- The plan is more accessible to and portable for the employee than benefits in a defined benefit plan.
- There is funding flexibility even though there are some limitations.

The disadvantages are as follows:

- The plan may not appeal to older employees and those with longer service.
- Since the employer's liability is not known precisely, there is the potential for unfunded liabilities.
- The investment risk remains with the employer.
- PBGC premiums are due each year.
- Compliance with changing laws and regulations can be difficult.

Target Benefit Plan Another type of hybrid retirement plan is a target benefit plan. These plans are qualified under government regulations as defined contribution plans but provide several of the advantages of defined benefit plans. Each employee has an individual account. The contribution to each employee's account is different in order to target a specific benefit for the individual employee. The employee assumes all investment risk. The employer calculates the targeted benefit amount at retirement age and then determines the contribution required to hit the target based on an assumed investment return. To the extent the investments are different than the assumed investment return, the actual benefit will be higher or lower than the targeted benefit amount.

RETIREMENT PLAN PROVISIONS

Once the type of retirement plan is determined, the employer must determine the specific plan provisions. Below are some key provisions to be determined.

- *Normal retirement age*. This provision defines when full benefits are payable to the employee.
- *Early retirement* This provision determines the age at which an employee may receive benefits and what reductions in benefit amounts are made for taking the benefits early.
- *Vesting*. This provision determines when the employee has full "ownership" of the plan benefits whether or not he or she continues to be an active employee.
- *Disability*. This feature may allow employees to receive an unreduced benefit

upon disability, or it may simply provide for the continued recognition of service during disability with the benefit still payable at retirement age.
- *Retirement death benefits.* This provision states what is due to an employee's beneficiary from the retirement plan in the event of the employee's death prior to retirement age.

Once the type of retirement plan and the key provisions are developed, perhaps the employer's most difficult task is to communicate. Employees should understand the value of the plan and be able to use it in planning for their retirement. Many organizations use a combination of communications media for this purpose.

Vacation Time and Holidays

Time off from work—for vacations, holidays, and illness—is another standard employee benefit. The standard vacation benefit in most companies is two weeks after one year of service, three weeks after five years of service, and four weeks after ten years of service. Earned, unused vacation time is paid on termination.

Sick Pay

The standard sick leave policy is a half-day earned per month, to a total of six days per year. Some companies let employees carry the time over from year to year but put a cap on it at a certain number of days. Other companies do not let employees carry the time over from year to year. Another practice is to eliminate sick pay after three days and offer a short-term disability plan through the insurance carrier, which starts paying after the three-day company-paid leave.

Paid Holidays

Most companies provide paid holidays for employees. Standard holidays are Christmas Eve, Christmas Day, New Year's Day, Memorial Day, Independence Day, Labor Day, and two days over Thanksgiving. Most companies now give employees two days off for Christmas and two days for Thanksgiving. Some companies give one or two days as floating holidays which can be used either on the employees' birthday or for religious holidays. Sick pay and holiday pay are normally not paid on termination.

Educational Assistance

This benefit is a common one for midsize and large organizations. The benefit varies from company to company, but it normally covers the cost of tuition and books for education or training taken outside company premises that relates to the employee's job. Some policies are broader and cover courses that do not relate to the job but are required in order for the employee to obtain a degree.

Relocation

Thousands of companies today are involved in corporate relocations. Most companies that ask employees to relocate pay their relocation costs, including the cost of selling their old home and buying a new one. Various relocation benefits include, but are not limited to, the following:

- Paid moving expenses
- One month's salary to cover incidental expenses
- Mortgage interest differentials
- Cost-of-living differentials
- Relocation taxation policies
- Up-front bonuses to move

As part of their relocation policies, companies should emphasize how the transfer fits into the employee's career progression and furthers his or her career. In addition, the new job must be challenging as an incentive for the employee to accept a transfer. But companies should not "dead-end" employees who reject relocations. Many employees fear that refusing a transfer could damage their careers. In companies that explicitly state that transfer refusals will not result in dead-ending, employees have a greater feeling of control over their careers.

An important relocation benefit offered by many organizations is assisting the relocating spouse with job placement help at the new location. This benefit, called transplacement, provides the relocating spouse with job contacts in the new area, counseling in job search techniques, help with résumé preparation, and so on. In fact, getting the entire family involved is an important component of a successful relocation. To that end, many organizations pay for the entire family to make a trip to the new area to look at homes, schools, and so on.

Miscellaneous Work and Family Benefits

Because of the growing number of two-income families and the number of single-parent employees, companies are becoming more attuned to work and family issues. As a result, some companies are offering additional benefits related to family needs. Examples include child care, which can include providing information on child care services in the community, helping with child care expenses, and running on-site or near-site child care centers. Elder care benefits are also available in some companies, since so many employees are now responsible for caring for older relatives. These benefits, however, are not as widespread as child care benefits. Companies are also beginning to offer employees more liberal time off with pay, to be used after a baby is born or adopted (for both fathers and mothers) or as needed for personal situations. (See Chapter 15 for more information on work and family issues.)

Employee Communications

To a great extent, a benefits program's success relies on how employees perceive the program and how well they understand and properly use it. For example, if an employer is changing from a typical indemnity plan to a PPO program with a utilization review feature, employees will most likely react negatively to the change—unless a thorough communications campaign accompanies the plan change. One fact is clear: Employees react negatively to change unless they have a clear understanding of why that change is taking place and how it affects them and the organization.

A thorough communications campaign typically includes:

- Planning
- Listening to employees' concerns
- Drafting materials (print/audiovisual/face-to-face)
- Reviewing materials
- Testing
- Producing
- Distributing
- Finalizing
- Evaluating

Some campaigns may not include all steps, but the campaign's effectiveness is enhanced when all steps take place.

If an employer wants positive employee perceptions of the benefits programs, it is essential that an effective communications plan be developed. Most employees value the benefits plan in proportion to how effectively the employer communicates it to them. Investing time to plan and organize an appropriate employee communications campaign will result in increased employee understanding and more positive perceptions. A typical planning process is outlined in Exhibit 10-5.

The planning process will help the employer:

- Identify its communications objectives and philosophies.
- Determine for each benefits plan the amount of education that is appropriate and desired.
- Identify employees' current understanding of various plan provisions.
- Determine the most appropriate communications media.
- Outline all communications needs (legal requirements, forms, etc.).
- Define the audience so that materials will be developed that will be understood and appreciated by the majority of employees.
- Select an appealing graphic theme and design to add interest to the communications materials.

The planning process results in specific activities, timelines, and responsibilities that will ensure the project is on target. Following the planning process, the employer can develop an outline of communications components that may include any combination of the following:

- Listening to employees through surveys and/or meetings. More and more employers are utilizing these methods to gather employee input to increase their success in developing benefits plans that will be appreciated by employees.
- Announcement letters that introduce new plans or provisions.
- Articles in company newsletters that are used to reinforce announcements, keep employees informed, and remind employees of key items.
- Posters to add excitement and interest to communications campaigns.
- Brochures that provide plan highlights and key provisions.

Exhibit 10-5. Planning an employee communications program.

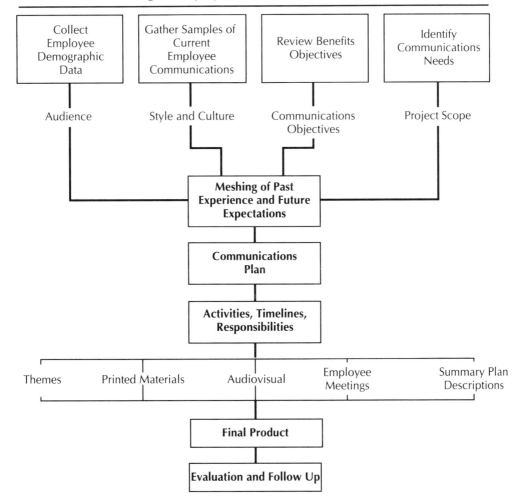

- Telephone hotlines to answer employees' individual questions.
- Audiovisual presentations to provide consistently delivered messages and highlights of plans and to add interest.
- Personalized benefits statements to show employees their individual benefits information and their value and cost.
- Summary plan descriptions to meet legal requirements.
- Forms for employees to make benefits elections.
- Employee meetings to explain plans, answer questions, etc.
- Management briefings and/or employee forums for sharing ongoing information.
- Employee involvement mechanisms, such as drawings and contests.
- Interactive communications tools, such as telephone voice response systems and computer modeling software.

In order to ensure that communications materials meet the employer's objectives of providing appropriate information in an understandable and interesting manner to employees, employee testing should be considered. Either by conducting group meetings or by distributing draft materials, employees can provide input before final materials are produced.

The above methods and many more can be effective in communicating benefits plans. It is important to remember that employees will become fully educated on plans and their provisions after multiple communications campaigns. An ongoing communications plan that builds on the initial information is best for increasing employee understanding.

11

Flexible Benefits

Carol Benjamin
Consultant
The Wyatt Company

The U.S. work force is changing dramatically—growing older and becoming more diverse with more women, minorities, and immigrants. In addition, studies reveal new views emerging about work and careers. We are seeing attitudes and values toward work and toward employers that have not been previously witnessed. These changes are the driving force behind a different psychological perception and work ethic in the United States today. These changes are causing employers to become more flexible in ways that impact employees. Specifically, as employers are becoming aware of the need to respond to employees' changing needs, there is greater flexibility in benefits.

Flexible benefits plans, which allow employees to choose a mix of benefits that best meet their particular needs, have been adopted by a large number of companies in recent years. Employers who do not give workers an opportunity to help select their own benefits may, in fact, find themselves at a competitive disadvantage in the future. An imaginatively designed flexible benefits plan can give a company a recruiting and retention edge in the new labor market.

More than 50 percent of 515 employers surveyed by The Wyatt Company in 1990 that do not currently sponsor a flexible benefits program indicate they are planning to implement one within the next five years. Flexible benefits plans are no longer the way of the future. They are already here.

Before going into detail about how flexible benefits plans (commonly called "flex") actually work, it is worthwhile to consider some of the many myths and realities about flex.

• Many people believe that flexible benefits plans can save a company a lot of money. Actually, they do not. But there are many reasons beyond cost saving for a company to implement flexible benefits plans, not the least of which is that with them employers can enhance positive employee relations, and can attract and retain a better work force.

• Many people believe that with flexible benefits, employees can take all cash and no benefits. Actually, most companies restrict the so-called cash option, with such restrictions written into the plan. Most plans require that a "core" level of benefit coverage be taken to protect employees against inadequate coverage.

• Many people believe that flexible benefits will end if tax advantages connected with them are legislated out of existence. Actually, tax advantages are rarely the major reason companies have for implementing flexible benefits. In fact, if benefits plans become taxable, there may be a boom in flexible benefits.

• Many people believe that significant in-house systems are needed to support the implementation of a flexible benefits program and that the current human resources staff will be unable to administer such a program. Actually, employers can use third-party administrators or relatively inexpensive software programs to support the implementation of a flex plan. As for the HR staff, if it is in good shape now, it probably will be able to administer a flexible benefits plan successfully. If it is having trouble administering standard benefits, it will have similar problems administering a flexible benefits plan. In general, flexible benefits often promote administrative efficiency.

• Many people believe that it is extremely expensive to implement flexible benefits. Actually, while it can be fairly expensive (but less expensive now than it was in the 1970s or 1980s), the investment is usually returned within two years.

To understand the concepts of flexible benefits fully, two terms need to be defined:

• *Pretax* literally means "before tax." The federal government allows certain types of benefits plans to offer employees the option of paying for some insurance coverage and contributing to regulated savings programs by taking funds out of the participants' paychecks before federal, most state, and Social Security taxes are withheld. This process generally results in more spendable income for the employee than if the same amount of funds were deducted on an after-tax basis. It has the effect of lowering the employee's taxable salary, which, in turn, reduces the amount of taxes due on that salary.

• *Reimbursement accounts* are flexible spending accounts included in many flexible benefits programs. These are accounts set up for each employee that offer a choice between taxable cash and nontaxable compensation in the form of payment or reimbursement of eligible, tax-favored benefits.

What Are Flexible Benefits?

A flexible benefits program offers employees a choice. Typically, plans include choices between taxable cash and nontaxable benefits (such as medical and dental care and disability). However, many plans have choices only among nontaxable benefits. Others include choices between taxable benefits (such as elder care and auto insurance) and nontaxable benefits. The benefits choices offered should reflect and support an organization's philosophies and objectives.

Without flexible benefits, compensation and benefits are independent of one another. When flexible benefits are introduced, benefits and pay relate to one another and essentially overlap, making a portion of each "flexible," as illustrated in Exhibit 11-1. The portion that becomes flexible represents the areas where employees can trade some benefits for other benefits, benefits for compensation, or compensation for benefits. However, most plans do not allow all benefits to become flexible. The nonflexible benefits are often referred to as the "core" benefits, which employees are required to continue to take.

Additionally, with flexible benefits, employers are able to separate *the form* from *the cost* of the benefits package. The amount of benefits dollars to be given to employees is budgeted each year, much like an organization budgets its annual salary increase

Exhibit 11-1. The overlapping of benefits and compensation in a flexible benefits plan.

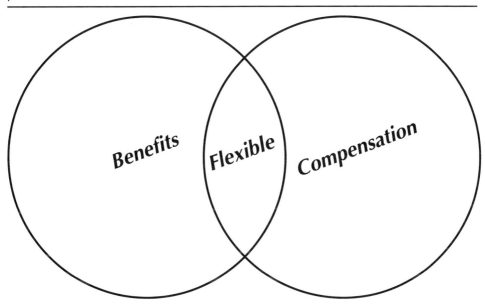

dollars. These dollars are allocated to employees based on a method established by the employer. Employees then are given benefits choices, each with an appropriate price tag, and choose how they want to spend their benefits dollars. Unlike traditional benefits programs, the employer defines the company's contribution amount to the benefits plan, rather than defining the benefit (regardless of the cost). The illustration in Exhibit 11-2 shows how a plan might work.

Employees are permitted to select their benefits choices annually and whenever they have a family status change. A family status change is typically defined as marriage, divorce, birth or death of a dependent, or significant change in work status by the employee or the employee's spouse.

Why Flexible Benefits?

Employers are implementing flexible benefits plans to:

- Provide a "total compensation" program where employees can see the total value of the cost of their pay and benefits. Most employees do not realize the cost of benefits provided by their employers. Flexible benefits helps employees gain an understanding and appreciation of benefits and their cost.
- Provide employees with choices so they can select benefits that meet their individual needs. Traditional benefits programs meet the needs of only a very small percentage of employees in our changing society.

Exhibit 11-2.   A flexible benefits plan in action.

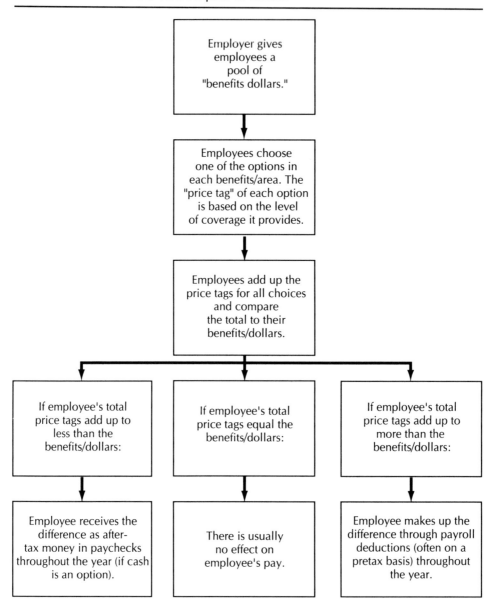

- Attract and retain employees in a tightening labor market. Providing a package that meets employees' individual needs makes the total compensation package more valuable to employees.
- Assist with cost management of the benefits program as health care costs continue to soar. Separating the form of benefit from the cost allows management to control benefits costs.
- Provide a unique competitive program. During the 1990s, competition for skilled

workers will increase dramatically. A well-communicated flexible benefits plan can differentiate an employer from competitors and is an excellent way for employers to increase the perceived value of limited benefits dollars.

• Address the issues of multiple work groups as businesses continue to diversify, creating needs for different benefits levels.

• Add new coverages that employees are requesting, without spending additional employer dollars. As pressure is added to provide more benefits, employers with flexible benefits programs can add new plans as choices that employees can buy using their allocated flexible benefits dollars.

• Provide employees with an opportunity to pay for benefits on a tax-effective basis. Allowing employees to trade taxable pay for nontaxable benefits is a tax-efficient method of adding value to dollars being spent on employees.

• Communicate and educate employees about various benefits options. When employees have choices to make, they learn more about their benefits.

Employers must assess their own reasons for implementing a flexible benefits program. These reasons will directly influence the type of flexible benefits program that is appropriate for that organization.

What Is Included in Flexible Benefits?

A full spectrum of flexible benefits plans is now available. These include *premium-only plans,* which allow a choice between cash or pretax payment of medical, dental, life, and/or disability premiums. *Reimbursement account plans* allow employees to choose between cash and paying uninsured health care and/or day care expenses on a pretax basis. *Modular flexible benefits plans* provide choice by allowing employees to select from one or two or three benefits programs. *Full flexible benefits plans* are the most complex. They offer a choice of benefits levels in most coverage areas. They may or may not incorporate a managed health care plan. Typically, such plans include reimbursement accounts for pretax payment of health care and dependent care expenses.

The following are nontaxable options that may be included in a flexible benefits plan:

• Medical care
• Dental care
• Vision and hearing care
• Group life insurance
• Accidental death and dismemberment insurance
• Long-term disability
• Short-term disability
• Prescription drug plan
• Vacation trading
• Dependent day care

Many plans also include a Section 401(k), Section 403(b), or Section 457 savings plan under the flexible benefits program. (These savings plans allow an employee to contribute to a retirement or salary-deferral account on a pretax basis. Employers often make tax-deductible contributions to the accounts.) Employers encourage employees to save for retirement by adding one of these plans. However, these plans cannot be *directly* linked to a Section 125 (of the Internal Revenue Code) flexible benefits program. To build one of these salary deferral plans into a flexible benefits plan, the employee must first elect between taxable benefits and cash (if cash is an option). Then, under the salary deferral plan, the employee decides between keeping the taxable cash or deferring that amount into the 401(k), 403(b), or 457 plan, depending on which plan the employer is able to offer.

In addition, there are several taxable options that are included under flexible benefits plans. Even though these items are taxable choices, their popularity is continuing to grow. Some of the most common taxable options are:

- Cash
- Dependent life insurance
- Universal life insurance
- Automobile insurance
- Homeowners insurance
- Elder care
- Long-term care
- Wellness

Organizations not including a cash option in their flexible benefits plans find that providing other taxable options can help meet employees' needs and support corporate objectives, such as encouraging wellness.

Cost Issues

As previously stated, flexible benefits alone cannot stop cost increases, which continue because of new technology, increasing utilization, and inflation. Medical costs are rising nearly twice as fast as the rate of inflation, in spite of all the efforts made by employers, insurance companies, and health care providers. People are living longer, and new technology is expensive. Frequently, consumers use sophisticated, expensive health care services freely—often for problems that could have been solved with simple, less expensive remedies.

Flexible benefits plans do have cost-saving characteristics. They include:

- Reducing pressure to add new employer-paid benefits. New options can be added and employees can choose which benefits they want. The employer does not need to increase the dollars provided to employees for "buying" the benefits.
- Slowing the rate of increase for total health care costs. When employees elect medical options with greater first-dollar costs but lower price tags, utilization typically decreases. This generally results in a slower rate of health care cost increases.
- Shifting a greater share of the cost to employees. As employees have to pay more of the total cost for health care, they tend to become better consumers of health care services.

- Reducing duplicate dependent coverage. Flexible benefits encourages employees whose working spouses can move to their employer's plans to do so.

Design Considerations

When developing a flexible benefits program, an organization must study each benefits area and determine what options, choices, and price tags will support the organization's benefits philosophy. Careful consideration needs to be given to the:

- Allocation of flexible benefits dollars.
- Breadth of plans to be included, e.g., medical, dental, disability, and life insurance.
- Depth of options: How many choices will be included for each benefits area of the plan?
- Pricing of options, taking into consideration possible adverse selection, the organization's objectives, etc.
- Communication: Educating and involving employees.
- Administration: Will the plan be administered internally or externally?

You must identify the source of flexible benefits dollars—where the dollars come from for employees to use to purchase benefits. There are typically two sources of dollars: employer and employee. Employer dollars might come from current benefits, reduction of other benefits, or additional money the organization is willing to spend on benefits. Employee dollars come from salary conversion, which means using currently taxable pay for nontaxable and/or taxable benefits. When an organization determines the employer dollar allocation, the following organizational objectives should be considered:

- *Cost management.* What are the organization's objectives?
- *Profit sharing.* Should flexible benefits dollars vary based on the profitability of the organization?
- *Service recognition.* Should an employee's amount of service be reflected in the amount of flexible benefits dollars he or she is allocated?
- *Social responsibility.* Does the organization feel a responsibility for providing a certain level of benefits to all employees? To employees' dependents?
- *Pay equity.* Should all employees receive the same amount of benefits dollars, or should it vary?
- *Wellness.* Should an employee's good health and wellness be rewarded?

Most employers struggle with determining how to allocate employer dollars. In addition to the previous considerations, past practice usually influences what approach the organization eventually takes. Organizations often begin developing a flexible benefits plan with the following goals:

- Equal flexible benefits dollars for all employees. (This can be difficult if the organization has previously paid for or subsidized coverage for employees' dependents.)

- No winners or losers. (This is nearly impossible if changes are made.)
- Realistic price tags so employees begin understanding the true cost of benefits.
- No additional cost. (This is probably impossible if all of the above goals are to be met.)

Meeting all four of these goals is usually not possible, so the organization must prioritize the goals before setting a flexible benefits dollar allocation and pricing approach.

Options to Include in Flexible Benefits

Medical Option Considerations

Since the medical plan generates the single highest cost of the flexible benefits plan, a great deal of time is needed to design medical options that will help the organization meet cost objectives. These elements should be considered:

- *Deductibles.* How much should the employee pay before the plan begins paying?
- *Copayments.* How much of each expense should the employee pay?
- *Out-of-pocket maximums.* At what point should the plan pay 100 percent of eligible expenses for employees? For employees' dependents?
- *Cost management features.* What features have proven successful, and should they be incorporated into all of the medical options?
- *Wellness benefits.* Should any or all of the options encourage wellness by providing additional dollars for encouraging employees to be healthy?
- *Pricing.* How should all of the various options be priced in relationship to one another and for covering various family demographics? Also, most organizations develop a second and subsequent years' pricing strategy since health care is the largest cost-containment component of the plan.

In addition, the organization must determine if employees will be allowed to waive all medical coverage and use their flexible benefits dollars to buy other benefits. And, if so, will these employees receive the entire flexible benefits dollar allocation?

There are many types of medical plans: indemnity plans (fully insured, partially insured, and self-insured), preferred provider organization (PPO) plans, health maintenance organization (HMO) plans, managed care plans, and reimbursement account plans. Organizations must study all of these types of plans and consider their current plans in order to determine the types of plans that will work best in a new flexible benefits program. (See Chapter 10 for detailed information on medical plans.)

Savings Through Flexible Benefits Managed Care

Incorporating managed care with the flexible benefits program can help an employer better manage costs. With a managed care plan, the employer employs a staff of medical specialists who monitor proposed care to contain the costs of health care benefits plans. By negotiating preferential provider prices and tightly monitoring the use of services, the employer's cost objectives can be better met.

OTHER OPTIONS FOR SAVINGS

When designing medical options, some of the features that have worked very successfully in helping organizations meet their objectives, in addition to managed care, are:

- *A wide range of deductibles.* If the deductibles are too close together, employees tend to continue to elect the richest (lowest deductible) plan.
- *A small range of copayments.* The amount of copayments from one option to another tends to work best when the range is small.
- *Low family out-of-pocket maximums.* Employees are generally most concerned about their cost exposure for a major illness or accident.
- *High dependent cost.* This will help encourage employees whose spouses have coverage available through their own employers to move to those plans.

Dental Considerations

Developing dental options is much easier than developing medical options. Employers must consider how many options are appropriate, whether or not a no coverage option should be allowed, and the provisions of the current plan now in place. Consideration with regard to adverse selection is perhaps even more important when designing dental plans than medical plans. It is easier for an employee to select against a dental plan than to select against a medical plan. Therefore, certain rules and election restrictions typically accompany dental options (e.g., making dental elections every two years, rather than annually). The potential of adverse selection requires that significant thought be given to the design and pricing of dental options.

Vision and Hearing Considerations

When designing vision and hearing options, the most important consideration is the value of the benefit versus the price. Although many employees request vision and hearing plans, they are often disappointed in the value of the benefit they receive for the price they pay. An employer must determine if it is better to offer vision and/or hearing options or to encourage employees to pay for these expenses on a nontaxable basis through the reimbursement account.

Group Life Insurance Considerations

There are many types of group life insurance, including employee life, accidental death and dismemberment, dependent life (an after-tax benefit), and survivor income. An organization must determine the number of options, how the options will be priced (if age-related prices are appropriate), and how current plans will impact the design. Again, adverse selection is an issue, and plan restrictions should be considered.

Disability Considerations

There are both short-term and long-term disability plans that may be appropriate for a flexible benefits plan. Based on what type of disability plans the employer currently has in place and how well those plans are meeting objectives, a number of options may be appropriate to incorporate into the flexible benefits plan. The design and pricing of disability plans is important to control adverse selection. For example, additional short-term disability benefits may be very attractive for employees with "planned" disabilities, such as pregnancy. Therefore, the organization must carefully design and price short-term disability options.

Vacation Considerations

The single most important consideration when incorporating time-off benefits into a flexible benefits plan tends to be the current program an employer offers. Established policies toward accumulating vacation days and carrying them forward from year to year will impact the ability to incorporate the current plan into a flexible benefits program. An employer must determine whether or not buying and/or selling time-off days will help meet overall company objectives. This issue is becoming more important as we experience an increased labor shortage.

If buying and/or selling vacation time is deemed appropriate, the employer must decide how many days should be part of the flexible benefits plan and if the cost of each day that is bought or sold should be equal to 100 percent of employees' current pay. Providing time-off benefits is a soft-dollar cost, particularly with management employees. Allowing employees to use cash to buy other benefits becomes a hard-dollar cost. These considerations must be noted when pricing time-off benefits to be bought and/or sold.

Reimbursement Accounts

Most flexible benefits plans include reimbursement accounts. There are two types of allowable accounts: health care and dependent day care. Expenses that are eligible for a reimbursement account are paid on a nontaxable basis. There are two sources of contributions to the reimbursement account: employer (leftover flexible benefits dollars) and employee (through salary conversion).

In exchange for the nontaxability of these monies, there are certain rules imposed by the IRS, including:

- *Annual election.* The employee must determine annually what contribution, if any, he or she wishes to make to either or both of the reimbursement accounts. This election can be changed during the year only in the event of a family status change.
- *Nontransferrable funds.* Monies in either account cannot be transferred to the other account.
- *Forfeiture of unused funds.* Contributions made to either account must be used for eligible expenses during the year in which they are contributed, or the employee is required to forfeit them at the end of the plan year. Forfeitures can be used in the following manner: allocated to employees or plan participants on a pro rata basis, used to offset plan administrative costs, or retained by the employer.
- *Contribution limits.* The health care contribution limit is determined by the em-

ployer, but it must be equally available to all employees. The day care limit is $5,000 per year for employees who are married and filing jointly or are single employees, and $2,500 for employees who are married but filing separately.

Health Care Reimbursement Account

Eligible expenses payable from the health care reimbursement account include:

- Uninsured medical expenses, such as:
  —deductibles
  —copayments/coinsurance
  —ineligible expenses (well-baby care, physicals, chiropractic care, etc.)
  —expenses in excess of plan limits
- Uninsured vision expenses, such as:
  —deductibles
  —copayments/coinsurance
  —exams
  —lenses and frames
  —contacts
- Uninsured hearing expenses, such as:
  —exams
  —hearing aids
- Uninsured dental expenses, such as:
  —deductibles
  —copayments/coinsurance
  —orthodontia
  —expenses in excess of plan limits

An employee's annual election to the health care account must be available for employee use from the first day of the plan year.

Day Care Reimbursement Account

Expenses for dependent care incurred in order for an employee—and if married, for the spouse—to work can be paid pretax through the reimbursement plan. Key plan rules include:

- The annual amount of expenses for which an employee can be reimbursed must be less than the lower of the employee's income or the spouse's income.
- The expenses must be for the care of a dependent who is under age 13 and entitled to a dependent deduction under Internal Revenue Code Section 151(e), or a dependent who is physically or mentally incapable of self-care.
- The payments cannot be made to a person who is claimed as the employee's dependent on that person's federal income tax form.
- If the care is provided by a dependent care center or in an individual's home that provides for more than six individuals, the center or home must comply with all state and local laws in order for the cost to be eligible for reimbursement.
- The person providing care must sign the reimbursement claim form or provide a

receipt or invoice that includes his or her Social Security or care center license number.

Day care reimbursements cannot be used additionally as a tax credit. Therefore, employees must determine if they are better off paying for day care expenses through the day care reimbursement account or paying them and claiming a tax credit. To some extent, day care reimbursement accounts and the day care tax credit can be coordinated. Employers should be prepared to provide employees with guidelines and/or worksheets to assist them in determining whether the dependent care reimbursement account or the tax credit is best for their individual situations.

Day care funds are available for the employee's use as the employee's contributions are made to his or her account. Typically, only the amount of funds in the employee's day care account are reimbursable.

Encouraging Wellness

One of the newest and most exciting considerations for flexible benefits plans is encouraging wellness. Many organizations have become concerned about the amount of dollars that are spent on employees who do not take care of themselves and on how few dollars are directed toward employees who keep themselves well. When developing an approach within the flexible benefits structure to encourage wellness, an employer must: focus on demographics and culture, determine standards for evaluation, facilitate the evaluation process, and reinforce with employees that wellness is a shared responsibility. Employees are typically asked to complete a health appraisal, meet health appraisal standards, follow a course of treatment, and improve against health appraisal standards. If the wellness standards are met, the flexible benefits plan might:

- Increase the amount of the employer-provided flexible benefits contribution
- Decrease the cost for buying any of the medical options
- Decrease the amount of the medical plan deductible
- Provide a contribution to employee's reimbursement accounts
- Reimburse expenses for wellness activities, e.g., health club memberships and exercise equipment
- Reward the employees with additional paid time-off days.

Organizations are using wellness incentives to encourage employees to exercise, maintain weight and cholesterol standards, stop smoking, change eating behaviors, and so on.

Conducting a Feasibility Study

Many organizations conduct a feasibility study to determine if a flexible benefits program will complement the organization's business strategy and philosophy, and if so, what type. There are seven basic components to a flexible benefits feasibility study.

1. Project planning
2. Establishing benefits philosophy and objectives

3. Inventory of existing plans and practices
4. Design of preliminary flexible benefits program model
5. Implementation analysis
6. Cost/benefit analysis
7. Report and presentation to management

The results of each component will help management in determining if a flexible benefits program is right for the organization. A brief overview of each component follows.

Project Planning

Successfully completing a flexible benefits feasibility study is vitally important to the ultimate success of the project. To accomplish its objectives within a given time frame requires careful planning. Therefore, the first step in the flexible benefits planning study is to develop a detailed project plan.

Project planning involves identifying the project participants and tasks to be performed, determining responsibilities, and developing a work schedule. The organization's decision-making style and other such factors will also influence the work plan. This step may also involve educating project participants about flexible benefits and the process the project will follow.

Some of the key issues addressed in the project planning is to decide:

- What input is required for each of the objectives of the planning study, and who should provide that input?
- Do any special groups, task forces, or committees need to be formed?
- Who will the ultimate decision makers be?
- What decision-making process should be followed?

Establishing Benefits Philosophy and Objectives

The development of any cohesive, integrated employee benefits program (especially a flexible benefits program) can be best accomplished within the context of comprehensive benefits program objectives. For this reason, it is advisable to establish the organization's benefits philosophy and objectives at the outset of the planning study. A task force is typically utilized to accomplish this. Then, the results are reviewed and approved by top management.

Some of the issues to be addressed include:

- Determining the responsibility of the organization to provide for employee welfare and security
- Establishing the appropriate mix between salary, benefits, or other forms of compensation among groups of employees
- Determining the role of employee benefits in achieving organizational objectives
- Establishing the limitations, if any, placed on plan design by internal administration and communications capabilities
- Identifying the employee perceptions the organization wants to generate with its employee benefits program

- Agreeing upon the degree to which employees should have control over their benefits
- Determining the funding and cost containments
- Documenting the degree of fluctuation in benefits expenditures that the organization can tolerate

Inventory of Existing Plans and Practices

A review of the existing program and practices is essential to make a meaningful recommendation concerning the variability of a flexible benefits program or concerning possible modifications to the existing benefits program. This review is completed within the framework of the organization's benefits philosophy and objectives to identify any inconsistencies and to determine other opportunities for improvement. To aid in the understanding of the existing program, a certain amount of information must be compiled. This information includes:

- Detailed descriptions of existing benefits plan provisions, funding levels, and financing arrangements, including both employee and employer contributions
- Past and present benefits expenditures and future cost projections
- Demographic profiles of the organization's work force
- Participation statistics (current and historical) for all plans involving employee decisions
- Claims experience
- A description of the organization's payroll and human resources information systems
- Descriptions and examples of current employee communications practices
- Description of current employee attitudes, including results of any recent surveys
- Information about benefits practices at other organizations to which the organization wishes to be compared

The two most critical requirements for the successful implementation of a flexible benefits program are a sound administration package and a well-structured, meaningful communications package. The following should be completed to address these requirements and evaluate the organization's capabilities:

- Identification of the administration and communications requirements of a flexible benefits program
- Discussion of the impact of flexible benefits programs on administration and payroll systems
- Understanding of the organization's existing administration/payroll routines and administration/data processing environment and capabilities
- Evaluation of the organization's existing communications capabilities
- Identification of any budgetary limits the organization may have established for the administration and communication of a flexible benefits program

Design of Preliminary Flexible Benefits Program Model

When designing a flexible benefits program, attention must be given to the benefits areas to be included, the options to be offered in each benefits area, the source and allocation of credits, and the level of funding to be provided. Examples of the issues to be addressed are:

- Which employees will be eligible to participate in the program?
- What benefits choices should be provided?
- Should a minimum level of benefits coverage be required?
- What will be the source of funding?
- What method should be used for pricing options? What steps will be taken to counter adverse selection?
- How often should employees be allowed to change their choices?
- How will new employees and interim changes be accommodated?

The net result of this effort is a conceptual model of the new flexible benefits program. Based upon the results of the analysis, this model could be a comprehensive flexible benefits plan or a plan of lesser scope.

This conceptual design sets the stage for considering benefits funding needs, credits, and option price tags. It also provides a basis to evaluate the organization's benefits administration and communications capabilities and to develop preliminary administration and communications recommendations.

The impact of flexible benefits on overall benefits expenditures may then be analyzed. Taking the cost of adverse selection into account, rough estimates of the short-term and long-term cost implications are developed. Any additional hardware, software, or staffing required for the administration of a flexible benefits program can also be determined at this time.

Implementation Analysis

The purpose of this step is to identify the activities required to implement the flexible benefits program successfully, to determine who should be responsible for each activity, and to estimate the time and costs needed to complete each of the activities. This analysis is performed for each of the functional areas of plan design, financing, communications, and administration. The following should be addressed with respect to each of these areas of activity:

- What has to be done in order to implement the proposed flexible benefits program successfully?
- How should responsibility for accomplishing the activities be divided among the organization's personnel and external resources?
- What is the cost estimate of the implementation in terms of internal and external resources?
- How long will it take to accomplish all implementation activities?

Once the scope of the project is ascertained, an implementation plan is developed. This plan should include a timetable for action that encompasses all of the implementation activities required for plan design, communications, systems administration, and financing. It serves as a blueprint for the implementation of the entire flexible benefits program.

Cost/Benefit Analysis

In this step, the costs of the flexible benefits program should be projected over a five-year period. It is compared to the existing program, and the differences in net cost or savings are calculated on a present-value basis. Onetime implementation costs and increased ongoing administrative and staffing costs generated by the new flexible benefits program should be included in the comparison.

Report and Presentation to Management

All of the findings and recommendations resulting from the planning study should be documented in a written report and presented to the organization's management team. Assuming that the implementation of an expanded flexible benefits program is recommended, the written report should:

- Support the recommendation based on the organization's benefits philosophy and objectives
- Recommend an appropriate plan design
- Identify the steps remaining to implement a flexible benefits program along with a timetable for action
- Provide an estimate of the costs involved compared to the existing program

Implementing Flexible Benefits

Once an organization decides to implement a flexible benefits program, a staff team is required to implement the program successfully. Below is a summary of the key disciplines and tasks necessary to implement a flexible benefits program. Typically, a team of human resources, finance, systems, and legal representatives is necessary to complete these tasks.

Design

The team will need to redefine the plan design and develop detailed plan provisions, such as:

- Eligibility for current employees and new hires
- Definition of family status change and permitted enrollment changes
- Impact on other plans, such as pension plan, 401(k), or 403(b)
- Reimbursement account contributions, limits, reimbursement cycle, claim minimums, etc.
- Administration of adverse selection rules
- Default plans for employees failing to return enrollment forms

Flexible Benefits Dollar Allocation and Pricing

The flexible benefits dollar allocation—how many benefits dollars employees will receive—is the first component of making the plan design work. The second is the option price tags—how much employees will pay for each option they elect. The flexible benefits dollar allocation and option price tags are developed using the organization's objectives and strategies, past practice, and actual claims experience.

The method selected for allocating flexible benefits dollars depends largely on an organization's philosophy. The following issues need to be considered:

- Should equal dollars be given to all employees?
- Should dollars be based on whether an employee covers his or her family?
- What have been past practices of subsidizing benefits costs?
- Should dollars be based on the cost of current benefits plans?
- How should flexible benefits dollars given to each employee compare to price tags for various options?
- If permitted, will those employees who waive coverage receive a different amount of flexible benefits dollars?

The basis for setting option price tags also will affect how the flexible benefits dollars are allocated. In setting the price tags, employers must consider issues such as:

- Will options be priced by individual or by family unit?
- Will realistic price tags be used? If so, how will they be calculated? How will past claims experience be utilized?
- How will anticipated changes in items such as medical inflation, adverse selection, utilization, and plan design be used in calculating price tags?
- If employees are allowed to waive coverage, how will this impact pricing?
- Will any option price tags be subsidized to encourage enrollment in that specific option or to limit the potential of adverse selection?

An appropriate flexible benefits dollar allocation and price tag structure may be the most important factor to achieve an effective flexible benefits plan and to meet cost-management objectives. Therefore, these and other issues must be carefully considered and an appropriate strategy developed.

Communication

Effective communication of flexible benefits is critical to the success of the flexible benefits program. Generally, this requires:

- Informing employees so they become aware of the program
- Orienting them so they understand the program
- Motivating them so they have a positive attitude toward the program

Successful completion of this process can lead to employees making the "right" selections for themselves and their families and will facilitate a smooth enrollment process. The success of the communications effort is directly related to the media used to convey the program. A potential strategy that has often proved successful is to announce and reinforce the program through a coordinated but varied series of communications activities.

The beginning step is to develop a communications plan. The plan should include objectives for employee communications materials, development of an overall theme that reflects the organization's objectives, and a strategy that includes the most appropriate media and timing. There are several options when selecting the menu of media to be used to communicate the flexible benefits program. The most appropriate menu may vary, depending on the organization's culture, environment, in-house capabilities, and budget considerations. Consideration should be given to the following menu of communications items and to what will work best in the organization's environment.

PREENROLLMENT

- Send an announcement letter communicating basic program concepts and notifying employees of upcoming events.
- Circulate a series of time-released newsletters describing the different benefits options to be included in the flexible benefits plan.
- Display posters that announce the program, remind employees of upcoming events, and help build a sense of anticipation for the program.

ENROLLMENT

- Design a workbook to detail the flexible benefits options, "walk" employees through the enrollment process, and serve as a decision guide.
- Use a videotape or slide/tape show designed to communicate key flexible benefits plan messages, make the program seem real to employees, and leave employees with a positive feeling about the program and the organization, as well as to motivate employees to read the program materials and to get involved in the decision-making process.
- Distribute enrollment-related forms, including worksheets, personal reports, and enrollment forms to facilitate the enrollment process.
- Prepare employee meeting materials, such as an overhead or slide presentation and handouts, to assist the meeting leader in communicating the plan face-to-face.
- Circulate a question-and-answer brochure to address questions frequently asked by employees enrolling in a flexible benefits plan for the first time.

POSTENROLLMENT

- Draft a notice or payroll stuffer reminding employees to submit enrollment forms by a specified date.
- Provide confirmation statements to recap employees' choices and indicate the impact on employees' paychecks.

PART IV

EMPLOYEE RELATIONS AND RECRUITMENT AND RETENTION

12

Employee Assistance Programs

Dale A. Masi, D.S.W.
University of Maryland School of Social Work
and Masi Research Consultants, Inc.

In recent years, as employers found their problems with employees growing more complex and difficult to handle, employee assistance programs (EAPs) have been developed to deal with critical work issues. EAPs are a professional assessment and referral and/or short-term counseling service for employees with alcohol, drug, or emotional problems that may be affecting them on the job. Employees are either self-referred or referred by supervisors. Larger companies may retain EAP personnel on staff. Smaller organizations prefer to use off-site EAP consultants on an "as needed" basis.

EAPs help employees who are dealing with substance abuse, mental health problems, or other emotional issues—either their own or that of a loved one—by showing them how to cope with the anxiety, fear, and other emotions that emerge in response to these problems. EAP staff can work as team members with the personnel and medical staff of the organization, and they can also provide support services to unions for members who are dealing with personal problems.

A company's EAP can serve as a valuable resource in developing employee policies and in the long-term retention of valuable employees. As the workplace changes, it must be flexible and open in its commitment to help employees. And as society becomes more complex, the workplace must be prepared to offer employees help in coping with such issues as drugs, AIDS, sexual harassment, and prejudice. EAP personnel are in a unique position to offer this kind of support, since they are trained in mental health counseling, policy implementation, and education.

EAPs can also help companies to interpret and implement legislation pertinent to employees. For example, the Rehabilitation Act of 1973 and the Americans with Disabilities Act of 1990, which declared persons with certain illnesses to be handicapped, have been interpreted as extending to persons with AIDS. The EAP staff is already familiar with these laws as they pertain to persons with other handicapping conditions. That knowledge is an invaluable aid in understanding ramifications for employees who have AIDS, as issues arise concerning disability benefits and termination on medical grounds.

The Role of the EAP in Retention

As recently as the early 1980s, many troubled employees would have been reprimanded or even fired for lack of performance. Traditionally employers felt that employee problems were just that and should be dealt with privately, at a distance. Employees, on the other hand, felt that employers were disinterested in their personal concerns and difficulties. However, major changes in these kinds of attitudes and perceptions have occurred with the development of EAPs. Their major impact has been to change the view of the workplace from that of a producer of problems to a source of help.[1]

Employers are finding that in order to keep their most valuable asset, their employees, it is becoming necessary to identify troubled employees and assist them in their needs, while maintaining a productive, cost-effective work force. It is in this identification that the role of the EAP becomes critical. If troubled employees are identified and offered assistance and then regain their equilibrium, they will not become a burden or loss to the organization.

Need for EAPs

EAP experts estimate that 20 percent of any work force is affected by personal problems that can have an impact on job performance. Of the affected employees, statistics from the 1989 NIDA *National Household Survey* indicate that 12 percent have alcohol- and drug-related problems, and 6–8 percent have emotionally related problems. These problems can result in a 25 percent decrease in productivity and increased costs for the company. The annual costs to productivity for companies in the United States are over $50.6 billion for alcohol and drugs. Exhibit 12-1 lists the measurable, hidden, and legal costs to the organization arising from job performance problems. Proper utilization of the EAP concept can greatly reduce the financial costs, the costs associated with liabilities to the company, and the all-important cost of human lives.

Just as personal problems can have a negative effect on individuals, work can have a positive influence because self-esteem is tied to job and occupational concepts. An employee may deny a personal problem only until threatened with the loss of a job. Many alcoholics, for example, are motivated to seek help and address their problems only after their jobs and livelihood are in jeopardy.

History of EAPs

Employee assistance programs developed out of the concept of occupational alcoholism programs (OAPs), which began in the 1940s. OAPs were developed through the efforts of recovering alcoholics. They were based on the premise that a troubled employee should be confronted while still on the job; the employer should not try to cover up the problem. In this way the addiction could be treated and the job could be saved.

The fact that the job could be an important factor in confronting and treating alcoholism was the original premise behind occupational alcoholism programs. In the 1940s, Kemper Insurance, Eastman Kodak, and Du Pont Corporation, among others, started OAPs, headed primarily by staff who were themselves recovering alcoholics. With the passage of the Hughes Act (Public Law 91-616) in 1970, these programs received an important boost. The Act established the National Institute for Alcoholism and Alcohol Abuse (NIAAA) as distinct from the National Institute of Mental Health and mandated the establishment of an occupational branch for the NIAAA that granted funds to each state to hire two occupational program consultants (OPCs) charged with developing programs in both the private and public sectors.[2] The Hughes Act also man-

Exhibit 12-1. Losses to organizations from job performance problems.

Measurable Losses

Absenteeism
Overtime Pay
Tardiness
Sick Leave Abuse
Health Insurance Claims
Disability Payments

Hidden Losses

Diverted Supervisory/Managerial Time
Friction Among Workers
Waste
Damage to Equipment
Poor Decisions
Damage to Public Image
Personnel Turnover
Premature Death

Losses Related to Legal Claims

Workers Compensation
EEO Complaints
Disciplinary Actions
Grievance Procedures/Other Legal Actions
Threat to Public Safety
Illegal Drug Trafficking on the Job
Security Issues

dated the development of programs for the prevention, treatment, and rehabilitation of federal employees with alcohol and drug problems.[3]

The next year, a group of individuals in the OAP field met in Los Angeles to found the Association of Labor-Management Administrators and Consultants on Alcoholism (ALMACA). ALMACA began as a nonprofit international organization of practitioners involved in occupational alcoholism and employee assistance programming. This organization continues to serve as the professional body for OA/EAP practitioners.[4] Recently, it was renamed EAPA (Employee Assistance Professionals Association) to signify a broader representation than alcohol.

Passage of the Rehabilitation Act in 1973 served to promote awareness of the need for OA/EAPs.[5] Section 504 of the Act guarantees the rights of handicapped people; in other words, employers must offer reasonable accommodation to employees with handicapping conditions. In 1978, the U.S. attorney general defined *handicapped* to include alcoholism and drug addiction.

As OAPs developed, practitioners changed their focus from alcohol to job performance and found that programs dealing with a broader base of employee problems were more effective. This evolution into a broader model was the birth of the modern employee assistance program, which now includes such areas as parent-child relationships, emotional and life crisis, drugs, gambling, and eating disorders.

In the evolving EAP, supervisors were trained to focus on and confront employees whose job performance was falling, but they were cautioned not to try to diagnose the problem. This form of assistance focuses on supervisory referral to the EAP, based on observation of poor job performance. This shift of diagnosis from untrained staff to professionals developed as rising health care costs became of such concern to employers. It was found that furnishing counseling within the EAP was a way to limit mental health costs.

The EAP field expanded again in the 1980s as large numbers of employees—from Wall Street to factories, from hospitals to small companies—became exposed to drugs at the worksite. CEOs became aware of and alarmed at having pushers on their payroll. Moreover, the National Transportation Board found that an increasing number of transportation accidents were related to drugs. As a result, the Drug-Free Workplace Act of 1988 was passed, encouraging companies to implement EAPs.

By developing and maintaining a strong EAP, an organization significantly reduces the many costs, financial and otherwise, that it would have incurred because of employee's personal problems. When considering the more abstract costs, there is no way to measure the savings in relief from anxieties, fears, and distress; however, this savings clearly has a positive effect on overall morale, team spirit, loyalty to the organization, and public image.

Program Models

There are many different EAP models specifically designed to meet the needs of a wide variety of companies, but all of them fall into one of the following categories:

• *In-house model.* The entire assistance staff is employed by the company. A company manager directly supervises the program's personnel, sets policies, and designs all procedures. The program can be housed physically in the company or located in offices away from the worksite. A recent study suggests that top management believes that these programs provide service at a lower cost, with increased control, greater identification of alcoholic employees, increased supervisory and medical referrals, and more positive acceptance by unions.[6]

• *Out-of-house model.* The company contracts with a vendor to provide an employee assistance staff and services. The vendor might provide services in its own offices, the company's offices, or both. This model is viewed as providing better accountability, lower legal liability, and ease of start-up and implementation.

• *Consortium model.* Several companies pool their resources to develop a collaborative program and thus maximize individual resources. Generally, this model works best for companies with fewer than 2,000 employees. Services may be provided on-site or in separate offices. Running these programs may be more complex and may require a difficult decision-making process.

• *Affiliate model.* A vendor subcontracts with a local professional rather than use salaried staff. This enables the vendor to reach employees in a company location in which the vendor might not have an office. Usually this model is used in conjunction with a model that involves paid staff. With this model, the vendor may have less control over a subcontracted professional; however, this has become the vehicle whereby employees in various locations can be reached by one responsible vendor. Such programs may offer less accountability and decreased responsiveness.

In determining the best approach, each organization must ascertain how complex a program must be to fulfill its needs and the level of its commitment to it. Many companies prefer the contractual approach because the commitment need not be long-term. If evaluation deems the EAP is ineffective, it is easier to terminate a contract than to terminate members of the company's staff. Company size, geographic location and diversity, employee population, and values and goals are also important considerations. In many instances, a consultant is useful to help match company characteristics to a particular model.

Recent estimates reveal that there are now approximately 13,000 EAPs in U.S. work organizations, as compared to 5,000 in 1981.[7]

Essential Ingredients

The success of an EAP rests on the following essential ingredients. These elements are all equally important and are not listed in order of priority.

Policy Statement

The written policy statement clearly defines the purpose of the program, organizational and legal mandates, employee eligibility, the roles and responsibility of various personnel in the organization, and procedures. This statement should be endorsed by the highest level of management and should have the formal support of unions (if applicable).

The statement sets important parameters for the entire operation of the employee assistance program. It will indicate, for example:

• Who can use the services
• How confidential information is handled
• Credentials of the staff
• Methods for program evaluation
• Whether an employee should receive free time from work for appointments
• How client records should be kept and for how long

Services

The basic services an EAP can provide are information, assessment and referral, and/or short-term counseling with twenty-four-hour access to an 800 line. It is important for the counselor not only to listen to the employee but also to evaluate the nature and seriousness of the employee's problem before the employee is assisted and a focus for help defined.

Once the problem is defined, the service plan should include a range of options. In some cases, the employee may be helped by simply receiving written information explaining and defining certain difficulties and coping alternatives or resources such as listings of smoking cessation workshops or nursing homes. For more complex problems, program staff supply a referral to an agency or care giver and help the employee contact and use the services offered by the outside agency or provider. For this reason, the plan must have a system for identifying appropriate community resources and a method of evaluating credentials and skills.

Finally, it has become increasingly common for EAPs to offer short-term counseling. Early short-term counseling can prevent postponement of seeking help, decrease later treatment costs, and reduce confusion about locating services.

Professional Staffing

Staff should be required to have at least two years' experience working with alcoholism and other addictions. The staff should also have education and work experience in the recognized mental health professions—psychology, social work, psychiatry, or psychiatric nursing—and should have the appropriate credentials and/or license. In addition, these professionals must have previously demonstrated the ability and flexibility to work with difficult managers, supervisors, employees, and unions. Because of the difficult combination of the counseling and administrative components, many EAPs separate the EAP's administrative role from its counseling. The growth of EAPs has made it difficult to find qualified professionals.

Universities are only beginning to offer EAP-related programs. The University of Maryland School of Social Work is unique in offering an EAP specialization whereby M.S.W. graduates receive a certificate in EAP studies. In addition, the School of Social Work, in conjunction with the School of Business and Management, offers an annual EAP residential institute each spring.

The use of trained, licensed professionals protects the EAP and, ultimately, the company from the legal problems surrounding malpractice because unlicensed persons make an employer vulnerable to legal suit.

If the company has fewer than 2,500 employees at one location, the EAP may use a qualified affiliate or subcontractor from within the community. Subcontractors are used typically when an internal EAP program is too complex for small companies or for small branches of larger companies located in distant cities and states. It is important that the subcontractor have the same qualifications as would a regular EAP staff in a larger company.

Confidential Record-Keeping System

Most employees will not participate in the program unless they feel assured their case will remain confidential. Therefore, secure records and training for professional and support staff are essential. Everyone—secretaries, interns, and volunteers—must understand the importance of confidentiality and how easily it can be violated. Files should be locked, access should be limited and monitored, and identifying information kept to a minimum. The staff should be aware of federal and state regulations governing confidentiality and client-professional privilege. Proper release forms should be used at all times.

A Community Resource Referral Network

One of the EAP's responsibilities is to evaluate community resources for appropriate employee referrals and keep the list up to date. For example, in the case of an employee with AIDS, support groups for the employee and family are appropriate.

Attention to community resources has been neglected and even misused. Too often, company officials and supervisors suggest than an employee go to an organization on a resource list without researching and monitoring the qualifications of the organization. This must be done through the expertise of an EAP practitioner. Often companies have considered the compilation of a list of referral agencies to be a sufficient company EAP. It clearly is not.

Appropriate EAP Location

An EAP located within the organization should be under the auspices of the company's human resources or personnel department or occasionally the medical department. It should be situated so that it is accessible to the handicapped and inconspicuous enough to increase confidentiality and with well-furnished and well-maintained surroundings to demonstrate the company's commitment to the EAP. If the EAP is located off-site, there should be an office on the premises where supervisors and clients can meet with the EAP counselor.

Funding

There are two options: The company maintains an in-house staff, or it contracts out all functions on a per capita basis. The fees, regardless of the option used by the company, range from $22 to $30 per employee per year, depending on the location of the company. This fee is based on the total number of employees in the company regardless of how many use the program and how much they use it. This fee structure runs contrary to the traditional fee-for-service mental health medical model. It is more cost-effective because fee for service provides no motivation to move treatment toward a goal and eventual completion and therefore often results in unnecessarily longer treatment.

Union Support

Historically, unions have been concerned that employee counseling programs might be a management method for circumventing collective bargaining agreements. Companies can gain union support by including them in program planning.

Supervisory Training

Supervisors, especially if they make referrals to the assistance program, must be properly trained. They should understand the program policies, procedures, and services and be clear about their role in relation to the plan. That is, they should identify performance problems, not make clinical diagnoses, and should encourage employees to use the EAP services.

Supervisors must understand that the use of these services is voluntary but that it could be used as a step before a disciplinary process. An assistance program can provide an opportunity for the employee to get help before dismissal. Therefore, it is important that the supervisor be trained to view the referral as a service that helps rather than one that will embarrass or humiliate the employee.

Supervisors should know that referring an employee is a sign of supervisory skill rather than failure. Because of the chronic denial of the addictive person, the role of the supervisor is key in reaching such employees through the possibility of job loss.

Employee Outreach and Education

If the EAP is to be effective, employees must be informed of its availability and services. Memos, posters, and programs, including slide shows or films, can all be used to inform employees about the EAP's existence. They are usually more effective and well received if they are presented on company time, such as a lunch hour or coffee break. These should be offered regularly, perhaps several times a year.

In addition, the EAP should provide separate educational sessions and material on substance abuse as well as updated relevant medical research. Many employees, for example, might be only minimally aware of what is troubling them. In the case of substance abuse, denial prevents them from recognizing their problem. Therefore, they must have some basic education regarding when recreational use of alcohol and drugs is really dependence, when fatigue is depression, and when edginess is stress. Employee education programs could use written materials, short talks, workshops, or films and should have a good fit with the company's other communication dissemination methods.

Plans that encourage family members' participation should send information to each employee's home.

Sensitivity to Special Populations

By the year 2000, many culturally diverse groups and special populations will be in the workplace. Reaching these groups—women, minorities, gays and lesbians, the physically challenged, and the developmentally disabled—requires attention, knowledge, and sensitivity to their particular needs and problems in order for counselors to deal with group-specific issues such as sexual harassment, family violence, and role conflicts. Female and minority counselors may be more sensitive to the gender and cultural nuances of a particular behavior or problem area.

Outreach material should be designed so it reaches these groups. However, it is crucial that such groups are not singled out on the basis of cultural or sexual stereotypes.

Legal Issues

The design and implementation of the EAP must be done in accordance with current laws, regulations, and rulings, both state and federal. Issues concerning confidentiality of client records and drug testing legislation are important for EAP professionals to know.

State statutes mandate the disclosure of child abuse to the appropriate state agency. The threat of harm to another made by a participant of the assistance program could require warning the potential victim.

Program policies and procedures should clearly and explicitly reflect all relevant laws and regulations, and all program staff in-house, as well as vendor personnel, should be covered by professional liability insurance.

Program Evaluation

All EAPs must be evaluated to justify their existence and demonstrate their effectiveness. (It is estimated, however, that less than 1 percent of the 13,000 existing EAPs are evaluated, a major weakness in the field.) An evaluation allows the company to assess the extent to which its objectives are being reached and to find ways to improve the effectiveness of the plan's performance. In addition, an evaluation can help ensure that the company EAP is legally protected. Because of the confidentiality issues intrinsic to such programs, a third party evaluator—an individual or corporation without connection to the company—may be necessary to preserve confidentiality and to make an adequate evaluation.

Although a variety of evaluation methods can be used, a truly comprehensive EAP evaluation should include the following two components: (1) a process evaluation, which is the monitoring of the implementation of the program, and (2) an outcome evaluation, which is a study of the effectiveness of the program.

A *process evaluation* encompasses the review and analysis of monthly EAP statistics, including the number of cases, categories of diagnosis, and supervisory referrals. The purpose of this evaluation component is to ensure that the EAP reaches the appropriate number of employees, including those with alcohol and drug problems; that the client population reflects the work force composition in relation to age, sex, race, job level, and so on; and that there is a baseline date in job performance for comparing performance after going to the EAP.

Diagnosis and referral decisions made by the EAP counselors can be monitored in many ways. One recommendation is that an alcohol/drug history be conducted for each client, regardless of the presenting problem, in order to assist the counselor in detecting employees with symptoms of alcohol/drug abuse and to determine whether the counselor's decision has been appropriate.

An *outcome evaluation* includes both quantitative and qualitative analysis. The quantitative evaluation determines whether the EAP is cost-effective. Specific elements are measured and compared with information on costs incurred before the company EAP was in place; subsequent quarterly and annual comparisons are used as well. Areas to be evaluated may include:

- Absenteeism
- Advanced leave
- Leave without pay
- Performance appraisal records
- Disability insurance claims
- Sick leave
- Industrial accidents
- Health insurance claims
- Workers compensation claims

These data are matched to control groups, which are refined by age, sex, and managerial level. Data collection procedures vary for each contract, so the evaluation should be designed with data accessibility, the agency's interest, and cost in mind.

A quantitative evaluation is also made of supervisory referrals. They are accomplished by evaluating performance criteria furnished by supervisors at the point of the employee's referral and after three months and one year. Matched to a salary figure, these evaluations have consistently resulted in a $13 to $1 return on the EAP investment.

EAPs can be evaluated qualitatively through a peer panel approach conducted by recognized experts in the fields of psychiatry, psychology, and social work who provide a professional, comprehensive, and constructive review of individual case records. Concern for the employee as well as possible liability considerations make this an essential part of any program evaluation. The panel should review a number of randomly selected EAP records and provide a written and oral report to management.

Under the Alcohol and Drug Regulation, evaluations are allowed by bona fide evaluators. The author has consulted with U.S. Department of Health and Human Services attorneys, and all such procedures for the safeguarding of records, as well as the evaluation process, have been approved.

Peer review, as developed by the author, has precedents in the medical profession and has four major components: (1) a general orientation session, (2) a review of case records, (3) direct dialogue with company vendors (optional), and (4) a company debriefing with a final written report. The individual review of case reports includes a protocol instrument that reviews cases for questions about assessment of problem outside referrals, quality of counseling, and a full discussion of the employee's options.

This method has been used successfully with such organizations as IBM, the American Management Association, Bristol Myers, the Internal Revenue Service, and others to address the following factors:

- Accuracy of diagnosis
- Treatment planning
- Referrals to community resources for treatment
- Employee follow-up after referral for treatment
- Client and/or supervisor satisfaction with the program

The EAP and Case Management

AIDS and other catastrophic illnesses have been responsible for the acceleration of a relatively new and atypical approach to health care known as case management, a system of assessing and monitoring client needs throughout treatment. It is a process specifically designed to customize care for individual patients with catastrophic illnesses. Its elements include assessment of the patient's needs, referral to the appropriate resources, follow-up, and consultation. Extended follow-up is necessary because of the chronic nature of the disease and the potential for varying stages of psychological and physical stresses.

The patient is assigned a coordinator, who is an experienced health care professional, to provide psychological and sociological support for the patient and the patient's family. The EAP counselor can perform this role effectively. The coordinator acts as a liaison among the patient, the physician, and the family and helps plan details of medical care and finances. Case managers also strive for a timely discharge from hospitals and utilize atypical health care venues, such as hospices or home care settings. The estimated average daily cost for home health care or hospice is estimated to be $100 to $300 per day, in contrast to the average daily cost of hospitalization, which stands at $880 to $1,000 per day. Ironically, only 50 percent of U.S. insurers cover home health care, and only 30 percent cover hospices. In the alternative long-term care situation, the case manager would explore the appropriate options given the insurance plan or perhaps investigate other insurance options. The case management approach has two obvious advantages: it allows clients to achieve their optimum recovery faster, and it greatly reduces the number of unnecessary hospital days.

In their roles as case managers for the employee, EAP practitioners should reach out to the following groups to make their status known: family members, managers and supervisors, employees, medical department personnel, and senior management. The EAP practitioner coordinates with the insurance company, physicians, and psychological experts and acts as an advocate for the employee.

The EAP and Cost-Containment Efforts

In 1989, companies in the United States spent about $91 billion for health care, an increase from $25.5 billion a decade ago. Faced with these increases and the rising cost of employee health benefits, business, with the support of the federal government, has sought more control over the health care marketplace and has put in motion a whole range of new service delivery systems. Companies and insurance carriers are trying out a variety of cost-containment techniques.

Nearly two-thirds of U.S. corporations offer health maintenance organizations (HMOs) as part of their benefits package, but most HMOs offer very limited mental health services, so they are unable to help curtail a significant health care expense. Preferred provider organizations (PPOs) have also emerged. PPOs, however, offer too loose an arrangement of services and have proved unsatisfactory in the issue of coordination of care.

Because of the lack of viable alternatives, the EAP is beginning to be seen as the entity that can fill the void. A separate but related issue is that the growth, cost, and confusion in health care delivery systems is creating the need for a fourth party—a quality assurance manager—that can ensure that employees are receiving the best and most appropriate services at reasonable prices. The EAP is beginning to serve the dual functions of service provider and health care manager.

Future Directions of EAPs

Certain major trends in the organization of EAPs and in the larger social and economic picture have implications for the future of EAPs. Four factors in particular will affect the development of EAPs in the workplace: (1) the role of EAPs in managed mental health, (2) the focus on drug abuse in the workplace, (3) the increasing number of persons with or affected by AIDS, and (4) the need to address the needs of working women, the handicapped, and diverse populations in the workplace.

Managed Mental Health

At one end of the managed mental health continuum, EAPs are becoming the health maintenance organizations of mental health services. Increasingly, companies request that the EAP provide up to eight counseling sessions for employees who need this service. As a result, the EAP is able to facilitate problem resolution without referring the client to outside resources. Thus, the client avoids the use of costly health care benefits while receiving qualified professional assistance. However, given that the EAP emphasizes short-term self-referral mental health services, it is in danger of losing its original mandate of aggressive outreach to addicted employees.

Increasing health insurance costs have sparked a greater interest in developing methods for monitoring and managing the use of covered services, and concurrently, EAPs are beginning to serve as controls for mental health benefits utilization. Some companies have begun to request that troubled employees be seen by the EAP staff for a second opinion prior to approval of a lengthy inpatient hospitalization or long-term outpatient therapy sessions. EAPs therefore can be both an alternative to the use of outside professional services and a gatekeeper for the use of outpatient and inpatient services. In the future, EAP staff may have the ultimate responsibility for planning and monitoring the entire mental health package.

Alcohol and Drug Abuse

Both public and private companies are seeking to combat alcohol and drug abuse in the workplace. Drug testing is considered one of the most viable solutions to this growing workplace issue, and EAPs will be called on to assist employers in developing policies surrounding employee drug testing and related issues.

Companies have tried to control the problem by using drug screening in preemployment physical examinations and "for cause" and random urinalysis. EAP practitioners need to be skilled in the areas of security questions, employee and public safety, and legal issues surrounding drug screening. EAPs should not be the enforcers of anti–drug use policies and procedures but instead need to work in conjunction with personnel, medical, and security departments for the elimination of legal and illegal drug abuse in the workplace.

One of the most important pieces of legislation that directly relates to the role of the EAP practitioner in the workplace is the Drug-Free Workplace Act of 1988. It states that "agencies shall initiate action to discipline any employee who is found to use illegal drugs, provided that such action is not required for an employee who . . . obtains counseling or rehabilitation through an employee assistance program." Organizations are required to publish and provide a copy of the required statement to all employees, establish a drug-free awareness program for all employees, and sanction or require any employee convicted of a drug violation in the workplace to participate in a rehabilitation program. In addition to drug testing, drug screening instruments for assessments should be utilized by EAP counselors.

AIDS in the Workplace

Increasingly employers are having to address the issue of AIDS in the workplace. The EAP could take the lead in assisting companies with this highly sensitive issue by providing a number of services. EAP intervention in the workplace can include ongoing AIDS education, supportive counseling to coworkers and supervisors of employees with AIDS, and facilitating the implementation and maintenance of the company's policy and educational program on AIDS.

Education about AIDS will be the key means of intervention and should not wait to begin after AIDS is identified within a company. Short-term EAP counseling should be made to family, friends, and coworkers on how to cope with the problems presented by the disease on a day-to-day basis.

Diversity in the Workplace

The workplace of the future is changing dramatically, and as a result, companies must be receptive to the needs of people with different backgrounds, cultures, and values.

The EAP must address the unique role of women in the workplace and the additional stresses they face. These stresses may include the responsibility of being a single parent, having to secure adequate day care facilities for their children, receiving an inequitable salary in relation to their male counterparts, and working in some of the most stressful jobs (including secretarial and clerical work). Many working women also suffer psychological and economic pressure because child-related constraints make it difficult for them to develop their careers. To help women, an EAP should have at least one female counselor, in addition to running special programs like support groups and career planning workshops. It can also provide referrals for those who need child care. In addition, the EAP can serve a very valuable function by making upper management more aware of the special problems of working women and by recommending policies that accommodate the needs of working parents, such as adequate maternity leave, flexible work hours and leave time, and day care reimbursement policies.

EAPs must also demonstrate concern for minorities and the handicapped. EAP counselors should encourage employers to modify their policies and programs to address the unique concerns of diverse populations. If a company employs a large minority population, counselors must be trained in the appropriate language and culture. Minority counselors should also be sought in program administration and staffing. In addition, programs must be adapted to the needs of the handicapped.

Professionalization and the EAP

Because the EAP field is a new one, there is no accreditation of programs, and as a result, there is wide diversity in delivery of services. Some programs have clinically licensed personnel, and others have employee relations people wearing an EAP hat without any human resources training. This makes it difficult to generalize on the appropriate role of the EAP. However, there is no doubt that as an emerging profession, it has a responsibility to assume a major role in the workplace. It is incumbent upon corporate management to see that their EAP people are trained appropriately to deal with the company's most valuable asset: its employees.

Since the emergence of the broader-based employee assistance programs, the EAP field has been infused with a variety of professionals and paraprofessional practitioners who vary in their educational level and their amount of experience. One reflection of this move is in the emergence of university-based course work for EAPs. This move toward professionalization is positive. However, care must be taken to ensure that these professionals have the necessary experience and knowledge of addiction problems to identify and refer troubled employees.

The world of work and the world of human services have been joined through the common ground of EAPs. Employers who have brought EAPs into their workplace have demonstrated that they care for their employees, as well as the productivity of the company. To be successful, however, an EAP cannot stand alone. Even the most established programs depend on the support and allegiance of other key departments in the organization.

Notes

1. D. Masi and S. Friedland, ''EAP Actions and Options,'' *Personnel Journal,* June 1988.
2. U.S. Congress, ''Comprehensive Alcohol Abuse and Alcoholism Prevention, Treatment and Rehabilitation Act of 1970,'' December 31, 1970, Public Law 91-616 (42 USC 4582).
3. D. Masi and M. Goff, ''The Evaluation of Employee Assistance Programs,'' *Public Personnel Management* 16, no. 4 (Winter 1987): 324–325.
4. D. Masi, *Designing Employee Assistance Programs* (New York: AMACOM, 1984).
5. Office of Personnel Management, *Handbook of Selected Placement of Persons With Physical and Mental Handicaps in Federal and Civil Service Employment,* Document 125-11-3 (Washington, D.C.: U.S. Government Printing Office, March 1979).
6. S. Straussner, ''Comparison of In-house and Contracted-out Employee Assistance Programs,'' *Social Work,* January–February 1988.
7. Conversation with R. Bickerton, ALMACA clearinghouse manager, February 1989.

Suggested Reading

Berry, C. *Good Health for Employees and Reduced Health Care Costs for Industry.* Washington, D.C.: Health Insurance Association of America, Health Insurance Institute, 1981.

Byers, W., and Quinn, J. ''Alcoholism as a Major Focus of EAPs.'' In *The Human Resources Management Handbook.* New York: Praeger, 1985.

Clark, A., and Covington, S. ''Women, Alcohol and the Workplace (Part III).'' *ALMACAN* (February 1986).

Masi, D. *Designing Employee Assistance Programs.* New York: AMACOM, 1984.

———. *Drug Free Workplace.* Washington, D.C.: Buraff Publications, 1987.

———. ''Employee Assistance Programs.'' *Occupational Medicine,* October-December 1986.

Masi, D., and Goff M. ''The Evaluation of Employee Assistance Programs.'' *Public Personnel Management* 16, no. 4 (Winter 1987): 324–325.

National Institute for Alcoholism and Alcohol Abuse, Occupational Branch. Forum on Occupational Alcoholism, ''Rights of Alcoholics Under Federal Law,'' Fall 1976.

Office of Personnel Management. *Handbook of Selected Placement of Persons With Physical and Mental Handicaps in Federal and Civil Service Employment.* (Document 125-11-3.) Washington, D.C., U.S. Government Printing Office, March 1979.

Straussner, S. ''Comparison of In-House and Contracted-Out Employee Assistance Programs.'' *Social Work,* January-February 1988.

13

Performance Management

Andrew M. Geller, Ph.D
Managing Director
Hay Management Consultants

Performance management is a process for establishing shared understanding about what is to be achieved in an organization and an approach to managing people to increase the probability that it will be achieved. Organizations usually do not view it in this way. In the majority of cases, the management of employees' performance is an administrative matter. Performance must be evaluated for legal reasons and for the practical reason that there must be some reasonable way to divide up the merit increase budget. However, there is usually little understanding that the same administrative systems can be used very effectively to direct and motivate people.

This lack of understanding would be a pity if it meant only that the time and effort expended on performance management was not being utilized to its fullest, and managers were not taking advantage of a powerful tool to help them motivate their subordinates. But in the 1990s, failure to utilize performance management techniques effectively will have even greater consequences.

For almost the entire Industrial Age, the key aspects of competition were physical resources, technology, and capital. Labor was important only in that a shortage of workers hampered growth. Today, well into the Information Age, this is no longer the case. Physical resources are increasingly less important in an era in which many new innovations are the products of someone's garage, and facilities exist around the world to produce them. Technology changes so fast that today's patents are often worthless only a few years later. Capital is generally available to all. We have finally reached the stage in which saying that people are the only real competitive advantage has gone from being lip service to being the absolute truth.

Performance management is important not only because people are more important in the competitive marketplace, but because the nature of the work force is also changing, and methods and operating styles that worked ten or twenty years ago are not effective today. In particular, with the growing trend toward employee empowerment and flattened organizational hierarchies, it is essential that bureaucratic approaches to performance management be replaced by more imaginative processes that integrate individual development with corporate goals in order to retain valuable employees.

The performance management concept should focus on the organization both as an entity and as a collection of diverse human beings. As an entity, the organization must have well-articulated goals and strategies. These strategies, however, must be translated into individual performance objectives so that people throughout the organization can set meaningful personal objectives and know how their efforts contribute to the wider business goals. One way of institutionalizing this concept is through the performance management process.

It is critical to realize that performance management is not just a system, nor is it just another way to administer pay or a means to divide up the organizational objectives among all the managers. Performance management is a continuing *process*. It is a framework within which the plans and strategies of the organization can be turned into action and results. The process entails continual, tactful monitoring that keeps the organization focused on these plans and strategies. Hence, the key to a successful process is management. Effective and committed managing will not only enable the organization to stay focused on its goals and tasks, but it will also create information that can help develop the people being managed through better training and development, career pathing, and pay administration.

Few if any organizations are truly satisfied with their present performance management programs. The reasons for this dissatisfaction are many, but they often boil down to the same thing: Performance management is not an integral part of running the business. For it to be effective, it must be taken seriously by line management and fully integrated into the overall management of the organization.

Why Performance Management?

Performance management is a process that is ideally suited to support the key managerial challenge of planning, managing, and implementing organizational change. In particular, it can provide a clear means of interpreting a corporate change initiative at business unit work group and finally at individual level. Bringing these ideas and strategies down to the individual job level, especially to lower-level employees, has been a typical problem for most organizations. Usually, corporate strategies are discussed at the business unit levels, but rarely do the employees below the level of top business unit management understand how their responsibilities are linked to these overall goals. Often senior management has not carefully thought this out either. The performance management process, if properly developed and implemented, can deal with this problem. In particular, it will:

- Help communicate strategic and operational priorities
- Help managers focus on areas that provide the best "returns" and "value" to the organization
- Foster a more productive dialogue between managers and subordinates
- Emphasize clear accountability for actions
- Secure better performance by means of setting stretching objectives and providing supportive management behavior, including efficient training and developing
- Encourage managers to accept responsibility for securing results within areas
- Reinforce a "results-driven" culture

The benefits generated from the performance management process help to ensure that corporate strategies are carried through and "owned" by all levels of the organization. In the 1990s this sense of ownership is critical in two ways. Employees will not be motivated only by the promise of a paycheck or a secure job (which in fact often can no longer be promised). They want to feel that they have a say in what goes on and a clear stake in the outcome. By creating a sense of ownership, management accomplishes this and also creates the entrepreneurial spirit so necessary for innovation, high-quality performance, and retention of good employees.

Performance management is not a quick fix. It cannot be instituted in response to an immediate organizational need and then discarded as soon as the need has passed. The impact of performance management is not immediate; it can easily take a year or more for significant results to emerge. The core of performance management is the way that individuals are managed and motivated to achieve the most that they can in their jobs. It is this way of managing and motivating that makes people want to stay with an organization or prompts them to leave.

The process itself is applicable to many different areas and levels of an organization, yet it employs the same basic elements:

- Understanding the overall business planning framework
- Performance planning at business unit/work team level linked to performance planning at individual level
- Performance feedback and management (continuous monitoring of business performance, motivating, and coaching of individuals)
- Performance review and appraisal
- Rewards

This chapter focuses on performance management as an ongoing process that essentially links corporate strategies, goals, and objectives to individual jobs down through all levels in the organization. It ties together the interdependency of the organization by functions and accountabilities. Not only does the performance management process consciously open the avenues of communication; it also induces action. Management, along with its subordinates, can set meaningful goals that are ultimately linked to the corporate objectives.

The Performance Management Framework

The key to effective performance management is the link between the organization's strategy and plans and individual jobs. Therefore, the prerequisite of effective performance management is that the organization has a clear idea of where it is going and how it wishes to get there. In brief, an organization must have a clear, workable strategy if performance management is to work to tie all of the elements of the organization together to meet common goals.

A clear link with organization strategy is provided by starting with operational team or business unit objectives and performance measures. These in turn need to be framed with reference to the wider business goals and strategies of the organization. In doing this, the operational team or business unit has a blueprint upon which to build its strategy and objectives, linking them to the larger picture. Focusing at this level allows individuals to get a general sense of the direction in which the organization is headed. Concentrating at the team level is not always necessary, but it is a good source for hearing the organization's thinking firsthand. Once these unit levels have been established, usually through a team decision-making process, indiviudals can plan their own performance objectives more meaningfully.

It is important to note that operational team and individual performance planning are highly interdependent. The two processes should not be confused. Each should work to support the other, with the result that individual performance is effectively linked to corporate achievement. After the unit objectives have been reviewed and successfully linked to corporate strategies, individuals along with their managers need to devise their own objectives, incorporating job accountabilities, duties, and activities that link them to their wider business goals of the organization.

In the process of planning, standards for performance feedback and review also need to be established. It is upon these basic principles and planning processes that the performance management framework is built.

Using the Framework to Create Leverage

Whether applied at the organization, business unit, or individual level, performance management is about creating leverage. Simply stated, creating leverage means giving extra attention to the areas of business that are central to the organization and where the extra effort imputed is equal to or greater than the outcomes. This means setting performance objectives that balance business impact with organization, team, or individual influence. Business impact is measured in terms of bottom line results or performance improvements; influence relates to the ability of the individual or business unit to influence directly those particular results or improvements.

It would clearly be futile to set performance targets for outcomes that theoretically would make a difference to business performance but over which the unit or individual concerned has little influence. Equally, choosing to focus on areas over which strong influence can be exerted but in which excellent performance will make only a marginal difference in business terms will not achieve results for the business.

The performance management philosophy is that every operational team and every individual is capable of both impact and influence (otherwise there would be no justification for the team or the job existing). The creative challenge for management is to help people discover their potential for leverage by helping them to relate their individual performance to the next level organizational objectives.

Exhibit 13-1 is an overview of the performance management process. It is clearly a two-way process in which the manager and employee meet several times a year to plan, review, monitor, and appraise all aspects of the employee's total performance against objectives they have set.

Beginning With Performance Planning

The first area of concentration in the performance management process is performance planning. Performance planning is the stepping-stone for opening communication among managers and subordinates. This is where the tone of the relationship is developed.

The performance management process begins with establishing a relationship between corporate strategy and objectives down through the business units to individual job duties and accountabilities. First, business units or operational teams need to develop a strategic action agenda, deriving it from an understanding of the team's purpose in contributing to corporate goals. This process applies to the top management team and also to any group within the organization that must integrate its efforts around a com-

Exhibit 13-1. Overview of the performance management process.

- Manager shares corporate and departmental goals with employee.
- Employee submits proposed list of objectives.
- Manager reviews objectives, makes adjustments as appropriate, and discusses how objectives will be achieved and how performance will be measured with employee.

↓

- Manager and employee informally discuss and review performance.
- Employee keeps manager informed about major accomplishments during the year.

↓

- Manager and employee review interim results and revise and reprioritize objectives. Manager and employee may also prepare development plan to improve skills/knowledge areas.

↓

- Manager and employee continue to discuss and review performance informally on a regular basis.
- Employee continues to keep manager informed of major accomplishments during the year.

↓

- Manager prepare for formal performance review by summarizing and rating employee's performance on objectives, and evaluating and rating employee's skills/knowledge. Manager considers development needs as input to an individual developmental plan.

↓

- Salary recommendations are reviewed by next higher level of management.

↓

- When formally approved, manager conducts formal performance review and salary treatment with employee.

mon aim or activity. Second, individuals need to develop their strategic plan, goals, and objectives congruent to both corporate and business/work unit thinking. The focus of individual planning varies depending upon the level within the organization. Upper management levels are primarily concerned with "what" the organization is doing; lower levels focus on "how" it is accomplished.

The next step is developing job accountabilities, duties, and activities, linking the individual to the corporate scheme. Finally, measures for performance need to be negotiated and agreed upon.

Performance planning at operational team or business unit level requires bringing the different perspectives of the team members together to assess the present and plan for the future in light of the "whole team" performance. The team decides how it will measure its performance against the agreed team objectives and strategies, and it takes a collective, synergistic responsibility for attaining those performance targets (i.e., failure and success are equally shared). The team concept in performance planning is not necessary with all businesses, but in most cases it is the best source for integrating efforts around a common aim or activity. The corporate goals and objectives need to be discussed and defined first in order to assemble an operational team or business unit plan effectively. After establishing this base, the team collaborates on deciding the areas where they can create the most leverage. Without disregarding the necessary but less "impactful" areas, operational team or business unit goals, objectives, and plans are then defined.

After filtering through corporate and team strategies, individuals along with their manager have the necessary direction for their own planning. Individual performance planning takes the team objectives as a significant input: The individual assesses how he or she can best contribute to the team goals and frames performance targets in the light of these goals.

However, one may be a member of more than one team, so it is important to exercise judgment as to what commitments are realistic and achievable in the light of "whole job" accountabilities. This balancing of individual and team objectives is particularly relevant when dealing with middle management task force teams. Having drafted individual performance objectives (with the assistance of the manager, where appropriate), the individual is then ready to confirm his or her team commitments at a follow-up team meeting. The objective of this meeting is to try to reach a fit between the priorities of the individual team members and the objectives and performance targets of the team as an entity. Some adjustment, by mutual agreement, may be necessary to ensure a proper alignment between individual and team priorities with no significant weak spots.

Managers work with employees to help them to translate the business unit or operational team objectives into measurable, attainable individual goals and objectives. These performance objectives, and the measures developed to track them, will differ greatly depending on factors such as the nature and scope of the job and the planning horizon involved. However, the general criteria for effective performance planning are applicable to both individuals and organizational teams. The key questions to be addressed are:

- To which part of the business plan must I contribute?
- What personal objectives and actions are most likely to achieve the agreed upon business plan "ends"?

- What is the priority for these personal objectives?
- Who else must I work with to maximize the chances of achieving my (and their) agreed performance objectives?
- How can I track progress?

In a simple organization, these issues can be addressed one-on-one by management and the outcomes of those discussions kept in written form or perhaps recorded only informally. Most organizations are more complex, either because they are larger and more diverse or because they employ a matrix structure. In these cases, the interrelationships between each individual's objectives are complicated enough that a more formal process for identifying interrelationships and a computerized database for storing and analyzing them must be employed.

The process for identifying interrelationships between objectives usually requires both individual and then group efforts. First, each individual lists his or her objectives and the people who must contribute in order for the objectives to be achieved. The computer is then employed to compare the responses of each individual, highlighting inconsistencies. The individuals then meet as a group to reconcile these differences. The outcome of such a meeting is a list for each individual describing his or her own objectives, the people who have committed to helping with the attainment of these objectives and the nature of their contribution, and the people whom he or she must help accomplish *their* objectives.

On a daily basis, the individual will know he or she is contributing in some way to the larger outcome of the organization. This is where the sense of ownership is derived and the individual is directly connected to accomplishments or results. The next step, once these job elements are created, is to develop a means for tracking progress: Upon what basis can performance be judged?

Measures for Performance

The final piece in the performance planning process involves setting measures for performance and guidelines for monitoring progress. General performance measures need to be mutually designed to show how and on what basis progress is tracked. Generally, there are two approaches used in measuring performance: the objective and subjective. The third approach, used often, is some combination of the two.

The objective-based approach is appropriate for those jobs that are linked to the delivery of the bottom-line objectives of the organization, such as sales, profits, productivity, and quality. Obviously, this applies to most if not all top and middle management posts. The accountabilities of upper management usually are most closely linked to outcomes or quantitative results. Success in the job can clearly be judged depending upon whether the goal is accomplished. Top management has control over "what" the organization is doing and should be committed to attaining these goals.

Setting Objectives

As management starts the process of setting objectives, a checklist like the one that follows should be used.

- Does the objective stem from and/or support key corporate business plans or values?

- Is it significant enough to be a key objective?
- Can results be measured and verified?
- Is the objective specific?
- Is the goal realistic and attainable?
- Is the objective under the control of the employee?
- Is the level of performance expected set at the competent performance level?
- Will the objective require the employee to "stretch" to attain it?
- Is the time frame clearly understood?

To be useful as a guide to action, the number of individual objectives should be limited. Rather than try to focus attention on all the possible objectives one could identify, you should identify only the most important to be achieved in any particular period. As a rule of thumb, this is usually no more than ten objectives.

PRIORITIZING OBJECTIVES

Once the manager and employee have agreed upon the employee's performance objectives, establish priorities among the objectives identified for the performance period. Establishing priorities helps to ensure the achievement of the most critical objectives. Objectives focus an employee's activity, and priorities help determine the relative effort to be expended toward the achievement of each goal. The simplest and most practical approach in determining which objectives are critical is to ask for which objectives below average performance would hurt the department or corporation the most. Keep the corporation's business plan in mind in reaching a decision.

DEVELOPING ACTION PLANS

Action plans can aid in accomplishing objectives by describing the methods by which the employees will achieve each of their performance objectives. It is not necessary to document the action plans unless you decide to include them in your formal process.

In developing action plans, consider how the objectives will be achieved, what the needed resources will be, and the assumptions that must be met. The parts of an action plan are as follows:

- *Key assumptions.* These are the basic conditions upon which the objective is based. These could either be conditions within the company or external conditions, such as economic predictions or demographic trends. It is important for the employee to discuss key assumptions with the manager before proceeding. If an assumption proves false, it is a signal that the objective may no longer be realistic.
- *Possible obstacles.* What events or circumstances may prevent the employee from reaching the objective? You will notice that there is an overlap between the concept of assumptions and the concept of obstacles. The concepts are often opposite sides of the same coin. It is not important whether you state an event in the positive (key assumption) or the negative (possible obstacle).
- *Action steps.* These are conscious, planned actions that should be taken to ensure achievement of the objective. For each performance objective, consider the re-

lated action steps or tasks, resources that are needed, critical interfaces, and completion dates. Identifying needed actions makes all the difference between an objective being merely a wish or hope and it being a realistic, achievable result.

When the objectives have been agreed upon and discussions completed, it's time to write them down. Documentation is important to this whole process.

MOVING FROM OBJECTIVES TO COMPETENCIES

Moving down the levels within the organization, the definition of performance moves from the accomplishment of quantitative objectives to competencies and/or tasks that are more subjective in nature. Competencies include knowledge, skills, abilities, and attitudes relating "how" a job is done, measured more in qualitative terms than quantitative.

In the performance management process, most problems occur in this area. At these levels, individuals have less control on "what" is accomplished and more impact on "how" the job is accomplished. The organization has already set team goals and requires contribution from all team members. Though individuals may not have quantifiable goals, tasks and activities must be accomplished properly and in a timely fashion in order to contribute to the success of the team. Measuring success becomes more of a variable without tangible results, and standards for success need to be devised.

The qualitative/competency-based approach looks at the key competencies that make for outstanding performance in the job, and these standards (if known) should be the benchmark for the performance contract with the individual. A competency-based approach will be most appropriate in the following jobs (or a combination of them):

- *Low-level jobs.* Task, not plan related. These jobs require activities to accomplish a certain outcome with quality, neatness, promptness, and attitude as some standards for measuring success.
- *High know-how jobs.* Performance = input. These are knowledge jobs, i.e., scientists or researchers, where input is the basic function.
- *Reactive jobs.* Turbulent environment, little planning. For instance, a stockperson reacts to a customer's demand by keeping shelves full.
- *Service delivery jobs.* Customer focus behavior is the key. Again, appearance, promptness, and attitude are the main standards.

The competency-based approach identifies the type of skills and behaviors necessary for "good" performance and compares them to the job holder's. In the jobs mentioned, knowledge, promptness, neatness, and attitude lead the list of qualities examined.

Obviously, it is more difficult to appraise by these qualities than by quantity, but standardized measurements can be defined. This is particularly true if one views the organization as a system in which everyone produces something for a customer, whether external or internal. For example, the accounting function produces data and analyses for their line management "customers" who need the information to make decisions and to protect the assets of the business. These customers can then be asked to rate the quality and usefulness of the information. These ratings, like the sales numbers or profits measured by their line colleagues, can serve as quantitative measures for jobs that are usually not thought of in that way.

In addition to jobs that must be judged in a largely qualitative way, there are also situations in the business environment that require the competency-based, qualitative approach for appraisal:

- *Poor management information systems (MIS).* If the MIS is poor, nobody believes management control data, and thus quantitative measures will not work.
- *Cultural change.* The emphasis is on managers behaving differently. This requires attention to the behavioral components of work, even when quantitative outcomes can be measured.
- *Training development.* An analysis of the strengths and weaknesses of employees is required for the development of training programs. Knowing the quantitative output of their work alone will not suffice for this purpose.

In situations where competencies might be used, the key questions for the job holder are:

- What are the critical measures of success in my job?
- What are the key competencies that make for outstanding performance in the job (and future job)?
- How do I rate against these? What are the critical gaps?
- What should be my personal development objectives, if I am to display improved competence?
- What is the priority order among these agreed personal objectives?
- How can I track progress?

By answering these questions and using them as guidelines, performance measurements can be designed. Even though some standards will be more difficult to define, a basis framework can be created. Once the key outputs of behaviors of the job have been defined, the next stage is to decide the appropriate measures of performance: How will "success" be recognized, and are there different "standards" of success? Some of the criteria to be addressed are listed below.

- *Measurable*
  —Is it clear how performance will be tracked?
  —Are different degrees of success calibrated?
  —Are the qualitative measures (if any) as rigorous as possible?
- *Alignment*
  —Do the objectives of subordinates line up with those of their managers?
  —Do they reflect the critical interdependencies with colleagues?
  —If the objectives are successfully completed by everyone in the work unit, will the work unit's objectives be achieved?
- *Stretch*
  —Is there a real but achievable challenge?
- *Time Related*
  —Is there a defined time scale for their completion? Or are there at least milestones throughout the year, if final completion extends beyond a year?
- *Encompassing*
  —Are all the important issues covered?

——Do they cover all the important aspects of the work unit's/individual's job purpose?
* *Results Oriented*
——Are they focused on a definite end result?
* *Support and Training*
——What assumptions are made about support and training required and/or expected from colleagues and managers?
* *Creativity*
——Is there any ''new'' thinking here, i.e., an innovative approach, rather than ''just'' maintaining the status quo?

All that has been written above about the definition of objectives, interrelationships, and measurements is important. However, it must be emphasized again that this structure is less important than the process of performance management. There must be continual discussion between each manager and his or her subordinates about the appropriateness of the objectives and measures. Even after they are set, the process continues.

Jobs may change, or new ones are created; promotions occur, or responsibilities are added. The entire process of performance management must anticipate changes and accommodate them. As long as the lines of communication are open between managers and subordinates, integrating changes becomes routine.

Integrating changes becomes more difficult when the changes are external rather than internal: The economy hits a recession, interest rates rise or fall, new products are created, etc. The decision whether to stay with the goals as planned or to modify them in midstream is a complex one. Certain issues need examining:

* Do these external realities have an impact on the business? And if so, are they significant?
* Are there ways in which these changes can be offset, e.g., internal price changes or increased research and development?
* Should or can these changes be worked through in order to stay focused on goals set previously?

Oftentimes these questions are not easily answered, and some market analysis is necessary. Generally, the more impact external changes have on certain businesses and the less individuals have internal controls, the more likely replanning of goals is necessary.

At this point, the individual has participated in essentially formulating the job within the confines of the organization and also in determining how performance will be measured. Involvement in all these critical facets ultimately results in the individual's sense of ownership. In the process of creating this sense of ownership, the links between the organization's strategies down through individuals' daily activities are recognized. The next step in the process is monitoring the progress toward which these goals, strategies, and plans are being carried out.

Management of Performance: Monitoring and Feedback

In keeping with the principle of allowing employees a greater degree of responsibility and control, the traditional ''core'' performance management activities—performance planning and appraisal—are augmented by a new emphasis on frequent coaching and information feedback. This helps to ensure that the formal, end-of-cycle performance review is a constructive and well-planned event with few surprises on either side.

Performance monitoring and feedback is a vital component of the performance management process. The ability to track performance against targets on a continuous basis provides the key to proactive management. Again, this applies equally to organizations, operational groups, and individuals. Feedback enables the entity or individual to adjust effort or behavior incrementally in response to changing circumstances, rather than waiting to be overtaken by events. It also allows for the implementation of needed training and development programs that are now recognized as a result of the information gathered in the performance management process.

During the performance period, the manager has several obligations to his employees.

- Observing and documenting performance
- Giving guidance and coaching: providing training and development programs when necessary
- Giving feedback against objectives
- Renegotiating accountabilities as required by changes
- Providing positive reinforcement or warnings with explanations for appropriate behaviors

At the individual level, the key to improving the effectiveness of performance management is frequent manager–job holder interaction. This includes communicating, coaching, and motivating: the "what," "how," and "why" of individual performance. A creative and integral part of performance planning is establishing an atmosphere where coaching, monitoring, and feedback is a compatible routine. Managers need to develop a style to monitor the success of plans and a style to relay the message back to the organization. Consistent yet tactful performance feedback as well as formal end-of-cycle review tie together the operations team and individual performance plans and objectives. Too often managers dominate the relationship, causing a negative influence on performance. By nature, individuals resist when they feel controlled. Effective management of people for performance requires managers to spend time with their people, not in controlling but empowering them. Empowering them means giving freedoms, choices, and the ability to participate in governing their destiny.

Components of Performance Feedback

COMMUNICATING

Effective communication is the essence of the performance management process. Hence, timely, proper, and tactful communication determines the quality of feedback and reinforcement. The evolving roles of managers stress the importance of providing regular feedback on the performance and progress of direct reports. This can be accomplished by frequent, casual interactions or by one-on-one meetings dictated by the necessity.

In addition to daily or routine monitoring and observations, an important aspect of the feedback process encourages formal, midperiod reviews of individual performance plans to accommodate unforeseeable changes. Changes to the original plan can be triggered externally (e.g., by changing organization objectives or environmental threats) or by the employee (e.g., by development of new skills leading to a changed focus). Interim reviews midway through the planning cycle help to ensure that the performance plan is still on target in aligning individual talent with corporate needs.

Another avenue of communication is through information systems, which have an important role to play in the feedback progress. They should be designed so that the individual knows his or her own results first and the data can be used as the basis for constructive discussion about ongoing performance, not a device for attributing blame for mistakes made long ago. Ideally, obtaining the results before the meeting enables the individual to analyze and assess his or her performance prior to discussion. The meeting then begins with the individual explaining the results. If the performance management process is successful, the self-analysis will be on target with the manager's, and further analysis becomes unnecessary. The discussion can revolve around the future and possible development programs where appropriate. If the two are significantly different, the performance management process is somewhat flawed, and revisions are necessary. Currency and relevance of performance-related information along with its proper channeling are therefore of prime importance to the performance management process.

COACHING

The art of coaching involves sharing the manager's expertise and insight to help shape the job holder's behavior and style, thereby improving performance. The coach is a model for a different type of teaching. His or her coaching allows for personalized, hands-on learning in addition to the necessary classroom training. The benefits of personalized training are twofold: First, it helps in the relationship between manager and subordinate, communicating a collegial atmosphere. The manager proves his or her role is to work with the subordinate through development, not control. Second, it induces learning by experience, congruent to the ways of the manager with whom the subordinate works. Seminars, when appropriate, are adequate for general training but cannot incorporate personalities. Effective coaching combines teaching the necessary information along with the style preferred by the manager.

At any level, effective coaching depends on the quality of the relationship between the manager and the subordinate. In a healthy relationship, one-on-one coaching is often the nucleus for the development of individuals. In contrast, a competitive or clashing relationship greatly reduces the effect of coaching because the learning process is hindered by the negative atmosphere. Most often when reflecting on a career, people recall individuals who singlehandedly shaped their development; effective coaching has this type of impact.

MOTIVATING

The third critical component of performance feedback is motivating. While frequent performance communicating and coaching can be intrinsically motivating, sometimes more direct approaches are needed. Some major factors need to be examined and present if motivation is to occur.

- *Management style.* Do managers have the leadership qualities to motivate employees? More importantly, do these qualities fit the nature of the job? Though an enthusiastic, dynamic speaker can move sales forces, he or she cannot necessarily motivate financial analysts or accountants.
- *General climate.* Is the operational unit performance-oriented, or are people there just for the pay? Generally, people can fit into two categories. Either they are focused on achievement and a successful career, or they are more concerned with "paying the bills."

It is important to ensure that motivation is built into the environment. In addition to these factors, managers can create motivation in a couple of ways.

- *Job design/enrichment.* Exploring which jobs can be made more challenging and enriching
- *Training.* Developing people's abilities to increase their opportunities

These above elements are all related to the period between performance planning and performance review and must be the true focus of a viable, working performance management process. Performance management is far more extensive than a simple change in the performance appraisal system; creating a learning, coaching environment may require radical alterations to an organization's underlying culture and management styles. To reinforce this change in behavior, all levels of management should be evaluated on the ability of managers to provide performance information, coaching, and motivation for their direct reports.

Again, the goal of the performance management process is to link individual jobs to the wider business goals of the organization and to integrate this process as part of the routine business plan. The managerial role of providing feedback by communicating, coaching, and motivating generates information, direction, and enthusiasm and leads to the success of the process.

Frequency of Feedback and Review

There is no universal standard for the period of time between performance planning and formal performance review. However, matching individual planning cycles to the natural cycles of the business makes good sense. For example, some jobs (indeed, some businesses) are essentially project-driven and therefore it makes more sense to plan and review performance at the start and end of a project cycle than on a traditional midyear or annual basis. In fast-changing business environments, individual job objectives and priorities may change rapidly over time, and this, too, would suggest a somewhat shorter planning cycle. On the other hand, a top-level executive of an oil company whose planning horizons tend to stretch out over a period of several years could be justified in arguing for a much less frequent formal review of progress than the midyear or annual appraisal system allows. Continual feedback, whether semiformal or routine, keeps the plans on track.

Whatever the individual planning period suggested by the business cycle, with frequent feedback and coaching in between, formal reviews become less concerned with attributing personal blame (or praise) for actions past, and more concerned with planning for the future of the individual and the organization. The test of the feedback/

review process is that there should be no surprises in the formal review at the end of the performance.

Performance Review

When frequent performance feedback is the norm, the end-of-period performance review is less threatening and contains no surprises: Job holders should already know how they are performing. Why, then, have a formal review of performance? There are two main reasons for the formal review.

1. Any planning cycle requires a phase to give closure to the activities undertaken in the planning period and to enable fresh thinking to begin about the new planning period ahead.

2. Many organizations are now basing variable pay schemes on individual performance over a given period. The formal review provides a clear summary statement of performance achieved over a planning cycle, thus providing an objective, defensible basis for variable pay decisions. However, the advisability of varying the length of the performance planning cycle according to the natural business cycle argues for other summary performance documentation to be produced at regular intervals (applicable to all employees) to ensure an equitable companywide basis for variable pay assessment.

The frequency and quality of communication between manager and subordinate has been emphasized repeatedly in this chapter as the most critical element in the performance management process. However, the formal performance review provides the opportunity to add another valuable dimension that some innovative organizations are bringing to the review process: the concept of the multidimensional review. Although the single most important key to improving individual performance is the quality of manager–job holder interactions, there are jobs for which supplementary inputs to the review process are appropriate.

Self-review is a central notion behind the review of most job holder types—in particular, professional and managerial employees. The job holder needs to ask:

- What quantitative data exist relating to any achievement of objectives? How reliable is it? What qualitative data can supplement?
- What parts of the job received the greatest emphasis during the year? Were these explicit priorities stated at the start of the year?
- To what extent can successes and failures as reflected by the evidence be attributed to my performance? With whom should credit be shared?
- What major obstacles or constraints hampered performance? What steps were taken to overcome these difficulties?
- What important lessons have been learned from performance this year that need to be reflected in next year's plans?
- What personal development activity should I undertake and/or request to help improve my performance?
- What help do I need from my manager to aid performance? What suggestions could be given on what activities might be initiated, stopped, or continued?

As mentioned earlier, analyzing oneself prior to the review is the most effective endeavor for testing the success of the performance management process. Having the manager disagree with the self-analysis presents an obvious communications gap. The expected result is a mutual agreement on performance.

Peer review may be used to evaluate performance where interdependencies and teamwork among peers are critical. It is less necessary when job positions are significantly different and more appropriate when an individual contribution to the team's success is not clearly identifiable. More importantly, the business environment dictates whether or not this type of review is beneficial. In competitive circumstances, for obvious reasons, peer review is not a useful tool.

Subordinate review is applicable to most managers and at the most senior level is the only formal internal review that is possible, but it is relatively rare. When subordinate ratings are not accepted at top management levels, it sends a clear message down through the organization. This is unfortunate because the opinions of subordinates are often less well understood and more important than those of others in the organization.

External and internal customer review is relevant where the job holder has frequent interactions with outside and inside customers and these exchanges form a central component of his job. User surveys can be used to gauge the general level of satisfaction with a particular service that the job holder provides for a wide internal audience. However, care should be taken to ensure that such surveys are not designed in such a way that they place undue blame on the job holder for shortcomings that may be outside of his or her control. In general, surveys may be more relevant to team or functional performance assessment than to individual performance review.

Rating and Ranking

All employees should be rated as individuals, without regard to the ratings of others (unless they compromise a team whose ratings should be interdependent). Yet most organizations insist that, when the individual ratings are completed, the distribution of those ratings should conform to some predetermined pattern. There is good reason for this insistence. Supervisors and other raters seldom like to give bad ratings; most work hard to avoid them. Without a predetermined pattern, an organization's ratings would inevitably be skewed, perhaps wildly so, toward the high end.

In most cases, this would not be an accurate representation of the facts. In large organizations, there are some superstars and more than a few poor performers. The majority of employees are good at what they do, no better or worse than that. The predetermined pattern, usually a normal distribution, forces managers to recognize this and give higher than average ratings only to those who truly deserve them. On the typical 1 to 5 rating scale (with 5 at the top), the manager must assign the 3 rating to 50 percent or more of employees, 20–25 percent can be rated higher as 4s, and fewer than 10 percent can be given the highest rating of 5. The rest are rated 2 or 1.

There are a number of problems with this approach.

- The expectation that ratings will be distributed normally holds only in a large population. If the manager's work unit is small (fewer than thirty people), accurate ratings may not conform to this pattern.
- Many organizations have a culture that insists that to be average is not good

enough. This conflicts with the performance rating requirement that the majority of employees be rated in the middle.

* The notion of a forced, one-number-explains-all rating does not fit with the highly interactive performance management process described above. It takes all the discussion and coaching and creates a rating that may seem artificial and perhaps unfair to manager and subordinate alike.

Some organizations have attempted to deal with this problem by having managers rank-order, rather than rate, their subordinates. The rationale for this is that while it might not be right to insist that a manager have only two 5s or four 4s, there is nothing wrong with requiring one of his or her subordinates to be the top; the next, one down from that; and so on. In practice, this approach is not much better than forced distribution.

There seems to be no perfect solution to this problem. Some have suggested, therefore, that rating and ranking be abandoned entirely but this is quite rare. Employees *need* a rating; they want a bottom line to their performance evaluations. Personnel managers need ratings or rankings in order to link pay to performance.

The best approach may be a compromise of all of the above. Each employee should be rated—not on a numerical scale, but in words (such as "fully meets all requirements of the job" or "consistently exceeds job requirements") that summarize the manager's more detailed written description of performance. This rating is the formal communication to the employee of how well he or she did. At the same time, employees are grouped into large enough units and then are rank-ordered by their managers, not for rating of performance, but for pay purposes only. Even among ten employees who received the highest rating possible, one can be the best, another next best, and so on. In this fashion managers can convey to employees an accurate description of their performance and also ensure that rewards are divided differentially among employees based on performance.

Rewards

Pay is one of the strongest communicators of how much an organization values the contributions of an individual or group. A well-structured and implemented performance-related pay strategy gives clear messages about the direction and values of an organization. Timely and equitable reward practice is essential to stimulate outstanding individual performance; therefore, compensation should be aligned with performance wherever it is feasible. Individual acts of reward are a powerful reinforcer of behavior and can help to drive organizational change or retard it.

In understanding the key links between performance-related pay and the broader and strategically important process of performance management, there are six issues that need to be taken into account.

1. Performance-related pay needs to match the culture and value systems of the organization.
2. The design has to fit the organization. It should not be an "off the shelf" product.

3. Performance rewards need to be closely linked to the business, support overall strategy, and be flexible enough to respond to changes in strategic direction.
4. The process is not a "one-off" exercise. It needs to be monitored, evaluated, and reviewed.
5. It is important to manage expectations about what performance rewards can and will deliver.
6. It is important to avoid being too mechanistic and simplistic about setting performance targets.

In view of the potential hazards of a poorly aligned reward policy, many organizations wisely decide to link pay decisions explicitly to the performance management process until the latter has had a chance to become an established and accepted way of life in the organization. Whether or not a variable pay policy is to be implemented as an explicit reinforcement of performance management, a review of the organization's reward systems may well be advisable to ensure that they do not undermine the performance management process.

In a major organization change intervention, close links should be forged between the performance management process and the organization's reward strategy. The latter can act as a powerful, incremental reinforcer of an organization change program structured around a phased, organizationwide approach to performance management.

Documentation

A variety of forms are needed to document the performance management process. Exhibit 13-2 is a sample management appraisal form to be completed by the manager (and by the group, if a group review is done) prior to the formal performance review with the employee. Exhibits 13-3 and 13-4 are alternative forms to use in reviewing employee performance. Since it can be difficult to write open-ended, descriptive assessments, Exhibit 13-5 provides sample phrases to help managers complete appraisal forms.

Exhibit 13-2. Sample management appraisal form.

Name of Employee _____

Department _____

Appraisal Date _____

Supervisor's Overall Statement of Performance:
(Note: Supervisor should rate employee on performance, skills, knowledge, ability, experience, potential for promotion, and so on.)

_____

_____

_____

_____

_____

Supervisor's Statement of Development Needs:

_____

_____

_____

_____

_____

Group Review of Performance:

_____

_____

_____

_____

Names of participants in group review: _____

_____

Current Annual Salary _____

Proposed Salary Recommendation _____

Exhibit 13-3. Annual performance tracking form.

Employee Name _____ Performance Year _____

Performance Planning	Midyear Evaluation	End-of-Year Evaluation	
Record agreed-upon objectives here. (These should number no more than ten.) Attach extra sheets, if necessary.	Enter Evaluation Outstanding (O) Fully Meets (FM) Needs Improvement (NI)	Comment on the degree of achievement for each objective, including all contributions to corporate priority. Consider degree of difficulty and supervision required in determining if the objective was met.	Enter Evaluation Outstanding (O) Fully Meets (FM) Needs Improvement (NI)

Employee Comments: _____

Signatures

Supervisor _____ Date _____ Employee _____ Date _____

Exhibit 13-4. Performance appraisal worksheet.

Employee Name		Report of Performance From To	
Department	Position	Employment Date	Date this report completed

INSTRUCTIONS

All employees should be appraised annually. Consider the employee's performance on the basis of the standards you expect to be met. Place a check by the area you feel best describes the employee's performance. Provide a narrative review of performance for each category listed.

QUALITY OF WORK—Consider standard of work, accuracy, neatness, skill, thoroughness, economy of materials, organization of job.

☐ Exceeds job requirements   ☐ Fully meets job requirements   ☐ Meets minimum job requirements   ☐ Does not meet minimum job requirements.   ☐ Other (Specify)

Reason: _____
_____
_____

VOLUME OF WORK—Consider use of time, volume of work accomplished, and ability to meet schedules under normal conditions.

☐ Exceeds job requirements   ☐ Fully meets job requirements   ☐ Meets minimum job requirements   ☐ Does not meet minimum job requirements   ☐ Other (Specify)

Reason: _____
_____
_____

JOB KNOWLEDGE AND SKILL—Consider understanding of job procedures and methods, ability to acquire necessary skills, expertness in doing assigned tasks, and utilization of work experience.

☐ Exceeds job requirements   ☐ Fully meets job requirements   ☐ Meets minimum job requirements   ☐ Does not meet minimum job requirements   ☐ Other (Specify)

Reason: _____
_____
_____

ADAPTABILITY—Consider ability to meet changing conditions and situations, ease with which the employee learns new duties and assignments.

☐ Outstanding   ☐ Very good   ☐ Satisfactory   ☐ Needs improvement

Reason: _____
_____
_____
_____

(continued)

Exhibit 13-4. *Continued.*

JUDGMENT—Consider ability to evaluate relative merit of ideas or facts and arrive at sound conclusions, ability to decide correct cours' of action when a choice can be made.

☐ Outstanding   ☐ Very good   ☐ Satisfactory   ☐ Needs improvement

Reason: _____

_____

_____

ATTITUDE—Consider cooperation with supervisor and co-workers, receptiveness to suggestions and constructive criticisms, attitude toward company, enthusiasm in attempts to improve performance.

☐ Outstanding   ☐ Very good   ☐ Satisfactory   ☐ Needs improvement

Reason: _____

_____

_____

TEAM EFFORT/LEADERSHIP—Consider ability to inspire teamwork, enthusiasm to work toward a common objective, desire to assume responsibility, ability to originate or develop ideas and get things started.

☐ Outstanding   ☐ Very good   ☐ Satisfactory   ☐ Needs improvement

Reason: _____

_____

_____

SELF-DEVELOPMENT ACTIVITIES OF THIS EMPLOYEE (to be completed jointly during interview)

_____

_____

_____

PRESENT STATUS—NEEDS—PLAN OF ACTION

OVERALL EFFECTIVENESS—Check the rating that most accurately describes current performance.

☐ Exceeds job requirements   ☐ Fully meets job requirements   ☐ Meets minimum job requirements   ☐ Does not meet minimum job requirements

WHAT ASPECTS OF PERFORMANCE, IF NOT IMPROVED, MIGHT HINDER FUTURE DEVELOPMENT OR CAUSE DIFFICULTY IN PRESENT JOB?

_____

_____

WHAT ARE GREATEST STRENGTHS OF THE EMPLOYEE? _____

_____

_____

DESCRIBE SPECIFIC PLANS YOU AND THE EMPLOYEE HAVE MADE TO IMPROVE WORK PERFORMANCE

_____
_____
_____

Evaluated By:	Title:	Date:
Approved:	Title:	Date:
Employee's Comments	Employee's Signature: (Does not necessarily indicate concurrence)	Date:

_____
_____
_____
_____
_____

Exhibit 13-5. Statements to help supervisors complete appraisal forms.

Communications Skills

Communicates with credibility and confidence.
Excels in interpersonal communications and interactions.
Communicates confidently with peers, subordinates, and superiors.
Conveys a positive impression that reflects favorably with the public.
Encourages open communications to achieve mutual understanding.

Competency

Resolves problems quickly and effectively.
Combines technical and professional competence with dependability and loyalty.
Effectively applies skills and abilities to the position.
Demonstrates strong personal competence on the job.

Dependability

Consistently accurate and dependable.
Consistently achieves results.
Can be counted on to achieve results even in difficult circumstances.
A self-starter who displays a strong personal commitment to completing projects successfully.

(continued)

Exhibit 13-5.   *Continued.*
Goals

Effectively implements personal and departmental goals.
Establishes and achieves relevant performance standards.
Excels in planning and determining courses of action.

Maturity

Displays a high degree of emotional maturity.
Keeps situations in proper perspective.
Displays good emotional adjustment and stability.
Can deal with ambiguity.

Mental Capacity

Understands both theoretical and practical concepts.
Uses common sense to reach workable conclusions.
Grasps difficult concepts.
Is quick and responsive.
Thinks logically—uses common sense.

Performance

Demonstrates credibility.
Demonstrates positive self-concepts.
Turns negatives into positives.
Maintains an optimistic outlook when faced with difficulties.
Competes with confidence.

14

Training and Development

William R. Tracey, Ed.D.
President
Human Resources Enterprises of Cape Cod, Inc.

Too many organizations fail to focus their attention on their most valuable resource: their people. Organizations must continually improve their ability to attract and retain good workers if they want to remain competitive, and one way to do that is to train and retrain their work force. In addition, they must create a work environment that will attract and hold highly motivated and productive employees. This requires a positive company image, forward-looking management practices, attention to employee values and priorities, viable feedback systems, total employee involvement, and unremitting teamwork. Even all these actions can't provide the 100 percent solution.

Organizations must continually reevaluate and restructure their training and development programs. They must be prepared to *make* competent workers, not just hire them ready-made. They must use company-sponsored and company-conducted training and development programs to get and hold the kinds of workers they need. They must be prepared to accept the fact that a majority of the work force will require training rather than the estimated 10 percent who currently receive it. And then they must provide that training!

What kind of people are needed? The people an organization must have today are intelligent and talented—the most difficult people to get and keep. Insightful and resourceful people have clear goals. They have more than a vague idea about career progression and where they want to be five, ten, or more years in the future. They are not attracted and retained by promises of promotion and higher salaries. They want to know how the organization will support and further their goals—how it will help them achieve their vision of the long-range and near-term future. Specifically, they expect to be told what training and development they will receive at corporate expense, what they will be required to do on their own, and how corporate and outside resources will help them to develop and fulfill their career aspirations.

In addition to explicit minority recruitment, workplace changes, alternative work schedules, job splitting, and job sharing, training must have priority: entry-level training for new employees, training for supervisors to deal with cultural diversity, training for women and minorities to get them ready for supervisory positions, coaching and mentoring programs, English-as-a-second-language courses, and remedial training.

Companies need to recruit, hire, and retain employees of child-rearing age (because there will be more of them in the 1990s) if they are to become employers of choice and remain competitive. They need to assimilate people from different cultures into the work force as well as the socially and educationally disadvantaged—those with dysfunctional attitudes and low expectations. And they need to make use of the large and largely untapped pool of disabled persons. This chapter describes how training and development can help an organization attract and retain competent and highly motivated people.

The Dimensions of the Challenge

Organizations today face a multidimensional challenge: Demographic and work force changes, advancing technology, and changes in the business environment are only three of its facets.

Work Force Changes

Organizations must prepare now for the unprecedented changes occurring in the work force. Few are doing so. U.S. business and industry are on the verge of a critical labor shortage in terms of both quality and numbers. Not only is there a smaller pool of potential workers, but also the supply is becoming increasingly diverse. There will be more women, more immigrants and minorities, and more Hispanics and Asians in the work force. There will be more single-parent, middle-aged, older, disabled, disadvantaged, and functionally illiterate people. And the values, life-styles, and expectations of this work force will be significantly different from those that have characterized the U.S. worker in the past. The expected labor shortage will not be brought about solely because of a smaller pool of people. There will also be a talent/job mismatch. The jobs that will be available will require skills and abilities that the worker pool will not have.

Advancing Technology

The years ahead will continue to be a period of rapid and pervasive technological change. Jobs will become obsolete, and the content of most jobs will change. There will be less dependence on manual and manipulative jobs and a growing need for conceptual, technical, and human skills. Advancing technology will create a new workplace where, in addition to math, reading, and writing, the average worker must use problem solving, teamwork, listening, and other skills formerly required only of supervisors and managers. In addition, even the lowest-paying jobs require basic computer skills. Fast-food employees and retail store clerks must have some basic knowledge of computer input. And these new requirements come at a time when our educational system is in crisis. If schools can't turn out the kinds of entry-level workers that business and industry need, organizations are going to have to develop those skills—as well as help local, state, and federal governments and agencies change the current educational system.

The Business Environment

Domestic competition for markets over the decade of the 1990s will remain intense. Foreign competition will increase dramatically with the activation of the European Community in 1992. Pacific Rim countries will continue to press for a larger share of the market. Meanwhile, the productivity of corporate America continues to falter. The soaring costs of pay and entitlements, particularly medical and health benefits, compounded by the increasing demands of collective bargaining units for a bigger share of enterprise profits, make productivity improvement a critical need. Restructuring and downsizing, as well as Chapter 11 bankruptcy filings, remain favored strategies for business survival and make the situation even worse. Certainly part of the solution to these problems lies in increasing the productivity of the work force through training and development.

The Training and Development Solution

One of the most promising solutions to the problem of attracting and retaining a competent, qualified, motivated, productive, and loyal work force involves a carefully designed and painstakingly implemented career development and assessment system, complemented by forward-looking, workable, and effective training and development programs.

Career Planning and Assessment

Employees need to see career ladders that define clear paths for development and promotion: carefully sequenced series of jobs available in the organization in their career fields from the lowest to the highest levels, in terms of responsibilities, compensation, and challenges. They also need help in career planning, the process of establishing short- and long-term career goals and objectives. And they need help in defining the specific knowledge, skills, and steps required to achieve them: the position, training, development, and other experiences that will allow them to attain their goals and objectives.

Career planning workshops are needed to help people understand where the opportunities lie. And, in addition, individual assessment is required to obtain a comprehensive perspective on individuals and identify the knowledge, skills, and abilities they will need to qualify for the openings that are likely to occur. Workshops should focus participants' attention on the skill and knowledge areas of greatest need, and individualized learning priorities must be established by the assessment program.

Training

Training consists of formal or informal, group or individual, short-term learning experiences designed to impart or improve the skills, knowledge, and job performance of employees. Its immediate goal is the development of new job skills or improved competency: the ability to do something new or do it better. It takes place *before* it is needed. Today, corporate America spends an average 1.5 percent of payroll on training; training in Europe commands 5 percent of payroll. The United States must do better.

Development

Development consists of a planned and tailor-made set of learning experiences designed to improve the skills and job performance of individuals in their current positions in a defined career field and a specific job or to prepare them for advancement to higher-level, more responsible positions in the organization. Development strategies include coaching, counseling, mentoring and networking programs, job rotation, appointment to committees, detail to special projects, attendance at professional or technical conferences, and participation in self-development activities such as community projects, public speaking, and writing for publication.

Benefits of Training and Development

Training and development systems offer many benefits to the organization, it owners, its managers, and its people. Here are some of those benefits.

• *Demonstrate concern.* Training and development provide one of the most effective means of letting your people know that they are understood and valued, that their needs and concerns are significant. It is a way of saying, "You're important. Your aspirations matter." People are not machines. They need more than periodic mainte nance to do the things that the organization needs to have them do. It's far more than just telling people what is expected of them, giving them a pat on the back when they do it, and firing them when they don't.

• *Lower the potential for failure.* Of course employees need clear job descriptions and standards of performance. They need to know exactly what is expected of them. They also need immediate feedback and recognition and reward for doing well. But, more than that, they need assistance and support when they falter. That includes training, coaching, development, and other experiences that will prevent failure.

• *Maximize talents and abilities.* Managers must encourage, inspire, and lead the people who work with and for them and, in concert with them, create an environment in which their people can become the very best their talents and abilities will allow. That requires a primary focus on viable and appropriate training and development programs, tailored to the needs and wants of the individual worker as well as the requirements of the organization.

Characteristics of a Viable Program

What are the essential features of a workable training and development program? There are several.

• *It is linked with corporate goals, plans, and systems.* Training and development must be tied to the corporate strategic plan, the management succession plan, the derivative human resources strategic and operational plans, and the performance appraisal system.

• *It addresses workers at all levels.* The training and development program provides training and development opportunities and programs for people at all levels of organization: executives, managers, scientists and engineers, staffers, supervisors, technicians, clerical and administrative personnel, and hourly workers.

• *It meets the needs of employees and the organization.* The program is designed to meet the changing needs of both the organization and its people. It is not set in concrete. It is monitored continuously, and it is subjected to critical review at least annually in light of the most recent forecasts of corporate requirements and periodic assessment of workers' needs.

• *It uses effective delivery systems.* Delivery systems provide the vehicle or medium for conducting training and development: the means of organizing, packaging, and getting the program to employees. They must be effective; that is, they must do their job well. They must also be efficient, that is, they must meet needs with minimum resources and without unforeseen consequences. They must take full advantage of new delivery options, such as CD-ROM, computer-based training, and satellite.

• *It controls costs.* All training and development programs cost money. A direct link must be established, by means of objective and valid statistical data, between the resource requirements for training and development and the impact they will have in dollars and cents on the bottom line. Managers need to be certain that programs, services, and activities are tied to business needs. They need to be very careful about how training and development dollars are spent.

• *It uses the systems approach.* The systems approach to training is composed of five phases.

1. Design, which includes the processes of conducting occupational, job, and task analyses; needs assessment; selecting and writing learning objectives; analyzing behavior into its components of knowledge, attitudes, and skills; and identifying and sequencing required content.
2. Development, which involves the processes of selecting the training delivery system; choosing or developing and validating instructional strategies, methods, techniques, and media; constructing evaluative instruments and criterion measures; and preparing training documents and trainer guidelines.
3. Implementation, which includes overseeing the delivery of the instruction, including the conduct of learning activities, use of lesson plans and media, and administering and analyzing test results and the outcomes derived from other evaluative instruments.
4. Evaluation, which involves the process of monitoring the training system in action; analyzing trainee test results, performance, and achievement; assessing the impact of training on organizational performance; and carrying out a benefits-cost analysis to measure return on training investment.
5. Follow-up, which is the process of checking and measuring the on-the-job performance of the products of the system, identifying performance shortfalls, and revising the system as needed.

Training and Development Needs Analysis and Assessment

Needs analysis is a means of identifying current or projected skills or deficits among employees. Needs assessment is a means of determining the training and development systems and programs needed by the organization, employee groups, and individual employees. Assessment identifies gaps in capabilities, abilities, and on-the-job performance, and places the identified needs in priority order for resolution. Some of the most useful assessment strategies are described in the paragraphs that follow.

Advisory Committees

Here, committees representing all levels of management (first-line supervisors, middle managers, and executives), functional specialists (marketing, sales, production, and so on), or organizational levels (supervisors, technicians, staffers, and other workers) are convened to identify and set priorities for training. A variant of the method is to convene a panel of outside experts to perform the same function.

Assessment Centers

This is a structured method of diagnosing training and development needs. Over a period of a day or two, and under the direction of a team of evaluators, employees deal with a variety of realistic problems and situations. They engage in simulations, in-basket exercises, and role playing; undergo psychological tests; and engage in group discussion and self-evaluation. Evaluators observe, assess, and record participants' behavior and performance, interview participants, and combine their appraisals in a formal report.

Company Records and Reports

Review and analysis of existing corporate reports, records, and other documents can reveal the level of performance of critical functions and jobs and pinpoint targets for improvement. Records of absenteeism, accidents, break-in time for new employees, customer complaints, employee suggestions and grievances, machine downtime, projections of position vacancies, rejects and reworks, and so on, are all useful in identifying training and development needs.

Critical Incident Surveys

With this approach, statements are collected from supervisors or designated observers based on direct observation of job incumbents or by recall of job behavior by employees. Incidents reported typify both competent and incompetent performance of a job or task. The technique underscores critical job behaviors for emphasis in training.

Exit Interviews

Exit interviews are individual meetings conducted by trainers or others upon the termination (through resignation, dismissal, or retirement) of employees to obtain information pertaining to training needs and problem areas. The interviews are structured, and written notes are made of responses to carefully worded questions.

Group Interviews

Here, several job incumbents are called together to provide specific information about their jobs, their competencies, and common problems and pitfalls. A trained needs analyst asks questions designed to elicit job performance data. Following the interview the job analyst combines the data into a single composite report of findings.

Individual Interviews

These are face-to-face meetings with individuals (superiors, peers, employees, customers, suppliers, and dealers) to collect information, identify areas and skills requiring training and development, get leads to new or unperceived problems, and determine the seriousness of problems identified by other means.

Job Description/Applicant Specification Analyses

These documents identify the skills, knowledge, training, and experience required for success in specific jobs. By analyzing the documents and comparing them with personnel records, discrepancies between job requirements and the knowledge and skills of job incumbents can be identified.

Needs Inventories

These are instruments that describe the skills and abilities of a specific group or class of workers (for example, computer programmers) and ask employees from that group to rate independently the extent to which the skills and abilities apply to themselves or their subordinates. Ratings are tallied by item. The distribution of scores yields a rank order, reflecting the relative importance of specific skills. Decisions on training can then be based on a cut score; for example, all items above a selected score will be included in training.

Nominal Group Technique

This is a structured group meeting designed to develop a list of problems that can be addressed by training. Five to nine participants write down as many problems as they can identify and then, in turn, present one idea from the list. The process continues until all lists are exhausted. Structured discussion of each idea follows. The session concludes with individual, independent, private, and silent balloting to select items and establish training priorities by rank order.

Observation and On-Site Inspection

This option involves periodic planned visits by training and development managers and specialists to locations where specific jobs are being performed: the plant, the assembly line, the shop, the laboratory, the office, the classroom, the clinic, the retail store, the warehouse, the operating room, and so on. The observer-inspectors concentrate on observable behavior and characteristics: whether sales personnel are truly serving the customer, managers are really coaching and counseling, and instructors are actually involving trainees in learning activities. The process is directed toward fact-finding and is systematic in terms of the timing, length, and number of observations. Results are recorded.

Performance Appraisal Analysis

Information can be gained from analyzing performance appraisals because they include (or should include) notations pertaining to the developmental and training needs of employees as well as observations and ratings pertaining to the performance of job duties and tasks. Discrepancies can then be identified between results and the required level of performance. Performance appraisals should also be reviewed as they relate to the management succession plan (if you have one) to ensure that those employees identified as successors to key management people get the training they need to move up in the organization.

Questionnaires

One of the most commonly used means of collecting data on training and development needs is the administration of a questionnaire to all employees or to selected categories of employees. The questionnaire may list several employee skills and ask respondents to rate their importance (on a scale of three, five, or ten points) and how well they currently perform those skills. Alternatively, the questionnaire may be addressed to the supervisors of employees and ask the same questions.

Types of Training

Most organizations need several types of training. The most common are compensatory, uptraining, and special training.

Compensatory Training

BASIC SKILLS TRAINING

It is patently obvious that radical change is needed in U.S. education. Schools in the United States are and have been badly troubled for years (witness the *A Nation at Risk* report of the secretary of education in 1983 and more recently the Bush administration's *America 2000: An Education Strategy*, designed to improve U.S. elementary and secondary schools). As a result of the fact that students are graduating with serious gaps in basic skills, employers must try to fill those gaps. Traditionally seen as encompassing only basic literacy training (reading and writing) and computation, basic skills are now defined as training provided to upgrade workers' skills and equip them to deal with changes in technology and work processes, as well as overcome educational deficits in reading, writing, computation, and interpersonal communications.

REMEDIAL TRAINING

This is training designed to provide repeat instruction and guided practice for workers to remedy or correct deficiencies in their performance. It is given when needed and may target deficiencies in work habits, attitudes, knowledge, skills, or job performance.

RETRAINING

This is training provided to older workers, people who have returned to the work force after a long absence (called reentry training), plateaued employees, or other workers in a specific job or occupation to enable them to perform new processes and procedures or work with new or unfamiliar tools, equipment, and materials. Retraining also includes programs for employees who have been assigned to new jobs because their old jobs are obsolete and no longer required. For example, assembly-line workers might be retrained as sales clerks.

Uptraining

CROSS-TRAINING

This is training designed to improve employees' performance of current skills, teach new skills, or help workers become ready to assume more responsible or more demanding positions. Sometimes called upskilling or redeployment, it is a means of developing multiskilled workers, people who can adapt to changes in job requirements and advancing technology. It is essentially a strategy to make an organization more competitive, increase productivity, promote stability, respond more rapidly to change, avoid layoffs, and compensate for the shrinking pool of qualified workers.

INTERCULTURAL/CROSS-CULTURAL TRAINING

This is training provided by public and private organizations, institutions, and agencies for managers and supervisors, immigrants, foreigners, foreign-born Americans, or even Americans from different cultural backgrounds. For managers and supervisors, its purpose is to increase managerial and supervisory effectiveness in dealing with minorities and people of diverse backgrounds. For immigrants, intercultural training is provided to help them adapt to working, living, and learning environments in the United States. In addition, some organizations are providing workshops for immigrants or English as a second language. These workshops are a positive way to help these new employees become more comfortable in their new country and the job.

Special Training

TRAINING FOR FAST-TRACK EMPLOYEES

Fast-track employees are usually knowledge workers, people whose work is for the most part intellectual: planners, problem solvers, decision makers, managers, scientists, course developers, instructors, technical writers, and so on. The way to increase the number of knowledge workers and their capacity to contribute to organizational growth, development, and bottom-line results, is through individual training and development. There are at least twelve critical skills employees in knowledge-based companies must possess to sustain organizations in the decade ahead: strategic planning, problem sensing, problem solving, inquiring, innovating, managing change, negotiating, coaching, training, empowering, team building, and developing oneself.

TRAINING FOR THE DISABLED

Disabilities fall into four categories, each of which can be further subdivided:

1. *Learning disabilities:* Problems with acquiring knowledge and skills, ranging from dyslexia to less severe disorders that can obstruct, encumber, or hamper learning success.
2. *Mental disabilities:* "Slow learners" (IQ range of 75–90), "retarded" (IQ range of 50–75), "severely retarded" or "trainable" (IQ below 50), and "perceptually disabled" (brain-injured).
3. *Emotional disabilities:* Attention-deficit disorders (short attention spans), psychotic disorders (schizophrenia, paranoia, and manic-depressive psychotic reaction), psychoneurotic disorders (anxiety, hysteria, hypochondria, phobic reaction, and depression), personality disorders (antisocial personality), and substance dependence and abuse, including alcoholism.
4. *Physical disabilities:* Totally or partially deaf, totally or partially blind, speech problems, orthopedically handicapped (loss of normal use of limbs, bones, or muscles due to disease, injury, or deformity, such as cerebral palsy, muscular

dystrophy, congenital deformities, and amputation), and health or medical problems (such as AIDS, asthma, epilepsy, diabetes, and heart conditions).

Basically, there are four reasons for establishing training programs for the disabled. First, it is the right thing to do because challenged individuals must be treated as people who need to express their individuality. They have the right to live as rewarding and independent lives as their disabilities will permit. Second, disabled workers are badly needed to augment the work force during a period of acute labor shortages. Third, the difference between the disabled and so-called ''able-bodied'' employees is mainly one of degree; the disabled are more like other employees than unlike them, and it is impossible to prejudge what most disabled persons can learn. Fourth, at least by implication, the Americans with Disabilities Act of 1990 mandates training for the disabled.

When a company makes the decision to hire a person with a disability, it's a good idea to do two things. First, find out immediately what type of physical accommodation (if any) the new employee will need in order to do the job. Second, mutually discuss and arrive at a decision as to what type of special training will be needed (if any). Since almost all new employees need some initial job training, it is just a matter of identifying any changes that will need to be made in delivering that training to the disabled employee.

Commonly Offered Training Programs

There are numerous types of training programs to provide the specific skills needed by employees in particular situations.

Adventure Training

This is training conducted in the wilderness or the woods, rather than in a traditional classroom setting. It is used to ease employees through corporate change, build teamwork, improve problem solving, encourage risk taking, or strengthen leadership abilities. Participants learn by doing: swinging from ropes, scaling four-story-high trees, going white-water rafting, running obstacle courses, and engaging in group problem solving of physical problems. Some companies offer this type of training only to higher-level managerial employees.

Assertiveness Training

Assertiveness training is provided to build assertiveness, improve the job performance and satisfaction of managers and supervisors, establish models of managerial behavior, reduce anxieties in handling interpersonal relationships on the job, and enhance employees' self-image. Strategies include inventory of participants' skills, attitudes, habits, and values; self-analysis and self-evaluation exercises, group interaction, assertiveness exercises; and feedback on assertive-responsive behavior patterns.

Behavior Modeling Training

This is training that focuses on specific situations that the worker must deal with on the job. For example, training may be provided to help supervisors improve the work en-

vironment and the behavior and productivity of their people by demonstrating and practicing the proper methods of correcting performance. Strategies include small-group
discussion, demonstration and performance, simulations and role playing, team training,
case studies, exercise and practice of skills, and feedback.

Communication Training

Communication training is offered for workers at any level to improve their ability to
generate, transmit, and receive information. It includes training employees to listen,
speak, write, or read to avoid misunderstanding and get the desired response or action
from others. It is usually provided by means of small group seminars and workshops
using job-related exercises, printed materials, multimedia presentations, and video recording, playback, and critique.

Computer-Related Training

This type of training is provided to employees at all levels of organization to ensure
optimum and effective use of corporate data-processing facilities and services. It includes computer literacy training for supervisors and managers and computer programming, computer operation, and computer troubleshooting and repair for other types of
employees. It invariably involves hands-on experience and practice with computers or
computer terminals.

Customer Service Training

This is a relatively new type of training now being provided in many organizations for
all levels of employees from managers to front-line employees, from marketing people
to sales clerks. It is designed to improve customer service by focusing on service basics:
what service is, how to empathize with customers, how service can provide a competitive edge for a company, how to exceed customer expectations, how to handle complaints, and how to measure service performance.

Decision-Making Training

Decision-making training is provided for supervisors and managers to improve their
decisions. Typically it focuses on the processes and procedures of problem solving and
the nature of risk taking. It makes use of simulations, case studies, and role playing.

Ethics Training

Ethics training is provided for executives, managers, supervisors, and sales personnel
to promote integrity and ethical practices within and outside the organization, prevent
unethical conduct or practices, and avoid violations of community standards and values.
Coverage typically includes ethics in interpersonal relationships; rules regarding giving
and receiving gifts; the consequences of tolerating violations of policies, rules, and
regulations; how to confront unethical behavior; and proper relationships with clients,
customers, dealers, suppliers, and contractors. Primary methods used are case studies,
role playing, panels and group interviews, study assignments, and problem-solving exercises.

Financial Training

This is training in finance and accounting terminology, concepts, principles, processes, and procedures. It is provided for nonfinancial managers and executives who must understand the finance function, interact with financial professionals, use the balance sheet, analyze income and profit and loss statements, and be able to communicate the quantitative aspects of performance and results. Programs are designed to meet the needs of corporate officers who must produce, analyze, oversee, or approve plans, policies, systems, goals, or objectives.

Instructor Training

This is instruction provided to train managers, supervisors, staff personnel, technicians, sales personnel, and operative employees in the principles, methods, and techniques of instruction or to orient and retrain professional teachers in the procedures and techniques of job training and organizational development. It is sometimes called "training the trainer." It typically includes training needs analysis, instructional planning, preparation of instructional materials and lesson plans, and methods and techniques of presentation and evaluation.

Negotiating Skills Training

This is training for executives, managers, corporate negotiators, and members of negotiating teams designed to improve their ability to reach successful agreements and mutually advantageous contracts with clients, collective bargaining units, consultants, customers, financial institutions, and suppliers. The focus is on concepts, principles, procedures and techniques, preparation and planning, recognizing and dealing with conflict, overcoming barriers, and resolving issues, problems, and impasses.

Office Skills Training

Office skills training is given to office support staff who provide administrative support services, such as reception, clerical, secretarial, and word-processing activities. It may include keyboard skills, telephone skills, filing, correspondence, interpersonal communication, and receiving visitors. Primary methods used are hands-on equipment, drill and practice, case studies, role playing, and problem-solving exercises.

Presentation Skills Training

This is training provided for employees who must speak to groups and face cameras and microphones. It is designed to build skills, confidence, and control in facing an audience or the media. It focuses on planning, organizing, and delivering the presentation; projecting a professional image; maximizing persuasive power; managing anxiety and stress; building and maintaining rapport with listeners; handling questions and objections; and dealing with hostility.

Problem-Solving Training

Problem-solving training is provided for employees (managers, supervisors, technicians, and others) to develop their ability to resolve troublesome situations or issues by following a deliberate, logical, reasoned thought process; keeping emotions and personal values in check; and using previously acquired or newly gained knowledge, skills, and experiences. Primary methods used are case studies and problem-solving exercises.

Project Management Training

This is training designed for project managers responsible for construction, corporate planning, corporate relocation, engineering, new products, research and development, and systems development, and for other executives, managers, and staff officers who may be assigned to project teams. Training focuses on project planning, scheduling, implementation, and control concepts; principles, processes, and procedures for resource allocation; performance measurement; and reporting procedures.

Safety Training

Safety training is provided for employees, clients, and customers to promote safe and healthful working conditions and reduce accidents, injuries, and illnesses. Strategies, processes, and techniques include formal training involving demonstrations and the use of multimedia, meetings, and conferences; safety publications, bulletins, and posters; safety contests, signs, and slogans; immediate correction of errors; and the elimination of hazards.

Sales and Dealer Training

This training is provided for the sales force, franchisees, and dealers to teach them what they need to know about the products and services they market and sell, how to demonstrate the effectiveness of their products and services, and how to conduct their business. Training also helps them develop the attitudes, skills, and habits they need to influence prospects and customers to make decisions to buy. Strategies include demonstration, multimedia, role playing, and case studies.

Sensitivity Training

Sensitivity training, sometimes called T-Group training, involves small-group interaction under stress in an unstructured group composed of volunteer learners and a trained and skilled leader using a permissive and supportive environment. Participants, guided by an experienced trainer, are encouraged to act their own roles, receive feedback, examine their concepts of self, and experiment with and practice new patterns of behavior. Content of the training varies with the nature of the individuals and groups participating.

Stress Management Training

This is training conducted to reduce the consequences of excessive stress to individual employees, their families, and the organization. Strategies and techniques include medical referral, psychotherapy, exercise and fitness programs, counseling, diet consultation and nutritional assays, relaxation tapes and exercises, breathing techniques, meditation, discussion groups, and spouse or couples workshops.

Technical Training

Technical training focuses on the application of mathematical and scientific principles to the creation of products, services, or processes. It is provided for workers who use technology in their jobs. Most technical training in industry is geared to upgrading and updating skills in jobs that require certification or licensing, for example, health care. Such training makes extensive use of demonstration and performance, equipment, tools, models, mock-ups, and multimedia, task lists, and job aids.

Time Management Training

Time management training is offered for employees at all levels to improve their use of and control over time on and off the job. It focuses on a systematic approach to the control of time, identifying and analyzing time problems, avoiding procrastination, eliminating time wasters, making the most of delegation, and developing and implementing action plans.

Training Delivery System Options

Trainers now have an imposing array of options for delivering training where only a few years ago the choices were limited to a few alternatives. The choices today enable trainers to select the delivery system or systems that will provide effective training at an affordable cost.

Selecting a delivery system should never be based on expediency. A sounder, more objective method of making such an important decision must be employed. The costs of mistakes are too high. Choosing a delivery system requires not only knowledge of what is currently available but also some firm criteria for the selection of the optimum means of getting training to those who need it.

What are the options now available to training managers and trainers to deliver training to employees? In general, they fall into six categories: one-on-one training, interactive training, distance training, centralized training, learner-controlled training, and other types of training. Although there is some overlap among these alternatives, for the sake of convenience they will be treated here as discrete delivery options.

One-on-One Training

One-on-one training invariably involves two persons: one, the learner; and the other, a coach, supervisor, mentor, instructor, or facilitator. It provides day-to-day learning experiences using such learning strategies as telling and explaining, questioning and probing, showing and demonstrating, drilling and practicing, providing feedback and reinforcement, and following up.

INDIVIDUALIZED INSTRUCTION

This option, also called self-paced training, involves the use of instructional systems, programs, or lesson modules designed to allow individual trainees to proceed at their own rates through a sequence of learning activities. An instructor is available to answer questions and help trainees who are experiencing difficulty. Activities are designed to provide for individual trainee differences in learning style, experience, aptitude, ability, interest, and needs.

ON-THE-JOB TRAINING, COACHING, OR TUTORING

This alternative involves planned and organized training conducted by a coworker or supervisor at the workplace; in the office, shop, laboratory, or the field; on the production line or the construction site; or behind the counter. It is a one-on-one, face-to-face teaching/learning/counseling relationship designed to develop job-related knowledge and skills and improve performance. The coach or tutor demonstrates, assists, motivates, encourages, and rewards the trainee and provides guided practice and feedback on performance. The approach requires a continuous flow of instructions, comments, explanations, and suggestions from coach to employee, with the coach or tutor listening, questioning, relating learning to the learner's experiences, and providing guidance.

Interactive Training

Interactive training systems (ITS), sometimes called interactive performance systems, performance support systems, or on-demand learning systems, are systems that support workers by providing immediate and on-line access to information, advice, and learning experiences. ITS is provided at the work site, on the bench, or at a workstation by other than a live instructor. The training vehicle may be multimedia or a computer. The systems can be designed to provide interactive advice on how to perform a task or operation or make a decision. The information bases of computer-driven performance support systems contain test, graphics, audio, and traditional (alphanumeric) databases.

JOB AIDS

These are materials that provide step-by-step direction for performing specific technical tasks to reduce training time, error rates, and dependence on instructors. They may be in paper form (documents, procedures manuals, or job instruction sheets) or audiovisual (slides, motion pictures, or videocassettes). Job aids provide several benefits. They are relatively inexpensive to produce in quantity and are reusable. They sometimes are provided by the supplier of the equipment. Their principal disadvantage lies in their applicability, which is primarily in technical areas. An additional disadvantage is that they typically rely on only one medium.

EMBEDDED TRAINING

Embedded training (ET) is training that is built into the software of computer applications programs (the programs the employee uses on the job), rather than provided in a separate training package. ET is on the same terminal or delivery device as the product it supports. A program that teaches an employee how to use a spreadsheet while using the spreadsheet itself is an example of ET.

MULTIMEDIA

Multimedia is the output provided by combining a variety of formerly independent sound and visual media with a computer in control. Multimedia consists of combinations of hardware, software, and learningware in one easy-to-use package that can deliver still and dynamic imagery, text, audio, graphics, animation, video, and even full motion at one workstation or learning carrel. It can bring together text, graphics, animation, captured screen images, and video, as well as digitized audio and CD-ROM.

INTERACTIVE VIDEO SYSTEMS

Interactive video technology offers new opportunities for involving learners. It enables trainees to communicate with and control a video training program by using a computer to interface with videocassette or videodisk recorders. The most sophisticated systems provide random access to the contents of the training or other program through a keyboard, mouse, or touch-screen (finger touch of the CRT) and where responses of the system are determined by the user's input. However, it is also possible to create interactive circuits composed of videotape, an instructor, and the trainee. Interactive video and television training programs will be the hottest training techniques in the future. Generations of children who have been raised watching TV and playing video games relate to this medium.

COMPUTER-BASED TRAINING

Computer-based training (CBT) involves the use of computers to deliver instructional packages either at a central training facility or at the workplace through local area networks (LANs),* modems and telephone lines, or satellite. It can be used in tutorial, drill, practice, games, modeling, simulation, and problem-solving modes to teach a great variety of content and job knowledge and skills: complex analytical skills, manipulative or cognitive skills, deductive inference, and advanced problem solving. Originally, CBT was touted as one of the most effective means of presenting single-topic, stand-alone training programs. Today it is more likely to be found as one component of a larger training package that might include video, multimedia, workbooks, and even classroom training.

Distance Training

This option is education and training provided for adults at remote locations by such means as correspondence courses, teleconferencing, business television, microwave, and satellite-delivered training.

---

*A local area network (LAN) is a multiuser electronically linked system for communicating data in the same format, one-way or interactive, in one building or at many sites in the same general area. In training, a LAN is a means of facilitating, distributing, or delivering training to individuals and groups at several different locations.

Correspondence Study

This is education or training conducted by mail or other means of delivering training packages. It uses books, manuals, workbooks, tests, and sometimes audiocassettes or videocassettes. Correspondence study typically involves the completion of reading, writing, viewing, and problem-solving assignments and tests, which are returned by the trainee to the sponsoring organization for review, correction, grading, or other form of feedback. Correspondence study can be used to provide almost any type of training, although if equipment is involved, it must be made available to trainees.

Teletraining

This delivery system uses satellite, microwave, or phoneline TV point-to-point communication links established between two or more groups at two or more locations to provide instantaneous interchange of aural and visual information for training. It may take any of four modes: (1) video conferencing, which uses TV images plus sound at all locations; (2) computer conferencing, where computers at several sites are netted; (3) audiographic conferencing, where two-way audio via telephone and visual images via fax are the means of communication; and (4) audio conferencing, which is voice communication by means of telephone or radio. Of course, all modes of communication can be distributed by satellite.

Centralized Training

Instructor-Led Training

This is the conventional approach to training. It involves an instructor, a group of trainees, and a classroom or laboratory and employs the standard lecture, conference-discussion, demonstration, and performance (practical exercise) methods of instruction and such techniques as questioning and audiovisual aids. In other words, the option makes use of the presentation, discussion, and question-and-answer approaches. It may be provided internally by staff or by external contractors.

Learning Centers

This option employs a resource facility that offers materials in a variety of formats for individual study: audio- and videocassettes, computer-assisted and computer-managed instruction, interactive video, compact laser disks, 8mm and 16mm film, programmed and conventional books and workbooks, periodicals, manuals, organization documents, and a large number of programmed materials in audiovisual forms (sound-filmstrip, 35mm slides, overhead projections, and so on).

Learner-Controlled Training

This alternative is an approach in which the learner, rather than an instructor, plays the primary role in such activities as planning; setting objectives; selecting the delivery system, instructional methods, and techniques; and evaluating results. It may include any or all of the conventional instructional strategies as well as special participative methods, such as case studies, role playing, and simulations. It is self-motivated and self-managed planning and execution of the process of learning, changing, and improving. It may be undertaken with the assistance of an adviser, mentor, or trainer, but it always involves learner control over the learning goals, strategy, methods and materials, and evaluation.

AUTOMATED LEARNING CENTERS

A new development is the automated learning center (ALC). An ALC facility puts trainees in control of their learning activities. Automated learning centers contain multimedia workstations equipped with PCs, VHS player/monitors, audiocassette players, CD-ROM players, and interactive laser disk systems. The workstations are supported by a library of courseware.

SELF-DIRECTED LEARNING

Here the learner, more or less completely on his or her own, develops a study program using whatever resources are available in the organization and in the surrounding community. The program may involve formal courses, professional reading, networking, or a host of other strategies.

Other Forms of Training

SUITCASING

Suitcasing is a traditional method of delivering classroom training to groups of workers at remote locations. All materials required to conduct the training are packaged and either sent or hand-carried to the training location, where they are used by a "traveling" trainer to conduct the training. Itinerant trainers, although an expensive option because of the travel and subsistence costs involved, are a viable option when there is a shortage of instructors in numbers, pedagogical skills, or subject matter competencies. It can also provide human interface when that is critical to trainee motivation and the instructional objectives. It has all of the advantages of conventional classroom or laboratory training.

CONTRACT TRAINING

Here outside sources (either on-site or off-the-premises) are used to provide training programs for operative, supervisory, or managerial personnel. Sources of training include colleges and universities, professional societies, management institutes and associations, and management and training consultants. Most contract training programs are conducted by conventional lecture, demonstration, discussion, and practical work in a seminar or workshop format.

CUSTOMIZED TRAINING

Customized training involves programs designed specifically for a particular group of people in a particular organization. It employs problems, situations, and other content that are unique to the target group. It may be self-instructional or require an instructor or facilitator.

OFF-THE-SHELF TRAINING PROGRAMS

These are training programs or packages, in a variety of audiovisual formats, produced for other organizations or available commercially that are judged to match the needs of an organization well enough to use them, although they may not fit either the organization or the industry precisely. They may be computer- or media-controlled, trainee-controlled, or require an instructor.

TUITION-AID PROGRAMS

These are formal corporate programs and plans that provide financial assistance to employees who take credit or noncredit courses from accredited schools and colleges on their own time. In some cases financial backing is provided only for training and education programs that are directly related to the employee's current job. In other organizations, tuition aid is granted for high school equivalency courses, general postsecondary education programs and cultural courses, and advanced degree programs for employees. Aid is sometimes also provided for the employee's spouse and/or children.

INSTITUTIONAL PARTNERSHIPS

These are contractual partnerships established with area technical schools, colleges, and universities by corporations to develop programs, including undergraduate and graduate degree programs, tailored to the needs and requirements of the organization. The institution and the corporation jointly determine enrollment requirements, plan and develop the curriculum, and establish course or degree completion standards and requirements. The school, college, or university provides the instructors (although some courses may be taught by employees of the corporation) and organizes and administers the program. Courses may be conducted on the premises of the corporation, at the institution, or both.

Factors in Delivery System Selection

Several factors must be taken into account when deciding which of the available delivery systems is to be implemented.

TRAINING OBJECTIVES

The important thing here is to consider the real thrust of the training without getting into detailed lesson- or module-level training objectives. For all practical purposes, instructional objectives may be cataloged as orientation and induction, concept development, skill building and practice (physical and mental), skills mastery, problem solving and decision making, creative endeavor, enrichment, individual development, retraining, team training, review, and makeup. But there are some additional considerations. Is standardization of instruction critical? Is the content subject to change? Are there problems of integration with other enterprise operations, programs, and activities?

TRAINEES

Here the deciding factors relate to the nature of the trainee population. Is the trainee group relatively homogeneous in terms of aptitude, ability, communication skills, prior training, and experience? Or is it relatively heterogeneous in terms of those same attributes? Are the numbers of people to be trained large or small? Are they to be trained simultaneously, or doesn't it matter? Are they all at one location, or are they widely scattered?

INSTRUCTORS

How many instructors are available? Where are they located? Can they be moved? Are they technically qualified? Are they experienced? Are they trained in the use of the delivery systems, strategies, methods, and techniques they will be called upon to apply? What are their pedagogic strengths and shortcomings? Do they have strong preferences for any training strategy or method of instruction?

INSTRUCTIONAL FACILITIES, EQUIPMENT, AND MATERIALS

Some of the most critical questions here are as follows: Is instructional space of the right kind available? Are there classrooms, conference rooms, shops, laboratories, food services, and hotel/motel accommodations? Is all of the available space in one location or in several separated locations? Are facilities such as offices, breakout rooms, library/learning center, and storage available adjacent to the primary instructional space? Is equipment, such as audiovisual, computer, and operational equipment and tools, on hand and in good repair? Is there enough equipment to accommodate the desired or required group size? Are materials, such as software, books and manuals, and film and tapes, available and in adequate supply?

TIME

Here there are many important questions. What is the best estimate of the duration of the training in weeks or hours? How much lead time for training is available before the products of the training system must be productive members of the work force? Must all trainees complete the training at the same time, or doesn't it matter? How much time will be required to develop and validate the training system?

Development Programs and Delivery Options

Employee development may take several forms, some formal, but most informal. That doesn't mean that informal programs are unplanned and unstructured. On the contrary, good development programs are carefully plotted, painstakingly configured, and systematically implemented. Although there may be a considerable amount of overlap in the types of programs and the options for their delivery, they will be treated here as separate and distinct entities.

Types of Development Programs

EXECUTIVE DEVELOPMENT

Executive development consists of formal and informal education and training programs, either managerial or functional, designed to improve the performance and potential of selected managers and executives. Most common strategies are formal institutional training, seminars and workshops, coaching, special assignments, and self-study.

EXECUTIVE TRANSFORMATION

This option involves learner-centered programs designed to convert functional managers and specialists into general managers: people who can manage across several organizational functions and make strategic decisions that overcome the inherently insular and conflicting goals of those functions.

LEADERSHIP DEVELOPMENT

Leadership development programs are designed for all levels of management—supervisors, middle managers, top-level managers, executives, and those preparing for such positions—but they are conducted separately for each group. Programs focus on identifying the differences between management and leadership, inventorying and identifying leadership abilities and types of leadership, analyzing organizational culture, fostering innovation, learning to use a variety of leadership styles in different situations, and gaining the support and commitment of subordinates.

MANAGEMENT DEVELOPMENT

These programs are designed to meet the needs of an organization for successors to current managers, to help current managers to become more effective, and to provide additional managers to meet the need for expansion of the industry or organization. The programs develop knowledge and skills in leadership and group dynamics, strategic planning and goal setting, organization theory and applications, leadership styles, motivation theory and applications, coaching and team building, and managing change and innovation.

ORGANIZATIONAL TRANSFORMATION

This is a general term covering programs designed to reshape or transform organizations by stimulating motivation, innovation, and excellence through teamwork, empowerment, and participation. It is viewed as the final stage of a continuum consisting of management-employee development, organization development, and organizational transformation. In essence it is a long-range program to involve all employees in a major effort to change an organization's culture, values, and management processes and thereby improve productivity, product/service quality, results, and employee satisfaction.

ORGANIZATION DEVELOPMENT

Organization development (OD) is a systematic strategy for improving the management and operation of an enterprise to increase effectiveness, productivity, and return on investment, improve the quality of work life, and raise the level of employee job satisfaction. The OD process is designed to clarify the mission, goals, and objectives of the organization; align and integrate individual employee and enterprise goals; deal effectively with technical, managerial, and human problems; and improve cooperation, communication, and teamwork between managers and their subordinates and among enterprise units.

PERSONAL DEVELOPMENT

This option involves development opportunities provided on a voluntary basis to workers at all levels to promote their self-knowledge and self-acceptance; improve their mental and physical health and well-being; improve their ability to work with others; reduce absenteeism, tardiness, accidents, and injuries; improve productivity; reduce tension and stress; and provide positive personality development. Personal development typically includes medical evaluation and may take such forms as health and fitness programs, physical and recreational activities, introspective exercises, stress management, and small-group interactions.

PROFESSIONAL DEVELOPMENT

Professional development involves a continuing and deliberate organization-sponsored process aimed at assisting, encouraging, and enabling professionals as individuals to improve their performance and potential by developing their knowledge, skills, abilities, and values. It aims to help workers keep current in their occupation or profession, maintain competence in their practice, and remain open to new theories, techniques, and approaches.

PROFESSIONAL MEMBERSHIPS

Membership in professional and technical societies, both national and local, offers a fruitful means of staying abreast of developments in one's profession or technical discipline and opportunities for cultivating important and useful networks. Some organizations pay membership dues for their employees, and others offer support in the forms of providing time off with pay to attend meetings, paying attendance fees, and even reimbursing travel expenses.

PROFESSIONAL MEETINGS AND CONFERENCES

Whether organization-supported or paid for by the individual employee, this option centers on employee attendance at professional and technical meetings, conferences, exhibitions, and trade shows. The option offers a stimulating, interesting, and fruitful means of staying current in one's profession or technical discipline.

PROFESSIONAL READING, RESEARCH, AND WRITING

These are also means of remaining current in one's profession or technical discipline. The option involves the development and practice of a regular program of reading (professional and technical books and journals), on- or off-the-job study and research, and writing for publication.

SCIENTIST AND ENGINEER DEVELOPMENT

This option consists of programs conducted to update and refresh the professional and technical vitality of scientists and engineers, improve their productivity, retrain personnel whose skills and knowledge have become obsolete or unneeded in the organization, and promote and support learning and growth. Delivery systems include attendance at programs and conferences sponsored by professional societies; enterprise-sponsored seminars, workshops, lectures, and tutorials; laboratory observation and experimentation; industrial, government, and university exchange programs; and sabbatical leaves for study and research.

SELF-DEVELOPMENT

Self-development is a means of planning and carrying out strategic career and life planning. It inventories an individual's strengths, aspirations, and opportunities and seeks to identify and remedy deficiencies and integrate strengths and aspirations into an optimal career plan. Self-development includes all dimensions of self: personally, socially, professionally, intellectually, physically, emotionally, experientially, and spiritually. It makes use of such means as correspondence and home-study courses; technical school, college, and university study; membership in trade, technical, and professional associations; membership in civic and community groups, service clubs, and personal improvement groups; and professional reading.

SEMINARS AND WORKSHOPS

This option involves attendance at company-sponsored or public seminars and workshops offered by professional societies, public and private institutions, public and private training organizations, and private consultants either at corporate or employee expense. Programs are designed to involve participants directly in the learning process. They make use of panels, discussions, group interviews, group problem solving, and role playing.

SUPERVISOR DEVELOPMENT

This is training and development provided to selected employees with the potential for promotion to supervisory positions, to employees who are newly appointed to supervisory positions, or to incumbent supervisors to remedy their performance deficiencies. It typically covers the rudiments of managerial planning, organizing, staffing, directing, and controlling with an emphasis on legal responsibilities, employee relations, and performance evaluation.

WORK TEAM DEVELOPMENT

Work team development is provided for leaders and members of committees, project teams, quality circles, self-directed work teams, and task forces to improve their performance. It focuses on the selection and development of members, how to structure and manage the team, how to resolve conflict, and how to increase collaboration and productivity.

Development Delivery Strategies

ASSISTANT-TO ASSIGNMENTS

Sometimes called understudy assignments, this is a method of providing management development that involves assignment of the trainee to a competent senior manager or executive who tailor one-on-one training and coaching to the needs of the individual, providing carefully selected experiences, frequent guidance, and immediate feedback to enhance skills development.

CAREER COUNSELING

Career counseling is one-on-one counseling designed to help employees learn about their own capabilities, limitations, and objectives; what opportunities are available to them within and outside the organization; and what they need in the way of training and development to make the most of their opportunities. The employee is then assisted to develop career plans, using information on specific career requirements, career ladders, organizational needs, available development opportunities, and employee interests and needs.

CAREER PLANNING

Career planning is the process of establishing short- and/or long-term career goals and objectives and defining the specific steps required to achieve them (the positions, training, development, and other experiences that will assist in attaining the goals and objectives). It may be done by the employee alone or in concert with a mentor or adviser.

COACHING

Coaching is a one-on-one, face-to-face teaching/learning/counseling relationship designed to develop job-related knowledge and skills and improve performance. It involves a continual flow of instructions, comments, and suggestions from coach to employee: listening, questioning, relating learning to the learner's experiences, and providing guided practice.

COMMITTEE ASSIGNMENTS

This option develops managers by involving them in policy making and decision making. They are assigned to committees established to perform a specific function or carry out a project. Such committees may take the forms of standing (permanent) or ad hoc (temporary) committees and perform such functions as policy making (legislative), executive (administrative), judicial, advisory (consultative), or research (investigative).

JOB ROTATION

Job rotation is an informal method of development, often used in conjunction with coaching. Potential managers receive diversified training and experience under close supervision through rotation for specified periods of time in nonsupervisory or managerial jobs, observational assignments, or training, assistant-to, or managerial positions. In some cases, managers are rotated through all major departments in an organization for one month each.

MENTORING

Mentoring programs involve appointing a senior, experienced, and respected manager or staffer to serve as a role model, coach, counselor, adviser, and advocate for a younger or less experienced employee. Through frequent face-to-face contacts, mentors provide personal and professional guidance and assistance to their assigned workers. Although mentors may be employed by the organization, they are not directly involved in their charges' personal or work lives.

NETWORKING

This option involves encouraging executives, managers, scientists, engineers, and other professionals to exchange advice, information, assistance, contacts, and referrals with their counterparts or peers inside and outside the organization to foster self-improvement and generate ideas, new products, or innovative solutions to problems. Some networks are electronically supported by means of modems and computers.

SPECIAL ASSIGNMENTS

This is a strategy for developing employees and building their expertise by bringing them into contact with new and different people, situations, problems, and ideas. They include assignments to projects, investigations, studies, audits, quality circles, and temporary positions, as well as travel.

Training Costs

Costs are usually the most critical of all the considerations when reevaluating and restructuring training—but not always. Costs are not always measured in dollars. Sometimes dollar costs must be given lower priority than other criteria, particularly when the lack of an immediate response to a training requirement is likely to result in increased employee turnover, failure to win a large and lucrative contract, or a destructive drop in competitive status. But the root question is this: How much can the organization realistically budget for training and development and for the conduct of training over the time required? Although you may have a difficult time coming up with firm numbers, good estimates are absolutely essential if the final costs are to be considered and approved by management.

Many companies ask the training manager to provide a cost-benefit analysis of training activities.[1] This is not an easy task, since so many things go into the total training activity. If you are asked to produce such an analysis, here are the key elements to consider.

- Number of students being trained
- Course length in days
- Student salary per day
- Lost work costs
- Number of instructors
- Instructor salary
- Instructor travel and other costs
- Facilities costs
- Administrative costs
- Instructional development costs
- Materials costs

Focus your analysis on tangible benefits to the organization, such as decreases or reductions in absenteeism, accident rates, machine downtime, and operating costs *and* increases or improvement in production, profit, return on investment, and sales. But don't make the mistake of failing to report intangible benefits, such as reductions in customer complaints, policy violations, substance abuse, and work backlogs, or improvements in customer relations, customer service, employee job satisfaction, or new products.

It's also a good idea to ask yourself and the management group, "What are the long-term costs to the organization if we don't train?" Those costs may actually be more significant. One thing we know for sure: Everyone wants to save money on training. Following are ten ideas for meeting your training needs and saving money.

1. Get managers involved up front. Ask them to identify the training needs in their areas first, before you start looking at company-wide training. Ask them to review the training needs of each of their employees. Have them ask employees what they feel their personal training needs are, then ask the manager to prioritize these needs for the department. This rather simple task can save a great deal of money when done throughout the company.

2. Conduct training programs in-house, using current staff. For example, an accounting manager can teach a course on budgeting, and an employment manager or interviewer can conduct a workshop for managers on interviewing. By allowing your staff to participate in training and development activities, you give them a growth opportunity and save training dollars.

3. Trade services with training professionals in other companies. For example, if your trainer has expertise in communications skills, and a trainer in another company has expertise in time management, it's cost-effective to trade out the training time on an hour-for-hour basis rather than teaching each trainer to present a new program. Maintain contact with other companies in order to facilitate trades in expertise.

4. Cut training costs by charging outside seminars and conferences back to the department. When department managers know that outside seminar costs will show up in their budgets rather than the personnel budget, they are more selective when sending employees to outside programs.

5. Develop formal cross-training programs in-house in order to double your on-staff expertise. Include formal shadowing and mentor programs to use the expertise you already have.

6. Use local community colleges to provide training programs. They are usually less expensive than programs offered by large commercial companies.

7. Use more video- and audiocassette programs. They cost less and can be used over and over to offset initial development costs. An audiotape course can be taken while on the job or driving to and from work.

8. Set up a system of formal written critiques (provided by both the trainee and his or her immediate supervisor) of all courses or seminars that the company sponsors for any employee. These critiques will tell you which programs are worthwhile and which are not. They will help you maximize the return on your investment.

9. Check with department managers before you schedule training programs to make sure the programs will be held when the largest number of employees are available, to make the best use of the trainer's time. Classes that are not full are not cost-effective.

10. Use films, filmstrips, and slide programs that can be borrowed free of charge from companies, associations, and governmental agencies.

Producing a Training Plan and a Training Schedule

After you have decided the types of training you need, what your budget will be, and when the training will take place, you will want to produce both a training plan and a training schedule. When you start this process be sure to work out the timing and logistics with your managers to ensure that you are planning your training programs at the most opportune time for all departments. Exhibit 14-1 is a sample training plan. Exhibit 14-2 is a sample training schedule.

Training and development programs, tailored to the needs of the organization and its employees, represent the most promising and productive means of improving the quality of an organization's work force and retaining it. A great variety of training and development options are available today, as are efficient and effective delivery systems. Organizations must be willing to invest in these systems and give training and development of human resources a high priority.

Note

1. For detailed instructions on the calculation of cost-benefits, see "Calculating Costs and Benefits," in William R. Tracey, *Designing Training and Development Systems,* 3d ed. (New York: AMACOM, 1992) and Lyle M. Spencer, Jr., "Calculating Costs and Benefits," in William R. Tracey, ed., *Human Resources Management and Development Handbook* (New York: AMACOM, 1985).

Exhibit 14-1. Sample training plan.

Training Programs	Hours Scheduled	Dates Scheduled
Skills Training		
Bluepring Reading		
Lathe Operation		
Purchasing/Warehousing		
Welding		
Safety and Health		
Safe Driving		
Word Processing		
Supervisory Training		
Supervisory Skills I, II, III		
Interviewing Workshop		
Performance Appraisal Workshop		
Communication Skills Workshop		
Data Processing for the Non–Data-Processing User		
Management Development		
Planning, Organizing, and Controlling a Function		
Written Communication—Track I		
Technical Writing—Track II		
Coaching and Developing Employees		
Financial Forecasting and Budgeting		
Advance Communication Skills for Managers		
Middle-Management Development Program		

Exhibit 14-2. Sample training schedule.

MARCH	APRIL	MAY	JUNE	JULY
7, 8 Effective Technical Writing Workshop	12, 13, 14 Interviewing Skills Workshop (in-house)	4, 5, 6 How to Manage by Objectives	13, 14, 15, 16 The Manager's Job: How to Plan, Organize, and Control Your Function	11, 12 How to Manage Conflict
10, 11 Effective Presentation Skills	19, 20 AMA Course: Finance for the Nonfinancial Manager	23, 14 Project Management	27 Secretary's Workshop in Communications	26, 27 Motivation and Productivity

AUGUST	SEPTEMBER	OCTOBER	NOVEMBER	DECEMBER
18, 19 Train the Trainer (in-house)	21, 22 Communication Skills Workshop for Supervisors (in-house)	12, 13 Time Management	10, 11 Positive Discipline for Supervisors and Managers	7, 8, 9 Creating Productive Work Relationships
25 First Aid for Suprvisors and Managers		17, 18 Safety and Health Workshop		

15

Work and Family Issues

Raymond C. Collins, Ph.D.
President
Collins Management Consulting, Inc.

Work and family have become increasingly interdependent in the past generation as a result of a series of demographic, social, and economic developments in the United States. The traditional "Ozzie and Harriet" style family, with a working father, homemaker mother, and children cared for at home, is being replaced by diverse family structures. The norm in the neotraditional family is that the mother works out of economic necessity.

A 1989 nationwide survey by Louis Harris and Associates found that 89 percent of all people are convinced that "most women of childbearing age continue to work while bearing and raising children," and 78 percent of parents indicated that they accept the emerging norm. Both men and women are adopting "new generation" work values, favoring a balanced life: work *and* family, not work or family. As a result, out-of-home child care is expanding rapidly, with center-based care and family day care by nonrelatives supplanting care by grandmothers. Some families find themselves in a "sandwich generation," faced with elder care concerns for parents and other aging dependents while trying simultaneously to cope with child care responsibilities. These pressures can produce heightened levels of stress, sometimes resulting in absenteeism from work, divorce, or physical or mental illness.

Employers have begun to focus on these changes in the family in terms of the potential adverse impact on the workplace. Some firms have adopted programs and policies that are responsive to family needs. CEOs and human resources managers are beginning to take work and family issues into account as part of a total plan for investing in human capital development. This chapter discusses these issues and outlines a step-by-step approach employers could follow to develop their own work-family strategy as it relates to the recruitment and retention of a productive work force.

Shifting Patterns of Work and Family Life

The pivotal change in today's U.S. family is the transformed role of women, particularly in relation to the job market. Women have always performed a vital economic function, but in past generations this was primarily as homemakers and in rearing their own children. Some women still choose to stay out of the labor force and to remain at home with their offspring. However, women now are viewed (and see themselves) as key players in the paid labor force and as breadwinners or indispensable secondary wage earners on the home front. This realignment of women's role is the twin consequence of the pull and push of economic and social forces.

The pull comes from the marketplace. Female managers and workers are essential to the ability of the United States to compete abroad and to prosper domestically. The aging of the labor force means that new workers must be found to replace those who retire. Nonwhites, immigrants, and women will account for most of the net growth in the labor force during the 1990s. More than 70 percent of women aged 25–34 are now in the labor force, double the ratio a generation earlier. Heightened labor force involvement is occurring among women of all ages, socioeconomic groups, and racial-ethnic backgrounds.

The push for women entering the work force comes from the shifting economic circumstances of families. According to the U.S. Bureau of Labor Statistics (BLS), the roughly one-half of working wives who have year-round, full-time jobs contribute 40 percent of annual family income. The average working wife produces 30 percent of family income. Without income from working wives, families could not meet the sky-rocketing costs of housing, food, and bringing up children.

The grim reality is that the take-home pay of men, after adjusting for inflation, has leveled off or dropped. This is the first generation of Americans that can no longer anticipate that they will be better off than their parents or assume that their children will be better off than they are. The contribution of the working wife tends to make the difference in whether the family's standard of living goes up or down and can shape their offspring's future life chances.

For single-parent families, the overwhelming majority of which are headed by mothers, the economic prognosis is even worse. Single parents were associated with a large share of the increase in child poverty that occurred during the 1980s. According to the Bureau of the Census, in 1986, one out of five children lived in families with incomes below the poverty line, a total of 12.7 million children. Children who only have mothers have a higher probability of being poor than those in two-parent families. Child poverty has not lessened in the 1990s.

Other radical social changes impacting the family are spiraling divorce rates and increases in births to unmarried adolescents and other single women. All races and socioeconomic groups are affected by these trends, each in slightly different ways. Nearly one-half of white children and over four-fifths of black children are expected to live some portion of their childhood with only one parent.[1]

Children

The brunt of these shifts in family culture and mores is felt by children. The percentage of children with mothers in the labor force rose to 60 percent in 1988 from 39 percent two decades earlier. Labor force participation of mothers with young children has not yet peaked, and it is not clear when it will level off. By 1995, two-thirds of preschoolers and three-fourths of school-age children are projected to have working mothers.[2] The steepest increases in labor force participation have been occurring among women with infants and toddlers.

The most direct effect of these trends on child and family functioning stems from who looks after the children and where. The tendency is for caregiving to occur outside the home and to be performed by someone other than the child's parent, grandparent, or other relative. More than two out of three children under age five were cared for outside their homes, according to a 1988 survey by the National Center for Health Statistics. Participation in a child care center, nursery, or preschool program involved

31 percent of children. Care in other out-of-home settings accounted for 33 percent, nearly two-thirds of which was by a family day care provider or other nonrelative. Care in the child's home was the least common form, affecting 29 percent of children. Most of the remaining children were cared for by their mothers at work. Parents and grand-parents accounted for less than one-third of total care across all settings.[3]

The problem is not that parents are unhappy with their child care arrangements. In fact, surveys uniformly report high levels of satisfaction with care arrangements. It is typically when child care is disrupted as a result of a caregiver moving away, grand-mother taking a job, or other reasons that dissatisfaction gets voiced.

In an earlier era, parents worried that children who were in child care outside the home might be in jeopardy. Today's evidence demonstrates conclusively that there are no dangers for children in high-quality child care. The National Research Council (NRC) had indicated, "Developmentally appropriate care, provided in safe and healthy envi-ronments, has been shown to enhance the well-being of young children."[4] Care of low quality, on the other hand, can pose risks, particularly for infants and for children from poverty environments.

Child care is a necessity for the majority of U.S. families, but adequate care is not readily available, particularly for infants and toddlers, sick children, children with dis-abilities, school-age children, and children whose parents work nontraditional schedules. Cost pressures put child care out of the reach of many families of modest means. Fam-ilies may also be hindered in obtaining adequate child care that meets their youngster's needs and conforms to their work schedule because of inadequate information about what constitutes quality care and shortage of time to track down suitable caregivers.

A gap exists between the best that can be attained in early childhood education and child care programs, as exemplified by the impressive long-term benefits produced by research-oriented preschool programs, and the results obtained in run-of-the-mill chil-dren's programs. Any child care program can produce valuable developmental gains for children, but this doesn't occur automatically. Quality requires investments in recruit-ment of capable staff, ongoing training in child care and early education, carefully designed child-oriented curriculum, spacious and safe facilities, playgrounds, health and nutrition services, parent and family involvement, and staff wages and benefits sufficient to minimize turnover.

Employers should not conclude, however, that quality child care needs to "break the bank" of either society or the corporate community. Creative proposals have been developed for public-private partnerships that envisage "child care as the new business of business."[5] A wide variety of family-friendly program options has been described, including direct child care services, resource and referral programs, parent education seminars, and financial assistance for child care. These practical workplace policies are intended to produce a wide range of benefits for the corporation and its employees.

The Elderly

Contrary to popular belief, not all of the work-family pressures center on child care, important as that issue is. Modern families also have responsibilities for care of disabled and elderly family members. By the time adults reach their forties, elder care for parents and aging dependents is likely to become a consideration. This creates a double whammy, since they may have dependent children needing child care at the same time. Approxi-mately 6 million older persons today require assistance with activities of daily living, and it has been estimated that 80 percent of such care is provided by a relative or friend.[6] If it's true that demographics is destiny, U.S. families are in for a rough time. As the population ages, elder care will become a crisis on a par with child care. The proportion of persons over the age of sixty-five, numbering 28.5 million in 1985, is projected to increase to over 13 percent of the population by the year 2000.

In parallel with child care, the elder care burden tends to fall most heavily on working women. The person receiving care is typically in her seventies and is the mother, mother-in-law, or other female relative of the caregiver.

In 1989, *Fortune* and the John Hancock Company surveyed a nationwide sample of employees. Employees reported that the majority of caregiving is for parents (58 percent) and parents-in-law (27 percent) and averages thirteen hours per week. Over half of employees with elder care responsibilities reported emotional stress associated with caregiving.

The Public Policy Response

Although business leaders have mixed feelings about "big government," there is a tendency among CEOs to look first to Washington or to the state capital to solve major social problems such as those stemming from changes in the family and the labor force. For their part, policy makers are becoming aware of the need to respond to work-family challenges. But government alone cannot be expected to solve these problems. Corporate executives must do their part. Responding to work-family challenges must be included in the agenda for a viable free enterprise system. The Conference Board and the Committee for Economic Development have been in the forefront of business groups setting forth concrete proposals for public-private partnerships. Universal Head Start and expansion of early childhood education have been endorsed as the foundation for a total program of investing in human capital. A few business leaders have begun to grasp the notion that planning for early childhood education and child care must be carried out in tandem and that these can be complementary strategies for supporting families and the goals of the corporation.

More can be done in the social policy arena in planning family-responsive programs for the year 2000 and beyond. Tax resources are finite, however, at all levels of government. Public policy should not be the only, or necessarily the first, area to which CEOs turn in addressing work-family issues. The place to start with work-family issues is the same as for other issues that have a strategic impact on the company's future viability and profitability. CEOs should ask what can they do in their own corporation with their own resources.

CEOs and human resources managers should place the primary emphasis on what work-family developments entail for their organization. The key questions for top management are:

- How can we reconcile the needs of our employees with the responsibility to ensure that our company earns a profit and has a secure future?
- What are immediate actions that our firm could take to address work-family concerns within the framework of an overall human capital development strategy that is designed to facilitate recruitment and retention, improve productivity, and enhance profitability?

Implications for the Workplace

In considering these questions, it is useful to review what other employers have done in the 1970s and 1980s, since work-family issues have come to the fore. What has been the response of employers to transformations of the family and its relation to the world of work? The principal areas of dependent care services that attract the most attention are child care, and, more recently, elder care. Maternity leave arrangements and parental leave subsequent to birth or adoption are belatedly being considered.

Child Care

Estimates of the extent of corporate involvement in child care are that over 4,000 of the larger private firms have an organized program of child care options.[7] The best available data on employer involvement in child care come from a 1987 survey by the Bureau of Labor Statistics of all establishments with ten employees or more (including government agencies and nonprofit organizations, such as child care centers, public schools, colleges, and universities). According to the BLS, 11 percent of establishments provided such direct benefits as employer-supported child care, financial assistance directly related to child care, or information and referral services. Sixty-one percent of establishments had work scheduling or other policies designed to support child care. A little over one-third (37 percent) had neither direct child care benefits nor work scheduling poli-

Exhibit 15-1. Percentage of establishments providing child care options, by number of employees.

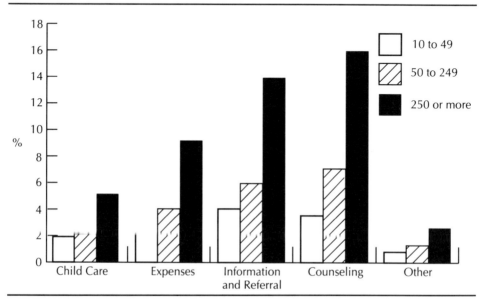

Source: Adapted from BLS data in Howard V. Hayghe, "Employers and Child Care: What Roles Do They Play?" *Monthly Labor Review,* September 1988.

Exhibit 15-2. Percentage of establishments providing child care–related policies, by number of employees.

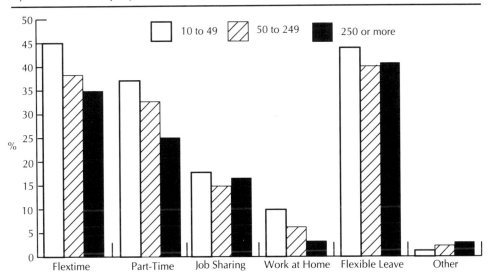

Source: Adapted from BLS data in Howard V. Hayghe, "Employers and Child Care: What Roles Do They Play?" *Monthly Labor Review*, September 1988.

cies. Exhibits 15-1 and 15-2 provide summary data on the types of child care benefits and related policies, with the proportions of firms of different sizes providing each type.

Larger firms (with over 250 employees) have consistently taken the lead in providing child care. There is a role for smaller employers, however, as documented by a study conducted for the Small Business Administration. The research revealed that a wide variety of smaller firms could implement child care programs to meet their needs, if their approach was tailored to the specific circumstances of the firm, the labor market, and the community. Small firms that tended to provide child care benefits had certain characteristics that distinguished them from other small businesses:

- Management placed a high priority on retaining employees, especially when a substantial investment in employee training had been made.
- Child care benefits were part of a broader commitment to making the workplace responsive to employee needs.
- Companies in tight labor markets felt child care was an important recruiting tool.
- Women made up a high proportion of the work force and also occupied top management positions.
- The companies had stable finances and were experiencing rapid and sustained growth or a desired level of stability in the work force.[8]

Elder Care

There is a growing appreciation of the impact of child care (or its absence) on the corporate bottom line among employers of all sizes and types. However, only recently have CEOs and human resources managers begun to become aware of elder care as an emerging work-family issue. Elder care confronts both employer and employee with a fundamentally different situation from child care. Nevertheless, both modes of care should be considered as part of an overall dependent care approach to ameliorating work-family tensions.

Few major studies have been conducted on employment-related elder care, building on the foundation of a pioneering survey by The Travelers in 1985, which found that one out of every five employees over age 30 provides some care to an elderly relative. Caregiving includes activities ranging from shopping to tending to a bedbound or home-bound person. The person receiving care may live alone, with the caregiver, or in a nursing home.

Surveys of employers reveal less interest in and concern about elder care as an issue than child care. However, involvement with child care sometimes leads to an awareness of other work-family issues. Company executives frequently mention that elder care activities have grown out of work force surveys or program activities initially targeted on child care.

Only a few dozen firms have been included in most major studies of elder care, so any conclusions about the corporate role are preliminary. Employers seldom offer elder care benefits. Information and referral (sometimes called resource and referral) is the most common program. This is in response to the preferences of employees who tend to express interest in such services.

The 1989 survey by *Fortune* and John Hancock referred to earlier polled senior executives in the largest 1,000 U.S. companies as well as the nationwide sample of employees. The executives reported concerns about employees who have responsibilities for care of the elderly. They cited employee stress, unscheduled days off, tardiness, and absenteeism among the work problems associated with elder care.

In a 1990 survey of employers regarding elder care, conducted by the American Management Association (AMA) and analyzed by the author and Dr. Renee Magid, elder care program options were rated in terms of practicability. Options rated the most practical included the development of printed information related to elder care services and the provision of referral and counseling, either through an existing employee assistance program or an outside contract. This option is low in cost, comparatively easy to carry out, and provides readily perceived advantages to employees. Another favored option was liaison with one or more community organizations providing day care, nursing services, or other services for the elderly. Reimbursement for a percentage of elder care expenses (for example, day care) was ranked the least practical option. The most costly option, it was given a low rating by many employers for that reason alone, even though, from the perspective of those beset by work-family issues, it would presumably provide the most tangible benefits.[9]

In addition to the above, other elder care programs reported by AMA respondents as in effect or under consideration included the following:

- Using the recreation department to develop a half-day program for the elderly
- Long-term care insurance

- Allowing the employee flexibility to use sick leave to care for an aging parent
- Including elder care in surveys of employee needs targeted on child care
- On-site day care for the elderly
- An employee spending account, using employee tax-free dollars for home care for the elderly
- Other types of dependent care plans focused on the elderly

A further indication of emerging interest in the issue is the report from 33 percent of respondents to the AMA survey that their company had given serious consideration to development of a benefit or support program related to elder care. An additional 14 percent indicated that they had not yet engaged in such planning but felt that they should. Nevertheless, half of the companies had done no elder care planning, were providing no services, and did not express a need to deal with the matter.

The American Association of Retired Persons (AARP) surveyed workers in five organizations. Results showed that a majority of care was provided by 42 percent of the caregivers; paid persons were involved in only 5 percent of the situations. As a result of a crisis with the elderly who were cared for, 18 percent of respondents lost time from work, but only 5 percent of caregivers reported that caregiving regularly interfered with work responsibilities. Overall, employees were functioning well in the caregiving role; 27 percent reported needing some assistance, and 8 percent needed a great deal of assistance.[10]

The National Association of Area Agencies on Aging surveyed thirty-five employers and a sample of caregivers in those firms. Approximately one in sixteen employees was providing care for an elderly relative. The typical caregivers were white, married, female, full-time workers with children living at home. They missed an average of 12.8 hours of work annually because of elder care responsibilities. A majority of caregivers reported physical strain, fatigue, or emotional strain associated with care for the elderly. Factors associated with increased absenteeism as a result of caring for the elderly were the number of hours spent per week in caregiving, gender, and occupational level of the caregiver. Professional and managerial women missed the most hours of work.[11] These findings contrasted with the AARP research, in which female managers showed no differences in absenteeism due to elder care.

Corporate planners should be mindful that work-family issues evolve over time. As couples choose to marry and have children later in life, the numbers of those forced to deal simultaneously with child care and elder care can be expected to increase. With an aging labor force, child care problems gradually get easier and disappear after several years. Elder care burdens progressively worsen.

Parental Leave

Pregnancy and infant care parental leaves as well as health and other benefits have begun to move to the forefront of concerns of employers as well as state legislatures and the Congress. For better than a decade, employers have been aware that they could not legally discriminate against employees who are pregnant or unable to work because of complications of pregnancy, childbirth, or recovery following birth. Now they are confronting pressures to broaden the array of benefits focused on pregnancy and parental leave. At stake are both considerations of sound social policy and corporate interests.

Like other work-family questions, these benefits are sometimes linked to the provision of corporate child care.

A survey commissioned by the Small Business Administration reported that fewer than 14 percent of employees in large companies have maternity or parental leave benefits; fewer than 4 percent of employees in small firms have such benefits. Most workers with families meet their need for such leave by piecing together sick and disability leave along with vacation or personal time.[12] (According to federal law, maternity leave must be the same benefit the company provides for any type of disability.)

The Center for the Child of the National Council of Jewish Women interviewed a nationwide nonrandom sample of working women during the third trimester of pregnancy and again four to seven months after childbirth. One out of seven mothers did not return to work after childbirth. About 15 percent of employed married couples with newborns met all or part of their child care needs themselves by working different shifts from one another. For most other families, problems in arranging child care figured prominently in the mother's decision not to return to work following maternity leave.[13]

The presence of employer support for child care in the workplace was associated with significantly higher rates of return. For employers offering no support, 55 percent of women reported child care problems. The proportion of women with child care problems fell to only 20 percent when child care support was present in the workplace. Apart from child care assistance, the single most important workplace predictor of retention was whether or not employers offered job-guaranteed maternity leave. Health insurance was also highly valued.

Research on parental leave by Catalyst, a New York City–based organization that helps corporations further women's career development, indicates that the cost of not providing parental leave is turnover and losing valuable employees.[14] Turnover can also result from providing leaves that are inadequate or inflexible.

Family and medical leave laws in most states do not lead to significant cost increases for most employers, according to a survey conducted by the Families and Work Institute of New York.[15] In Minnesota, 73 percent of employers reported that health care benefits costs had not increased as a result of state family leave legislation (comparable proportions in other survey states were Oregon, 72 percent; Wisconsin, 71 percent; and Rhode Island, 66 percent). In Oregon, 77 percent of employers reported no change in training costs (as did 75 percent of employers in Rhode Island and 74 percent in Minnesota and Wisconsin). Eighty-four percent of Minnesota employers reported no change in unemployment insurance costs (similar responses came from 83 percent in Oregon and Wisconsin and 56 percent in Rhode Island).

Benefits of Work-Family Programs

Most of the evidence on what the corporation and the employees gain from work-family options pertains to child care. Three studies have gathered nationwide information from employers on child care benefits: a 1978 study by Katherine Perry of fifty-eight employers, a 1983 survey by Renee Magid of 204 employers, and a 1984 study by Sandra Burud and her colleagues of 415 companies, with usable information from 178 employers.[16] The author has reanalyzed data from these three surveys and compared the results to findings from other studies to develop an overview of the benefits of employer-supported child care.[17]

There were twelve principal benefits of providing child care options, as judged by employers. In declining order of importance, they were:

1. Improved recruitment
2. Higher employee morale
3. Reduced absenteeism
4. Lowered job turnover
5. Employee work satisfaction
6. Favorable publicity
7. Attracting new or returning workers
8. Better community relations
9. More productivity
10. Less tardiness
11. Equal employment opportunity
12. Improved quality of products or services

The top six benefits included recruitment, absenteeism, and job turnover. All three are easily measurable variables that are directly related to effective human resources management. Employers are more likely to maintain accurate records in these areas than on some of the other variables, and intuitive judgments by corporate executives on these three factors can probably be trusted. What remains difficult to assess, however, is how much of the credit goes to the child care program, and how much can be accounted for by other factors.

The priority given recruitment, absenteeism, and job turnover outcomes across these three nationwide studies and their prevalence in other work-family research enhances the likelihood that these benefits are real. Barbara Resiman, executive director of the Child Care Action Campaign, has estimated that businesses lose nearly $3 billion each year in child care–related absences alone.[18] This is an area where child care can be expected to have a direct effect on corporate performance.

The other three benefits in the top six are morale, job satisfaction, and publicity. These factors are subjective and harder to assess. Confidence in these findings is buttressed by the frequency with which they show up in discussions with CEOs and in case studies.

Employers tend to rank the outcomes of child care policies in enhancing productivity or improving the quality of products or services relatively low. Both variables were measured in only two of the surveys. What is noteworthy is not that productivity and product quality are given relatively low rankings, but that they are mentioned at all. Corporations invest billions of dollars in the attempt to improve productivity and product quality. Even modest gains can have a dramatic impact on a company's profitability. If low-cost investments in child care lead to measurable gains in productivity and quality, that is good news.

Dana Friedman and Ellen Galinsky, copresidents of the Families and Work Institute, have done extensive syntheses of studies on child care "productivity" (which they interpret to include reduced turnover, improved recruitment, reduced absenteeism, and reduced tardiness). Their findings confirm the positive interpretations from other sources that there are clear improvements in outcomes that relate to productivity, at least for some types of firms.[19]

Burud's 1984 survey included an analysis of costs and benefits of operating a child care center in four companies. The total savings attributed to child care outweighed the cost in each of the companies. Neuville-Mobil Sox, Inc., added a hosiery mill in North Carolina and opened an on-site child care center. Savings were documented in recruitment, turnover, absenteeism, and hourly productivity. The other three companies—Intermedics, in Freeport, Texas; PCA, Inc., in North Carolina; and Sioux Valley Hospital, in South Dakota—identified benefits in recruitment, turnover, and absenteeism. Burud and Associates also conducted a productivity impact study for the Union Bank's child care center in 1987. The savings were estimated at over $138,000. Positive effects were retaining employees; reducing absenteeism, tardiness, and the length of maternity leaves; helping to recruit new employees; improving morale and work performance; and increasing positive public relations. Turnover reductions accounted for approximately half of the savings.[20]

Retention benefits of child care tend to be substantial. Doug Phillips of Merck & Company has devised an approach for estimating the costs of turnover to a firm. He calculates that the turnover cost is about 150 percent of annual salary. An investment of $100,000 with a twelve-month payback could be recouped by reducing turnover by four employees, assuming an annual salary of $30,000. Phillips regards child care as the optimal strategy for U.S. industry to reduce turnover in the 1990s.

Not all employers operate on-site child care centers. In fact, other child care options are more common, but these other program approaches can lead to benefits as well. Polaroid had identified contributions to employer productivity from paying employees a direct subsidy to cover a portion of child care costs. IBM has pointed to benefits as a result of its program of child care resource and referral to assist employees to locate affordable, quality child care providers.

A Wisconsin survey obtained information from thirty-six employers, representing the manufacturing, office, and health care sectors, about their use of three program options: a child care center, a flexible spending account for child care costs, and child care resource and referral. All three program options provided benefits as perceived both by employees and employers. The rankings of employer benefits for child care centers, as rated by corporate executives in the Wisconsin study, were roughly comparable to rankings reported in the national studies reanalyzed by the author and discussed above. Seventy-nine percent of employers (only fourteen employers responded to this part of the survey) reported positive influences on recruitment; 64 percent reported lower absenteeism; 79 percent, lower job turnover; 86 percent, improved productivity; 86 percent, improved morale; and 93 percent, favorable publicity.[21]

Effects of the lack of adequate child care arrangements on absenteeism and tardiness were reported in research conducted by Portland State University covering 103 companies in five cities. Having children in self-care (that is, without a baby-sitter or care center) can result in employees missing an average of nine days per year. Women with such "latchkey" children tended to be late 18.5 times during the year, and men, 8.3 times.[22] Studies by Portland State and other researchers report that family stress, sometimes leading to physical illness, can be a product of the breakdown in child care or unsatisfactory arrangements such as self- or sibling care. One of the principal indicators associated with work-family stress is insensitivity on the part of supervisors.

Caution should be exercised in generalizing positive findings about productivity and related work-family benefits because of the weak methodology of existing research on employer-supported child care. The direction of available evidence is positive, nonetheless. What must be determined is what work-family options promote those benefits, in what types of organizations, and under what conditions.

How Employers Can Develop Their Own Work-Family Strategy

The weight of the evidence is growing that companies that have adopted responsive work-family programs have begun to experience tangible advantages. Employers report, however, that they still lack hard data on the discrete cost and payoff of specific work-family options and how such programs impact companies comparable to their own. A nationwide survey of HR managers conducted by the American Society for Personnel Administration (now the Society for Human Resource Management) revealed that the lack of research evidence on the benefits of providing child care was a major obstacle to their companies initiating child care program options.[23]

Top management faces the not unfamiliar dilemma of how to react in the face of uncertainty. It can sit on the sidelines assuming one or more of the following: (1) that its work force is not materially affected by these human capital development issues; (2) that the community's response alone will be sufficient to resolve any work-family problems confronted by its employees; or (3) that any actions taken by the company would not justify the return on investment. Since stockholders rarely calculate the opportunity costs of inaction, this "trust to luck" approach may suffice.

Alternatively, corporate leadership can proactively explore the pros and cons of work-family policies. Many businesses elect a trial and error approach to employee-family issues, generally starting with child care. Sometimes a foundation is laid, perhaps by conducting an employee survey. Often some type of dependent care option is selected with few preliminaries. Dependent care could indicate child or elder care or both. Rarely does the process entail formal advance planning with subsequent evaluation of costs and outcomes.

Odds are trial and error will work out better than the trust-to-luck gambit. But both are high-risk, low-payoff ways of dealing with employee family matters. Neither way is consistent with the prudent stewardship that top management would be held accountable for applying to other important corporate issues. Why should human capital development be subjected to looser standards than other investments?

What is required is a step-by-step procedure that enables executives to begin to explore dependent care and related issues within the context of their own company, collecting the necessary data as events unfold. The author and his colleague Dr. Renee Magid (president of Initiatives: the Center for the Advancement of Work and Family Life, in Doylestown, Pennsylvania) have begun developing such a methodology, called the *work-family audit*. The work-family audit is based on the premise that corporations should apply similar management principles to the planning and evaluation of child care and other dependent care programs as for other priority investments. Some adaptation is called for to take into account the unique features of family issues.

The work-family audit is performed in two stages. The first stage entails preplanning. During this stage, the company should address key aspects of the company, the labor force, and the community. This exploration should produce answers to such questions as:

- Is the nature of the firm, considered in the context of market forces and actions of competitors, such that it is a likely candidate for work-family programs?
- Do the characteristics of the work force and key managers make such factors as recruitment, turnover, training costs, and absenteeism critical indices of cost and productivity?
- Is the community infrastructure for supporting families (assessed in much the same way as the transportation, health care, or educational systems) adequate to address the needs of the organization's employees?

If a decision is made to proceed based upon preplanning, the work-family audit involves five steps.

1. Identify work-family options or program models.
2. Spell out objectives of each work-family program.
3. Develop an implementation plan.
4. Specify outcomes and benefits of each program model.
5. Put in place a methodology for measuring outcomes and costs.

Work-family programs pose novel programmatic issues. A small cottage industry has grown up of benefits consultants and other groups eager to provide information about options. Employers are becoming generally familiar with the principal dependent care program models, tax advantages, etc.

Less help has been available for complex management issues dealt with in the work-family audit, such as:

- How to forecast the cost and savings of particular courses of action
- How to make optimal use of periodic employee surveys
- How to measure changes in employee performance
- How to modify personnel records to track pivotal indicators such as recruitment, turnover, and tardiness
- How to modify accounting and other cost control systems to deal with total true costs (e.g., the executive time spent in work-family planning and administration) as well as out-of-pocket expenses of dependent care programs
- How to estimate true benefits and track outcomes using rough data and expert estimates
- How to use process auditing techniques where performance measures are hard to obtain or expensive (e.g., using intermediate outcome measures)

A quick checklist a CEO or human resources manager could use in assessing the adequacy of the work-family audit or alternate planning and evaluation strategy is:

1. Is the system complete?
2. Is it face valid: Can the data be believed?
3. Are the findings easy to interpret?
4. Can management actions be taken in response to the findings?

Blueprint for the Work-Family Audit*

This section provides a detailed, step-by-step blueprint for conducting a work-family audit.

There are two phases to the work-family audit: (1) preplanning needs assessment, and (2) planning and implementation. During preplanning the company addresses key aspects of the company, its work force, and the community in which it is located. The planning and implementation phase includes five steps. Each step has specific objectives; however, the steps are interrelated and may occur simultaneously.

The work-family audit is segmented into separate planning phases for two reasons, both having to do with cost containment. First, the company should assess the potential for joining forces with other groups in the community in order not to make the mistake of attempting to address work-family issues from a self-defeating and wasteful "go it alone" philosophy. Second, the company may conclude, following the Phase One preplanning needs assessment, that it does not wish to proceed with Phase Two of planning and implementation at this time.

Phase One: Preplanning Needs Assessment

The purpose of Phase One is to provide the organization with an understanding of the potential need for and payoff from responsive work-family programs. A common misconception about work-family programs is that the corporation needs to go it alone and launch its own on-site center for child or elder care. This might be optimal in some cases and generally brings the company positive publicity and other benefits, but there are innumerable alternatives to on-site center-based programs. Preplanning needs assessment should consider the full array of work-family options.

Aspects of the company, its employees, and the community are considered in this phase. The information will be used to decide whether to proceed with further planning or to defer action until a later date. The following items are addressed.

KEY ASPECTS OF THE COMPANY

- What business is the company in? Analyzing the nature of the business and corporate goals should reveal how sensitive human capital and work force issues are to the company's bottom line. (To date, banks, insurance companies, hospitals, high-tech firms, and other service industries have predominated among involved companies, although all types of employers have reported benefits of work-family programs.)
- What is the corporate culture? What does top management value?
  —Is there a pragmatic openness to move participatory or humanistic management styles?
  —Is innovation viewed as a plus?

*The author would like to acknowledge the financial support of the New York State Department of Economic Development under a contract with Collins Management Consulting, Inc., for some of the developmental costs associated with the work-family audit methodology described in this chapter.

—Are employees encouraged to discuss work-family problems openly, without fear of reprisal? (For example, would a female employee tell her boss or co-workers that she was late because her child was ill, or would she claim to have had car trouble?)

—Do supervisors value work force diversity as opposed to expecting workers to adapt to the norms of the dominant group (frequently white males)?

—Is career development based on merit rather than membership in a white male–dominated inner circle?

- Are executives effective "people managers"? Good people managers are open and honest about their expectations, especially with employee caregivers who need to know whether they will be penalized simply because they have family problems.
- Does the company operate more than one shift? (It is extremely difficult to find child or elder care that operates all evening.)
- Where is the company located? Is it accessible to public transportation and community services such as child and elder care centers?
- How large is the company? (If the company has fewer than 250 employees, on-site care might be too costly to implement alone. A consortium with other companies in the area might be an option.)
- How vulnerable is the organization to a tight labor market? How do the company's costs for recruitment, staff retraining, and turnover compare with those of leaders in the industry? What is the forecast for trends on human capital–related productivity factors among the company's major competitors over the next five years?
- Do other local employers provide work-family options, and if so, might these employers attract the company's work force?
- What is the company's financial condition? Is it prepared to invest resources in support of work-family programs?

KEY ASPECTS OF THE WORK FORCE

- Is there a local labor shortage? (Work-family options might make it easier to recruit and retain qualified staff.)
- Is a recruitment effort needed to fill positions at a new facility?
- Is the work force stable or constantly changing?
- Are there employee morale problems?
- Do skilled, experienced workers and managers require high salaries or other benefits?
- What proportions of the employees are female and/or working parents?
- What is the age distribution of the work force?
- Do employees report difficulty in finding suitable child care?
- Do workers worry about care for elderly parents, disabled spouses, or older children with handicapping conditions?
- When do employees return after birth or adoption? Do employees promise to return but change their minds when they cannot find suitable child care?
- Are there indications of worker stress related to family issues such as high rates

of absenteeism, requests for leaves of absence or part-time status, tardiness, or conflicts with supervisors?
* What major work force changes are forecast for the next two to five years?

KEY ASPECTS OF THE COMMUNITY

* What community resources exist to address the family needs of employees? (This issue can be approached in the same way that many corporations routinely analyze the school, health care, and transportation systems in the community. Informal discussions with community leaders and employees provide clues to the adequacy of the social infrastructure to support families. Formal needs assessments might be conducted, or the firm might elect to carry out its own, possibly in concert with other business and community groups or with the help of a consultant.)
* Is there a separate infrastructure in the community, or is much of the infrastructure supported by the company?
* Is there a local tradition of corporate community involvement?
* Are there strong child care and elder care systems in the community? Is there a child care resource and referral program?
* What steps have been taken in the community to plan for expanding child care and Head Start services?
* To what extent have public-private partnerships developed around the JOBS (Job Opportunities and Basic Skills) program to assist AFDC (Aid to Families with Dependent Children) parents to move off welfare through adult education, job training, child care, and other support services? (Such collaboration might involve the business community working together with the Private Industry Council, the welfare department, Head Start, and child care providers. Lessons learned from such alliances can be helpful in planning work-family services focused on all employees, including low-income families.)

After the preplanning needs assessment is completed, the company must decide whether to proceed with the second phase of the audit or postpone formal planning until a later date. Planning might begin again when specific circumstances trigger a future need—for example, when there are problems with recruitment, staff turnover, or market share.

If the choice is to continue the work-family audit, it is best to institutionalize planning at an appropriately high organizational level (if this has not already been done). Work-family planning should be an ongoing responsibility of a human resources manager or other top executive with ready access to the CEO and the clout to ensure policy resolution and organizationwide coordination. A work-family planning task force or team could be created as an extension of the corporate unit with the leadership role. Planning is most successful when it is a coordinated effort involving management and employees (including union representatives). Whenever feasible, planning should also involve community agencies. Assuming a decision is made to proceed with the work-family audit, the five steps in the second phase, planning and implementation, are next.

Phase Two: *Planning and Implementation*

STEP ONE: IDENTIFY WORK-FAMILY OPTIONS OR PROGRAM MODELS

The purpose of this first step is to identify realistic program options by assessing employee needs. A useful approach for gathering information is through employee focus groups and seminars, where employees discuss the work-family needs and program preferences. Employees participating in the focus groups or seminars can gain a better appreciation of management's attitudes toward family issues and a more realistic awareness of the possibilities and limitations of the family options the company might elect to support. Face-to-face sessions, when facilitated by experienced discussion leaders, can be useful alternatives or supplements to written questionnaires. Findings from these sessions can provide the basis for designing insightful survey instruments.

Employee surveys can collect follow-up information from focus group participants and new information from employees who were not participants. Planners should be aware, however, that surveys can raise worker expectations prematurely and typically overstate the actual usage of proposed child or elder care programs. It is common for fewer than one-fifth of those who say they will utilize on-site child care to do so once it becomes available. By the time programs are operational, the employees have made other arrangements. Despite this drawback, surveys can provide insights into patterns when employees share a common problem, such as a lack of information about how to locate elder care or family care providers of good quality.

The attitudes of the local labor union, if one exists, also should be considered. Although unions have a history of supporting family programs, this cannot be taken for granted. The union might have concerns about equity for employees who do not need these programs or might be fearful of diverting attention from other priorities. When a union does support work-family programs, it might have clear views as to which option is most responsive to its members' needs.

After completing Step One, planners should be able to make some preliminary decisions regarding which work-family options the company should implement. Some examples of work-family programs appear in Exhibit 15-3.

STEP TWO: SPELL OUT THE OBJECTIVES OF EACH WORK-FAMILY PROGRAM

The purpose of this next step is to analyze and define the company's objectives for each selected work-family option. The following issues should be addressed:

- Are all employees with particular characteristics targeted or only certain groups? For example, are the programs targeted to top and middle management or workers at lower levels? Are they designed to meet the needs of female employees, males and females, employees in a specific age range, and so on?
- What benefits are expected for the target employees? For example, will they feel less stress from their conflicting work and family responsibilities?
- Do employees share these expectations? What expectations have they expressed in focus groups or employee surveys?
- What are the anticipated levels of participation?
- Which of the organization's operations will be affected by the plan? Will the work-family programs compete for top management time and attention?

Exhibit 15-3. Work-family program examples.

Personnel Policies

- Flexible work scheduling
- Part-time employment
- Job sharing
- Work-at-home
- Family leave
- Job-guaranteed maternal and paternal leave
- Liberal personal phone call policies (to check on the status of an older relative or to talk with a child or caregiver)

Benefits Plans

- Family health insurance coverage
- Temporary disability insurance
- Cafeteria-style flexible benefits plans
- Subsidies or vouchers so employees can purchase child or elder care in the community
- Direct subsidies to family services providers
- Tax benefits (dependent care assistance program and flexible benefits program)

Resource and Referral

- Reliable information concerning available care (cost, quality, hours, type, and accessibility)

Parent Education and Counseling and Support Services

- Counseling and case management for employees who care for an aging parent, disabled spouse, or chronically ill child
- Parent education programs on parenting, aging, and building an effective working family

Direct Care

- On-site child care
- On-site elder care
- Participation in a child or elder care consortium
- Family day care
- Emergency child care
- Sick child care
- School-age child care

Management Training and Development

- Supervisory training
- Management awareness seminars
- Orientation training and other support for work-family issues

- What advantages to the company are assumed? For example, does the company assume there will be improved recruitment, greater employee retention, lowered training costs, greater productivity, less use of sick leave, and so on?
- To what extent does the plan depend on external factors over which the company may have little or no control, such as the responses of local government, the community service delivery system, or actions by competitors?
- What is the basis for planning estimates: projections based on existing data, expert opinion, or another source?
- Is the margin of error in these calculations within acceptable bounds?

At the end of Step Two, planners should have delineated the objectives, for both the employees and the firm, of providing each work-family option.

Step Three: Develop an Implementation Plan

The purpose of this step is to develop a detailed implementation plan for each work-family program, including the anticipated costs. The planning team needs to complete the following tasks:

- Develop a budget specifying operational costs. If it is not feasible to collect precise information or if the firm lacks a sophisticated cost accounting capability, the general nature of the costs should be listed. For example, estimate the cost of time during board meetings to consider work-family plans. In some instances expert opinion can provide estimates based on the experiences of other companies. In other cases (for example, facilities, equipment, and staff expenses for an on-site center) planners can make more precise estimates.

- Develop a realistic project timetable indicating when each task needs to be completed.

- Inform employees of progress at each stage of development through newsletters, memos, meetings, mass media, and so on.

- Provide orientation and training for supervisors regarding the new programs and related policy changes. (Supervisors play a critical role in the success or failure of work-family programs and in alleviating or exacerbating worker stress.)

The planning stage is the time to begin thinking about how to collect cost data and how to "keep score." In the next step, planners translate the benefits for each work-family option into measurable terms.

Step Four: Specify Options and Benefits of Each Program Model

Building on the program expectations identified in Step Two, planners need to pinpoint outcomes, benefits, and related costs for both the company and the employees. Some examples follow.

- Assess outcomes that can be readily measured:
  —Recruitment
  —Absenteeism

—Job turnover/retention
—Tardiness
- Assess other outcomes, such as:
—Productivity/quality of services
—Employee morale
—Job stress
—Supervisor-employee relations
—Employee work satisfaction
—Favorable publicity
—Community relations
—Equal employment opportunity
- Consider unexpected side effects, including the potential for employees not covered by the program to feel that their needs have been ignored by management.

At the conclusion of this step, planners will be ready to set up a system for tracking and measuring the outcomes and costs related to each work-family option.

Step Five: Establish a Methodology for Tracking and Measuring Outcomes and Costs

The purpose of this step is to establish a system for tracking and measuring the outcomes and costs of the work-family program so that the company can determine whether a program results in a favorable return on the company's investment. Benefits for employees should be identified in parallel with benefits for the firm. Some suggestions for completing this step follow:

- Modify personnel records to include recruitment, turnover, and absenteeism and to identify beneficiaries of the work-family program. If this is not feasible, then information will have to be gathered through special surveys, through supervisors' estimates, or by other means.

- Develop a means to record qualitative assessments for outcomes that are not readily measurable, such as employee morale or company image. Expert opinion might be a source of this information.

- Convene an in-house group of specialists to develop strategies for measuring productivity and quality of services.

- Take particular care to engage union representatives at an early stage in determining the methodology to be used for measuring outcomes. This will provide safeguards against the data being misused to effect particular employees adversely.

- Conduct periodic employee surveys and focus groups to validate in-house record keeping. Such soundings are often the most reliable techniques to address such outcomes as employee attitudes, behaviors, and stress. Employee surveys might also identify changing work force characteristics, indicating the need to reexamine ongoing family programs. Ultimately, these are the best ways to identify employee outcomes and related factors.

- Modify accounting systems (when cost accounting procedures exist or lend themselves to this purpose) to include relevant cost and benefit data. If the company lacks a sophisticated cost accounting capability, ballpark cost estimates can be tracked on a regular basis through a systematic written protocol. Consult expert opinion in the absence of specific cost data. Responsive work-family programs can lend themselves to modern methods of cost-benefit analysis if such activities are a priority of the CEO and if the proper planning and evaluation tools are utilized.

• Use information collected from internal corporate records and expert judgments to measure the ongoing benefits to the company.

Concluding Thoughts

Work-family programs that respond to the needs of the changing U.S. labor force are prerequisites for the country's future economic growth, and/or considerations for the recruitment and retention of a productive work force. Such programs are becoming a central component of private sector efforts to mobilize female workers, to broaden the talent pool for top management positions, and to recruit and retain a talented and diversified work force. Concrete benefits can be achieved for companies and for employees through work-family options such as child care, elder care, and parental leave policies. The business community and the larger society have a shared interest in devising innovative strategies for human capital investment to sharpen America's competitive edge.

Formal planning and evaluation frameworks such as the work-family audit are designed to complement the instincts of CEOs and human resources managers. Such tools are not substitutes for "gut level" judgments. Instead, they reinforce preliminary decisions based on intuition and help determine what aspects of the company are significantly different from other companies that may or may not offer work-family benefits. Some of these differences—for example, the size of the company and the age range of the targeted employees—are likely to have a great impact on the company's decisions about work-family options.

The success of the work-family audit is dependent on several critical elements. First, the process should be supervised by a senior human resources director or manager with decision-making authority. The ongoing involvement of the CEO is also essential. Next, a company should be prepared to allocate sufficient staff and resources for the six months to a year that it may take to complete the audit. Lastly, union and employee representation on the planning group will ensure that the work-family options selected and implemented meet the needs of both the company and its employees.

The work-family audit can be used by companies willing to begin in a pragmatic fashion to consider the implementation of family policies rather than waiting indefinitely for definitive proof of what works. This management tool can fill the gap in critical data that would enable a CEO or human resources manager to conclude that work-family programs would result in tangible benefits and show a favorable return on investment.

Notes

1. Gerald David Jaynes and Robin M. Williams, Jr., eds., *A Common Destiny: Blacks and American Society*, Committee on the Status of Black Americans, Commission on Behavioral

and Social Science and Education, National Research Council (Washington, D.C.: National Academy Press, 1989).

2. Sandra L. Hofferth and Deborah A. Phillips, "Child Care in the United States: 1970–1995," *Journal of Marriage and the Family* 49 (1987).

3. "Who's Minding the Children?" *Washington Post,* November 6, 1990.

4. Cheryl D. Haynes, John L. Palmer, and Martha J. Zaslow, eds., *Who Cares for America's Children? Child Care Policy for the 1990s,* Panel on Child Care Policy, National Research Council (Washington, D.C.: National Academy Press, 1990).

5. Edward F. Zigler and Mary E. Lang, *Child Care Choices: Balancing the Needs of Children, Families, and Society* (New York: Free Press, 1991).

6. Donna L. Wagner et al., *Employees and Eldercare: Designing Effective Responses for the Workplace,* University of Bridgeport, Center for the Study of Aging (Bridgeport, Conn.: September 22, 1989); and Michael A. Creedon, ed., *Issues for an Aging America: Employees & Eldercare. A Briefing Book,* University of Bridgeport, Center for the Study of Aging (Bridgeport, Conn.: June 17, 1987).

7. Ellen Galinsky, "Update on Employer-Supported Child Care," *Young Children,* September 1989.

8. Victor Rubin et al., *Small Business Options for Child Care: Final Report,* Berkeley Planning Associates, prepared under contract with the U.S. Small Business Administration (Berkeley, Calif.: March 28, 1988).

9. Renee Y. Magid and Raymond C. Collins, "Elder Care: Everyone's Business," *Human Resources Forum,* June 1990.

10. American Association of Retired Persons, *Caregivers in the Workplace: Survey Results,* (Washington, D.C.: AARP October 31, 1986).

11. Janice L. Gibeau and Jeanne N. Anastas, *Breadwinners and Caregivers: Supporting Workers Who Care for Elderly Family Members,* National Association of Area Agencies on Aging (Washington, D.C.: 1986).

12. "New Push on for Parental Leave," *Washington Post,* March 21, 1991.

13. Terry Bond et al., *Medical and Family Leave: Benefits Available to Female Workers in the United States,* Center for the Child, National Council of Jewish Women (New York, March 1987).

14. Margaret E. Meiers, "Down With the Wait-and-See Approach: The Progress of Parental Leave Policy," *Management Review,* January 1989.

15. "In States With Family Leave Laws: Most Employers Report No Significant Cost Increases," *Compflash,* December 1990.

16. Kathryn Senn Perry, *"Employers and Child Care: Establishing Services Through the Workplace,* Women's Bureau, U.S. Department of Labor (Washington, D.C.: 1982). Renee Y. Magid, *Child Care Initiatives for Working Parents: Why Employers Get Involved* (New York: American Management Association, 1983); and Sandra L. Burud et al., *Employer Supported Child Care: Investing in Human Resources,* National Employer-Supported Child Care Project (Boston: Auburn House, 1984).

17. Raymond C. Collins and Renee Y. Magid, "Work/Family Issues: New Frontiers in Human Capital Development," *HR Horizons,* Summer 1990.

18. Barbara Reisman, "Child Care as Strategy," *Productivity,* October 1988.

19. Ellen Galinsky, "Child Care and Productivity," unpublished paper, Bank Street College (New York: March 1988); and Dana E. Friedman, *The Productivity Effects of Workplace Centers,* Families and Work Institute (New York: June 7-8, 1989).

20. Burud and Associates, *Productivity Impact Study Conducted for Union Bank Child Care Center: Executive Summary* (Pasadena, Calif.: 1987).

21. Kathryn Senn Perry, Laurie McGee, and Nancy Mullikin, *Wisconsin's Response to Families and Work: Final Report,* Office of the Lieutenant Governor, prepared for the U.S. Department of Labor (August 1989).

22. Arthur Emlen, *The Nature of Work-Family Conflict. What Aspects of Family Life Are Most Predictive of Work-Family Conflicts?* The Conference Board Symposium on Workplace Research on the Family (Arden House, New York: March 23-25, 1988).
23. American Society for Personnel Administration, *Employers and Child Care: The Human Resource Professional's View*, 1988 Child Care Survey Report (Alexandria, Va.: 1988).

16

Alternative Work Options

Barney Olmsted
Codirector
New Ways to Work

What do alternative work options have to do with employee recruitment, retention, and development? Consider these company experiences:

- Aetna Life & Casualty was losing 23 percent of its women employees who had planned to return to the company after maternity leave. Aetna reduced this number to 12 percent and improved its recruitment efforts by developing a family leave policy and expanding its use of flextime, part-time, job sharing, and telecommuting.
- Mutual of New York realized that "a lot of people with experience, knowledge, and key interpersonal skills were going on maternity leave." The company started a job-sharing policy because "we didn't want these people just walking out the door." In addition, Baybanks, Walgreen's, and Boeing Corporation, to name just a few companies, have offered new kinds of part-time options in order to attract skilled workers and recruit for hard-to-fill positions.

These firms and a growing number of others have learned that alternative work options can provide an important competitive edge for companies trying to recruit or retain good workers. Alternative work options are valuable tools that can be used to help employees resolve conflicts between their personal needs and their work responsibilities.

Finding and keeping good people has become a major issue for many companies. How to retain the best employees when economic downturns require cutbacks in labor costs is a recurring problem for firms in a variety of industries. Demographic projections have alerted employers to the fact that in all likelihood, recruiting, retaining, and retraining skilled labor will be an even more pressing problem in the future. To remain competitive, firms will need to develop policies better suited to attract and retain employees from a labor pool that will be composed predominately of women, minorities, and immigrants and one in which older workers will be in demand rather than encouraged to retire early.

As we move through the 1990s, most companies have had some experience with new scheduling options like flextime, job sharing, compressed workweeks, and telecommuting. For the most part, however, the experience has been minimal, confined to one or two options that affect a limited number of employees. This chapter will discuss briefly why these options have emerged in the first place, why they will grow in importance in the future, what the "menu" looks like now, and how organizations can begin to use new work options more effectively.

Why Not 9 to 5?

The reshaping of work hours in the United States began in the early 1970s. One of the major reasons was that reshaping of the work force had already begun.

By the end of the 1980s the impact on the bottom line of work-family conflict had led many companies to develop special task forces to study the issue and recommend solutions. The companies have found that conflicting work and family responsibilities lead to many kinds of stress—the kind of pressures that many employees are under today. A Travelers Insurance Company survey of home office employees showed that approximately 20 percent of the respondents were providing an average of 10.2 hours per week of care to an older relative.[1] A large number of these workers were in their thirties and forties and also had young children to care for. A Du Pont employee survey showed that the problems of dual responsibility are not limited to female employees: 25 percent of the men who responded reported having considered seeking another employer who would offer them more flexibility. And indeed, almost invariably, one of the recommendations of company task forces and policy groups studying such problems has been to implement a wider range of work time options.

Conflicting responsibilities are not the only reason that alternatives to standardized work time have begun to attract interest. Changes in worker attitudes and expectations about work are another factor in the emergence of alternative work options. The work force of today is better educated than that of a generation ago, has different hopes and expectations about work, and has a different set of work and life values. During the 1970s many workers began to show a tendency to have more allegiance to their careers than to any particular company; they began to show interest in having more control over the content of their work and even where and how they work. For many this meant having more control over their work time, or a different work schedule, in order to integrate work with the rest of their life.[2]

In the 1970s many people also began to reexamine the "linear life plan" that was the expected norm and to express a need for a more cyclical, integrated approach to education, work, and leisure activities. Major realignments in the nature of schooling saw adults returning to the classroom for skill renewal and retraining as well as basic education. Education became integrated with leisure time throughout people's lives, so that they thought in terms of lifelong learning rather than waiting for retirement. For many people, what made it possible to move toward lives that integrated work, education, and leisure was more control over the allocation of their time and more choice in the kind of work schedule that was available to them.

Finally, there is the shift from a production to a services economy and the concurrent growth of global competition. Just as the farm economy diminished in importance at the beginning of the twentieth century, the services economy is gaining ascendance over manufacturing as we move into the twenty-first. This change will have a great impact on where, when, and how people work and will reinforce the need for a wider range of work schedules. Improving productivity in the services sector will be an important factor in U.S. ability to compete successfully in a global economy. Two important aspects of improving productivity will be learning how to strengthen employee commitment to organizational goals and creating a context that will encourage managers to help individual workers to tap their fullest potential. Learning how to introduce and manage work scheduling flexibility will facilitate these objectives.

These trends and others have provided the impetus for the emergence of new forms of work. Many alternative work arrangements were introduced initially as a new form of employee benefit, in order to attract or retain good employees. In time, however, as flexibility became more of an organizational objective, managers began to realize that these new work options were not just employee driven but had the potential for helping organizations function better in a wide variety of ways.

So, if not just 9 to 5, what are the other scheduling options that companies are introducing? What issues do they pose for managers, and how are companies beginning to use them? They fall into two basic categories: restructured full-time schedules and new forms of reduced work time. (See Exhibit 16-1 for a glossary of alternative work options.)

Restructured Full-Time Schedules

The restructured full-time schedules include flextime, compressed workweeks, and flexiplace (or telecommuting).

Flextime

Flextime, the generic term for flexible schedules, was the first shift away from standardized work time. This kind of work schedule permits flexible starting and quitting times within limits set by management. Generally, flextime programs operate as a rescheduled forty-hour, five-day workweek, with flexible periods at the beginning and the end of the day and sometimes over lunch hour as well. A "core" time is usually established during which all employees must be present. Flextime programs vary from company to company and often from department to department. Variations in format occur regarding whether flexibility is a daily or periodic choice, how core time is defined, and whether credit and debit hours are allowed. Some of the variations on flextime that indicate the difference in degree of flexibility are:

- *Program A:* Employees select their starting and quitting times for a specified period of time (often twelve months). They work a five-day, forty-hour workweek.
- *Program B:* A daily variation in starting and quitting times is permitted, but the five-day, forty-hour week is maintained.
- *Program C:* The length of days within the week or pay period may vary (i.e., an employee can work six hours one day and ten the next) as long as the total hours worked meet the defined number of hours within the period.
- *Program D:* Credit and debit hours are allowed, and core time is not required on all days. This type of activity encompasses the concept of "banking" time; that is, employees are allowed to carry over, and bank for later use, hours in excess of their daily or weekly schedule.

Employers generally credit flexible schedules with reducing turnover and absenteeism, increasing productivity—at least in part because "morning people" can come to work earlier, while those who want to come in late and work later can—and improving employee morale with little or no cost to the organization.

Forty-nine percent of the 486 respondents to a 1989 Conference Board survey on

Exhibit 16-1. An alternative work time glossary.

RESTRUCTURED FULL-TIME SCHEDULES

Flextime: Schedules that permit employees to choose their starting and quitting times within limits set by management.

Compressed Workweeks: A standard workweek that is compressed into fewer than five days. The most common schedules are four ten-hour days, three twelve-hour days, or two-week pay periods that contain five nine-hour days in the first week and four nine-hour days in the second week.

Flexiplace, or telecommuting: Employees working off-site who may or may not be linked electronically to the office through a computer.

REDUCED WORK TIME

Regular Part-Time Work: Less than full-time work by employees on a company's regular payroll. Ideally, it includes job security and all rights and benefits available to the firm's full-time workers.

Job Sharing: A form of regular part-time work in which two people voluntarily share the responsibilities of one full-time job, with salary and benefits prorated. It is a way to create regular part-time employment opportunities where there is a need for a full-time position. It differs from regular part-time work in that it requires a team approach to performing job responsibilities and allows for greater continuity because partners can trade time or fill in for each other.

V-Time Programs: Voluntary reduced work time programs. They allow employees to make time/income tradeoffs by enrolling in a program, rather than negotiating an ad hoc arrangement with their supervisor. Full-time employees can reduce work hours for a specified period of time with a corresponding reduction in compensation. Their benefits are prorated.

Phased or Partial Retirement: An option for older workers to reduce the number of hours worked for a period of time prior to retirement.

Work Sharing: An alternative to layoffs in which all or part of an organization's work force temporarily reduces hours and salary. In some states this can be paired with short time compensation from unemployment insurance to partially offset workers' lost wages.

---

corporate use of flexible scheduling that used new scheduling arrangements offered flextime.[3] Most reported satisfaction with the programs and would probably have agreed with the southern life insurance company official who commented, ''Flextime has worked well. It allows employees to schedule according to their needs.'' The latter part of the statement probably explains why most organizations using this option report a high degree of employee satisfaction; a drop in absenteeism, tardiness, and turnover; and either a positive or a neutral effect on productivity.

ISSUES FOR MANAGERS

As with any new procedure, managers who have not experienced flextime have concerns about how it will affect their ability to manage. Some of the more common issues are that:

• *Everyone will be coming and going when they please and the work won't get done.* In practice, most employees don't vary their schedules that much even when they have the opportunity to do so. Also, most programs reflect the fact that the business needs of the work unit must be primary, and most employees understand and support that priority.

• *Supervisors will have to work longer hours in order to supervise everyone on flextime.* Initially, many managers feel that they must be on-site during the entire bandwidth period. This is clearly not the way to manage flexible schedules. Managers should be encouraged to think of themselves as a resource for their employees, rather than an overseer, and to delegate or rotate some of the responsibility.

• *There will be times when no one will be here to answer the phone.* Schedules must be coordinated. If everyone appears to want to ''flex'' at the same time, the schedules must be revised in order to assure coverage.

• *The system is bound to be abused. Employees will come in late or leave early without making up time.* Experience does not appear to bear the abuse concern out. However, flextime is a privilege, not a right. If employees abuse the system, they can be required to return to a standard schedule.

COMPANIES USING FLEXTIME

Some of the many companies using flextime include Merck & Co., a large pharmaceutical manufacturer, and Blackwell North America, a wholesaler located in the Pacific Northwest.

Merck began using flextime in 1979. It is now available in all areas of the company at the discretion of individual departmental supervisors or managers. Employees are expected to work the standard number of hours per day and per week and to be at work during the core hours of 9:30 A.M. to 3:30 P.M. With the approval of their manager, they can choose a starting time between 7:00 A.M. and 9:30 A.M. and a quitting time between 3:30 P.M. and 6:00 P.M. Daily flexibility is not allowed, however; they must maintain their chosen schedule for a minimum of one week. Merck has found that flextime has reduced tardiness and requests for personal time off. There has also been some decrease in overtime. Managers feel that employees seem to become more task-oriented and that morale has increased significantly.

Blackwell North America has a flextime option available to first-shift workers. The standard workweek for a regular full time employee is forty hours with five eight-hour days. With their supervisor's approval, first-shift workers may select individual starting and quitting times from the flexible schedule. Accepted starting hours are 6:30 A.M. to 8:30 A.M., with corresponding quitting times from 3:00 P.M. to 5:00 P.M. The workday includes two fifteen-minute breaks and a thirty-minute lunch break. An approved flextime schedule may allow for a longer lunch break.

With over 80 percent women workers, many of whom have children, the personnel director comments that she "would *never* recommend dropping this benefit." Almost every exit interviewee mentions the flexible hours as a reason for staying with the company.

Compressed Workweeks

Compressed workweeks, like flexible schedules, were introduced in the early 1970s. They are also variations of a standard workweek, one in which the standard number of weekly hours are worked in fewer than five days. In the most common form, the week's hours are accomplished in four ten-hour days (for a total of forty hours) or three twelve-hour days (for a total of thirty-six hours). Another increasingly popular arrangement is for employees to work five nine-hour days during the first week of the pay period and four nine-hour days the next.

Until recently, compressed workweeks have mostly been management-initiated as a means of using expensive equipment or plant facilities for longer periods of time or of making shiftwork more palatable. An emerging trend has been for individual employees to ask for a compressed schedule in order to have greater blocks of personal time or to cut down on commuting time. In some states, questions of air quality control and commuting patterns that increasingly involve traffic gridlock are also creating interest in this option.

ISSUES FOR MANAGERS

Compressed workweeks conflict with wage and hours legislation in those states that identify the eight-hour day as the maximum standard. The schedule that has employees working forty-five hours in five days the first week and thirty-six hours in four days the second week also conflicts with the forty-hour standard established by the Fair Labor Standards Act. Exemptions from the overtime provisions can sometimes be obtained by companies, depending on the individual wage order, but only if the scheduling change is approved by a two-thirds vote of the employees in the affected division or department. Some forms of the compressed workweek raise Occupational Safety and Health Act (OSHA) questions relating to fatigue and the number of consecutive hours or lengthy days worked.

Other questions managers raise about compressed workweeks include:

• *The need for five-day-a-week coverage.* Compressed workweeks are most often used in conjunction with other scheduling arrangements. There may be some employees who prefer a standard workweek, or you may have two overlapping shifts: one, Monday through Thursday, and the other, Tuesday through Friday. In some organizations, employees have designed a rotating coverage system.

• *Some employees don't like longer days because they are worried about fatigue or getting home too late.* It may be helpful in designing coverage to have some employees working a standard schedule. Make this an option.

• *The high failure rate of compressed workweeks.* Most studies have indicated that compressed workweeks take careful planning to ensure coverage and good communication. If a planning process includes employee and management input and encourages modifications to eliminate problems in the initial design, this kind of schedule can work well.

• *Employees may have difficulty with transit systems that do not run often enough during the earlier and later hours.* In some cases employers have contacted the local transit authority to see if there are alternatives or have suggested setting up a transit pool operated on a cooperative basis by the company or the employees.

• *Sick days and holiday schedules are based on the standard of an eight-hour day.* Fringe benefits often have to be refigured. Some firms alter their plan of ten paid holidays (eight hours each) to eight paid holidays (ten hours each). Others work with the concept of sick "hours" instead of sick days, providing a set number on an annual basis.

COMPANIES USING COMPRESSED WORKWEEKS

Companies using compressed workweeks include Osh Kosh B'Gosh, a large manufacturer of consumer products whose corporate office is in Osh Kosh, Wisconsin, and Levi Strauss & Co., an international apparel manufacturer with approximately 1,600 people employed at its corporate offices.

In addition to other options, Osh Kosh B'Gosh has a compressed work schedule at several of its rural Tennessee and Kentucky production sites. The compressed week consists of four nine-hour days worked Monday through Thursday and one four-hour day worked on Friday. About 900 people work this schedule at several plants. All workers at a plant follow the same schedule, including union and nonunion workers and plant management. One of the considerations influencing the company's decision to use a compressed workweek was geography. The plants in Kentucky and Tennessee are in very rural areas where many of the plant workers travel thirty miles or more, each way, to work. Home duties occupy a large amount of their time, especially for those who maintain small family farms. Because the plants work on weekly production quotas, they may close on a Friday if all quotas have been met, allowing employees an extra day off. If quotas have not been met, the extra hours available on Friday, after the close of the regular four-hour day, can be used for overtime. This generally eliminates the need for weekend work.

The company culture at Levi Strauss values a supportive climate for employees, and the company has a long history of experimenting with and adopting various new scheduling and staffing options. It was one of the first major corporations to use job sharing and has adopted policies that allow regular part-time employment, flexible schedules, and phased retirement as well.

In the summer of 1987 the company began a test program of using a compressed workweek for summer work hours. The option was designed by corporate personnel staff and then offered on a unit-by-unit basis. Managers of each individual work unit were responsible for evaluating the feasibility of their employees using it. The guidelines specified that nonexempt employees would be expected to work eight and one-half hours Monday through Thursday and five hours on Friday, for a total of thirty-nine hours. At 1:00 P.M. on Friday, those participating could leave for the week. Managers were encouraged to have their work unit participate and were also asked to evaluate the work performance of their units under the new schedule. At the end of the first summer, managers were surveyed to determine whether or not the program should be offered the next year. Ninety-five percent recommended that the program be repeated in 1988. It was, and after another positive response, it was established as a regular summer offering in 1989.

Flexiplace

Flexiplace, also called telecommuting, is an option that has attracted a great deal of interest since the advent of the personal computer. It refers to the practice of allowing regular employees to work at home or at an alternative work site during a part of their scheduled hours, with or without an electronic hookup. When discussing flexiplace options, it is very important to distinguish between arrangements related to a company's regular employees and independent or cottage industry workers who are employed as peripheral staff. As in differentiating between regular part-timers and hourly, on-call, part-timers, one group has flexibility within the regular work force, and the other is a member of the contingent work force.

Flexiplace options for regular employees allow them to work out of their home or a satellite office serving many individuals from different companies, for an agreed-upon portion of their work schedule. In many cases this is a regularly scheduled activity. Many flexiplace workers "telecommute"—that is, they are linked to the office with a telephone or through the use of a home computer.

The Bureau of Labor Statistics estimated in 1985 that approximately 9 million people worked at least eight hours a week at home. This figure, however, included those who were self-employed and independent contractors as well as regular employees of private and public sector organizations. In a 1990 Conference Board survey, only 29 of 521 respondents reported having any type of formal program. There was no way to judge, however, how many informal arrangements existed.

In a number of states with significant transportation or air quality problems, there is currently interest in exploring wider use of flexiplace options as a means of reducing the amount of work-related vehicular traffic.

ISSUES FOR MANAGERS

Flexiplace can be particularly difficult for a manager to support because it represents a radically different way to work and demands new kinds of management skills. However, it also represents an opportunity to help employees manage the interface between home and office in a new way.

Although many employees, particularly those in professional or management positions, have always "taken work home," the idea of formalizing the process and allowing part of some employees' regular work schedule to include at-home workdays is relatively new. Among the most common concerns that managers raise are:

• *Worries about whether employees are working "if I can't see them doing it."* Traditional supervising styles have depended on "line of sight." This kind of management style makes work-at-home stressful for all parties. The growing use of flexible, off-site, and part-time schedules has reinforced the need for establishing measurable objectives of defining and managing white-collar productivity. It has also led to the development of a new kind of supervisory style, one that encourages employees to take on more responsibility and managers to provide support rather than oversight. The "new" manager is learning to look at work produced rather than bodies present from 9 to 5. Regular contact, whether on the phone or during scheduled office workdays, keeps the contact current and alleviates much of managers' concern about off-site time.

• *How to evaluate someone who works at home part of the week.* Whether the work takes place at home, at the office, or at a client's office, an evaluation should focus on the employee's ability to produce quality work within an agreed-upon time frame. It is also helpful to remember that most work-at-home arrangements include regularly scheduled office work time. It is a manager's responsibility, with both on-site and off-site employees, to specify job responsibilities, tasks, and objectives as clearly as possible and to include timetables and checkpoints that allow for oversight at regular intervals. Once this is done, there should not be significant differences in monitoring and evaluating the amount and quality of work output whether the employee is down the hall, across town, or at home.

• *The issue of whose insurance covers an accident if an employee is working at home.* The reason many companies require an employee to establish a "dedicated work-space" that can be inspected by the employer and to have "regularly scheduled hours" is to assure that safety rules are being observed and to establish a basis for deciding whether an accident is work-related or should be covered by the employer's insurance. OSHA and workers compensation systems requirements must be satisfied when the employee is engaged in direct employment activities at home or at a third-party, leased site.

• *How to keep customer or company data private and confidential.* Managers should realize that, in this age of widespread personal computer use, this is not just an issue for telecommuting employees. Guidelines on access to confidential files need to be developed for all employees. Experts on telecommuting say that security has not been a problem to date in firms that have begun to introduce formalized telecommuting options.

COMPANIES USING FLEXIPLACE

Companies offering a telecommuting option include Pacific Bell. As a telecommunications company, Pacific Bell has a dual interest in telecommuting: They have employees who can benefit from the option, and they are marketing the concept to other companies. In 1986 the company established a telecommuting pilot project that was open to all management employees on a voluntary basis, with their supervisor's concurrence. Approximately sixty employees enrolled in the formal program. They included programmers, analysts, engineers, planners, product managers, and forecasters. They were interested in this type of work arrangement because they needed more time for family, had a temporary disability, or simply wanted more flexibility than a standard schedule afforded.

The program utilized both work-at-home and satellite options, and pilot participants were provided with standard business lines for voice communication that were equipped with custom features. Their work-related phone expenses were paid for as appropriate. The telecommuting project remained experimental until shortly after the San Francisco earthquake of 1989. The merits of telecommuting during that crisis period were dramatically illustrated, and the arrangement was formalized.

Reduced Work Time

Reduced work time arrangements have also increased. As more and more workers find themselves having to manage dual responsibilities—work and family, work and education or retraining, job and vocation—the demand for new forms of part-time work have begun to appear. Between 1970 and 1982 the overall labor force grew 27 percent, while the part-time segment grew 58 percent. At the same time, the nature of part-time employment was changing. By 1982 there were 2.5 million professional-level part-time jobs, four times the rate of increase for all part-time jobs during the same period.

It is interesting to note that while an estimated 18.6 million people work less than a regular full-time schedule today, there is little agreement as to what constitutes part-time employment. Employers identify a part-time job as one where fewer than forty hours are worked per week. The kinds of part-time scheduling options that companies are using today are regular part-time, job sharing, V-Time, phased and partial retirement, and work sharing.

Regular Part-Time

A regular part-time job, which is filled by a member of a company's regular work force, entails fewer than forty hours per week. It differs from hourly part-time in that employees in regular part-time are considered part of an organization's core work force and have pay rates comparable to full-time jobs in the same classification, prospects for upward mobility, and, increasingly (but not always), fringe benefits, including health insurance and paid vacation.

Ninety percent of the respondents to the 1990 Conference Board survey cited earlier offered part-time work as an option to their employees. Employee retention and controlling labor costs were the reasons cited most often for using part-timers. In spite of the growing acceptance of the role of part-time work, however, most employers still authorize the use of part-time in "regular" job classifications with great reluctance. (This is not true of hourly part-time employees, who are generally viewed as peripheral or supplementary workers and are usually hired as part-timers.)

ISSUES FOR MANAGERS

Although the use of part-time employment has increased in most companies in recent years, and a number of new forms of regular part-time work have emerged, managers are still often reluctant to consider most jobs as having potential for being part-time (or shared) positions. In large part this is because of long-held perceptions about the role of part-time work and the kinds of employees who work part-time. The realities of part-time are changing, however, and managers are having to reevaluate many long-held attitudes about this form of employment. Perceptions that need to be examined in the light of today's marketplace include:

• *The belief that many managers hold that part-time employees are not as committed as full-timers.* Research and experience indicate that exactly the opposite may be true. In one large survey of employers, a high proportion of senior management rated productivity better for part-time than for full-time employees. Another recent research project on regular part-time also indicates that voluntary part-timers are often even more committed than the average full-time employee.

• *The notion that most jobs are full-time and can't be done on a part-time basis.* Managers can't expect a job that takes forty hours a week to be done in twenty hours.

The job can, however, be restructured or filled by two part-time employees who share the responsibilities.

• *The idea that part-time is only appropriate for lower-level positions.* A recent study of corporate use of professional-level part-time uncovered part-timers in all different capacities and at all levels. Another illustration of how much the use of part-time has changed is the fact that at Harris Trust and Savings Bank in Chicago, there are twenty part-time officers, eight of whom are vice-presidents.

• *The belief that supervisors can't work part-time.* This has been a long-held view that is slowly eroding as more and more supervisors do work part-time. In New York State's Part-Time/Job Share program, approximately one-fourth of the part-timers supervise other employees. The New York State handbook for supervisors and managers notes, "Because jobs with supervisory responsibilities differ greatly from each other, it is important to define clearly what it is that makes the job in question a supervisory job and how each supervisory responsibility would be affected by part-time."

Because most jobs are based on a full-time model, there are policy issues that make it difficult to use part-time arrangements. The two most common are:

1. The use of time cards and a time clock
2. The inability to provide a full benefits package to part-time employees

As companies move toward a wider, more complex integration of full- and part-time schedules, they are modifying their policies in these two areas in order to facilitate the use of new work options.

Coverage is also of concern to managers. One important characteristic of a successfully restructured or shared full-time job is an ability and willingness to be flexible to ensure that coverage is maintained. Would a job-sharing arrangement be an acceptable way to arrange a part-time option? Are the employees willing or able to attend important meetings or sustain client contacts even if it means putting in extra time occasionally or doing some work from home? Are the communications techniques sufficient to ensure that things run smoothly during the time that the employee is not there? Is the employee willing to be called at home, if necessary?

COMPANIES USING REGULAR PART-TIME

Companies that have increased their use of regular part-time include BayBanks. This financial enterprise is based in the Boston area and has twelve locations, employing approximately 6,600 people. In 1982, in order to recruit quality employees for part-time, entry-level positions, the bank launched its Workstyle program. Unlike its competitors, BayBanks offers part-time employees a full-range of benefits: paid vacation, sick leave, training and promotion opportunities, and the same health benefits that full-timers have. Although originally a recruitment strategy, this regular part-time program has since expanded to meet the needs of parents, students, and soon-to-be retirees. As Ann Bernstein, the assistant vice-president for human resources, notes, "people's needs change throughout their careers," and the program recognizes that. Currently, approximately 39 percent of the company's employees are regular part-time employees; 78 percent of them are female and 22 percent male. Although most of the participants are in clerical positions, approximately 5 percent are in professional, managerial, and technical jobs.

When employees want to participate in Workstyle, they discuss the new scheduling change with their supervisor and assess how the change will affect their work within the department. The nature and amount of work to be completed, opportunities to expand the skills levels of other staff by delegating some responsibilities, and the possibility of needing to add new staff to the department are all considerations in designing the new schedule. In most cases, the division head makes the final decision.

Job Sharing

Job sharing is a form of regular part-time employment where two employees share the tasks, responsibilities, and compensation (wages and benefits) of a full-time job. Job sharers may divide the hours of the day, work alternating days or weeks, or arrive at any other configuration that is mutually agreeable to the employees and their supervisor.

The concept of job sharing grew out of the need to provide part-time employment opportunities in job classifications that cannot be significantly reduced in hours or split into two part-time positions. The Conference Board/New Ways to Work survey indicated that most job-sharing employees are previous full-timers who have converted to a job-sharing status and that the arrangement is generally initiated by the employees. There have also been instances of job sharers applying for a position and being hired from the outside as a team.

It is difficult to estimate the amount of job sharing that exists because, until recently, it was primarily an ad hoc arrangement between employees and their supervisor, and the sharers were designated as part-timers on payroll systems. The number of companies that offer job-sharing options is also unknown, but it appears to be on the increase. For the most part, the use of job sharing is related to retention of valued employees or recruitment for hard-to-fill positions.

Issues for Managers

Although job sharing offers a number of possible new advantages and opportunities, like improved coverage and more skills and experience in a single job title, it is still such a new concept that some managers express concerns that:

• *Job sharing will require more supervision.* When asked, however, most supervisors of sharers disagree. They say there is less need for supervision, not more—if you emphasize the sharers' responsibility to make it work. Sharers tend to supervise one another and compensate for skill deficiencies.

• *If one person is allowed to job-share, everyone will want to.* The reality is that most people either prefer a full-time job or can't afford to job-share. However, some employees really need this kind of choice, and the fact that the option is available can be motivational for everyone.

• *Job sharing will result in higher costs.* For companies that do not use many part-timers and have not established a prorated benefits policy, job-sharing arrangements can represent an added cost in terms of benefits because health and dental benefits will be extended to more employees and their families. However, a policy can be introduced to allow for proration, and—balanced against the reduced costs associated with lower turn-over, absenteeism, and overtime and increased productivity—the result may be cost savings in the long run.

• *There is no room in the staffing budget for another person.* This is generally a head count issue. If a full-time equivalency system is used, two job sharers are counted the same as one full-time employee and will not negatively impact a staffing budget.

COMPANIES USING JOB SHARING

Companies with job sharing policies include Steelcase Inc., located in Grand Rapids, Michigan. This is the world's largest manufacturer of office furniture and equipment and employs 13,800 people, 2,888 of whom are women.

Job sharing was first tried at Steelcase in 1982, when two full-time pricers asked to reduce their hours and became the company's first sharers. The company treated the sharers' first six months, from June 15 to December 15, as a pilot program. In January 1983, Steelcase evaluated the experiment and concluded that, in addition to offering advantages to the affected employees, job sharing provided many benefits to the company. They cited lower absenteeism and turnover, a positive impact on affirmative action, possibilities for peak period coverage, the ability to retain valued employees, the availability of a wider range of skills in the position, higher morale and more energy from "fresher" employees, the ability to offer new options to older employees, and full-time job coverage even during vacations and illnesses. On the negative side, the company cited the extra cost of providing full benefits for each sharer. In order to adjust the cost, Steelcase decided to prorate the cost of most benefits for sharers.

Job sharers must have at least one year of full-time service before they can submit a request to reduce their work load. Positions with supervisory and/or budgetary responsibilities are not eligible for job sharing. Most of the employees who have requested a shared arrangement have done so because of family responsibilities. Some, however, have done so in order to return to school or take advantage of a training opportunity or because of health reasons. One male employee wanted to use job sharing as a means of phasing in his retirement. Initially, most of the job sharers at Steelcase were exempt employees in clerical positions. In 1988, Steelcase expanded job sharing to all its employees, including 6,500 production personnel.

V-Time Programs

V-Time programs are the next step in the evolution of part-time opportunities for regular employees. This programmatic approach to facilitating voluntary reductions of work time by full-time employees was originally designed as a way for employers to integrate part- and full-time employment options and was first instituted as a way to avoid layoffs during slow periods. Its real importance is as a model that legitimizes part-time employment and affords workers a way to accommodate short-term needs for reduced working hours without having to negotiate an ad hoc arrangement with their supervisor. V-Time programs allow full-time employees to reduce their work schedule voluntarily for a defined period of time with a corresponding adjustment in compensation and some employment rights like seniority. After the agreed-upon time period, the employee returns to full-time work.

ISSUES FOR MANAGERS

V-Time programs raise the same issues for managers as other part-time options do.

• *The amount of reduction being requested and the form in which the employee would like to take it off will make it difficult to get the work done.* V-Time programs require that the amount and kind of reduction satisfy both business needs and the personal needs of the employee. Managers should feel free to negotiate the amount of reduction and whether or not it is taken as fewer hours per day or per week or a block of time off during the year in terms of the needs of the job, while keeping the needs of the employee well in mind.

• *The required work can't be done in less than full time.* If the job requires full-time coverage, the work can sometimes be reapportioned, or the employee may be amenable to sharing.

• *The employee's revised schedule could have a negative impact on client services or the work group.* Does the employee's proposal suggest effective ways to deal with these issues? If not, they should be discussed and solutions agreed upon.

• *What are the business ramifications of accepting or rejecting the request?* Employees request permission to enroll in a V-Time program because full-time work has become difficult or impossible. Supporting a request for V-Time can help managers retain good employees. Having a V-Time program available can also help in recruiting.

COMPANIES USING V-TIME

An example of a V-Time program is New York State's Voluntary Reductions in Work Schedules Program. Begun in 1984, this program permits eligible employees to reduce their work schedules (and salaries) a minimum of 5 percent, in 5 percent increments up to a maximum of 30 percent. (The state also has job sharing and part-time options for employees who need a larger reduction in time.) The employee submits a plan for a reduced schedule, which management reviews and approves if it is consistent with operating needs. The plan specifies the duration of the agreement, the percentage of reduction, the amount of V-Time that will be earned in exchange for the reduction in salary, and the way the earned time will be used: by shortening the workday or the workweek, taking it in a block of time, extending a vacation, or taking intermittent days off.

During the first two years of the program's operation, management estimated that it saved $4 million in salary. Agency heads have the option of using the realized savings in filling other, more critical, temporary positions without increasing their budgets.

Phased and Partial Retirement

Phased and partial retirement arrangements grew out of a recognition that many older workers would remain in the work force longer if they could do so on a part-time basis. Phased retirement is offered as a way for an individual to retire gradually over a period of months or years. The hours worked per week are gradually reduced over a defined period of time. Partial retirement is an option that allows an employee to work part-time for a period of time prior to accepting full retirement. In some cases the part-time employment is augmented with partial retirement income.

The Conference Board/New Ways to Work survey indicated that phased retirement was the option that companies were least likely to have considered. Only thirty-six of the responding companies had used it, while 323 had never even considered it. (No questions were asked regarding partial retirement.) As the aging of the work force becomes more evident, however, this is an option that should attract a great deal of interest as a means of retaining senior employees with specialized skills and strong work habits.

ISSUES FOR MANAGERS

Managers have many concerns about these arrangements.

• *Company philosophy may not support phased or partial retirement. Many companies' strategies have been to offer attractive early retirement packages.* The perception of older workers being a segment of the work force to target for downsizing is one that bears rethinking. Early retirement programs are proving to be expensive in the long run, and, with skills shortages being projected and the aging of the work force upon us, senior employees should be considered a valuable resource and encouraged to extend their work life.

• *Older workers cost too much.* This view takes into account only salary level. Older workers' experience, work ethic, and commitment to and knowledge of the organization are seldom considered. Nor is their replacement cost, particularly if the "learning curve" is factored in. With the cutback on paid work time resulting from phased or partial retirement programs, most seniors become a real employment bargain.

• *Senior employees don't have the technological skills needed to do the job.* Since policy is often oriented toward early retirement, many seniors are not given the technological training that their younger coworkers receive. Training opportunities designed for senior employees would quickly close any gap in expertise that does exist.

• *Companies with a phased retirement policy sometimes find that very few older workers take advantage of it.* Most firms compute retirement benefits on the basis of the employee's salary level during the last three to five years employed. Consequently, anyone working less than full-time during the final years of employment risks retiring at a lower pension. Some companies are beginning to investigate models that allow older employees to keep paying into pension plans as if they were working full-time so they can retire without a reduced income. Earnings limits for retired persons also act as barriers for seniors who want to work at least part-time after they have retired.

COMPANIES USING PHASED OR PARTIAL RETIREMENT

Companies with phased retirement programs include Corning, Inc., the manufacturer of glass products. At Corning, the phased retirement option is available to exempt or nonexempt workers in good standing who have been with the company more than twenty years and are fifty-five years of age and older. The program was initiated in the early 1980s as a means of reducing staffing levels without the enormous talent drain that goes with downsizing.

The phased retirement participant works 40 percent of full time for a contractually agreed-upon period of time. They are paid 40 percent of their base salary and begin to draw their pension. Participants receive 40 percent of holiday pay and full medical benefits and are still part of the company's pension plan. Participants are between the ages of fifty-five and sixty-one; they are not eligible after age 62. Seven years is the maximum time possible on the program, assuming the participant started at age 55. This option is not considered an employee right, but senior workers may request the option. Inclusion in the program is based upon the type of job and the employee and company need. Those who have already established a retirement date are encouraged to stick with that date and not to convert to phased retirement.

The reduced work schedule is determined by the job, the employee, and the manager, and it varies substantially. For example, in a plant maintenance position, a participant may be asked to work full-time during a plant refitting and then take time off during ordinary plant operation. Others may work a set part-time schedule year-round or a fixed on-off schedule. Thus far, none of the positions have needed to be filled full-time.

Initially, one of the major problems associated with the program was a lack of retirement planning on the part of the employees. The company has had a successful outplacement service for some time, but the service had not been used for retirement planning. Recently though, a Career Transition Service was added, staffed by human resources personnel and outside retirement consultants. All phased retirement participants must have preretirement counseling. The director of human resources says the results have been much better, and the retiree is able to make a much more informed decision about his or her work and retirement needs.

Work Sharing

Work sharing is not an option for an individual employee; it is an organizational strategy that provides an alternative to layoffs. When a company uses work sharing, all or part of the organization's work force temporarily reduces hours and salaries in order to reduce operating costs. This enables an employer to cut back on paid hours of work in response to an economic downturn without cutting back on the number of people employed. The flexible response of a firm, and its ability to remain competitive and productive, is greatly enhanced by ensuring that a trained labor force remains intact, committed, and ready to gear up when the economy picks up again.

In fourteen states,* private sector work sharing is encouraged and facilitated by the ability to use partial payments from unemployment insurance systems for those workers whose salaries have been cut back. This creative use of unemployment insurance to foster continued employment, rather than waiting until workers have been dislocated, is called short time compensation (STC).

Firms like Motorola, in Arizona, and Signetics, in California's Silicon Valley, have credited work sharing with significantly affecting their turnaround time during recessionary periods. Motorola conducted an extensive study of its program that indicated that employees were as enthusiastically supportive of this approach as management was

The decision about whether or not work sharing should be used is generally made

---

* Some states that have passed short time compensation legislation are Arizona, Arkansas, California, Florida, Kansas, Louisiana, Maryland, Massachusetts, Missouri, New York, Oregon, Texas, Vermont, and Washington.

by top-level management. If the issue is permanent downsizing of a division or the entire firm, rather than an economic fluctuation, then attrition accompanied by some layoffs may be more realistic. But if a company wants to retain top-level people during a downturn that necessitates cost cutting, work sharing has a number of advantages. Many companies lose their best people during a downsizing because they are the ones with the skills and confidence to find new jobs—often with competitors. Work sharing implies commitment to employees and faith in the company's future.

ISSUES FOR MANAGERS

Managers have concerns and questions about work sharing.

* *What kind of work sharing should be used: voluntary reductions of paid work time, mandatory ad hoc reductions, or full-scale work sharing supplemented with short time compensation?* Decisions about the work sharing strategy are determined by how long you expect the cutbacks to be necessary, the composition of the work force, union attitudes, and other factors. The work sharing plan can consist of a combination of schemes that are designed to achieve a certain level of savings.

* *Union representatives will object.* For the most part, unions today support the concept of work sharing as an alternative to layoffs, particularly if they are part of the work sharing plan's design team. (Union involvement in the design of STC plans is usually mandatory.)

* *Employees won't want to cut back voluntarily.* Companies that have tried work sharing have generally found that a certain percentage of employees are eager for the opportunity to have a little more family time or a partially paid sabbatical in which to take a course or do some community work. Charles Schwab & Co. found that almost 100 percent of its employees participated in a voluntary work sharing plan in 1988.

COMPANIES USING WORK SHARING

Companies that have used work sharing include Motorola, a major manufacturer of semiconductor products. Although its corporate offices are in Schaumberg, Illinois, much of its production is in Phoenix, Arizona. The company had been badly hurt by the severe layoffs it had experienced in the 1975 recession. Because of this, and also as a result of its favorable experience with work sharing in its European plants, Motorola executives had been watching closely California's pilot project on work sharing. (California was the first state to test the use of STC from unemployment systems as a means of encouraging work sharing as an alternative to layoffs.) Since the STC strategy can be used only in states that have enabling legislation, Motorola initiated discussions with the Arizona Department of Economic Security. (The company is that state's largest private employer, employing 25,000 workers in the greater Phoenix area at that time.) The Department of Economic Security agreed to conduct an extensive statewide survey on behalf of Motorola and the Arizona Association of Industries. The respondents overwhelmingly endorsed the concept of work sharing. Legislation was introduced and passed, and in 1982, Arizona became the second state to adopt STC legislation.

During the 1982 recession, instead of having to institute damaging, disruptive layoffs, Motorola developed a work sharing plan. According to Motorola, it succeeded far beyond expectations. In 1982 there was a reduction in working hours of approximately 10 percent. Almost 9,000 employees participated in the program, which was applied uniformly, from top management to production and clerical employees, and which resulted in labor savings of $3 million. According to a subsequent evaluation of the impact of work sharing on selected Motorola units, there were even more advantages. A report on the program states, "The use of work sharing also may increase the quality and quantity of output during economic downturns. This is the case because the use of work sharing reduces the need for bumping and its consequent disruption of established production processes." [4]

Meeting Employees' Needs

In the year 2000, time will be an increasingly scarce resource. A long time ago Benjamin Franklin noted that "Time is money." It's worth remembering today. The best way to recruit good workers and then retain them is to offer them something they can't get most other places: time. Today, work time options are in great demand and in scarce supply in most companies. The challenge for the 1990s and beyond will be to learn how to construct the right mix and match of various kinds of flexible scheduling and staffing arrangements in ways that are consistent with organizational culture and objectives and employees' needs. The successful companies in the future will be those that have developed a culture, supported by policy, that encourages managers to customize, rather than standardize, their response to employees' needs. In this way they will attract and keep quality workers and build a base of employee satisfaction and commitment that will enable them to meet their organizational objectives successfully.

Notes

1. *Travelers Employee Caregiver Survey,* The Travelers Company (Hartford, Conn.: June 1985).
2. *Exchanging Earnings for Leisure: Findings of an Exploratory National Survey on Work Time Preferences,* R&D Monograph, U.S. Department of Labor (Washington, D.C.: 1980).
3. *Flexible Staffing and Scheduling in U.S. Corporations,* The Conference Board, Research Bulletin No. 240 (New York: 1989).
4. Bennett Burgoon and Robert D. St. Louis, *The Impact of Work Sharing on Selected Motorola Units,* College of Business, Arizona State University (Tempe, Arizona: October 1984).

Suggested Reading

Axel, Helen. *Job Banks for Retirees.* The Conference Board, Research Bulletin No. 929. New York: 1989.

Flexible Staffing and Scheduling in U.S. Corporations. The Conference Board, Research Bulletin No. 240. New York: 1989.

Gordon, Gil, and Kelly, Marcia M. *Telecommuting: How to Make It Work for You and Your Company.* Englewood Cliffs, N.J.: Prentice-Hall, 1986.

The Gordon Report. Monthly newsletter published by Gil Gordon Associates, Monmouth Junction, N.J.

McCoy, Ramelle, and Morand, Martin J. *Short-Time Compensation: A Formula for Work Sharing*. New York: Pergamon Press, 1984.

Nollen, Stanley D. *New Work Schedules in Practice: Managing Time in a Changing Society*. New York: Van Nostrand Reinhold, 1982.

Olmsted, Barney, and Smith, Suzanne. *Creating a Flexible Workplace*. New York: AMACOM, 1989.

Olmsted, Barney, and Smith, Suzanne. *The Job Sharing Handbook*. Berkeley, Calif.: Ten Speed Press, 1985.

Workforce 2000: Competing in a Seller's Market. Is Corporate America Prepared? Survey report on corporate responses to demographic and labor force trends, Towers Perrin/Hudson Institute, Washington, D.C., 1990.

Work Times. Quarterly newsletter published by New Ways to Work, San Francisco, Calif.

17

Employee Relations, Communications, and Quality of Work Life

Mary F. Cook
President
Mary Cook & Associates

Employee Relations

We hear all kinds of talk about companies as "good" or "bad" places to work. Most of this talk has a lot to do with how people are treated and what kind of interaction takes place inside the organization on a daily basis. If we want to retain our best people, we must institutionalize a positive, interactive, participative, and honest environment.

Unfortunately, after the layoffs and downsizings of the 1980s, many organizations took a giant step backward to the human relations climate of the 1960s. Social pollster and commentator Daniel Yankelovich has gathered impressive statistical evidence that shows the workplace is getting worse in terms of working conditions and social climate. Most U.S. workers still want to do a good job. But there seems to be a discrepancy between what workers want to accomplish, what they are allowed to do, and how they are treated in the process. This mismatch translates in many organizations into a profound feeling of alienation, and in a business sense it represents a tragic waste of human potential and a huge loss in productivity.

There are many companies in the United States, however, that do a wonderful job motivating their employees and providing terrific places to work. Some of these companies are listed in the 1984 book *The 100 Best Companies to Work for in America* by Robert Levering, Milton Moskowitz, and Michael Katz. In these companies the experience of work is fulfilling rather than alienating. What makes a company a good place to work? What sort of employee relations, communications, and work life issues have to be addressed, and what are some of the common causes of employee relations problems?

Employee Relations Problems

As a consultant, I frequently work with companies conducting supervisory and managerial focus groups. I often ask about the most serious problems in the company. Here are some of the answers:

- Favoritism, or inconsistency in the application of personnel policies and procedures
- Lack of fair but firm discipline

- Failure of supervisors and managers to listen and to follow through to resolve problems
- Arbitrary changes in policies or procedures
- A stifling of personal creativity and innovation, a "we've always done it that way" mentality
- An autocratic management style, lack of participative management techniques
- A lack of two-way communication
- A lack of genuine concern, an unfriendly work environment; not a team or family atmosphere
- Too much organizational politics; the average employee doesn't get a "fair shake"

Looking at the other side of the coin, when employees are asked what makes a good workplace, they almost always say: "One where you're paid well, have good benefits, are treated like a human being, do interesting work. You know what's going on in the company, and you're not fired at the slightest downturn in the economy."

Most companies will do almost anything to retain their best workers, and one way to do that is to recognize when there are problems and deal with them quickly and effectively. That's why many organizations have an employee relations function in the human resources department—someone charged with the responsibility of recognizing problems and resolving them.

Employees who complain may help you identify problem areas. However, not all employees feel comfortable discussing a problem. In such cases, employees may indicate the existence of problems through changes in attitude, behavior, or job performance. Look for these signs:

- A drop in productivity
- A change in employee attitudes
- A change in the way people work
- Increasing absenteeism
- Increasing turnover
- More complaints
- Resistance to following new instructions
- A new level of employee activism

Many of the things you see or hear may have little meaning in and of themselves. However, put together with reports of other managers, your experience may reveal a pattern that will enable management to anticipate employee relations problems. The prompt and equitable review and resolution of employee problems at the lowest possible organization level is vitally important to the employee relations environment of the company.

An employee problem exists whenever an employee feels that there is a job-related problem (real or imaginary) that has not been resolved. In such instances, the employee should be encouraged to use a problem review procedure such as the one that follows. The manager is responsible for ensuring that the problem is promptly and fully dealt with until the employee is satisfied with the decision made or until the procedure is exhausted.

Sample Problem Review Procedure

- *Step 1.* The employee should discuss the problem with the immediate supervisor. If the employee is not satisfied with the results of this discussion, a meeting should be arranged with the next level of management.
- *Step 2.* If the problem has still not been resolved to the satisfaction of the employee, the employee may make a formal written complaint to the department manager. The human resources director should be available for guidance and assistance as needed.
- *Step 3.* If the employee is still dissatisfied after discussing the problem with the department manager, a meeting should be arranged with the vice-president. This appointment may be made by the employee directly or through the department manager or the human resources director.
- *Step 4.* If the situation is still unresolved after Step 3, the employee may submit a written statement to the president of the company. The final decision should be made at this level.

The employee may drop the complaint at any step of the procedure. It is recommended that there be no more than a ten-day time period between each step.

Positive Employee Relations

The success of your employee relations program will have a significant impact on your ability to retain your best employees. As a result, the employee relations function is taking on more importance. Organizations are looking for the best ways to motivate their employees at all levels of the company. Here are some ways to do that:

- Don't just say that people are your company's most important asset. Actually treat them as though they are. Communicate with them. Tell them how they are doing. Shake their hands. Be their mentors. Treat your employees the way you treat your customers.
- Balance your organizational objectives with the career objectives of your employees. Find ways to mesh the two goals by creating short-term project positions for training and development and allowing job shadowing and lateral moves.
- Teach supervisors and managers the skill of leveling with employees about their performance. Use a positive approach to performance problems and to discipline when it is needed. Ask employees how problems can be resolved, and work with them to obtain a mutually acceptable resolution.
- Create and utilize short-term small teams in which all the members share in the decision-making process and in which everyone's input is solicited and considered.
- Challenge and stretch people. Encourage them to take risks and to work at the highest and best level they can.
- Be flexible in management practices. Use flexible work alternatives, flexible benefits, and flexible HR policies.
- Create situations where the employees can have some fun at work: seasonal parties and covered dish lunches, picnics, Christmas parties, and so on.

- Establish mechanisms for upward communication such as employee surveys, suggestion systems, and employee hotlines.

Employee Communications

Employees want more and better communication at work. In a recent meeting of top management of a midsize organization, the training and development manager commented, "We have surveyed our people about their concerns on the job and ranked them in order of importance. Communication is number one." Communication on the job is almost always one of the major concerns in any organization. Yet polls show that as many as 60–70 percent of today's employees think that their organizations communicate no more effectively today than they did ten years ago.

It's been felt for a number of years that organizations that effectively communicate with employees have higher retention rates. Organizations that receive high scores on communication distinguish themselves in four ways.

1. They have established and institutionalized two-way communications through training and special programs.
2. They have effective communicators in the organization who are open, spontaneous, supportive, and interactive. These individuals are visible and available to people at all levels.
3. Their supervisors and managers work hard at letting all employees in on strategic developments such as new products, services, territories, delivery systems, philosophies, structures, and corporate events.
4. There are fewer surprises in organizations where people feel communicated with. There is more consistency and higher morale and a feeling of being "in the know."

Factors Affecting Employee Communications

DEMOGRAPHICS OF THE WORK FORCE

A variety of government statistics, including *Workforce 2000*, published by the U.S. Department of Labor, tell us that nearly half of the work force is under thirty-five years of age. Countless studies have confirmed that this population group, born after the television set became a household fixture, is more attuned to receiving information electronically or in face-to-face discussion, not through the printed word. In addition, there is the problem of illiteracy in the United States. Particularly hard hit by this problem are companies that employ many entry-level workers; for them, written publications are of limited value.

Yet today's technical and professional employees are for the most part well educated and seek involvement in the workplace. They need and want more information from their organizations. They have far less "automatic" loyalty to a company and, according to the National Opinion Research Center, have a work ethic more driven by desire for personal success than by a strong desire to help their companies succeed. These professional employees respond positively to a wide variety of communications media, including written, audio, and video presentations.

What does this mean for your company? In essence, it means that you must take a good look at the composition of your work force to determine the means of communication that will be most successful in reaching them. It also means that you have to study the work environment as a whole.

CHANGING TIMES

Today we are in fast-changing times both at home and internationally, and employers and employees have a greater need than ever to interrelate effectively. Employees feel that this is not happening in most organizations. Of 5,000 workers nationwide surveyed by The Wyatt Company, only 40 percent said that management seeks their input on important issues. About 25 percent said they have no freedom to express their opinions.

In another survey conducted by the International Association of Business Communicators, of 32,000 employees in twenty-six business organizations, only half thought that company communication was candid and accurate. Two-thirds said communication was incomplete, and more than half said communication was strictly from the top down, with no opportunity provided for discussion.

Employees want to know what is happening with the company, what is going to happen to them, how they are performing, and if the company wants to keep them. Again, as has been stated before, the demographics of the changing work force tell us that the name of the game in the 1990s will be retaining employees. If we want to retain the best people, we have to communicate with them and let them know that we are interested in them. And we have to encourage them to communicate with us!

The U.S. Army is an outstanding example of an organization that has made all the right moves recently in establishing communications links that work both in crisis and in less stressful times. All supervisory level personnel are trained in facilitating small group discussions and are sent frequent, regular newsletters and white papers on a wide variety of social and public issues to aid them in such discussions. In addition, supervisors are given training in face-to-face communication and motivation as a regular part of their skills development program. Private companies would do well to adopt this model as we move through turbulent times.

TROUBLED TIMES

It's easy to communicate when everything is going well for a company, but how about communicating when things are not so good? The responsibility for communicating with the work force during a crisis or troubled times usually rests with the top human resources executive. In difficult times organizations need more in the way of employee communications—not less. The usual reactive mode in a crisis is to stop communicating and keep your mouth shut, but that is exactly the wrong thing to do.

When an organization is having problems—maybe it's going through a merger, an acquisition, or a downsizing program—employees need and want to know exactly where they stand. If the company is less than candid and honest and says, "We have to trim staff. We're going to have a small onetime layoff," and then a few weeks later has a second layoff, employees won't believe anything the company says from that time forward. In order to be believable, companies have to decide why they want to communicate, what they will communicate, and when and how frequently communications will take place. And above all, they must be honest and provide timely information and follow-through if they want employees to listen.

Forms of Communication

It was much easier to communicate with employees when companies were smaller and when employees seemed to fit into a mold. Everyone pretty much knew what was expected of them and what the company was going to do for them. Today, changes in the makeup of the work force and changes in the size of organizations and the way they run create more opportunity for work crisis and for troubled times. Therefore, we need many forms of communication, but most importantly, we need honesty, consistency, credibility, and personal interaction at all times.

Effective communications must come from a variety of professionals who participate internally at many levels. It requires involvement from the CEO and other top executives, from the human resources department, and from managers and supervisors, all participating in two-way communications. The communications function can be organized in many ways, but no matter how it's organized, the best and most effective communications will always occur when the boss is out shaking hands, talking to people, and listening to what they have to say.

Group Communication

Human resources managers or even an individual's immediate supervisor can't always be on the scene and ready to answer when an employee has a specific question. That's why more companies are adopting management/employee committees or councils and employee-supervised counselor or ombudsman programs. In some cases, frequent management/employee team meetings are advisable. Some organizations have also instituted employee sounding boards, groups of employees that meet once a month to discuss issues that arise and ways to resolve problems in a proactive, positive work environment.

Many organizations are also using forms of communication which, while not always face-to-face, can be more interactive and response-inducing than a publication and can help fill in any gaps. Employee questions and concerns must be welcomed by supervisors, fed back up the pipeline, and answered candidly and promptly.

Suggestion systems and speak-out programs are increasingly common. IBM uses a mail-in system, called Speak Up, that allows employees to get individual responses to questions from high-level managers while maintaining their anonymity. Employees indicate their names and addresses, but these are removed by the Speak Up director and kept separately. When an appropriate executive has supplied an answer, the Speak Up director mails it to the employee's home. Alternately, the employee may request a face-to-face or telephone response. Many large companies, including Anheuser-Busch and Eastman Kodak, now have similar programs.

Some companies have telephone hot-line systems that record employees' questions anonymously and provide feedback for use by management and human resources. Some companies use regularly conducted employee surveys. When affordable, audio or videotaped news and comment shows with feedback opportunities can elicit a positive response from employees.

An electronic medium was employed at the Tennessee Valley Authority (TVA), the largest producer of electric power in the United States, after a new chairman called for a commitment to new organizational values, a major reorganization, and a downsizing that eliminated 20 percent of jobs. Satellite technology was used to carry major speeches by TVA board members to 33,000 permanent workers and 4,000 contract workers. The workers learned what was happening before the media broke the story (learning company news from the media first had become a major employee complaint). These were TVA's first-ever companywide meetings. The program's success caused top management to become more aware of how proactive employee communication would benefit the organization.

EMPLOYEE NEWSLETTERS

While printed media are not always successful with all employees, an employee newsletter is one way to encourage two-way communication within an organization. A newsletter is a challenge because it must be published on a regular basis and it must, at least in part, be written by employees even though the newsletter may be published by the HR department. Employee support and participation is one of the keys to its success.

Surveys have shown that internal publications are the primary source of information for most employees and that the contents of most company newsletters are reliable, accurate, and believable. A survey of 45,000 personnel at forty organizations in the United States and Canada, conducted by the International Association of Business Communicators and Towers, Perrin, Forster and Crosby, indicates that a high percentage of people (89 percent) find employee publications believable.

The following checklist for starting a company newsletter (or reinvigorating an existing newsletter that has become dull or obsolete) may be helpful.

- Establish the scope of the newsletter. Is it a total company information tool, or a publication that merely lists anniversaries, birthdays, safety awards, etc?
- Establish the format. Is is a tabloid or a magazine? How long will each issue be?
- Decide on the frequency of publication. Will it be weekly, monthly, or quarterly?
- Decide on the basic contents.
- Establish a budget.
- Evaluate and decide on the time restrictions of the staff. Will a new person be hired to produce the newsletter? Who will actually produce it?
- Determine how much participation there will be from employees.
- Decide what outside resources you will use, such as writers, graphic artists, and printers. Do you have desktop publishing capabilities?
- If outside printers are to be used, get three or four quotes on production costs.
- Determine if the publication has to appeal to local employees only, or if there is a national or international readership.
- Decide who will have editorial control of the contents.
- Establish the distribution of the newsletter.
- Determine how you will measure the newsletter's effectiveness over time

In planning the newsletter, think about how readability will be measured. How will you determine what employees want to read? What will be the style of the publication? Who will have the editorial and distribution control? Perhaps an employee task force could assist in the initial planning for the newsletter. Employees would then feel more involved in the entire project. It's also a good idea to set up a news-gathering network from all areas of the organization. Ask for employee volunteers to be reporters, and build a backlog of articles and fillers.

Ideas for Developing Communications Programs

Most organizations are always looking for new communications ideas. Here are a few to consider.

- Put together a communications task force of employees. Ask them to brainstorm on the subject of communications in your organization and on how communication, both up and down, can be improved. Ask the task force to appoint a spokesperson to present their results to top management. Be sure to follow through on their suggestions.
- Try interactive videodisk programs for outlying locations. They are a wonderful new communications tool.
- Use small group meetings in all areas of the company to bring people together to discuss current organizational issues. Mix people in the groups so that people at all levels—including top executives—and from all departments can participate. This is an important communications tool for the new work force that wants a more participative style of management.
- Use video newscasts to let employees know what is going on in the company. Send them to all locations on a regular basis.
- Implement a program of early evening meetings once a month for discussion of specific topics or current business books. Ask the CEO or top executives to lead the discussion groups.
- Use action-oriented bulletin boards with cartoons and messages on pertinent subjects.
- Start a newsletter or update your current one. Put in more information on what the company is doing and what you expect to occur in the future.
- Start lunch hour programs such as brown bag lunches. Have speakers on current topics.
- Install a company hot line for thirty to sixty days. Ask employees to call in twenty-four hours a day if they have any problems or questions. If they leave their name, they will receive a direct answer within a certain amount of time (usually two days). If they don't want to leave their name, you will provide an answer in the company newsletter.
- Have regular employee meetings where executives talk on various topics and open the meetings to question and answer sessions.
- Provide an annual report to employees on the state of the company. Provide information on personnel and benefits programs as well as critical company and work issues.
- Provide the mechanism for employees to volunteer to work together in the community. Small groups of employees donating their time to community projects communicate with each other in the process.
- Start a fitness program and sponsor athletic events. This can be done at little expense and may even cut your medical benefits costs as well as improve morale.

When employees get together in these programs, they inevitably communicate, and a positive interaction occurs.

These ideas can help improve communications up and down in the organization by bringing employees at all levels together with management. Be sure that managers and top executives participate in all your programs.

Quality of Work Life

When people refer to the quality of the work life (QWL) in an organization, that's literally what they mean: what the quality of life is at work. Companies have talked about QWL programs and quality circles for twenty years, but what has finally happened is that today's workers are putting a practical spin on the subject, asking themselves, "What is the quality of my life on the job?" The fact that employees are asking this question—and expecting employers to do something about it—is forcing companies to address the QWL issue in a more pragmatic way, taking steps to ensure that the quality is good. Here are nine workable ideas for effectively actualizing QWL practices.

1. Use small group worker-management problem-solving techniques. Set up structures that allow people to address problems in flexible temporary teams that are coordinated and systematically managed.
2. Provide multidirectional career options for employees at all levels. Create and develop a variety of possibilities for movement from every job so that no job is a dead end. Use lateral moves, bridging positions, rotation, and temporary and project management assignments.
3. Try a task redistribution program within work units. Gather data to ensure that each person's tasks make best use of the workers involved and each job provides adequate challenge.
4. Design more than one career ladder for professional development and succession planning programs. Most companies need a supervisory/managerial career ladder and a technical/professional career ladder. This serves the needs of both the company and the employee.
5. Institutionalize formal succession planning in your organization. Without it, performance appraisal and promotional opportunities are just a hodgepodge of subjective activity that tends to alienate employees.
6. Constantly work at improving the communications skill of first-line supervisors and managers. Communication is the key ingredient for the success of a QWL program, and it must work well at the lowest supervisory level.
7. Forge new definitions of "how we work in this organization" as part of the QWL program. Give the definitions visibility, and follow through to see that managers actualize your definitions.
8. Make sure that all top executives participate in QWL programs and show their commitment. If employees feel that QWL programs are just window dressing, your efforts will be received negatively.
9. Ensure that processes and programs are not static. Respond quickly to developments as they occur, and constantly revitalize your program. Make managers responsible for change, creativity, and ongoing commitment.

Organizational Culture and the Work Environment

The values, beliefs, and norms within a company that strongly influence everyone from top management on down make up the organizational culture. These things aren't written down anywhere, but everyone in a company knows them. Corporate culture directly influences a company's work environment and management style, creating a certain quality of life. In some companies, for example, it's expected that work will get done right away, and a good manager is one who supplies quick solutions. In other organizations, what's more important is working as a team or delegating work to employees and helping them grow—managing people for long-term results. The organization that creates a distinctive but effective culture and style, understands it, and successfully transmits it to employees, will be a long-term winner.

You may be missing out on one of the key ingredients for employee retention if you ignore the influence of culture on your organization. Too often a good person fails at a new job not for lack of ability, but because he or she didn't understand the culture of the work environment. In a strong culture, employees know exactly what is expected of them. They waste little time deciding what their behavior should be. In a weak culture, employees waste time trying to figure out what they should do and how they should do it. To define your corporate culture, ask yourself these questions.

- Has your organization articulated a clear vision of company goals and objectives? Has this vision been communicated to all employees?
- Does the company encourage discussion on tough issues, or does management "clam up" and refuse discussion?
- Is collaboration and teamwork routine? Or is it more customary to encourage competition and individual effort?
- Is information often shared and accessible? Or is it usually restricted and private?
- Is disagreement permitted and respected? Or is disagreement viewed as disloyalty?
- Are the values, norms, and management style of your company defined and communicated?

When you answer these questions, you are identifying your current culture. Put your ideas in writing, and ask other executives to do the same. Then make it the focal point of discussion at a special management meeting.

One reason for looking at culture is to evaluate its effectiveness. Sometimes the culture has to be modified in certain ways so it has a more positive impact on the general productivity and success of the organization. Organizations must establish and perpetuate a culture that retains the best, most productive workers. People will stay with a company where there is an open, honest, and friendly atmosphere and a participative management style. This is one of the conclusions of Terrence Deal and Allen Kennedy in their 1984 book *Corporate Cultures*. They state that a "strong culture has a major effect on the success of a business," and the results of their studies of nearly eighty companies reflect a direct relationship between culture and profitability. According to Deal and Kennedy, successful organizations appear to possess the following characteristics.

- They have a widely shared philosophy of management.
- They encourage risk.

- They emphasize the importance of people to the success of the organization.
- They encourage rituals and ceremonies to celebrate company events.
- They identify corporate heroes and sing their praises.
- They maintain a network of culture communicators.
- They have informal rules of behavior.
- They have strong values.
- They set high standards for performance.
- They possess a definitive corporate character.[1]

An organization's culture must be identified and communicated, so people will understand where they are and how they fit in. It is especially important to communicate any changes in culture. Take, for example, a company whose culture rewards employees for long-term results. A top management decision has been made to change the organization's marketing approach to emphasize short-term results. If management doesn't communicate this change in the expected performance norm, employees who have worked for the organization for many years and have structured their behavior around a value system that rewards long-term planning and marketing strategies may find pay increases or performance bonuses reduced and not know why. The employees will naturally become confused and dissatisfied.

Altering cultural norms is difficult, but when a decision is made to make such a change, senior executives must clearly define and communicate the new norms and establish appropriate reinforcement and reward systems. Although the most successful organizations use a variety of approaches and techniques to reinforce norms, they consistently emphasize:

- Key business and organizational values
- An effective up-down communications system
- A bias toward action
- Rewards for performance and productivity
- Simple organizational form and lean staffing
- Productivity improvement through people
- Operational autonomy to encourage entrepreneurship
- A participative management style
- Simultaneous loose-tight controls
- An open, trusting environment

You can identify your current culture and management style in the following ways.

- *Look at the physical setting.* An organization that is proud of itself will reflect this through its environment. Consistency among sites is important. Headquarters may look sharp, but are division sites consistent with the standards of headquarters? Look also at consistency across classes of employees. Department by department, physical settings indicate a company's attitude toward different employees.

- *Read what is said.* Statements made in annual reports and press releases offer clues. In addition, slogans go a long way in setting the tone for an organization. "Progress is our most important product," says GE. "Better things through better living," says Du Pont. But look beyond the slogan. A company may say it believes in certain things, but its statements may be merely lip service.

• *Observe how employees are treated.* Are their ideas listened to and accepted? Do employees seem happy? Are they complaining about their job and the company in general? Is the organization's style participative or autocratic?

• *Look at how employees spend their time.* This will show what their priorities are. Is the culture focused inward? Is there an overemphasis on budgets, financial analysis, and sales quotas? Do people spend a lot of time on internal politics and apple-polishing? Or is there ample talk about customers, competitors, trends, or other business matters that affect the company?

• *Observe who gets ahead.* Does the culture reward competence and skill productivity, performance, tenure, or loyalty? Are important positions filled by long-term employees, the president's relatives, top performers, or people with technical backgrounds? The answers will give you a clear idea about what the company believes in and values.

• *Consider job length.* If people tend to stay in their jobs only a short time, it may mean they'll be more likely to make their mark quickly to get promoted again. They'll steer clear of long-term, slow-payback activities. In such a culture, a short-term focus will dominate. This is a danger sign. If most people's time and attention is spent meeting short-term targets, then long-term business goals may never be achieved. If the top people seem more interested in their careers than business results, that tells you a lot about the future success of the organization.

• *Observe how strangers are greeted.* The reception area reflects the organization's values. It is messy, nondescript, or tastefully decorated, busy or relaxed, formal or informal?

• *Talk to employees.* If you want to find something out about a company you're not familiar with, ask the receptionist whether the company is a good one to work for. If the receptionist dwells on the wonderful opportunities available in the company, you'll get a different impression than if you're told it's steady work and close to home.

Corporate culture and style shapes one's responses in a strong but subtle way. They make people fast or slow workers, tough or friendly, team players or individuals. After working for an organization for several years, one can become so conditioned by the culture that it cannot be recognized without taking a step back and taking a concerted look.

STRENGTHENING ORGANIZATIONAL VALUES

Identify and strengthen your value systems and communicate them at all levels. What top management values, i.e., hard work, honesty, et al., is what all employees who want to be successful in that organization will also value and support.

Research suggests that there are two phases of value development. First, acceptance of the value: An employee ascribes worth to prescribed behavior and is willing to identify with it. Second, the individual is sufficiently committed to the value to pursue it, to seek it, and to accept it emotionally.

Values are extremely important to both the individual and the organization in that: (1) they are standards by which one behavioral alternative is chosen over another, (2) they are the personal criteria against which individuals weigh the success of their acts, and (3) they are an integral part of a person's self-concept. Values are motivating factors in determining goals. They also provide the personal definition for successful goal achievement and serve as reference points for positive feedback.

An important way to strengthen values and measure the quality of work life is to emphasize communications within the organization at every level: up and down, laterally, and within all departments and employee groups. Defining the culture and its values and creating a positive climate should be the mission of a good organizational communications program. To accomplish this mission, the communications program should:

- Identify existing corporate norms, and values
- Create management strategies based on defined culture, and values
- Identify and communicate an acceptable management style
- Monitor culture and style on a long-term basis
- Identify how values and style relate to the quality of work life in the organization
- Continually communicate and strengthen culture and organizational values

These functions can be achieved only through a comprehensive communications program. Many organizations already have communications programs that use various techniques to transmit information, but they do not always measure reception or response, nor are they as comprehensive as they need to be to ensure effective results.

The Work Environment

People are beginning to identify the best places to work as those where the atmosphere is pleasant and where working is actually enjoyable. Humor and a bit of serendipity are not uncommon attributes of the best companies. This may have all started in California's Silicon Valley, when Steve Jobs and other young computer entrepreneurs gave employees offices with ocean views and cut work short on Friday afternoon for beer breaks and social get-togethers.

The work environment goes beyond the emotional atmosphere to matters of ergonomics. In strictly functional terms, no one really thought much about the way the office looked or how well it worked for people until 1968, when the Herman Miller Company of Zealand, Michigan, changed the office landscape for good by introducing what they called the *action office*. The idea, revolutionary at the time, was standard by the 1980s. It used panels as structural elements to support work surfaces and storage as well as to partition open-plan office space. At first workers didn't like it but they got used to it, and it had an enormous impact on industry for over twenty years.

Today, however, offices are undergoing another revolution in design as we move from the office set up to process paper to the office adapted to process information. Today, many employees at all levels of the organization, from secretaries to CEOs, spend at least part of the day in front of a video display terminal (VDT). To support these changes, office systems are now being built to accommodate channels and troughs for wiring. Ergonomically designed chairs, once mainly for secretaries and clerical workers, are being made for managers and executives as well. The demand for ergonomically designed equipment has never been greater. The physical problems that can arise from working at a VDT workstation are many: fatigue, eyestrain, headache, muscle strain, back pain, and wrist and finger problems (notably carpal tunnel syndrome), not to mention the possible effects of extremely-low-frequency magnetic fields. Now that executives are suffering from these physical woes, corporations are becoming more willing to update their office environments. The 1989 *Office Environment Index* reported that facilities managers are beginning to describe the money spent on office renovations as "asset management" rather than as an expense.

Further research has shown office design can provide more than good functioning. In his book *Workplaces: The Psychology of the Physical Environment in Offices and Factories* (1987), Eric Sundstrom points out that when workers are satisfied with their surroundings, they not only tend to be more productive but also more loyal. It's actually to a company's advantage to provide its workers with comfortable environments.

In a movement called industrial democracy, European firms are allowing workers to have a voice in design decisions that affect them. Several countries have laws either on the books or pending that give the rank and file this right. In Sweden, the law actually mandates that office and factory workers be consulted on the design of their environments before planning permission is given. U.S. companies have not yet proven to be as progressive as their European counterparts. A survey by the Buffalo Organization for Social and Technological Innovation found that 81 percent of the U.S. workers interviewed were not allowed to participate in design decisions, even though 79 percent expressed a desire to be involved.

Some inroads are being made, however. Take the case of Chicago-based Leo Burnett Company, Inc., the largest advertising agency in the Midwest. When it commissioned ISD Inc. to design the office space for its new corporate headquarters, the ad agency consulted its nearly 2,000 employees about their office requirements. Worker input went into everything from the choice of office systems to the color schemes and lighting. This collaboration resulted in an office interior that employees found not only eminently livable but that dramatically improved the vital communication between different departments and improved the office's general efficiency.

Workplace 2000 will shatter old concepts of what an office should be. Japanese architect Isao Hosoe says that the modern office is obsolete. If the office of the future is to serve the needs of a high-tech work culture, it must be reconceived. At a conference at the Domus Academy, the postgraduate design school in Assago, Italy, he encouraged students to come up with daring designs for the office of the future and to break through the rigidity of the current corporate office structure.

We must also consider other more serious issues at work such as the sick building syndrome, exposure to toxic chemicals, on-the-job accidents, and even a significant increase in workplace murders. Quality of work life includes all of these issues. One of the basic rights of workers is the right to work in a safe and healthy environment. Providing it is a key step in ensuring the quality of their work life.

Note

1. Terrence Deal and Allen Kennedy, *Corporate Cultures* (Reading, Mass.: Addison Wesley, 1984).

PART V

REGULATORY ISSUES

18

Legal and Regulatory Considerations of Recruitment and Retention

Charles W. Newcom
Partner
Sherman & Howard

Until the early 1960s, employees and job applicants had very few legal rights, and employers had very few restrictions on their ability to make employment decisions. The passage of state and federal fair employment practice laws in the 1960s and the subsequent development of common law exceptions to the employment-at-will doctrine have limited the traditional rights of employers to hire and terminate the employment relationship at will. Consequently, the number of employment-related lawsuits has increased dramatically.

Every state and the District of Columbia now prohibit discrimination in employer hiring practices. Additionally, federal statutes and a number of state statutes prohibit employers not only from retaliating against their own employees, but also from refusing to hire applicants for employment who have engaged in certain protected activities such as union activities, pursuit of health and safety claims, or pursuit of other objections to employer conduct that was or arguably was unlawful.

Employers have a legitimate business interest in hiring competent, reliable, and trustworthy employees. A thorough screening of prospective employees can serve this interest and is one of the most effective ways to minimize the likelihood of postemployment litigation. The scope and content of preemployment inquiries, however, are limited by state and federal law, and certain inquiries may create the basis for state law defamation actions. Moreover, an inadequate screening process may subject an employer to liability for negligent hiring and retention.

This chapter provides an overview of the basic legal and regulatory considerations involved in recruiting, hiring, retaining, and terminating employees. Because these issues are governed not only by federal law but also by state law and sometimes by local requirements, particularly in larger cities, it is important to emphasize that this chapter is primarily an overview of issues requiring consideration. Accordingly, in analyzing any particular decision, it is essential to look to current requirements. Court decisions interpreting applicable statutes and common law principles also amplify and clarify requirements. While it is unlikely that any of the broad issues will dramatically change in the near term, it is certain that subtle changes will occur that might dramatically impact a particular decision. Therefore, it is important that ongoing judicial decisions and potential statutory changes be considered and that attorneys be consulted.

Regulations tend to be lengthy and difficult to understand. To make it easier for you to spot quickly the ones you need to be concerned with, Exhibit 18-1 provides information on key federal regulations, including coverage, basic requirements, posting provisions, and which federal agency or department has jurisdiction.

A Brief Overview of Considerations

Discrimination

Federal law and the laws of virtually every state prohibit discrimination of any sort in hiring, terms and conditions of employment, or the layoff or firing of individuals because of their race, color, religion, sex (including pregnancy), national origin, age, or handicap. These statutes also prohibit harassment of employees because of their being a member of a protected class. At the state level, a number of states prohibit discrimination based upon marital status, arrest records, or other factors. Increasingly, at the state level, sexual preference or orientation are being added to the list of prohibited forms of discrimination.

Wrongful Discharge

Wrongful discharge prohibitions are exclusively an issue of state law. Employees who have an express written or oral contract may sue for breach of contract. Additionally, an employee may sue on an implied contract/promissory estoppel* theory based upon company policies or procedures that have been issues regarding discharge or layoff of employees or oral promises of job security or other protections. Public policy claims may also be raised as a basis for wrongful discharge. Many states therefore now allow an employee to state a claim of wrongful discharge where the claim is that the employee was discharged in retaliation for exercising some right the employee has, based upon public policy of the state or federal government (such as the right to file a workers compensation claim or to complain about an unsafe or unhealthy work situation). An additional common law theory of wrongful discharge is a breach of implied covenant of good faith and fair dealing. The thrust of this theory is that the employer acted in bad faith or with malice. In California and Montana, for example, the theory has been developed to prohibit termination of employees with expectations of job security grounded in long-term service, promotions, raises, positive job evaluations, and other expressions of job security.

Whistle-Blowing Claims

This area of public policy wrongful discharge claims should be noted separately. It is common to see claims of improper termination by former employees who allege that they "blew the whistle" on some improper company conduct. This may include violation of discrimination laws, environmental laws, banking regulations, or any number of state or federal statutes. The False Claims Act Amendments of 1986 encourage government workers to report waste of taxpayers' dollars. The provisions of these amendments

(text continued on page 381)

*Estoppel is a legal bar to alleging or denying a fact because of previous words or actions to the contrary.

Exhibit 18-1. Key federal regulations on employment.

Statute	Coverage	Basic Requirements	Posting Provision	Jurisdiction
Fair Labor Standards Acts of 1938	Employers engaged in interstate commerce	Mandates minimum hourly wage and time and a half for work in excess of 40 hours per week. Also contains child labor restrictions, equal pay for equal work	Sufficient postings in conspicuous places to permit employees to observe readily on way to or from work	Department of Labor
Walsh-Healey Public Contracts Act of 1936	Establishments engaged on a government contract of $10,000 or more	Mandates minimum hourly wage and overtime after 40 hours per week. Also contains health and safety requirements and a notation on fringe benefits	In sufficient number of places to permit employees to observe on way to or from work	Department of Labor
Davis-Bacon Acts of 1931 and 1964	Employers on public construction contracts exceeding $2,000	Mandates minimum wages found to be prevailing in the area by Labor Secretary	Minimum wage to be paid must be posted in prominent and easily accessible place at work site	Department of Labor

(continued)

Exhibit 18-1. *Continued.*

Statute	Coverage	Basic Requirements	Posting Provision	Jurisdiction
Civil Rights Act of 1964 (Title VII)	Employers of 15 or more employees and engaged in interstate commerce	Prohibits job discrimination based on race, color, religion, sex, or national origin	In conspicuous places where notices to employees and job applicants will be seen. Bilingual postings required	EEOC
Executive Order 11246, as amended	Federal government contractors and subcontractors; contractors under federally assisted construction contracts	Prohibits job discrimination based on race, color, creed, sex, or national origin. Encourages affirmative action	In conspicuous places available to employees, job applicants, and union representatives	Department of Labor
Age Discrimination in Employment Act of 1967	Employers of 20 or more employees and engaged in interstate commerce	Prohibits job discrimination based on age against workers ages 40–70	In prominent and accessible places where readily observable by employees, job applicants, and union representatives	EEOC
Pregnancy Discrimination Act of 1978	All employers	Requires that women employees "affected by pregnancy, childbirth, or related medical conditions" be treated the same as other employees with medical disabilities in terms of leave and pay	Cover in personnel policy manuals and employee handbooks	EEOC

Occupational Safety and Health Act of 1970	Employers engaged in interstate commerce. Effective January 1, 1983, the following industries are exempt: retail trade, finance, insurance and real estate, and service businesses	Requires employers to furnish a place of employment free from recognized hazards that might cause serious injury or death. Employers must comply with the specific safety and health standards issued by the Department of Labor. Employees must comply with safety and health standards, rules, regulations, and orders issued under the Act	Post OSHA form 200 in a conspicuous place in each establishment, available to all employees. Injury and illness totals for previous year must be posted during month of February	Department of Labor's Occupational Safety and Health Administration
Rehabilitation Act of 1973	Federal government contractors and subcontractors with a contract of $25,000 or more	Prohibits job discrimination against handicapped persons. Mandates affirmative action to employ and advance in employment qualified handicapped persons	In conspicuous places available to employees and job applicants	Department of Labor

(continued)

Exhibit 18-1. *Continued.*

Statute	Coverage	Basic Requirements	Posting Provision	Jurisdiction
Vietnam Era Veterans Readjustment and Assistance Act of 1974	Federal government contractors and subcontractors with a contract of $10,000 or more	Prohibits job discrimination against Vietnam veterans. Mandates affirmative action to employ and advance in employment qualified disabled and Vietnam era veterans	In conspicuous places available to employees and job applicants	EEOC
Employee Polygraph Protection Act of 1988	Most private employers. Exempt are federal government agencies involved in intelligence functions and organizations involved with controlled substances, nuclear power plants, public transportation, currency, commodities, or proprietary information	Prohibits employers from requiring or requesting employees or job applicants to take lie detector tests	In conspicuous places available to employees and job applicants	Department of Labor
Drug-Free Workplace Act of 1988	Federal contractors with contracts of $25,000 or more and federal grantees	Requires employers to certify the contracting or granting agencies that they maintain a drug-free workplace by publishing and adminis-	Post company drug-free workplace notice and cover in personnel policy manuals and employee handbooks	Department of Labor

		tering specific drug-free workplace policies and drug awareness programs. Employers must notify agencies of employee convictions for illegal drug activity in the workplace		
Worker Adjustment and Retraining Notification Law of 1988	Employers with 100 or more employees excluding part-time workers	Requires notice of plant closings and mass layoffs	Notice must be posted for 60 days in advance of the layoff or plant closing	Department of Labor
Immigration Reform and Control Act of 1986	All employers	Requires employers to file form I-9, certifying that newly hired employees are not illegal aliens	Display poster obtained from Immigration and Naturalization Service	Department of Justice's Immigration and Naturalization Service
Immigration Act of 1990	All employers	Same requirements as Immigration Reform and Control Act of 1986, which it is counterpart to. Covers new areas including workers of "distinguished merit" and employer-sponsored visas	Display poster obtained from Immigration and Naturalization Service	Department of Justice's Immigration and Naturalization Service

(continued)

Exhibit 18-1. *Continued.*

Statute	Coverage	Basic Requirements	Posting Provision	Jurisdiction
Americans with Disabilities Act of 1990	Employers of 25 or more, effective July 26, 1992. Employers of 15 or more, effective July 26, 1994. Public employers January 26, 1992	Prohibits discrimination against an individual with a disability in hiring or promotion if the person is otherwise qualified for the job	Display ABA posters and notices in conspicuous places where notices to employees and applicants will be seen	EEOC
Civil Rights Act of 1991	Basically restores Title VII by overruling 5 major court cases		Display posters in conspicuous places where notices to employees and job applicants will be seen. Bilingual postings required	EEOC

protect employees from employer retribution and guarantee rewards of 15 to 30 percent of the recovered amount. New legislation will likely be proposed in the future. It should be remembered, that more than fifteen states now have state statutory protections for employees who report alleged unlawful conduct by their employers, providing a public policy wrongful discharge protection in such circumstances. This is an area of continuing legislative activity at the state and local level.

Tort/Personal Injury

A range of tort/personal injury issues may be raised in preemployment testing or other inquiries or in an employee termination. Questions of invasion of privacy or defamation often arise in this context. Additionally, many states would recognize a claim for intentional infliction of emotional distress or outrageous conduct where the employer's actions were particularly intrusive—for example, where sexual or other harassment had occurred. Also, fraud or misrepresentation claims may arise based upon a failure to carry through either on promises made in the hiring process or promises made to an employee during the term of employment.

The Hiring Process

Legal Limitations on Preemployment Inquiries

Preemployment inquiries—whether made while verifying information on the employment application or from an employment interview—are the traditional methods used by employers to collect information about job applicants and to assess an applicant's qualifications for employment. Depending upon the inquiries made and how the information is used, applications and interviews can have the unlawful result of restricting or denying employment opportunities for members of various protected groups. As a general rule, any employment inquiry that is not clearly job related is suspect. Although making inquiries in and of themselves is not a violation of the law, questions concerning suspect areas can constitute evidence of discriminatory intent. Therefore, the better approach is to have a business justification for all information requested. Fair employment practice (FEP) enforcement agencies assume that if an employer asks a question on an application form or elsewhere as part of the preemployment process, the information requested serves as a basis for employment decisions. Employers expose themselves to potential liability by asking for information that has no relevance to the job sought.

Federal antidiscrimination laws—such as Title VII of the Civil Rights Act of 1964, the Age Discrimination in Employment Act of 1967, and the Americans with Disabilities Act (ADA) of 1990—and most state laws prohibit employers from obtaining and using certain information as the basis for hiring decisions if that information has a disparate impact on members of protected groups and is not a valid predictor of successful job performance or cannot be justified by business necessity. When drafting or reviewing application forms and interview questions, employers should ask themselves two questions.

1. Will the answer to the question, if used in making a hiring decision, disqualify a larger percentage of members of a particular group than others?

2. Is the information necessary to judge an applicant's competence or qualification for the job in question—i.e., what is the business justification requiring the information?

The traditional wisdom has been that employers who request information other than that which is essential to evaluate effectively an applicant's qualifications make themselves vulnerable to charges of discrimination and legal action. Any inquiry not clearly job related or justified by business necessity should be modified or eliminated.

Suspect Areas of Questioning

Equal Employment Opportunity Commission (EEOC) guidelines and guidelines published by many state government agencies identify several areas of inquiry that are suspect. These are race, color, religion, sex, age, handicap, and national origin. Questions concerning race, color, religion, sex, age, handicap, or national origin are not considered violations per se, but as a practical matter, they send out red flags to virtually all government agencies. Unless the business justification for these inquiries is clearly established, inquiries that directly or indirectly disclose such information are treated by government agencies and the courts as evidence of a discriminatory intent. Moreover, it may be considered unlawful discrimination to deny equal opportunity to persons because of marriage to or association with others of a specific race or national origin, attendance at schools or churches, or membership in organizations identified with particular racial or ethnic groups.

An employer's business justification may be that the information is needed for affirmative action programs, government reporting requirements (EEO-1 forms), and internal audits to identify and resolve possible discrimination in the recruitment of minority groups or women. However, in any legal action where these inquiries are challenged, the burden will be on the employer to demonstrate that the information was collected for legitimate business reasons. Any information of this type that is collected should be kept separate from regular employee records, and access should be restricted to ensure that it is not used to discriminate in making personnel decisions.

HEIGHT AND WEIGHT

Minimum height and weight requirements have been held to disqualify a disproportionate number of minorities and women from jobs they can perform. Therefore, if the employer cannot show that the requirements are essential to safe or effective performance of the job in question, inquiries in these areas may be evidence of discrimination.

MARITAL STATUS AND CHILDREN

Questions concerning marital status, pregnancy, future childbearing plans, and number and age of children should be avoided because they are not job related. To the extent that such information is necessary for tax withholding or other purposes, it may be obtained after the applicant has been offered employment.

It is unlawful to require preemployment information about child care arrangements where the inquiries are made of female applicants only. The U.S. Supreme Court has ruled that an employer may not have different hiring policies for men and women with preschool children.

EDUCATIONAL REQUIREMENTS

An employer may inquire into an applicant's educational background. However, anytime one applicant is preferred over another on the basis of educational achievements, the level of education should be clearly relevant to the position the applicant will be filling—i.e., the information obtained must be job related. If the educational standard is not closely related to the performance of the job, and if application of the educational standard has a disproportionate impact on members of protected groups, an employer may be liable to applicants refused employment because of the educational standard.

FRIENDS OR RELATIVES WORKING FOR THE EMPLOYER

Information about friends or relatives working for an employer is not relevant to an applicant's competence. Requesting this information may be unlawful if it indicates a preference for friends or relatives of present employees where this preference reduces or eliminates opportunities for women or minority group members. Questions of this sort should be asked only to prevent nepotism if the employer has an antinepotism policy. However, an antinepotism policy that prohibits or limits employment opportunity of a spouse or other relative may be illegal if it has an adverse impact on job opportunities for either men or women as a group or for a racial or ethnic group.

A narrowly framed nepotism policy may serve a legitimate business purpose if designed to prevent conflicts of interest or favoritism. While there may be good reasons to hire relatives of employees, such as high morale and lower costs of benefits packages, employers should carefully consider the drawbacks. Hiring family members may lead to security problems, relatives generally cannot effectively supervise each other, and terminating one family member may result in the loss of other competent and valued workers.

Several states prohibit discrimination against the spouse of an employee. For example, in Colorado it is a discriminatory employment policy to apply an antinepotism policy to spouses if the policy fails to comply with certain narrow exceptions (i.e., one spouse would directly supervise the other, one spouse would be responsible for accounting for monies received by the other, or one spouse has access to the employer's confidential information).

ARREST RECORDS

FEP agencies and courts have taken the position that personnel decisions based on arrest records involving no subsequent conviction have a disproportionate effect on the employment opportunities of members of some minority groups because members of these groups are arrested substantially more often than whites in proportion to their numbers in the population. Accordingly, the courts have held that without proof of job relatedness, an employer's use of arrest records to disqualify job applicants is unlawful discrimination. Even if an employer does not consider arrest information, the mere request for such information has been held to discourage minority applicants and should be omitted from employment applications. Therefore, requests for arrest records are suspect.

CONVICTION RECORDS

An absolute ban on employment of anyone with a criminal conviction for all positions violates federal law against employment discrimination because of its probable disparate impact on minorities. However, consideration of an applicant's criminal record is permissible if the conviction is substantially related to an applicant's ability to perform a specific job. For example, convictions of certain crimes involving dishonesty would be relevant where the applicant was applying for a position requiring trust or confidentiality or involving access to items of value. Conviction records should be cause for rejection if their number, nature, and recentness cause the applicant to be unsuitable for the position. If such questions are asked, they should be accompanied by a statement that a conviction record will not necessarily be a bar to employment.

MILITARY SERVICE

As with conviction records, employers should not, as a matter of policy, reject applicants who have less than honorable discharges from military service. According to a Department of Defense study, minority service members receive a higher proportion of undesirable discharges than nonminority members. Thus, information regarding discharge status should not be used in making a hiring decision. Evidence of military service may trigger veterans preference requirements.

PHYSICAL AND MENTAL CONDITIONS

Refusal to hire based upon an individual's physical or mental condition(s) may violate federal or state law prohibiting discrimination against handicapped persons. All states prohibit discrimination on the basis of handicap or medical condition against any person otherwise qualified, and they impose an obligation to accommodate the handicap. States vary as to whether they include physical handicap only or also mental handicap. They also vary as to how much is necessary by way of economic or administrative action to accommodate to the handicap. The federal Rehabilitation Act of 1973, while not generally applicable to private employers who are not government contractors, prohibits discrimination in hiring against handicapped persons by recipients of federal financial assistance and by federal agencies themselves. The Americans with Disabilities Act, signed by President George Bush on July 26, 1990, addresses both public and private discrimination against individuals with physical or mental disabilities. The ADA takes effect on July 26, 1992, for employers with twenty-five or more employees, and on July 26, 1994, for employers with fifteen to twenty-four employees.

Both federal and state laws prohibiting handicap discrimination define the handicapped very broadly to include: (1) one who suffers from a physical or mental impairment that inhibits the performance of "major life activities," (2) one who has a record of such a physical or mental impairment, or (3) one who is regarded as having such a physical or mental impairment. These definitions are broad enough to include people with contagious diseases such as AIDS, psychological disorders, a record of hospitalization for mental illness, recurrent illnesses, physical conditions that substantially interfere with work attendance, and former alcohol or drug addiction. Federal and state law further require that if a handicapped individual is unable to perform all of the requirements of the job in question, his or her eligibility for employment is nevertheless protected by the law if any "reasonable" accommodation by the employer would enable the individual to perform those tasks.

State laws vary as to the extent of medical inquiries an employer can make in the hiring process. Those variations should also be evaluated. The ADA will prohibit an employer from conducting preemployment medical examinations or making inquiries as to whether the individual is disabled, or as to the nature or severity of a disability, except to the extent the employer makes preemployment inquiries into the ability of an applicant to perform job-related functions. An employer may require a medical examination after employment has been offered as a condition to commencing employment, provided all employees are subject to the examination regardless of disability. In addition, the medical information received must be retained in separate, confidential files, with supervisors or managers being informed only about necessary restrictions on the work or duties of an employee and necessary accommodations. Medical inquiries may be made only where the medical examination or inquiry is shown to be job related and consistent with business necessity.

Refusal to hire an individual for reasons related to but not strictly based upon a handicapping condition may also be illegal. A condition, such as a congenital back anomaly, that does not prevent an applicant from performing the essential duties of a job, but which does increase the risk of future injury, cannot generally be used as a basis for refusal to hire. Refusal to hire because the prospective employer may incur future costs because of the handicap has been rejected by some courts as a defense to a handicap discrimination claim.

Lie Detector Tests

The federal Employee Polygraph Protection Act of 1988 prohibits private employers from using lie detector tests on job applicants. The only private employers exempted from this federal law are those authorized to manufacture, distribute, or disburse controlled substances; employers providing security services; and those involved in the protection of nuclear power plants, public transportation, currency, or commodities. The prohibited tests include the polygraph, deceptograph, voice stress analyzer, psychological stress evaluator, and any other similar device used to give a diagnostic opinion concerning the honesty or dishonesty of an individual.

This law does not prohibit medical tests used to determine the presence or absence of controlled substances or alcohol in bodily fluids. It also does not prohibit written or oral tests commonly referred to as honesty or paper and pencil tests, machine scored or otherwise.

Citizenship Status

Asking new hires about their authorization to work in the United States is required by the Immigration Reform and Control Act of 1986 (IRCA). As such, the IRCA requires employment discrimination in hiring against undocumented aliens. Employers currently must require all persons hired to provide documentation necessary to complete properly the employment eligibility verification form I-9. There are no exceptions for professional, administrative, or executive employees or even for new hires the employer is certain are not aliens unauthorized to work in the United States.

The IRCA does not require employers to obtain completed I-9s from all applicants for employment. To avoid generating unnecessary statistics concerning the citizenship status of employment applicants, only those persons selected for hire should be required by the employer to complete an I-9. The hiring decision should, of course, be conditional upon satisfactory completion of the form.

The second feature of the IRCA applicable to hiring practices is its prohibition of discrimination against individuals (other than unauthorized aliens) with respect to hiring, recruitment, or referral for a fee where based upon national origin or citizenship status. The purpose of the antidiscrimination provisions of the law is to ensure that employers seeking to avoid the IRCA's sanctions for hiring unauthorized aliens do not go beyond the law's requirements and simply refuse to hire any person who appears or sounds "foreign." In some respects, the IRCA's ban on discrimination reaches further than Title VII. The IRCA is applicable, for example, to all employers with four or more employees; generally, Title VII reaches employers with fifteen or more employees.

The IRCA leaves in full force and effect the provisions of Title VII that ban discrimination in employment on account of national origin according to an EEOC policy statement on the relationship between Title VII and the Immigration Reform and Control Act. Long-standing equal employment requirements identified and reaffirmed by the EEOC in its policy statement include the items discussed above, as well as nondiscrimination due to accents or ways of speaking and citizenship requirements or preferences. English fluency requirements and rules that only English can be spoken may also be unlawful unless justified by business reason or necessity.

CLUBS OR ORGANIZATIONS

Inquiries into these areas may be evidence of discrimination based on religion or union or nonunion status. Special rules apply to "union shop" arrangements under the Labor-Management Relations Act.

Conflicting Demands for Information

As the discussion above indicates, an employer is restricted from inquiring into certain areas such as race and sex when screening applicants. At the same time, however, employers are faced with conflicting obligations where they may be required to make these same inquiries for EEOC record-keeping purposes and for compliance with affirmative action plans.

This apparent dilemma can be resolved. To begin with, employers need not request the information directly from employees or applicants. Instead, employers can acquire data on sex and racial or ethnic identity by conducting a visual survey of the work force and applicants. If visual inspections are not adequate, employers can request applicants and employees to supply the information voluntarily, as long as the following precautions are taken: (1) inquiries are requested on a separate form from the written application, and (2) the forms are maintained separately from personnel files or other records available to those responsible for making hiring decisions.

Employers who use "applicant flow" data or logs for affirmative action compliance may wish to generate the information as part of the preemployment process. However, relatively sophisticated controls need to be maintained with respect to access to the information. For smaller employers, information for EEO reporting or affirmative action compliance should be generated after employment and should be kept separate from other personnel documents.

Bona Fide Occupational Qualification

State and federal legislation provide a limited statutory defense to charges of discrimination if the employer can establish that the discriminatory criterion is a bona fide occupational qualification (BFOQ). However, this is an extremely narrow defense and has been strictly construed by courts and FEP agencies.

An employer should not refer to requested information during the preemployment process as a BFOQ because of the difficulty associated with proving the defense. If, for example, an employer hires only males for positions requiring heavy lifting based on a BFOQ, the employer has the virtually impossible burden of proving that all or substantially all women could not safely and efficiently perform the job. Therefore, any reference to a BFOQ during the preemployment process should be eliminated.

Common Law Considerations

If an employer's preemployment process fails to screen employees properly, an employer may find itself facing a lawsuit for defamation or negligent hiring or retention. Although beyond the scope of this chapter, employers may also be faced with wrongful discharge or employment discrimination lawsuits when employees are hired who are not qualified for their positions.

Common Law Limitations: Employment-Related Defamation Claims

Defamation is the unprivileged publication of a false statement tending to harm the reputation of another person. A statement may be either oral (slander) or written (libel). In the hiring stage, the potential for defamatory statements arises when a prospective employer contacts you concerning a former employee for an employment reference, or you are checking references of job applicants. The risks of defamation claims can be minimized if human resources personnel have a basic understanding of their state's defamation law.

ELEMENTS OF DEFAMATION

The common law elements of a defamation action are as follows: intentional or negligent communication to a third person, by the defendant (or an employee of the defendant) of an asserted fact, of and concerning the plaintiff, which tends to harm the reputation of the plaintiff. Although the final element of defamation requires that the plaintiff prove actual damage to his or her reputation, many states recognize five exceptions to this rule. These statements are defamatory per se, and the plaintiff need not prove any actual harm to recover damages. Damages are presumed if a statement imputes to the plaintiff one of the following:

1. The commission of some criminal offense involving moral turpitude
2. Affliction with some loathsome disease, which would tend to exclude the person from society
3. Unfitness to perform the duties of an office or employment, or the want of integrity in the discharge of the duties of such office or employment
4. Some falsity that prejudices the plaintiff in his or her profession or trade
5. Unchastity of a woman

An interesting development in the law of defamation relating to the employment context is the theory of self-publication. A few states have adopted an exception to the publication requirement whereby an employer may be liable for defamation where an employee is under a strong compulsion to disclose the contents of a defamatory statement made by the employer. The issue arises when an employee repeats reasons given for a discharge to a prospective employer, and then is not hired. For example, in one case, the plaintiff was terminated by the defendant for alleged dishonesty concerning absences from work for medical reasons. The court held that an employer could be liable for foreseeable or compelled self-publication if it had reason to believe that the employee would be under a strong compulsion to inform a third party of the contents of a defamatory statement. Thus, a claim was allowed to proceed based upon the "compulsion" to disclose the defamatory statement in applying for other jobs.

DEFENSES

In addition to truth being a defense, states have recognized numerous types of communications as being privileged from liability for defamation. A privilege may be absolute or qualified.

• *Absolute privilege.* An absolute, or unqualified, privilege extends to statements made during grievance arbitration proceedings, statements made in administrative unemployment compensation hearing, and statements made with the consent of the person defamed. An absolute privilege means complete immunity from liability for any defamatory statements. An absolute privilege has been extended to: (1) a judge or judicial officer performing a judicial function in a matter relating to such function; (2) parties to a judicial proceeding regarding matters relating to that proceeding; (3) legislators in the performance of their legislative functions; (4) witnesses testifying at or communicating preliminarily to a legislative proceeding regarding matters relating to that proceeding; (5) certain executive and administrative officers in communications made in the performance of their official duties; (6) one who is required by law to publish the defamatory matter; and (7) persons in statutory confidential relationships.

• *Qualified privilege.* An employer enjoys a qualified, or conditional, privilege to publish statements about an employee in good faith in the discharge of a public or private duty. A conditional privilege may be lost if abused. An abuse of the privilege occurs if: (1) there is actual malice on the part of the person making the statements, or (2) the statements exceed the scope necessary to accomplish the purpose. For example, in one case, the plaintiff was discharged after a security employee of the defendant reported to the store manager that the plaintiff had attempted to steal a television set. The plaintiff denied the charge and brought suit for defamation. The court held that even assuming the accusation of theft was untrue, the security guard was conditionally privileged to make the statements to his employer because they were made in the performance of his duty to protect store property. The security guard would have abused the privilege and would have been liable for defamation, however, if he had lacked belief or reasonable grounds for belief in the truth of the accusation or if he had made the statement to someone who lacked a legitimate interest in the subject matter of the statement.

Another case illustrates the difference between an absolute and qualified privilege in the context of an employment reference. The plaintiff applied for a job as a nurse-anesthetist. On the employment application, the plaintiff authorized the hospital to contact her former employer. The defendant (the former employer) told the prospective employer that the plaintiff "lacked professional competence." The plaintiff was denied employment because of a less than desirable reference and brought suit for defamation against her former employer. The court held that the defendant's conversation with the prospective employer was absolutely privileged because the prospective employer initiated the conversation pursuant to the plaintiff's consent contained in her employment application. What is interesting about this outcome is that while the plaintiff gave the consent to the prospective employer, the privilege protected the former employer. It is therefore important that former employers determine whether an employee has given his or her consent before responding to requests for references. Thus, if consent has been given, a communication given in this context may be subject to an absolute privilege. Where there is an absolute privilege, the statements could be false and malicious and they still would not be actionable.

Negligent Hiring and Retention

Negligent hiring and retention claims are recognized by many states and illustrate the importance of thoroughly screening applicants. Otherwise, an employer may be liable to third parties if it fails to exercise ordinary care in selecting and retaining employees.

A negligent hiring claim is different from a claim based upon the theory of *respondeat superior,* which is the general principle of law that holds an employer liable for the negligent or wrongful acts of an employee if such acts were done in the course and scope of employment. In contrast, under a negligent hiring or retention claim, an employer may be liable for acts of employees *outside* the scope of their employment if the employer knew or should have known that the employee posed an unreasonable risk of harm to others. For example, these claims commonly occur when an employee commits a crime against a third party where it was reasonably foreseeable that the employee and third party would come in contact as a result of the employment.

To support a claim for negligent hiring in New Mexico, for example, there must be evidence (1) that the employee was unfit for the nature of the job, (2) that it was foreseeable that the employee posed a risk to those with whom he or she would associate, and (3) that the employer knew or should have known that the employee was unfit. New Mexico courts have focused on the employer's inquiry or lack of inquiry into the employee's past and the employer's actual knowledge of the employee's past criminal record. The employer's knowledge of a criminal record alone may not be enough to impose liability; however, this knowledge, combined with other factors such as a background of violent behavior or an employer's knowledge of a drinking problem, may subject the employer to liability.

The cases in New Mexico thus far have focused on the foreseeability of an employee's misconduct. In one case, the plaintiff purchased a television set from the defendant, who sold and serviced appliances in customers' homes. Three nights after delivering the plaintiff's television, the defendant's delivery man broke into the plaintiff's home and raped her. Although the employer knew of the employee's past criminal record, there were no specific indications of violent behavior on the part of the employee to conclude that the employer could have foreseen that the employee would rape a customer during his off-duty time.

It should be emphasized that, as a general matter, where the conduct complained of occurs while the employee is on duty and on the employer's premises, courts are more likely to find the employer liable. In another case the court found the employer liable by the fact that the plaintiff was sexually assaulted by an on-duty hotel employee on the hotel premises. The employee had a history of alcohol abuse and violence on the job. In fact, after being terminated once by the employer for drinking on the job, the employee came to the hotel drunk to ask for his job back and became violent when asked to leave. Despite this, the defendant rehired the employee. Subsequently, the employee sexually assaulted the employer's son (the plaintiff), who was present on the employer's premises. The court held that the employer's knowledge of the employee's drinking problem and propensity for violence might make the possibility of a sexual assault foreseeable to the employer.

The principal difference between negligent hiring, supervision, and retention as a basis for employer liability is the time at which the employer is charged with the knowledge of the employee's unfitness. Negligent hiring occurs when, prior to the time of the employee's actual hiring, the employer knew or should have known of the employee's unfitness. Negligent supervision and retention focuses on whether or not an employer failed to train and supervise an employee reasonably, particularly in light of accusations of prior misconduct. For example, the Colorado Supreme Court recognized a claim for negligent supervision in the context of a Catholic priest accused of engaging in sexual intercourse with a female parishioner to whom the priest was providing marriage counseling. The plaintiff stated a claim against the Diocese of Colorado Springs on the ground that the diocese knew or should have known that the priest was engaging in conduct that was outrageous, negligent, and a breach of his fiduciary duty.

Practical Suggestions for Avoiding Liability

The following are some practical suggestions for avoiding liability that can be easily implemented.

- Review employment applications and components of the preemployment process to ensure that all inquiries are job related or have business justification.
- Avoid inquiries in areas that are on their face suspect.
- Get consent on preemployment inquiries. (This is extremely important.)
- Restrict access to EEO and affirmative action information.

• Keep I-9 forms and supporting data out of personnel files.

• Keep EEO and affirmative action information out of personnel files.

• Include a statement on application forms that the applicant must specify the position for which he or she is applying and that the applicant will not be considered if the applicant applies for ''any'' position. Otherwise, it is difficult to pair the application with a given position or to identify the applicant pool for purposes of assessing qualifications.

• Insist that employment application forms be filled out completely. Look for any gaps or unacceptable lost time in the application. The failure to fill out the form completely should alert you immediately to the possibility that important information has been omitted. Moreover, the failure to make sure all information has been supplied may be evidence of negligence giving rise to liability on negligent hiring and retention theories. The absence of complete information also makes refusal to hire and termination lawsuits much more difficult to defend.

• Applications should contain a provision making the application effective for only a specified period of time, e.g., thirty days. Without such a provision the relevant applicant pool for a given position is unnecessarily expanded. Furthermore, without such a provision, a charging party or plaintiff may point to an employee hired months after the rejected application was made and make this the basis of an employment discrimination charge. By limiting the effective date, an applicant could compare him- or herself only to another employee hired within thirty days of the date of the application.

• Include a statement on the application that you are an equal opportunity employer and/or affirmative action employer if you have an affirmative action plan in place.

• Include ''employment at will'' disclaimers. While disclaimers may prevent inquiries or statements in the employment application from forming part of an employment contract, it may not prevent a contract from being implied from the subsequent conduct of the parties. Moreover, disclaimers may not protect you from liability for wrongful termination based on tort theories (public policy cases). Make sure that the disclaimer is properly drafted to take into account conflicting oral or written statements.

• Don't hire off résumés. Applicants, particularly for exempt or professional positions, may conceal information by submitting a résumé in lieu of filling out an application. Employers who hire off résumés without obtaining information normally requested in a job application and a thorough background search are asking for trouble because résumés tend to conceal factors that are unfavorable to the candidate. Moreover, lawsuits involving professional, executive, or administrative employees are particularly difficult to defend because these plaintiffs tend to be sophisticated, better able to afford the costs of litigation than hourly employees, and more articulate. Also, employment decisions involving exempt employees are more difficult to begin with because of the greater amount of subjectivity inherent in the selection process for exempt positions.

• Do not release information about current or past employees or respond to reference queries about them without their written consent. If an employee refuses to execute a release, do not provide information other than verification of employment, dates of employment, and positions held.

• Provide training to persons involved in the hiring process and to supervisors regarding the most obvious pitfalls associated with the preemployment process.

Drug and Alcohol Testing

A major issue faced by employers in both the preemployment and employment context is whether to test for drug and alcohol use. This critical topic is addressed here at length, as well as being covered in Chapter 5.

The Drug and Alcohol Abuse Problem

Although statistical studies on drug and alcohol abuse are necessarily imprecise, the reported statistics are very troubling. The National Institute on Drug Abuse (NIDA) estimates that up to 7 percent of employees are daily substance abusers. It is further estimated that 5 percent of the population is addicted to an illicit drug. According to a survey of *Fortune* 500 companies that screen for drug use, performed by the National Institute on Drug Abuse, drug use by employees rose from 3 percent to 30 percent between 1982 and 1985. It has been estimated that 25 million Americans have tried cocaine, and 50–60 million Americans have tried marijuana. It is also estimated that 2 million Americans regularly use other stimulants, more than 1 million use sedatives without a prescription, and 100 million regularly use alcohol. The NIDA estimates that on any given day, 12–25 percent of employees ages 18 to 40 would test positive for illegal drug use.

Based on these statistics, every employer must necessarily assume that a significant portion of its employees abuse controlled substances and/or alcohol. Indeed, the workplace may provide the perfect opportunity for a drug dealer to distribute his or her product, since it is a natural location for drug transactions between employees. Buyers prefer to deal with sellers with whom they work, because they know the dealers and are thereby assured a high-quality product. Buyers can also obtain credit on purchases from dealers with whom they are friendly. For their part, dealers have a ready and captive market for their product in the work force. Dealers are able to extend credit because they are less likely to be ripped off when they see buyers on a daily basis and when the buyers have a source of income from continued employment.

The costs of drug and alcohol abuse to employers are high. A few years ago, the Research Triangle Institute estimated that the United States lost $26 billion annually from drug abuse, including $16.6 billion in lost productivity, $6.9 billion in theft, and $2.2 billion in medical costs. One study in 1986 estimated that the total cost to employers annually is close to $100 billion. These costs are manifested in numerous ways.

- Increased absenteeism. A Firestone Rubber Company study found that employee drug users are two and one-half times as likely to be absent as nonusers.
- Increased on-the-job injuries and workers compensation claims. The Firestone study found that drug users are four times as likely as nonusers to have accidents, and file five times the workers compensation claims of nonusers.
- Employee theft.
- Higher medical benefits costs.
- Lost productivity.
- Loss of customers.
- Liability for injuries caused to others by impaired employees.

Drug and Alcohol Tests

There are a variety of tests available to detect drug or alcohol use.

- *Urine tests.* The most widely used urine screening test is the Enzyme Multiplied Immunoassay Technique (EMIT). The EMIT test is inexpensive and can detect the presence of enzymes into which drugs metabolize. It is highly accurate but has a high false-positive rate (indicating drug use when no drug has been taken). False negatives have also been detected.
- *Gas chromatography and mass spectrometry.* This is the superior screening test. It is highly specific and very accurate and, accordingly, is much more expensive than the EMIT ($50–$100).
- *Blood tests.* Blood tests detect the presence of drugs or alcohol in the bloodstream but are of little value a few hours after the substance is ingested.
- *Saliva tests.* These tests are extremely nonspecific and are of questionable accuracy.
- *Hair tests.* These involve radioimmunoassay analysis of metabolites imbedded permanently in hair. Such tests can be performed on a single strand of hair, and according to companies offering the test, rough estimates can be made of the quantity of drugs consumed by the subject and of the date the drug was consumed. This test is more expensive than the EMIT test and is of unknown accuracy.

To Test or Not to Test?

ARGUMENTS IN FAVOR OF TESTING

Various arguments have been put forward in favor of drug and alcohol testing. It is claimed that:

- Testing will deter employees from drug and alcohol abuse.
- Testing will support educational efforts to increase public awareness of substance abuse.
- Testing will increase safety, reduce on-the-job accidents, and cut sick leave and medical costs.
- Testing will increase productivity.
- Testing will reduce on-the-job drug dealing and employee theft.
- Testing may result in lower insurance rates.
- Testing will reduce absenteeism and employee turnover.
- Testing will help the employer evaluate the character of applicants and employees (on the assumption that people who use drugs are not trustworthy).

ARGUMENTS AGAINST TESTING

There are also arguments against drug and alcohol testing.

- Under the best of circumstances, tests reflect only the presence or absence of drugs but do not discern whether the subject is impaired. Nor do the tests discern the time (or location) of the ingestion of drugs.
- False positives may result from laboratory errors, over-the-counter medications, prescription drugs, tea with coca leaves, poppy seeds, and Vicks inhalers. False positives can inaccurately stigmatize an individual as a drug user.
- By definition, testing involves an invasion of an individual's privacy. But if privacy is not invaded, there may be false negatives because the specimen was tampered with (by being diluted, substituted for, mixed with another substance, etc.).
- Drug tests may detect off-duty drug use, which may have no relationship to job performance. Many employers share the philosophy of employees who assert that "what I do on my own time is my business alone."
- Testing programs may have a negative impact on employee morale and union relations.
- Testing programs may spawn time-consuming and expensive litigation.
- A difficult philosophical question is whether drug abuse should be treated the same as alcohol abuse. Alcohol is far more prevalently abused than illegal drugs, but most employers do not focus their testing efforts on alcohol abuse.
- At present, the political winds are blowing in favor of employer drug testing, because of the nationally declared war on drugs. But what if the political winds should shift? Is it better to have tested and then stopped or never to have tested at all?

Potential Legal Liabilities Arising From Drug Testing

UNCONSTITUTIONAL SEARCH AND SEIZURE

The Fourth Amendment to the U.S. Constitution declares that unreasonable searches and seizures by the federal government are unconstitutional. Because the Fourteenth Amendment extends the Bill of Rights to the states, it is also unconstitutional for state and local governments to conduct such unreasonable searches and seizures. (This search and seizure theory is applicable only to public, not private, sector drug testing programs. But note that state constitutional provisions protecting privacy may be interpreted to encompass private as well as governmental action.)

Until two recent U.S. Supreme Court decisions, public sector employees were generally quite successful in court cases attacking drug testing as an unconstitutional search. In those cases where a constitutional attack failed, certain extenuating circumstances were present. First, if facts created a "reasonable suspicion" that a government employee was using illegal drugs, the testing of the employee was not unconstitutional. This line of cases strongly suggested that random drug testing *was* unconstitutional. However, a second exception to the unconstitutional search and seizure theory was when public employees were involved in highly sensitive or dangerous occupations, such as air traffic control, law enforcement, weapons manufacturing, or nuclear power plant operation. On March 21, 1989, the U.S. Supreme Court issued two decisions which—at minimum—express strong approval of these exceptions to the Fourth Amendment and may indicate that the Fourth Amendment simply does not prohibit public sector drug testing.

In the first case, *National Treasury Employees Union* v. *von Raab,* the Supreme Court upheld the U.S. Customs Service's suspicionless drug testing programs for employees who applied for promotion or transferred to positions involving the interdiction of illegal drugs or requiring the use of firearms. The Court recognized that a urinalysis test is a search under the Fourth Amendment, but it held that neither a warrant nor particularized suspicion is required for testing, because the government's compelling interest outweighs the individual employee's privacy concerns. The Court recognized the governmental interests in making sure that interdiction personnel were of unimpeachable integrity and that armed Customs Service employees do not have impaired perception and judgment.

In the second case, *Skinner* v. *Railway Labor Executives' Association,* the Court upheld Federal Railroad Administration regulations that required private railroads to administer blood and urine tests to railroad employees involved in certain train accidents and fatal incidents, and further authorized railroads administer breath and urine tests following certain accidents, incidents, and rule violations. The Court held that the testing was reasonable and constitutional, even without a warrant or reasonable suspicion that particular employees might be impaired. Essentially, the Court held that the governmental interest in railroad safety outweighs employees' privacy concerns. In reaching this conclusion, the Court noted that the railroad industry is pervasively regulated, and it alluded to the "administrative search" exception to the Fourth Amendment.

Most state constitutions contain search and seizure provisions similar to the Fourth Amendment or other provisions arguably limiting drug testing. Such challenges have had mixed results. Some state constitutions apply to private employers, but the vast majority are only applicable in the public sector.

COLLECTIVE BARGAINING AGREEMENTS

Private sector employers who have a collective bargaining relationship with a union are required by the federal labor laws to negotiate with the union concerning terms and conditions of employment. In mid-June 1989, the National Labor Relations Board ruled that an employer is legally required to negotiate with a union about a drug or alcohol testing program for incumbent employees, but the employer is *not* legally required to bargain about a drug testing program for job applicants. When a unionized employer unilaterally implements a drug testing program, it should expect an unfair labor practice charge as well as grievances under applicable labor contracts. Numerous arbitrators have ruled that a standard "management rights" clause in a collective bargaining agreement does not authorize an employer to implement a drug testing program.

HANDICAP DISCRIMINATION LAWS

The federal Rehabilitation Act of 1973 prohibits employment discrimination against "otherwise qualified individual[s] with handicaps" by government contractors and recipients of federal assistance, and it further requires such entities to make "reasonable accommodation" for such individuals. Most states have similar restrictions in their antidiscrimination laws. Although the law is not settled, drug or alcohol dependency or addiction is probably a handicap under the federal Rehabilitation Act and may also be a physical handicap under many states' laws. This likely means that former abusers and current alcohol or drug abusers who are undergoing rehabilitation must be afforded "reasonable accommodation," unless they pose a direct threat to property or the safety of others in the work environment.

The Americans with Disabilities Act (ADA) of 1990 also addresses drug issues.

- *Current drug users.* Employees or applicants who are currently engaging in the illegal use of drugs are specifically excluded from the protections of the ADA.
- *Former drug users.* A qualified person who has successfully completed a drug rehabilitation program, has otherwise been successfully rehabilitated and no longer uses illegal drugs, is participating in a supervised rehabilitation program and no longer uses illegal drugs, or is erroneously regarded as using illegal drugs is protected by the ADA.
- *Prohibition of drug and alcohol use.* An employer may prohibit the illegal use of drugs and the use of alcohol in the workplace, may require that employees not be under the influence of alcohol or using illegal drugs in the workplace, and may hold an employee who uses drugs or who is an alcoholic to the same standards of performance and behavior as other employees, even if unsatisfactory performance or behavior is related to drug or alcohol use.
- *Drug testing.* An employer may require drug testing, but not a test for prescription drugs taken for a disability, before a conditional offer of employment is made, without showing that the test is job related and consistent with business necessity. An offer of employment may be made strictly contingent upon a negative result for illegal substances.

INVASION OF PRIVACY

An invasion of privacy occurs if there is an intrusion into another person's private affairs that would be highly offensive to a reasonable person. The concepts developed under federal and state constitutional claims are increasingly being borrowed for use in invasion of privacy tort claims against private employers, and employees are challenging suspicionless drug testing as an unreasonable invasion of privacy. In such cases, therefore, we can anticipate the outcome to turn on factors such as whether the person is reasonably suspected of illegal drug use, the extent of the illegal drug problem in the employer's workplace, the extent of other regulations applicable to the employment relationship, the amount and type of notice to employees (for example, whether there is a written program), the employer's business justification for drug testing, and the reasonableness and sensitivity of the drug testing procedures.

Invasion of privacy claims may be based upon allegations of:

- "Substantial" and "offensive" intrusion
- Unreasonable search
- Interrogation or polygraph
- Use or dissemination of personnel files or medical information
- Inquiry into conduct outside the workplace
- State constitutional privacy provisions that may also apply

WRONGFUL DISCHARGE

Public policy and implied contract claims may be asserted in cases involving drug testing, depending upon the surrounding circumstances. However, plaintiffs to date have not been successful raising such claims.

The analysis of wrongful discharge claims arising from termination based on work-related drug and alcohol abuse or refusal to participate in screening is generally the same as that for any other termination.

Even where the employment relationship is not subject to a "just cause" standard for termination, an employer must act reasonably in light of applicable constitutional, statutory, and common law restrictions. An employer should also act consistently with stated personnel policies regarding drug testing, the employee handbook, oral representations, and termination procedures to avoid breach of an express or implied contract. If a drug and alcohol abuse policy is in effect and communicated to employees, the employer should follow its policy in each termination case.

In jurisdictions recognizing a public policy tort exception, state handicap discrimination laws, privacy statutes, or polygraph statutes might be considered sufficient expressions of public policy to support a claim for wrongful discharge. Where a "just cause" standard applies, a terminated employee may allege that termination for drug or alcohol use or refusal to participate in screening does not meet the standard.

INTENTIONAL INFLICTION OF EMOTIONAL DISTRESS

The existence of a drug testing program, and the termination of an employee based on drug testing results or the refusal to take a test, would not likely be considered extreme and outrageous conduct, giving rise to liability for intentional infliction of emotional distress. However, in at least one case, the procedures utilized in obtaining a urine specimen gave rise to such liability.

There are two theories on which a cause of action for emotional distress might be based: (1) distress caused by subjecting an employee to the choice of submitting to a medical examination or losing his or her job, and (2) distress caused by conducting an investigation and testing in a careless and undignified manner. A search or drug test performed pursuant to notice, based on reasonable, individualized suspicion and conducted in a way to maintain privacy and decorum, is not likely to give rise to a valid claim for intentional infliction.

LIBEL AND SLANDER

A plaintiff establishes a *prima facie* case of libel or slander by proving that a defamatory statement about him or her was communicated to a third person. An allegation of illegal drug use undoubtedly is defamatory.

Communication of medical test information, without first obtaining a release from an employee or applicant, risks a suit for defamation. In general, results of drug and alcohol tests should not be communicated outside the company for any reason. Internal communication must be limited strictly to a "need to know" basis.

Risk of liability for defamation is highest in responding to requests for references.

Generally, an employer's response to references is given a qualified privilege. But the privilege may be lost if there is malice or excessive publication.

ASSAULT AND BATTERY

Under traditional tort law, a battery is the unwanted and offensive touching of another, and an assault is an individual's apprehension of such an unwanted touching. Any type of physical or verbal force used by an employer or any agent of an employer in the process of obtaining a blood or urine sample may give rise to tort liability.

Tests should not be conducted if consent is not given. Torts of drug testing agents or polygraph examiners may be attributable to the employer.

NEGLIGENT HIRING OR RETENTION OF EMPLOYEES

An employer that fails adequately to screen applicants for employment or retains employees who have a drug or alcohol problem may be subject to liability, particularly third-party liability. A number of cases illustrate the point. In one case, an employee was awarded damages because the employer had assigned him work without first inspecting the employee for intoxication and physical disability. Because the employee had been drinking and was not physically able to do the work assigned, he was injured. In another case, an employer was sued for wrongful death by the surviving spouses of two persons killed in a car accident by an employee who appeared intoxicated and was sent home by the employer.

EQUAL EMPLOYMENT OPPORTUNITY CHALLENGES

An employer's practice of excluding all narcotics users from certain safety-sensitive positions, assuming the policy has a disparate impact on certain minority groups, is justified by business necessity. Some plaintiffs have theorized that drug testing programs have an unequal impact on certain racial or ethnic groups because a greater amount of skin melanin can cause false positives. Most drug testing cases have been disparate treatment cases, and drug testing programs have been held lawful as long as they were administered on a nondiscriminatory basis.

EMPLOYEE RETIREMENT INCOME SECURITY ACT

The Employee Retirement Income Security Act (ERISA) prohibits employers from discharging, suspending, or otherwise discriminating against employees "for the purpose of interfering with the attainment of any right" to which the employee is entitled or might become entitled. If an employer were to discharge drug abusers for the purpose of keeping anticipated medical costs down, the action arguably would be a violation of this provision of ERISA. Although this may pose a problem with regard to employee drug testing programs, ERISA nondiscrimination rules are inapplicable to applicants for employment.

MINE SAFETY AND HEALTH ACT

The case of *Secretary of Labor on Behalf of Price and Vacha* v. *Jim Walter Resources, Inc.* addressed issues of drug testing and its implications under Section 105(c) of the Mine Safety and Health Act. Jim Walter Resources, Inc., had a substance abuse program that applied to all hourly and salaried employees in its mining division. The program provided in part that an employee "whose duties, whether by job title or by reason of elected office, involve safety, shall be subject to random testing for substance abuse up to four times per calendar year." The only hourly employees affected by this provision were union safety committeemen. Judge Broderick concluded that this provision of the drug testing program violated Section 105(c). The EEOC granted review of this case in September 1988 and had not yet issued its ruling as of this writing.

STATE AND LOCAL LEGISLATION

Some states and cities have enacted statutes and ordinances to prohibit or restrict drug testing. Some prohibit drug testing without reasonable suspicion, some require advance notice to employees of a test, some require one or more confirmatory tests after positive test results, some control who receives the test results, and some require that any employer with such a program also have an employee assistance program (EAP). States with some statute on the books regarding drug testing include Connecticut, Florida, Iowa, Louisiana, Maine, Maryland, Minnesota, Montana, Nebraska, North Carolina, Rhode Island, Utah, and Vermont. Examples of state laws are as follows:

- *Minnesota*. Minnesota requires a written policy for any testing and sharply limits testing, generally to situations where there is reasonable suspicion of drug or alcohol use. An employer cannot fire an employee after the first, confirmed positive drug test unless the employee has been offered and refused participation in a drug or alcohol counseling or rehabilitation program.
- *Montana*. Montana law allows preemployment testing only for employment in hazardous work environments or for jobs the primary responsibility of which is security, public safety, or fiduciary responsibilities. Employees may be tested only if the employer "has reason to believe that the employee's faculties are impaired *on the job* as a result of alcohol consumption or illegal drug use" (emphasis added).
- *Utah*. Utah has adopted legislation that allows testing if the employer has a written policy, confirms positive tests, and maintains proper documentation. When these safeguards are followed, the employer is immune from liability.

Drug testing programs may also face indirect challenges under other state employment statutes. For example, the Oregon Court of Appeals in two cases involving the same company has ruled: (1) that off-the-job drug use is *not* misconduct that would warrant a denial of unemployment benefits, absent some showing that the off-duty conduct reasonably related to the employer's business; and (2) that an employee who quit his job rather than take a mandatory random drug test may be entitled to unemployment compensation benefits if he can establish that the random drug test requirement was an unreasonable job requirement.

Local ordinances should also be reviewed for possible limitations on testing programs.

Proposed federal legislation would preempt state and local restrictions on drug testing. Under proposed legislation, testing would have to be done by laboratories certified by the Department of Health and Human Services. Employers that test would have to have a written antidrug policy and a drug education program. The bill would allow testing of all job applicants, provided tests were consistently done in a nondiscriminatory manner. Testing of employees would be allowed when:

- The employer has reason to believe the employee is using or is under the influence of drugs or alcohol
- It is a part of a required scheduled physical
- Employees have been in an accident or near-accident involving significant threat to life or property
- Employees are undergoing drug or alcohol treatment

The bill would also allow random drug testing of employees in certain higher hazard positions and of professional athletes. The bill may open new areas for legal challenges to employers' drug testing procedures. Federal regulations over drug testing might give rise to constitutional challenges to private sector testing programs because federal regulation governing such policies could constitute government action.

Specific Federal Laws

DRUG-FREE WORKPLACE ACT OF 1988

The Drug-Free Workplace Act of 1988 covers all businesses that contract with the federal government to provide property or services worth $25,000 or more, within the United States. Although it is not completely clear, it appears that subcontractors of covered federal contractors are not subject to the Act. The Act also covers any recipient of federal grants, such as financial awards, cooperative agreements, block grants, and entitlement grant programs, regardless of dollar amount. Recipients of loans, veterans benefits, and services given in lieu of money are not subject. If a grant recipient passes funds through to subgrantees, the subgrantees are not subject to the legislation, but the initial recipient is.

The Act became effective on March 18, 1989, and is not retroactive; it applies only to contracts and grants awarded after that date. The legislation will probably also apply to contracts and grants that were awarded before the effective date, when and if they are modified after the effective date.

Employers covered by the Act must certify to the contracting agency that they have complied with the following, as a condition precedent to receiving the contract or grant.

- *Notice to employees.* The employer must publish a policy statement that notifies employees "engaged in the performance of" the contract or grant that unlawful manufacture, distribution, dispensation, possession, or use of a controlled substance is prohibited in the workplace. Sanctions for violations must be specified. The term *workplace* has been defined as "a site for the performance of work done in connection with a specific grant or contract." The policy statement must also notify employees that they must abide by the above policy and must inform the employer of any criminal drug statute conviction for a violation in the workplace, within five days of such conviction. (No action must be taken by the employee when a conviction relates to a drug statute violation away from the workplace.)

• *Notice to federal authorities.* The employer must notify the contracting agency within ten days after receiving actual notice (from any source) that any employee has been convicted of a criminal drug statute violation occurring in the workplace.

• *Drug-free awareness program.* The employer must also establish a drug-free awareness program, informing employees of the dangers of drug abuse in the workplace, the employer's policy on substance abuse, the penalties for violations, and any available drug counseling or rehabilitation program or employee assistance program. (The act does not require a covered employer to provide a counseling or rehabilitation program or EAP.)

• *Appropriate sanction.* The employer must also impose an appropriate sanction or require satisfactory completion of a drug assistance or rehabilitation program, within thirty days of notice of an employee conviction.

In addition, the employer must make good faith effort to continue to maintain a drug-free workplace. The Act does not require drug or alcohol testing. Employers who violate the Act may be subject to penalties: suspension of payments, termination of contract or grant, or government disbarment for up to five years.

TRANSPORTATION DEPARTMENT REGULATIONS

The U.S. Department of Transportation in November 1988 issued regulations affecting a wide range of employers governed by the Federal Highway Administration, Federal Aviation Administration, Federal Railroad Administration, Urban Mass Transportation Administration, Research and Special Projects Administration, and the U.S. Coast Guard. Such regulations require employees whose jobs include safety- or security-related functions to be tested for illegal drug use.

The District of Columbia Court of Appeals recently upheld certain of the DOT regulations, but it ruled that the Urban Mass Transportation Administration (UMTA) has no authority to require recipients of federal mass transit funds to adopt drug testing requirements because Congress did not give the UMTA regulatory authority over urban mass transit authority.

DEPARTMENT OF DEFENSE INTERIM RULE ON DRUG-FREE WORK FORCE

The interim rule applies only to Department of Defense (DOD) contracts involving access to classified information, or whenever a contracting officer determines it necessary for national security, health, or safety. The rule does not apply to subcontractors or to contracts performed outside the United States. The interim rule became effective on October 31, 1988.

Under the rule, contractors must have a drug awareness program that includes, at minimum, the following.

• Random testing of current employees in ''sensitive positions.'' The DOD has stated that the adequacy of the program will be judged according to the nature of the work being performed, the employee's duties, the employer's resources, and the risk to the public welfare if the employee should fail to perform his or her duties adequately. The contractor may establish a program for employee testing when there is a reasonable suspicion that an employee is using drugs, when an employee has been involved in an accident or unsafe practice, or as follow-up to counseling or rehabilitation. Similarly, the contractor may establish a program to test applicants for illegal drug use.

• An EAP to deal with drug abuse.

• Personnel procedures to deal with drug abusers. Contractors may not allow an employee who tests positively to remain in a sensitive position until such time as the employee is satisfactorily rehabilitated.

The DOD has stated that it will not monitor or inspect contractors covered by the rule unless it has reason to suspect noncompliance.

EXECUTIVE ORDER 12564

Each federal agency is covered by Executive Order 12564, which President Ronald Reagan signed on September 15, 1986. It was effective immediately. It has been estimated that approximately 1.1 million federal civilian employees are affected by the executive order.

Under the order, each federal agency is required to establish a drug testing program for its civilian employees. The program must include cocaine and marijuana testing and may include testing for opiates, amphetamines, and phencyclidine. Testing for other drugs is not permissible without special permission unless reasonable suspicion, an accident, or an unsafe practice exists. Testing techniques must follow guidelines issued by the Department of Health and Human Services, which include privacy in the collection of specimens, the reporting of test results to a medical review officer of the agency for interpretation, confirmation of positive test results, use of certified laboratories, and retention of positive specimens for at least one year.

The United States Court of Appeals for the Fifth Circuit has upheld the executive order, saying any challenges must be directed to the individual agency's plans promulgated pursuant to this order.

Considerations Regarding Drug Testing Programs

Many factors should be considered before a drug testing program is established. Legal issues must be taken into account.

• *Check state and local restrictions.* Check state and local laws to determine if any statutes or ordinances may limit or regulate testing.

• *Are you a public or private employer?* Because of the constitutional theories discussed above, public sector employers have less latitude than private employers when adopting and implementing drug testing programs. Public employers can anticipate legal claims in all of the areas discussed in this chapter. Private employers at present can operate without undue concern over federal constitutional restrictions, but they are still vulnerable to claims under state statutory and common law theories.

• *Do you have a union?* If the employees to be tested are not represented by a union, you have much greater freedom to implement drug testing programs than if the employees are represented by a union. If employees are represented by a union, the employer must comply with existing collective bargaining agreements and negotiate with the representative union.

• *Do you want to test applicants and/or employees?* The testing of applicants is legally safer than the testing of employees, simply because they have not developed "squatter's rights" in employment.

• *Why do you want to test?* This is an important question. If you have public safety concerns, your testing program will be relatively easy to defend. Likewise, issues of the safety of the individual employee and his or her fellow employees may be a major factor in a testing program. This is especially true in heavy industries such as mining and construction. Your business justification for testing may ultimately be weighed against your employees' privacy interests. The answer to this question will also help you to decide which employees or applicants are to be tested, the circumstances under which they should be tested, the appropriate penalties for positive test results, and whether a disciplinary or rehabilitative response will be taken by the employer.

• *When do you want to test?* Private sector employers have more latitude than public sector employers in choosing whether to test on random, reasonable cause, periodic, or across-the-board occasions. Testing is most defensible when it is based upon some form of reasonable cause. For example, observation of aberrant behavior, erratic attendance, or involvement in an accident may be listed as justifications for reasonable cause testing.

• *Prepare a comprehensive written policy.* Eliminate any doubt that use, distribution, possession, or sale of controlled substances or alcohol during working hours or on the employer's premises are prohibited by preparing a comprehensive written policy against drug and alcohol abuse. The policy should expressly prohibit the switching or adulteration of any urine sample submitted for testing. It should also state that a refusal to submit a urine specimen for testing, when requested by management, will not be tolerated. Last, indicate that any of the above will result in disciplinary action, at the discretion of management.

• *Give notice to employees.* Employers should give written notice to applicants and employees that they will be subject to drug and alcohol testing.

• *Get employee consent.* If an employer is able to obtain an employee's consent to a test, the employer will have obtained a valuable defense in much litigation.

• *Are physical examinations required?* An employer that has mandatory physical examinations for applicants or employees, particularly if the examinations include urinalysis and blood tests, is better able to defend drug testing than those employers without such examinations. If you have been considering such examinations, you may wish to implement a comprehensive physical examination program. Realize, however, that your physical examination program must comply with the provisions of the ADA. Employees should be advised if drug testing is to be done as a part of a physical. It may not be enough to have consent to do urinalysis or blood tests if the employee is not advised of the fact that a check for drugs is included.

• *Train personnel who are charged with enforcement.* A well-designed policy is worthless if it is not properly followed. Those whose job it is to administer the policy must be carefully and thoroughly trained in order to minimize any risk of liability that might arise from inconsistent or incomplete testing procedures.

• *Select a certified, reputable, and independent laboratory.* Carefully select the laboratory that will conduct your drug and alcohol tests. It should employ state-of-the art quality control and be under the direction of a board-certified toxicologist. If possible, have all of your work performed by the same laboratory for uniformity, and if possible, use a federally certified laboratory. A chain of custody procedure should be rigorously observed.

• *Set in advance the types of tests you will use.* Consider that the less intrusive the test, the more specific and accurate the test, the safer the program from litigation.

• *Set cutoff levels in advance.* Confer with the laboratory in advance and set in writing what cutoff levels will result in a positive test finding. Advise your employees of that standard.

• *Avoid the adulteration of urine samples.* Confer with your laboratory about procedures that will be followed to prevent the adulteration of urine specimens. Personal observation of the employee giving the specimen is probably necessary if precautions are taken, such as testing the sample's temperature.

• *Afford employees the opportunity to explain a positive test result.* When the specimen is given, employees should be given the opportunity to list drugs or medications they have taken in the previous thirty days and allowed to explain the circumstances. Don't wait until after the employee has tested positive.

• *Conduct at least one confirmatory test.* Based on current scientific data, no employer should take any adverse employment action based on a single positive test result. Confirm a positive test with a second test (with a new sample) that is at least as sensitive and more specific than the first. (Using an EMIT test to confirm positive results on another EMIT test results in 98 percent accuracy.) You must rely on the results of the second test. If the first test is positive and the second test is negative, the employee tested negative.

• *Assure confidentiality of test results.* Test results should be disclosed on a strictly "need to know" basis. Employment decisions based upon test results should also be kept confidential. Keep any employment records reflecting the results of drug testing in locked or restricted access areas.

• *Give employees the test results.* You should give employees the opportunity to explain or challenge positive test results. You might wish to afford this opportunity to applicants as well.

• *Enter into a written agreement with any employee in rehabilitation.* If you give an employee a chance at rehabilitation, enter into a written agreement with the employee outlining the conditions for continued employment, including random postrehabilitation testing, immediate termination on any positive test result (with a positive confirmation test), and immediate discharge for any refusal to provide a urine sample at management's request.

• *Do you need to do more than test?* Many employers are beginning to question whether additional steps should be taken against substance abuse and illegal drug trafficking. Consider whether you need to search lockers, lunch boxes, purses, backpacks, briefcases, and so on. If you decide that such searches are necessary, formulate a written policy providing for such unscheduled searches, and distribute the policy to employees in advance.

Epilogue

19

Issues for Tomorrow

Mary F. Cook
President
Mary Cook & Associates

Facing Critical Issues

Destined for change, U.S. companies are concerned about how the future work force will affect business and ultimately the bottom line. As we move through the 1990s and beyond, recruitment and retention will become increasingly critical elements of the HR function. Here are some of the most critical issues we will have to confront and how they affect recruitment and retention.

Changing Demographics

As stated earlier in this book, the work force is getting older, and more women and minorities are holding jobs than ever before. They will make up the primary entrants to the workplace in the 1990s, and the diversity of the work force will create the biggest challenge for organizations. Companies will need a variety of new programs and processes in order to attract and retain these workers. Older workers, for example, need more medical coverage and realistic retirement plans. Families may want extended maternity or parental leave and more time off with pay to attend to family matters.

Pressures of Family and Work Life

Organizations will need to adopt new programs to support employees and their families—not only day care assistance, but elder care and a larger concern for the integration of home and work life. The average worker in the 1990s will be a single head of the family or half of a dual-career couple and have family assistance needs of one kind or another. Increasingly, work will move from the normal workplace to a variety of unconventional sites and arrangements, in part to serve these family needs.

Immigrant Work Force

The United States is a nation of immigrants, almost as much today as it was one hundred years ago. Julian L. Simon, author of *The Economic Consequences of Immigration,* believes that immigrants of every class and skill level invigorate the economy These immigrants are needed, especially in certain industries that face serious shortages of skilled workers. Congress is working to address these shortages through immigration relief. An example is the Immigration Nursing Relief Act of 1989, designed to benefit health care facilities experiencing a shortage of registered nurses by exempting from the annual national quota for permanent U.S. residency status those foreign nurses who have legally worked as registered nurses in the United States for at least three years, and who began work before September 1, 1989.

Supervisors and managers will need to become bilingual and cross-cultural as more foreign companies build operations in the Untied States and more foreign workers embark on our shores. New York State is already trying new programs to assimilate this growing immigrant work force. New York City's five-month Training Program in Human Services Counseling, funded by the state's Refugee Entrant Assistance Program, prepares immigrants to become paraprofessional bilingual counselors and helps them to find jobs. Although not targeted specifically at older people, fifty-one out of the program's 418 graduates have been forty-five years old or older. Representing more than fifteen cultural and linguistic groups, program participants have been employed as interpreters, bilingual case aides, educational assistants, and case workers in the city's health, educational, social service, and child welfare agencies. The program makes a unique contribution. It enables immigrants to find stable employment and economic self-sufficiency. At the same time, it helps agencies expand their bilingual staff capacity, while improving services to clients. Corporations may decide to try this type of program to attract badly needed technical and professional applicants.

Women in the Executive Suite

There is still a condescending attitude in some organizations toward the promotion of women into top management positions. But as the need for talented, high-performance individuals increases, this attitude and practice will change. It will also change because of the sheer force of numbers. Over the next few years women will force open the doors to the executive suite and will demand higher positions and equal pay.

Some organizations are already ahead of the game when it comes to promoting qualified women. At Fannie Mae, the work force is 60 percent women. Former CEO David Maxwell consistently provided promotion and recognition for qualified women by placing them in highly visible job positions. During his tenure in the 1980s and early 1990s, Maxwell increased the number of women in management from 4 percent in 1981 to 32 percent in 1991. Placing women in highly visible jobs where they will be successful sends a signal to the rest of the organization. The culture at Fannie Mae was solidified when Maxwell hired a woman to be the company's general counsel and secretary.

Literacy and Technical Competence

The United States is the center of scientific and technical education and has the world's largest technically educated work force. Yet a critical issue for companies in the 1990s will be finding and retaining a literate, technically competent work force. Critical skills are already in short supply, and corporations are reaching into the educational system to influence the quality of workers. At a time when the U.S. work force as a whole is better educated (one in four U.S. workers is a college graduate), corporations are still having problems with deficiencies in workers' basic skills level. More organizations will find themselves teaching basic reading, writing, math, and computer skills as the 1990s continue.

Retraining

More than 8 million workers have been laid off or terminated since the late 1980s. These workers may never work again in their fields. If organizations do not take action to help retrain this work force, these workers will eventually join the welfare ranks or be part of the chronically unemployed. This is a growing and serious issue and should be a serious concern of U.S. industry. Management must rethink its prejudices about hiring and retraining older workers and displaced workers, because they will be badly needed by the year 2000.

MOBILITY

The average American moves every six years, and eleven times in a lifetime. Now more than ever before, people are moving in order to get jobs. A mobile work force means that employers can attract skilled workers to new sites, making it easier to relocate closer to markets and resources.

The Emerging Global Society

In recent years, U.S. business has not thought much about hiring foreign nationals or about sending more American workers overseas to offshore operations. In the future, with an increasingly global society, these elements of recruitment will be commonplace, and organizational policies and systems will accommodate the global work force. We will need improved expatriate policies and procedures and well-developed systems of pay, benefits, and perks for employees going overseas.

The Costs of Labor

U.S. companies will have to confront growing competition at home and abroad from organizations with lower labor costs and faster product-to-market rates. Employers must contain labor costs while producing higher-quality goods and services with a smaller work force—not an easy task. More companies are moving offshore for lower labor rates, but unemployed U.S. workers are getting angry, and there is bound to be a backlash. Labor and management must work together to find a better solution.

Health Care Costs

The U.S. system of health care is now the costliest in the world. According to the U.S. Department of Health and Human Services, the United States spends over 171 percent more on health care per person than Great Britain, 124 percent more than Japan, and 38 percent more than Canada. In 1990 the medical bill in the United States totaled approximately $666 billion, or about $2,664 for each man, woman, and child. Health care spending consumes 11.5 percent of the gross national product, and yet the United States ranks seventeenth in life expectancy, behind Italy, France, Japan, and the Scandinavian countries.

The cost of medical care has forced insurance premiums so high that thousands of companies and millions of people can't afford coverage. In the 1980s, most CEOs believed employee insulation from health care costs was the major cause of escalating costs. To address that issue and to cut their expenditures, most companies have increased the portion of health benefits costs paid by their employees. They have also incorporated cost management techniques into their health benefits programs, such as managed care programs, hospital precertification, second opinion surgery requirements, and alternative delivery systems like HMOs and PPOs. No one strategy has emerged as a long-term solution to controlling health care costs, and employers are concerned about the future of health care as an employee benefit. Since most attempts at cost containment have not worked and since there has been little substantive direction from Congress or the White House, costs are not likely to decline anytime soon. This is a significant issue when it comes to the recruitment and retention of good people.

Increased Use of Industrial Robots

General Motors has 5,000 robots on the job and plans to have at least 14,000 in the 1990s, replacing 28,000 assembly line workers. The growth of robots is taking place for three primary reasons: (1) the development of the microprocessor, a computer small enough to use as the "brains" of a robot; (2) wage inflation, which is causing companies to look for cheaper labor alternatives; and (3) the fact that robots can do dangerous work that would otherwise expose people to workplace hazards. In the 1970s, a typical assembly line robot cost about $4.20 an hour to operate (averaged over its lifetime), just slightly higher than the average factory worker's wages and benefits. Today the robot can still be operated for under $5 an hour, while most employees in the auto industry make between $15 and $25 an hour.

Most large industrial countries today are planning giant steps in the design and utilization of robots. The technology is moving so fast that it's difficult to keep track of the numbers and types of robots actually in place worldwide. Both labor and management are taking steps to soften the impact of increasing numbers of industrial robots by providing resources for the retraining of displaced workers and the maintenance of current salary levels for workers placed into lower-rated jobs. Still, robot usage will become a labor issue as more workers are displaced.

The Changing Worker

Changes in the workplace and in society at large have caused the American worker to change as well. New attitudes and perceptions held by employees pose a challenge for employers that will grow as we near the year 2000.

Worker Frustration

Frustration is growing among employees as they begin to demand a better work environment and solutions to workplace problems. The problems that are important to employees—work and family issues, health care costs, pay equity, benefits for unmarried and same-sex partners, drug abuse, job security, employer surveillance—are not being fully addressed by most employers or the federal government. Workers are becoming activists, and they demand solutions to problems that management seems to be neglecting. This is a retention problem, but also a recruitment issue: Savvy applicants today are asking some tough questions before they accept a job.

The Effects of Downsizing

Downsizing began with the industrial work force, went on to hit the energy industry, proceeded to white collar workers, and now affects the composition of all industries and all types of companies in all areas of the United States. This drastic downsizing has caused a huge change in the way people think about the companies they work for. Employee loyalty has been significantly impacted. So has the hierarchical structure. The middle-management level was almost completely eliminated in some organizations, and companies will likely stay lean in the middle-management ranks. Downsizing has had its effects beyond those who lost their jobs. The people who are left after a layoff are almost as traumatized, making ongoing retention programs especially important.

Rebuilding Employee Loyalty

When U.S. organizations started downsizing, reorganizing, pushing early retirement, and cutting entire levels of management, they lost an important element of success: employee loyalty. This taken-for-granted relationship has been ruptured. Employees once thought that as long as they worked hard and were loyal to their organization, they had a job for life. Then huge numbers of workers were fired or laid off. Now, as these workers move back into the work force, their commitment to an organization is tentative—as is that of employees who kept their jobs but lost their sense of security when they saw how quickly others were let go. Businesses must rebuild that sense of loyalty and commitment in employees who have experienced the trauma of unemployment.

Part-Time Workers: The Shadow Work Force

Hourly part-time work is keeping a huge segment of the work force in low-pay, no-benefits jobs. (This is not the same as regular part-time work, for which employees get some benefits and salaries.) There is rising dissatisfaction among the more than 6 million Americans who are part-time workers but who want the pay and benefits of a full-time position. On average, hourly part-time workers make $5.00 per hour, compared with the $7.80 per hour average pay of full-time workers. At this level, part-timers who are lucky enough to work a full 2,000 hours a year are still only at the federal poverty level. This is an issue that will lead to labor-management conflict, as part-time workers begin to seek higher pay and benefits.

Employer Surveillance

Big Brother seems to be alive in many U.S. companies. Even though at least seven states have passed laws that give employees the right to inspect their personnel files, most workers are uninformed as to what kind of information those files contain. The Medical Information Bureau in Greenwich, Connecticut, says that employers keep medical files on at least 11 million workers. In addition, according to a report entitled the *Electronic Supervisor* prepared by the congressional Office of Technology Assessment, computers monitor more than 7 million workers, keeping track of their rest breaks and productivity. As this type of employer surveillance increases, workers will rebel, and Big Brother issues will have to be addressed. This is certainly going to be an employee retention issue.

A New Look at the Environment

In recent years we have seen the greening of corporate America, after decades of irresponsible behavior on the part of some corporations with regard to the environment. Companies are looking for credibility in their environmental actions because they know they can win points with their employees and the public if they effectively manage pollution control programs, recycle materials, and alter toxic processes, technologies, and products. Employee opinion and public opinion are turning against companies that are not conscious of the environment, and are doing something about it. Consumers may favor "green" companies by buying their products. And employees may prefer to work for companies that act in a responsible, committed way toward the environment.

The Fastest Growing Jobs in America

As we look at the key issues impacting the United States in the 1990s, we should also look at the areas of job growth. What jobs will organizations be recruiting for most often by the year 2000? The U.S. Bureau of Labor Statistics, in its publication *Job Outlook in Brief*, from the *Occupational Outlook Handbook 1991*, lists the fastest growing jobs through the year 2000. (See Exhibit 19-1.)

Health care services will be among the fastest growing jobs in this decade, with health-related jobs composing seven of ten of the fastest growing jobs. Overall, employment in health industries will grow from 8.2 million jobs in 1988 to 10.2 million by the year 2000.

Topping the list of the fastest growing jobs in the United States are paralegals, with a projected 75 percent increase in the number of jobs that will open up in the 1990s; 62,000 new jobs are expected. In the health field, other hot careers include medical assistants (104,000 new jobs), homemaker/home health aides (207,00 new jobs), and medical secretaries (120,000 new jobs). Outside the health area, we find securities and financial services representatives (109,000 new jobs), computer-system analysts (214,000 new jobs), and computer programmers (250,000 new jobs).

While the fastest growing jobs will be an important part of the overall growth of the labor market, it is important to understand the effects of major trends within the society and within major occupational groups as well. One of these major trends is that many jobs will require more education, particularly specialized training beyond high school. Three of the fastest growing occupational groups will be the executive, admin-

Exhibit 19-1. The fastest growing jobs in the United States, 1988–2000.

Occupation	Number of New Jobs	Percentage Increase
1. Paralegals	62,000	75%
2. Medical assistants	104,000	70
3. Radiologic technologists	87,000	66
4. Homemaker/home health aides	207,000	63
5. Medical record technicians	28,000	60

6. Medical secretaries	120,000	58
7. Physical therapists	39,000	57
8. Surgical technologists	20,000	56
9. Securities and financial services representatives	109,000	55
10. Operations research analysts	30,000	55
11. Travel agents	77,000	54
12. Actuaries	8,500	54
13. Computer-system analysts	214,000	53
14. Physical- and corrective-therapy assistants	21,000	52.5
15. Social welfare service aides	47,000	51.5
16. EEG technologists	3,200	50
17. Occupational therapists	16,000	49
18. Computer programmers	250,000	48
19. Service sales representatives	216,000	45
20. Human services workers	53,000	45
21. Health services managers	75,000	42
22. Corrections officers	76,000	41
23. Respiratory therapists	23,000	41
24. Receptionists	331,000	40
25. Electrical and electronics engineers	176,000	40
26. Employment interviewers	33,000	40
27. Registered nurses	613,000	39
28. Flight attendants	34,000	39
29. Licensed practical nurses	229,000	37
30. Recreational therapists	9,500	37
31. Management analysts and consultants	46,000	35
32. Computer and office-machine repairers	44,000	35
33. Podiatrists	5,700	35
34. Information clerks	441,000	34
35. Guards	256,000	32
36. Engineering, science, and data-processing managers	83,000	32
37. Nursing aides and psychiatric aides	405,000	31
38. Aircraft pilots	26,000	31
39. Dispensing opticians	16,000	31
40. Lawyers and judges	188,000	30
41. Child care workers	186,000	30
42. Actors, directors, and producers	24,000	30
43. Nuclear-medicine technologists	3,000	30
44. Meteorologists	1,800	30
45. Social workers	110,000	29
46. Computer and peripheral equipment operators	92,000	29
47. Underwriters	30,000	29
48. Landscape architects	5,500	29
49. Engineering technicians	203,000	28
50. Physicians	149,000	28

Source: Job Outlook in Brief, 1990–1991, and *The Occupational Outlook Quarterly,* 1991, both published by the U.S. Department of Labor.

istrative, and managerial; professional specialty; and technicians. Not surprisingly, these occupations usually require the highest levels of education and skill.

Meanwhile, jobs that require less education and skill are disappearing. Office and factory automation, changes in consumer demand, and increased use of imports will cause employment to stagnate or decline in many occupations that require little formal educational. Laborers, assemblers, and machine operators will decline in number. Opportunities for high school dropouts will become increasingly limited. Illiterate workers will find it difficult, if not impossible, to find jobs.

Tomorrow

What's obvious to human resources professionals is the fact that most workers today no longer respond to the old "carrots and sticks" approach to motivation. As the nature of work changes (and it is changing drastically), so does our motivation for doing it. Today's workers value autonomy. They value time off to be with their family. They want to combine work, leisure, family, and physical well-being in a balanced life that has continuous self-improvement and growth as its goal.

Michael Maccoby, in his book *Why Work: Leading the New Generation,* calls this new breed of workers "self-developers." How can employers keep these extremely independent people happy? Maccoby says, "Self-developers dislike jobs that only offer money as a reward. They prefer work that allows for development and exercise of their skills and abilities . . . they are also rewarded by a sense of being needed, of having a unique, necessary, meaningful role."[1]

Tomorrow brings unique challenges to recruiters. There are people of all sorts ready to work—people of all ages, of both sexes, of many diverse groups—but they won't jump at our jobs. They will be more questioning of our corporate values and practices, and it will be even more difficult and challenging to retain this tremendously independent and diverse work force.

Note

1. Michael Maccoby, *Why Work: Leading the New Generation* (New York: Simon & Schuster, 1988).

Resources for Recruitment and Retention

A variety of resources are listed to aid in your recruitment and retention efforts. The magazines and newspapers can be used for the placement of recruiting ads, and the ads they run can serve as models.

Magazines

Advertising Age
220 E. 42nd Street
New York, NY 10017
(212) 210-0167

Aero Space Engineering
400 Commonwealth Drive
Warrendale, PA 15096
(412) 776-4841

Affirmative Action Register
8356 Olive Boulevard
St. Louis, MO 63132
(314) 991-1335

Affirmative Journal of Nursing
555 W. 57th Street
New York, NY 10019
(212) 582-8820

American Scientist
99 Alexander Drive
Research Triangle Park, NC 27709
(919) 549-4691

Automation
1100 Superior Avenue
Cleveland, OH 44114
(216) 696-7000

Aviation Week & Space Technology
1221 Avenue of the Americas
New York, NY 10020
(212) 512-2294

Black Careers
PO Box 8214
Philadelphia, PA 19101
(212) 387-1600

Black Employment & Education Journal
6433 Topanga Canyon Boulevard, Suite 401
Canoga Park, CA 91303
(818) 716-0071

Black Resource Guide
501 Oneida Place NW
Washington, DC 20011
(202) 291-4373

Byte
1 Phoenix Mill Lane
Peterborough, NH 03258
(603) 924-9281

Careers and the Handicapped
44 Broadway Street
Greenlawn, NY 11740
(516) 261-8899

Chemical Engineering
1221 Avenue of the Americas
New York, NY 10020
(212) 512-4653

Chemical Week
810 Seventh Avenue, 9th Floor
New York, NY 10019
(212) 586-3430

Civil Engineering
345 E. 47th Street
New York, NY 10017
(212) 705-75514

Communications
6300 S. Syracuse Way, Suite 650
Englewood, CO 80111
(303) 220-0600

Communications News
120 W. Second Street
Duluth, MN 55802
(218) 723-9531

Communications Week
600 Community Drive
Manhasset, NY 10030
(516) 562-5000

Computer
10662 Los Vaqueros Circle
Los Alamitos, CA 90720
(714) 821-8380

Computerworld
Box 9171
375 Cochituate Road
Framingham, MA 01701-9171
(508) 879-0700

CPA Journal
200 Park Avenue, 10th Floor
New York, NY 10166-0010
(212) 973-8300

Data Communications
1221 Avenue of the Americas
New York, NY 10020
(212) 512-2039

Design News
275 Washington Street
Newton, MA 02158-1630
(617) 964-3030

Electrical World
11 W. 19th Street
New York, NY 10011
(212) 337-4060

Electronic Business
275 Washington Street
Newton, MA 02158-1630
(617) 964-3030

Electronic Buyers News
600 Community Drive
Manhasset, NY 11030
(516) 562-5000

Government Computer News
8601 Georgia Avenue, Suite 300
Silver Spring, MD 20910
(301) 650-2000

Help Wanted Weekly
1008 E. Baseline, #925
Tempe, AZ 85283
(602) 839-5627

Hispanic Engineer
729 E. Pract Street, Suite 504
Baltimore, MD 21202
(301) 244-7101

Hispanic Times Magazine
PO Box 579
Winchester, CA 92396
(714) 926-2119

Hospitals
211 E. Chicago Avenue, Suite 700
Chicago, IL 60611
(312) 440-6800

Industrial Engineering
25 Technology Park
Atlanta, GA 30092
(404) 449-0460

Information Week
600 Community Drive
Manhasset, NY 10030
(516) 562-5000

Infoworld
1060 Marsh Road
Menlo Park, CA 94025
(415) 328-4602

Journal of Accounting
1211 Avenue of the Americas
New York, NY 10036
(212) 575-6200

Journal of the American
Medical Association
515 N. State Street
Chicago, IL 60610
(312) 464-2456

Management Accounting
10 Paragon Drive
Montvale, NJ 07645
(201) 573-6275

Mechanical Engineering
345 E. 47th Street
New York, NY 10017
(212) 705-7722

Mining Engineering
8307 Shaffer Parkway
Littleton, CO 80127
(303) 973-9550

Minority Engineer
44 Broadway Street
Greenlawn, NY 11740
(516) 261-8899

Nursing Career Directory
1111 Bethlehem Pike
Springhouse, PA 19477
(215) 646-8700

Nursing Opportunities
600 Kinderkamack Road
Oradell, NJ 07549
(201) 262-3030

Oil & Gas Journal
1421 S. Sheridan Road
Tulsa, OK 74112
(918) 835-3161

Omni
1965 Broadway
New York, NY 10020
(212) 496-6100

PC Week
800 Boylston Street, 11th Floor
Boston, MA 02199
(617) 497-2526

Peterson's Recruiting Guide
PO Box 2123
202 Carnegie Center
Princeton, NJ 08543-2123
(609) 243-9111, Ext. 400

Petroleum Engineer International
PO Box 1589
Dallas, TX 75221
(214) 691-3911

Software Magazine
1900 W. Park Drive
Westborough, MA 01581
(508) 366-2031

Systems Integration
275 Washington Street
Newton, MA 02158-1630
(617) 964-3030

Telecommunications
685 Canton Street
Norwood, MA 02062
(617) 769-9750

Unixworld
444 Castro Street
Mountain View, CA 94041
(415) 940-1500

Voice of Physically Challenged
1211 N. Westshore Boulevard, Suite 702
Tampa, FL 33607
(813) 874-5550

World Oil
3301 Allen Parkway
Houston, TX 77252
(713) 529-4301

Newspapers

Akron Beacon Journal
44 E. Exchange Street
Akron, OH 44328
(216) 375-8503

Albany Times Union
News Plaza
645 Albany-Shaker Road
Albany, NY 12205
(518) 454-5410

Albuquerque Journal
Box J-T
Albuquerque, NM 87103
(505) 823-7777

Arizona Republic/Gazette
120 E. Van Buren
Phoenix, AZ 85004
(602) 271-8704

Arkansas Democrat
Capital Avenue & Scott Street
Little Rock, AR 72201
(501) 378-3469

Atlanta Journal and Constitution
72 Marietta Street
Atlanta, GA 30303
(404) 526-5151

Baltimore Sun
501 N. Calvert Street
Baltimore, MD 21278
(301) 332-6000

Baton Rouge State-Times
PO Box 588
Baton Rouge, LA 70821
(504) 383-1111

Birmingham News
2200 N. Fourth Avenue
Birmingham, AL 35202
(205) 325-2222

Boston Globe
135 Morrissey Boulevard
Boston, MA 02107
(617) 929-2000

Boston Herald
1 Herald Square
Boston, MA 02106
(617) 426-3000

California Job Journal
2535 Capitol Oaks Drive, Suite 10
Sacramento, CA 95833
(916) 925-0800

Canada Globe Media
444 Front Street West
Toronto, Ontario M5V 2S9 Canada
(416) 585-5415, (800) 387-9012

Charleston Post/News and Courier
134 Columbus Street
Charleston, SC 29403
(803) 577-7111

Charlotte Observer
Box 32188
600 S. Tryon Street
Charlotte, NC 28232
(704) 358-5000

Chicago Sun-Times
401 N. Wabash Avenue
Chicago, IL 60611
(312) 321-3000

Chicago Tribune
435 N. Michigan Avenue
Chicago, IL 60611
(312) 222-3232

Cincinnati Enquirer
617 Vine Street
Cincinnati, OH 45201
(513) 721-2700

Cincinnati Post
125 E. Court Street
Cincinnati, OH 45202
(513) 369-1874

Columbus Dispatch
34 S. Third Street
Columbus, OH 43216
(614) 461-5043, (800) 282-0263

Courier-Journal
525 W. Broadway
Louisville, KY 40202
(502) 582-4011

Daily Oklahoman
Box 25125
500 N. Broadway
Oklahoma City, OK 73125
(405) 232-3266

Dallas Morning News
508 Young Street
Dallas, TX 75202
(214) 977-8222

Dayton Daily News
Fourth & Ludlow Streets
Dayton, OH 45401
(513) 225-2000

Denver Post
1560 Broadway
Denver, CO 80201
(303) 820-1010, (800) 525-9502

Desert News
PO Box 1257
30 First Street
Salt Lake City, UT 84110
(801) 237-2188

Detroit Free Press
321 W. Lafayette Boulevard
Detroit, MI 48231
(313) 222-6400

Detroit News
615 Lafayette Boulevard
Detroit, MI 48232
(313) 222-2000

El Paso Times
PO Box 20
401 Mills Street
El Paso, TX 79901
(915) 546-6231, (915) 546-6208

Florida Times Union
1 Riverside Avenue
Jacksonville, FL 32202
(904) 359-4111

Fort Worth Star-Telegram
PO Box 1870
400 W. Seventh
Forth Worth, TX 76102
(817) 390-7400

Ft. Lauderdale News/Sun Sentinel
101 N. New River Drive
Ft. Lauderdale, FL 33301-2293
(305) 761-4741

Gannett Rochester Newspapers
55 Exchange Boulevard
Rochester, NY 14614-2001
(716) 232-4130

Gannett Westchester Rockland Newspapers
1 Gannett Drive
White Plains, NY 10604
(914) 694-5141

Globe Times
202 W. Fourth Street
Bethlehem, PA 18015
(215) 867-5000

Grand Rapids Press
155 Michigan Street NW
Grand Rapids, MI 49503
(616) 842-6400

Greensboro News and Record
PO Box 20848
Greensboro, NC 27420
(919) 373-7000

Hartford Courant
285 Broad Street
Hartford, CT 06115
(203) 241-6200

International Herald Tribune
850 Third Avenue, 10th Floor
New York, NY 10022
(212) 752-3890, (800) 572-7212

Kansas City Kansan
901 N. Eighth Street
Kansas City, KS 66101
(913) 371-4300

Kansas City Star
1729 Grand Avenue
Kansas City, MO 64108
(816) 234-4141

Knoxville News
PO Box 59038
208 W. Church Avenue
Knoxville, TN 37902
(615) 523-3131

Las Vegas Sun
PO Box 4275
Las Vegas, NV 89127
(702) 383-0316

Los Angeles Times
Times Mirror Square
Los Angeles, CA 90052
(213) 237-5750, (800) 528-4637

Miami Herald
1 Herald Plaza
Miami, FL 33132
(305) 350-2111

Milwaukee Journal
PO Box 661
333 W. State Street
Milwaukee, WI 53201-0661
(414) 224-2000

Nashville Banner/Tennessean
1100 Broadway Street
Nashville, TN 37203
(615) 254-1031

National Business Employment Weekly
420 Lexington Avenue
New York, NY 10170
(212) 808-6793, (800) 323-6239

New York Times
229 W. 43rd Street
New York, NY 10036
(212) 556-7226

Omaha World-Herald
World-Herald Square
Omaha, NE 68102
(402) 444-1000

Orange County Register
625 N. Grand Avenue
Santa Ana, CA 92701
(714) 835-1234, Ext. 4933

Oregonian
1320 S.W. Broadway
Portland, OR 97201
(503) 221-8482

Palm Beach Post
PO Box 24700
2751 S. Dixie Highway
West Palm Beach, FL 33416-4700
(407) 837-4343

Palo Alto Peninsula Times Tribune
245 Lytton Avenue
Palo Alto, CA 94301
(415) 853-1200

Philadelphia Inquirer
400 N. Broad Street
Philadelphia, PA 19101
(215) 854-5440

Pittsburgh Press and Post Gazette
34 Boulevard of the Allies
Pittsburgh, PA 15230
(412) 263-1181

Plain Dealer
1801 Superior Avenue
Cleveland, OH 44114
(216) 344-4596

Rocky Mountain News
400 W. Colfax Avenue
Denver, CO 80204
(303) 892-2676, (800) 345-7461

Sacramento Bee
PO Box 15779
Sacramento, CA 95852
(916) 321-1000

Salt Lake Tribune
PO Box 867
Salt Lake City, UT 84110
(801) 237-2800

San Antonio Express News
PO Box 2171
San Antonio, TX 78297
(512) 225-7411, (800) 456-1666

San Francisco Chronicle/Examiner
925 Mission Street
San Francisco, CA 94103
(415) 777-5700

San Jose Mercury News
750 Ridder Park Drive
San Jose, CA 95190
(408) 920-5000

Seattle Times
PO Box 70
Seattle, WA 98111-0070
(206) 464-2121

St. Louis Post-Dispatch
900 N. Tucker Boulevard
St. Louis, MO 63101
(314) 622-7000

Tacoma News Tribune
PO Box 11000
Tacoma, WA 98411
(206) 597-8551

Tampa Tribune
202 Parker Street
Tampa, FL 33606
(813) 272-7711

USA Today
535 Madison Avenue
New York, NY 10022
(212) 715-5350

Wall Street Journal
420 Lexington Avenue, 14th Floor
New York, NY 10170
(212) 808-6823

Washington Post
1150 15th Street NW, 6th Floor
Washington, DC 20071
(202) 334-5757, (800) 624-2367

Management Consultants

Directory of Management Consultants
Kennedy & Kennedy, Inc.
Templeton Road
Fitzwilliam, NH 03447
(603) 585-2200

Dun's Consultants Directory
Dun's Marketing Services
Dun & Bradstreet, Inc.
3 Sylvan Way
Parsippany, NJ 07054
(201) 455-0900, (800) 526-0651

Institute of Management Consultants
Directory of Members
230 Park Avenue
New York, NY 10169
(212) 697-8262

Networks for Job Searches

The Job Search Network (cable)
1650 Tysons Boulevard, Suite 570
McLean, VA 22102
(703) 506-9292

Jobtrak, Inc.
1990 Westwood Boulevard, Suite 260
Los Angeles, CA 90025
(800) 999-8725

Recruitment Software

Abra Cadabra Software
5510 9th Street N
St. Petersburg, FL 33703
(813) 525-4400

Abra Macdabra Software Co.
485 Pala Avenue
Sunnyvale, CA 94086
(408) 737-9454

Acker Associates/Reynwood
Software Systems
45 Shady Lane
Stamford, CT 06903
(203) 322-1118

Advanceware
1317-C Warner Avenue
Tustin, CA 92680
(714) 259-1761

Allied Business Systems
18350 Mt. Langley, Suite 211
Fountain Valley, CA 92708
(714) 261-1773

Alltrack Software Co.
4 Nutcracker Lane
Westport, CT 06880
(800) 822-0206

Bedford Microcumputer Consultants
595 Market Street, Suite 2750
San Francisco, CA 94105
(415) 495-8835

Career Communications, Inc.
PO Box 169
500 Main Street
Harleysville, PA 19438
(800) 346-1848

Career Design Software
1301 Avenue of the Americas
New York, NY 10019
(212) 258-5600

Computer Employment Applications, Inc.
606 Wisconsin Avenue, Suite 609
Milwaukee, WI 53203-1905
(800) 233-1015

Computerized Personnel Systems, Inc.
2 Executive Circle, Suite 240
Irvine, CA 92714
(714) 955-2601

Computing Management
2346 S. Lynhurst Drive, Suite C101
Indianapolis, IN 46241
(317) 247-4485

Comshare, Inc.
3001 S. State Street
Ann Arbor, MI 48108
(313) 944-4800, (800) 922-7979

Corporate Education Resources, Inc.
PO Box 2080
505 N. Third Street
Fairfield, IA 52556
(515) 472-7720, (800) 445-7181

Creative Research Systems
15 Lone Oak Center
Petaluma, CA 94952
(707) 765-1001

Cyborg Systems
2 N. Riverside Plaza, 12th Floor
Chicago, IL 60606
(313) 454-1865

Decision Technologies
17480 Dallas Parkway, Suite 120
Dallas, TX 75252
(214) 385-3523

Educational Technologies, Inc.
1007 Whitehead Road Extension
Trenton, NJ 08638
(609) 882-2668

Electronic Selection System Corp.
2300 Maitland Center Parkway, Suite 302
Maitland, FL 32751
(407) 875-1102

Firth Software
5301 Office Park Drive, Suite 215
Bakersfield, CA 93309
(805) 324-8324

Greentree Systems, Inc.
201 San Antonio Circle, Suite 120
Mountain View, CA 94040
(415) 948-8844, (800) 748-6334

Information Resource Group
PO Box 189238
Utica, MI 48318-9238
(313) 254-8500

Infotrieve Systems, Inc.
30 E. San Carlos Street, Suite 319
San Jose, CA 95113
(408) 294-7755

Interactive Systems, Inc.
590 Summit Avenue
St. Paul, MN 55102
(612) 224-1153

Joblink
12062 Valley View Street, Suite 239
Garden Grove, CA 92645
(714) 893-4454

Job Net
3 Haddon Hall
Melville, NY 11747
(516) 491-6595

McCormack & Dodge
1225 Worcester Road
Natick, MA 01760
(617) 655-8200

Microtrac Systems, Inc.
19 Needham Street
Newton Highlands, MA 02161
(617) 655-4660

Office Data Systems
745 E. Jericho Turnpike
St. James, NY 11780
(516) 366-3638

Omni Systems
3070 Lawson Boulevard, Suite 202
Oceanside, NY 11572
(516) 736-5413

PC Advantage
14215 Greenview Drive
Laurel, MD 20708
(301) 725-3519

Personnel Performance Systems
337 El Dorado Street, Suite 3B
Monterey, CA 93940
(408) 649-5030

Revelation Technologies, Inc.
2 Park Avenue, Suite 2300
New York, NY 10016
(212) 689-1000, (800) 262-HRIS

ROI Systems
17 Sherwood Place
Greenwich, CT 06830
(800) 876-6077

Searchflo
PO Box 925
Trabuco Canyon, CA 92678
(714) 858-1111

Simple Soft, Inc.
7155 S.W. Varns Street
Portland, OR 97223
(503) 620-3320

Spectrum Human Resource Systems Corp.
1625 Broadway, Suite 2800
Denver, CO 80202
(303) 534-8813

System Vision
PO Box 281857
San Francisco, CA 94128
(415) 355-7308

U.S. Datalink
6711 Bayway Drive
Baytown, TX 77520
(800) 527-7930

Wang Laboratories
1 Industrial Avenue
Lowell, MA 01851
(508) 656-6777

Workscience Corp.
7814 Carousel Lane, Suite 400
Richmond, VA 23229
(804) 273-1703

Search Firms

Allan Consulting Group, Inc.
4790 Irvine Boulevard, Suite 105-345
Irvine, CA 92720
(714) 856-5855

Anthony R. Byrne
14014 Moorpark Street, Suite 214
Sherman Oaks, CA 91423
(818) 783-5107

Ashley & Craig
11326 Isleta Street
Los Angeles, CA 90049
(213) 472-6395

The Atlanta Consulting Group, Inc.
2028 Powers Ferry Road, Suite 190
Atlanta, GA 30339
(404) 850-3900

Booz, Allen & Hamilton
4330 E. West Highway
Bethesda, MD 20814
(301) 951-2200

Boyden International, Inc.
260 Madison Avenue
New York, NY 10016
(212) 685-3400

Cambridge Group International
266 Elmwood Avenue
Buffalo, NY 14222
(716) 885-5902

Chicago Search Group, Inc.
1110 Lake Cook Road, Site 375
Buffalo Grove, IL 60089
(708) 520-7800

Christian & Timbers, Inc.
30050 Chagrin Boulevard, Suite 300
Cleveland, OH 44124
(216) 464-8710

Coopers & Lybrand Management
Consulting Services
203 N. La Salle
Chicago, IL 60601
(312) 701 5500

Directory of Executive Recruiters
Kennedy & Kennedy, Inc.
Templeton Road
Fitzwilliam, NH 03447
(603) 585-2200

Diversified Search, Inc.
2005 Market Street
1 Commerce Square, Suite 3300
Philadelphia, PA 19103
(215) 732-6666

Ernst & Whinney/Executive Search
2000 National City Center
Cleveland, OH 44414
(216) 861-5000

Fenwick Partners
57 Bedford Street, Suite 101
Lexington, MA 02173
(617) 862-3370

Gilbert Tweed Associates, Inc.
630 Third Avenue
New York, NY 10017
(212) 697-4260

Heath/Norton Associates, Inc.
16 E. 41st Street
New York, NY 10017
(212) 685-7474

Heidrick & Struggles, Inc.
125 S. Wacker, Suite 2800
Chicago, IL 60606
(312) 372-8811

Hispanic Business, Inc.
360 S. Hope Avenue, Suite 300-C
Santa Barbara, CA 93105
(805) 682-5843

International Business Services
630 N. Main Street, Suite 225
Walnut Creek, CA 94596-4609
(415) 937-9152

Intersearch Group
115 E. 87th Street, Suite 24-D
New York, NY 10028
(212) 831-5156

Kearney Consultants
222 S. Riverside Plaza
Chicago, IL 60606
(312) 648-0111

Korn/Ferry International
1800 Century Park E.
Los Angeles, CA 90067
(213) 879-1834

KPMG Peat Marwick
345 Park Avenue
New York, NY 10154
(212) 758-9700

Logic Associates, Inc.
170 Broadway, Suite 1206
New York, NY 10038
(212) 227-8000

Management Recruiters International
1127 Euclid Avenue, #1400
Statler Building
Cleveland, OH 44115-1638
(216) 696-1122

The Morris Group
40 Morris Avenue
Bryn Mawr, PA 19010
(215) 520-0100

National Logistics Recruiters, Inc.
3 Whitney Place
Princeton Junction, NJ 08550
(609) 275-1919

Paul R. Ray & Co., Inc.
301 Commerce Street, Suite 2300
Fort Worth, TX 76102
(817) 334-0500

Paul Stafford Associates, Ltd.
261 Madison Avenue
New York, NY 10016
(212) 983-6666

Robert Stevens & Associates
Route 1, Box 189
Rochester, IL 62563
(217) 498-7481

Sheridan Search/John Sheridan Associates, Inc.
405 N. Wabash Avenue, Suite 1707
Chicago, IL 60611
(312) 822-0232

Sigma Group
717 17th Street, Suite 1440
Denver, CO 80202-3314
(303) 292-6720

Spencer Stuart & Associates
55 E. 52nd Street
New York, NY 10055
(212) 407-0200

The Whitney Group
12 E. 49th Street, Tower 49
New York, NY 10017
(212) 421-4949

Reference and Background Checking

Equifax, Security and Resource Management
1600 Peachtree Street NW
Atlanta GA 30309
(404) 870-2500

Fidelifacts Metropolitan
50 Broadway, Suite 1107
New York, NY 10004
(212) 425-1520, (800) 678-0007

Information Resources
115 Torrance Boulevard, Suite 100
Redondo Beach, CA 90277
(213) 376-1399

Investigations Corporation of America
Personnel Screening
2964 Peachtree Road
Atlanta, GA 30305
(404) 239-9580, (800) 345-2607

James E. Van Ella & Associates
8420 W. Bryn Mawr
Chicago, IL 60631
(312) 693-6220

Murphy & Maconachy, Inc.
1851 E. First Street, Suite 1100

Santa Ana, CA 92705
(714) 547-6541

National Employment Screening
4110 S. 100 E. Avenue, Suite 200
Tulsa, OK 74146
(918) 627-1003, (800) 247-8713

Personal Employee Profiling
601 Lee Street
Des Plaines, IL 60016
(708) 803-2890

Pinkerton Investigation Services
507 Exton Commons
Exton, PA 19341
(800) 232-7465

Refcheck, Inc.
1383 Bethel Road
Columbus, OH 43220
(614) 459-1442

Verified Credentials, Inc.
1020 E. 146th Street, Suite 200
Burnsville, MN 55337
(612) 431-1811, (800) 325-5440

Testing Services

Aptitude Testing for Industry
100 W. Broadway, Suite 1140
Glendale, CA 91210
(818) 244-0077

Assessment Systems Corp.
2233 University Avenue, Suite 440
St. Paul, MN 55114
(612) 647-9220

Bigby, Havis & Associates Assessment
Psychologists
12201 Merit, Suite 420
Dallas, TX 75251
(214) 233-6055

Compulink
158 N. Glendora Avenue, Suite J
Glendora, CA 91740
(818) 505-3421

Consulting Psychologists Press
3803 Bayshore
Palo Alto, CA 94303
(415) 857-1444

CPP Pinkerton
65 Old Route 22
Clinton NJ 08809
(201) 730-8318

E. F. Wonderlic Personnel Test, Inc.
820 Frontage Road
Northfield, IL 60093
(708) 446-8900, (800) 323-3742

Handwriting Research Corporation
2821 E. Camelback Road, Suite 600
Phoenix, AZ 85016
(602) 957-8870

Health Evaluation Programs, Inc.
808 Busse Highway
Park Ridge, IL 60068
(708) 696-1824, (800) 323-2178

Human Resource Associates
300 C. Waters Building
Grand Rapids, MI 49503
(616) 458-0692, (800) 23SCORE

International Testing Services, Inc.
PO Box 9183
955 Massachusetts Avenue
Cambridge, MA 02139
(617) 661-4560

John E. Reid and Associates, Inc.
250 S. Wacker Drive, Suite 1100
Chicago IL 60606
(312) 876-1600

Key Functional Assessments, Inc.
1010 Park Avenue
Minneapolis, MN 55404
(800) 333-3KEY

London House
1550 Northwest Highway
Park Ridge, IL 60068
(708) 298-7311, (800) 221-8378

Med-tox Associates, Inc.
4125 E. La Palma Avenue, Site 300
Anaheim, CA 92807
(714) 996-5570

National Center for Forensic Science
Maryland Medical Labor
1901 Sulphur Spring Road
Baltimore, MD 21227
(800) 368-2576

National Computer Systems, Inc.
11300 Rupp Drive
Burnsville, MN 55337
(612) 895-7136, (800) 328-6172

Occupational Health Services
695 Atlantic Avenue
Boston, MA 02111
(617) 262-6888, (800) 533-9735

Personnel Decisions, Inc.
2000 Plaza VII Tower
45 S. Seventh Street
Minneapolis, MN 55402-1608
(612) 339-0927

Precis Corp.
1320 Harbor Bay Parkway, Suite 110
Alameda, CA 94501
(415) 748-6900

Psychemedics
1806 Wilshire Boulevard
Santa Monica, CA 90403
(800) 522-7424

The Psychological Corp.
535 Academic Court
San Antonio, TX 78204
(800) 228-0752

Psychological Services, Inc.
Test Publications Division
100 W. Broadway, Suite 1100
Glendale, CA 91210
(818) 244-0033, (800) 367-1565

Psychometrics, Inc.
4730 Woodman Avenue, Suite 401
Sherman Oaks, CA 91423
(818) 783-5731

Reid Psychological Systems
200 S. Michigan Avenue, Suite 900
Chicago, IL 60604
(800) 922-7343

Stanton Corp.
6100 Fairview Road, Suite 900
Charlotte, NC 28210
(704) 552-1119, (800) 528-5745

Substance Abuse Management, Inc.
2 Plaza E.
330 E. Kilbourn Avenue, Suite 1075
Milwaukee, WI 53202
(414) 273-7264, (800) 247-7264

Temporary Services

The Accountants Overload Group/
Accountants Overload/Accountants Unlimited
10990 Wilshire Boulevard, 14th Floor
Los Angeles, CA 90024-3905
(213) 208-7766

Accountemps
2884 Sand Hill Road
Menlo Park, CA 94025
(415) 854-9700

ADIA Personnel Services
64 Willow Place
Menlo Park, CA 90425
(415) 324-0696

Kelly Temporary Services
999 W. Big Beaver Road
Troy, MI 48084
(313) 362-5555

Manpower Temporary Services
5301 N. Ironwood Road
Milwaukee, WI 53217
(414) 961-1000, (800) 558-6996

Norrell Temporary Services
3535 Piedmont Road N.E.
Atlanta GA 30305
(404) 240-3440

Snap Temps
90 Madison Street, Suite 704
Denver, CO 80206
(303) 329-6693

Stivers Temporary Personnel, Inc.
200 W. Monroe Street, Suite 1100
Chicago, IL 60606
(312) 558-3550

Tempforce
1600 Steward Avenue, Site 700
Westbury, NY 11590
(800) 275-2750

Uniforce Temporary Services
1335 Jericho Turnpike
New Hyde Park, NY 11040
(516) 437-3300

Volt Temporary Services
8605 Westwood Center Drive, #201
Vienna, VA 22182
(703) 847-2996

Index

About the Editor

Mary F. Cook is president of Mary Cook & Associates, a Denver-based human resources management consulting firm established in 1983. Ms. Cook has twenty years' experience as a corporate human resources generalist and as a human resources consultant. Her clients include both public and private sector organizations. She is actively sought as a lecturer and has written many articles for business magazines, newspapers, and trade journals. Ms. Cook's HR trends forecasts are quoted in such notable publications as *Success, Management Review, Franchise Update, Federal Credit Union,* and annually in *The Human Resources Yearbook.* Ms. Cook is an award-winning author of eleven books on the subject of human resources management, including *The Complete Do-It-Yourself Personnel Department.*

Ms. Cook is a recipient of the top national research award from the Society for Human Resource Management. She has also received awards from the Colorado Society for Human Resources Management. She is a member of the Denver Woman's Press Club, the Colorado Authors' League, and The Authors' Guild, Inc.

About the Contributors

Diane Arthur is president of Arthur Associates Management Consultants, Ltd., a Northport, New York–based human resources development company. As such, Ms. Arthur consults with organizations regarding all facets of human resources. In addition, she designs and conducts training workshops in such areas as interviewing skills, equal employment opportunity, personnel policies and procedures, performance appraisals, and employment testing. Ms. Arthur is the author of numerous works dealing with human resources, the most recent of which is *Recruiting, Interviewing, Selecting, and Orienting New Employees*, 2d. ed.

Carol Benjamin is a senior total compensation and benefits consultant in The Wyatt Company's Dallas office. She assists clients in designing and communicating pay and benefits programs and has worked with many organizations in developing total compensation strategy, designing plan alternatives, communicating human resources programs, and developing and implementing flexible compensation plans. Prior to joining The Wyatt Company, Ms. Benjamin was a consultant with another major consulting firm for eight years, where she assisted many companies in designing and communicating all types of benefits programs. She was also a corporate benefits manager for Boise Cascade Corporation for eleven years.

Raymond C. Collins, Ph.D., is the president of Collins Management Consulting, Inc., in Vienna, Virginia, a general management consulting firm with a dual emphasis on human services and providing systems support to the business community. Dr. Collins's consulting focuses on organizational development, human resources training, strategic planning, survey research, training and technical assistance, and management information systems. He is a recognized authority on child and family programs and has developed a methodology called the work-family audit for planning and evaluating child care, elder care, and other work-family programs for private corporations. Prior to his full-time consulting, Dr. Collins was a federal official with the Department of Health and Human Services, the Office of Economic Opportunity, and the Department of State.

Steven E. Gross is a vice-president and managing director of Hay Management Consultants' Workforce Variable Compensation Practice. He is responsible for directing all of Hay's activities in the design and implementation of innovative variable compensation programs for all levels of employees. His personal consulting expertise is in the design of work force, executive, management, and sales incentive compensation plans; overall corporate compensation and benefits reward strategies; and the use of variable compensation to bring about and reinforce cultural change. Mr. Gross is a certified management consultant.

Robert M. James is an officer of the Hay Group and one of the principals in Hay's executive compensation, employee benefit, and total remuneration issues. He joined Hay in 1976 and is currently located in the Kansas City, Missouri, office. Since joining

Hay, Mr. James has provided consulting services to clients of all sizes in the industrial, financial, and services sectors. He frequently serves as a consultant to the compensation committee of corporate boards, assisting in the establishment and implementation of organizationwide total compensation strategies and programs. Prior to joining Hay, Mr. James had sixteen years of human resources experience in the industrial sector, working for International Harvester and Rohr Industries. He is a frequent speaker and has published several articles in the business press.

Dale A. Masi, D.S.W., is a professor at the University of Maryland School of Social Work and president of Masi Research Consultants, Inc., in Washington, D.C., a company that specializes in employee assistance programs, managed mental health design implementation and evaluation, and corporate training. Dr. Masi is the author of more than forty scholarly articles and five books, including *The AMA Handbook for Developing Employee Assistance and Counseling Programs* and *Designing Employee Assistance Programs.*

David C. McClelland, Ph.D., is the founder and chairman of the board of McBer and Company in Boston. A professor of psychology emeritus at Harvard University, Dr. McClelland has devoted a lifetime to research that has resulted in an internationally accepted theory of human motivation. His theory and research findings have been applied to management, small business administration, postsecondary education, mental health, behavioral medicine, economic development, and the modernization of developing countries. Dr. McClelland is widely published on human motivation and related topics.

Charles W. Newcom is a partner in the Denver office of Sherman & Howard and manager of the firm's Employment Law Department. Since his admission to the bar in 1974, he has been involved in all aspects of the practice of employment law, representing employers only. Mr. Newcom's experience in the range of legal problems facing employers includes employment discrimination and wrongful discharge, various aspects of health and safety law, wage and overtime pay disputes, union election campaigns, and unfair labor practice charges. He has published in legal journals and is a contributor to *Employee Dismissal Law & Practice,* and *The Human Resource Yearbook.* He is an active member of the Occupational Safety Health Law Committee of the American Bar Association.

Robert C. Ochsner is a vice-president of Hay Management Consultants and is director of compensation in the Philadelphia headquarters. He specializes as a consultant in executive compensation, management and nonmanagement incentives, stock-related plans, and benefits plans. Mr. Ochsner has consulted with and managed projects for a variety of clients, including large publicly held companies, privately held companies, and the federal government. Major emphasis has been in process industries, financial services, and business services. He has specialized in the tax consequences of both qualified and nonqualified deferred compensation and incentive plans. Mr. Ochsner writes the quarterly "Compensation Planning" column for *Compensation and Benefits Management* and edited a volume on *Linking Pay to Performance* for *Topics in Total Compensation.* He is also on the review board and is a contributor to *The Human Resource Yearbook.* Prior to joining Hay in 1976, Mr. Ochsner was a vice-president of Martin E. Siegal in New York City and Atlanta.

Barney Olmsted is codirector of New Ways to Work, a San Francisco–based resource development and research organization that she cofounded in 1972. New Ways to Work has been the leading pioneer in the field of work time options, promoting wider use of new arrangements like job sharing, flextime, flexiplace, phased retirement, and work sharing. At New Ways to Work, Ms. Olmsted consults, develops programs, and edits the newsletter *Work Times*. Her clients have included the state of California, the Women's Bureau of the U.S. Department of Labor, Illinois Bell, and the Royal Bank of Canada. She speaks and writes regularly on the subject of work time flexibility. Her most recent book, *Creating a Flexible Workplace,* won the Society for Human Resource Management award for the best book of the year.

Lyle M. Spencer, Jr., Ph.D., is president and CEO of McBer and Company, located in Boston, and technical director, human resource planning and development worldwide, Hay Management Consultants. Dr. Spencer has written many articles and books on human resource topics, including *Human Resource Cost Benefit Evaluation.* Dr. Spencer is a licensed psychologist in the District of Columbia and the Commonwealth of Massachusetts and a member of the American Psychological Association.

William R. Tracey, Ed.D., is the president of Human Resources Enterprises of Cape Cod, Inc., in South Yarmouth, Massachusetts, an international management and training consulting company serving business, industry, government, educational, and other nonprofit organizations and institutions. Earlier in his career he served as deputy commandant for training and education, U.S. Army Intelligence School, Fort Devens, Massachusetts, and professor of education and director of teacher training at Fitchburg (Massachusetts) State College. Dr. Tracey is the author of more than fifty journal articles and nine books, including *The Human Resources Glossary: A Complete Desk Reference for HR Professionals.*